LIVES LIVED AND LOST

The Holocaust: History and Literature, Ethics and Philosophy

Series Editor:
Michael Berenbaum (American Jewish University)

LIVES LIVED AND LOST

East European History Before,
During and After World War II as Experienced
by an Anthropologist and Her Mother

Kaja FINKLER and
Golda FINKLER (Posthumously)

Foreword by Michael Berenbaum

Boston 2012

Library of Congress Cataloging-in-Publication Data:
A catalog record for this title is available from the Library of Congress.

Copyright © 2012 Academic Studies Press
All rights reserved
ISBN 978-1-618112-17-0

Book design by Adell Medovoy

Published by Academic Studies Press in 2012
28 Montfern Avenue
Brighton, MA 02135, USA

press@academicstudiespress.com
www.academicstudiespress.com

*To my mother, my father, and all my loved ones
who were murdered on the pyre of evil
but live on in my memory
and with this book*

-Kaja

Acknowledgments

I wish to express my deep appreciation and thanks to Christopher Browning and Gerhard Weinberg, who assisted me in fact-checking and elucidating many of the events my mother described. I was extremely fortunate to have these two scholars as colleagues and to have the opportunity to draw on their vast knowledge of World War II and German strategies for the "Final Solution".

My thanks to Daniel Blatman for giving me his insights about the death marches.

I much appreciate Michael Berenbaum's very helpful comments, suggestions and insights on the initial draft of the manuscript.

I owe a very special dept to Margaret Diehl, who was kind enough to edit the manuscript, providing me with her insights and urging me on, especially to write more about myself. Her professional expertise as an editor and faith in the worthiness of this manuscript was invaluable to me.

Many thanks to Mel Hecker, Publications Officer at the United States Holocaust Memorial Museum, for his careful reading and comments on an earlier draft of the manuscript.

I owe special thanks to Christine Egan, for her helpful advice related to the publication of the book.

My thanks to Robert Dalton, Academic Affairs Librarian at Davis Library at the University of North Carolina, Chapel Hill, who assisted me with finding some of the towns passed by my mother on the death march on pre World War II maps, and calculating the distances between them.

Abbie Langston created the genealogical chart, and my thanks to her able work.

My thanks to Sheva Zucker for reviewing and correcting the appropriate transcriptions of Yiddish words.

Table of Contents

Dedication — 5

Acknowledgments — 6

Foreword: *Michael Berenbaum* — 9

Prologue — 22

Part I. In My Mother's Voice — 37
Chapter 1. My Childhood and Youth: In the House of My Grandparents — 38
Chapter 2. The War Begins — 80
Chapter 3. Working in a Slave Labor Ammunition Factory — 117
Chapter 4. Working in a Slave Labor Ammunition Factory in Germany: Liberation and Return to Chaos — 154

Part II. In My Mother's Voice — 198
Chapter 5. On Being a Refugee in the Land of Gold — 199

Part III. In My Voice: — 218
Chapter 6. A Child-Adult Remembers Home, War, Loss, and Liberation — 219
Chapter 7. The Child Becomes an Adult — 255

Epilogue — 279

Appendix 1. *Mother's World and Family before World War II* — 285
Appendix 2. *On Hasidism* — 306
Appendix 3. *Genealogy* — 312
Appendix 4. *Prayers and Calendar of Jewish Holidays reconstructed from memory by Golda Finkler in Hasag-Leiptzig* — 321

Glossary — 336

Bibliography — 340

Index — 342

Foreword

Survivors' memoirs are usually divided into three parts: *Before, During* and *After*. *Before* is often an idyllic depiction of a world that was lost. *During* takes us into the world of darkness which is alien to our world, or sometimes, more frighteningly, not alien enough. The depiction of *After* often takes the shape of a brief essay on the healing of wounds and the promise of freedom, of America or of Israel. It is often a story of resilience and defiance.

Lives Lived and Lost offers a very different narrative. Golda Finkler recorded her memories before she died in 1991, and in an act of fidelity and love, her daughter Kaja Finkler transcribed these tapes and fashioned them into a powerful story, preserving her mother's voice, perspective, and insight. She then supplemented and completed the narrative with her own testimony as a child survivor of the Holocaust, conscientiously distinguishing between what she actually recalled and what she knew from stories that had been told to her since childhood. Although the *Before* ended when she was but a young child under the age of six, there is much that Kaja remembers and much that she has pieced together from the fragments of memory, to create a coherent narrative based on family lore, diligent research, interviewing those who knew her, and listening time and again to her mother's recountings of her own experiences. Kaja is a trained scholar and applies all the tools of her academic training to this most deeply personal task.

The world of *Before* is especially rich. Golda and Kaja were born into a group of distinguished rabbinic families, among the spiritual elite of East European Jewry. Golda's mother's first marriage was a fusion of Hasidic dynasties, though the marriage did not last long: as Golda explained it, the divisions were too great, the outside forces too divergent. Golda's mother's second husband, who was formally Golda's step-father, was in actuality the father she really knew, who raised her and reared her, who loved her and whom she loved in return. He too was a Hasidic master surrounded by disciples and a court. Because of this background, the reader is offered a rare glimpse behind the curtain into the lives Hasidic masters lived with their families, without being impeded by the legendary qualities that their disciples often impart to them.

The world *Before* represented itself as quite stable and unchanging generation to generation, and yet one is reminded in this work that it was, even then, clearly in transition. Golda's mother married young in an arranged marriage that was a merger of two conflicting Hasidic dynasties with two very different schools of thought. The way of Golda's maternal grandfather was one of diligent study and intellectual mastery. The way taught to her paternal grandfather's Hasidim was one of song and joy. Golda blames the rival Hasidic courts for the split between the young couple. One suspects that had the marriage truly taken, had love blossomed after marriage—the couple barely met before marriage so if love were to grow, it would have to follow the marriage—the couple would have withstood the political/spiritual difference. And one also suspects that a generation earlier, divorce would not have been an option and Golda's mother would have lived her life dutifully, reverentially, and miserably. Her husband would have been admired and cherished by his disciples but in the rare moments of privacy in their home, husband and wife would have been alienated strangers living alongside one another.

Golda married in her twenties, not in her teens. In the Hasidic world couples are married at 18, just about the age that their non-Orthodox contemporaries are beginning to leave home and experiment sexually. As a young woman before marriage, Golda went to university in Warsaw and graduated as a lawyer despite the fact that she was the daughter of a Hasidic Master. This was a rare accomplishment for any Jewish woman of her era, even more so for one reared in the fervently Orthodox community, and still more unexpected for someone born with her *yichus*, her pedigree and stature. Golda's family was not only prestigious but affluent, and therefore her decision to attend the university was all the more startling. Of course, she could not do so openly, but the fact that she did so at all remains remarkable. Since exams were given on Shabbat, she had to take them orally or arrange for another testing time, not a simple accomplishment in a world where anti-Semitism was prevalent and where the cost of participation in larger society was expected to be assimilation, an option neither acceptable nor available to Golda.

Throughout her depiction of the world *Before*, one is struck by how fluid the boundaries were. Her world was far less rigid than the Hasidic world today and far more open in what she could read and in permitting attendance at theaters and operas—even a cinema. Her memories are warm and her pride in that world evident. Her fidelity to it were tested by fire time and again. Many times, Golda would ask her daughter, "Do your friends know who you are?" meaning, do they understand your unique and exalted stature? Kaja would dismiss the question. I suspect that Golda herself well knew who she was and had internalized the responsibilities of her distinguished lineage even as she traversed the different worlds in which she lived.

By providing a family tree to trace her lineage as well as a general description of Hasidism, Kaja is kind to those readers for whom both Hasidism and her *yichus* would be strange. For those less familiar with that world, reading the appendices before tackling the book might be advisable; it certainly will help one overcome the strangeness of this world.

Survival with dignity was not made up of grand gestures but of small deeds. Golda recounts that when the ghetto was being bombed and her family was forced to flee their home, the servant girl grabbed food; her brothers grabbed the family Torahs. Both were important; in fact, for this family both were essential for survival.

I might not have been struck by this passage or might have dismissed it by saying that the servant girl was concerned with material things and Golda's brothers lived in a world infused with the spirit, were it not for comment that was made to me by a woman after I had lectured in Boro Park, in the heart of the Haredi community, about the use of artifacts to record and transmit historical memory. To supplement my speech I had prepared a powerpoint presentation that illustrated the ideas I was trying to transmit. Among the items displayed were a bra stitched together from rags by a female inmate in Auschwitz and a Torah that was sewn together from disparate fragments found in the ruins of a synagogue. This woman spoke incredulously about an exhibition that might contain a ladies "undergarment"—she felt uncomfortable speaking to a man of a bra—and a Sefer Torah. She was taken aback when I did not back away from the inclusion of both as examples of "spiritual" defiance and of preserving one's dignity, both physical and spiritual.

Though Kaja has broken with her Hasidic heritage and chosen the secular life of a university professor, an anthropologist who studies strange societies even as she witnesses her own, she has not broken with the values of her society. She writes of her mother:

> My mother was not a mover and shaker in the common meaning of the phrase. Her acts were not recorded in history books. Her heroism rested not only in surviving the war but—what was most essential to her—surviving it honorably, and more so, recording her memories accurately. The world depends on unknown figures who live their lives gallantly and respectfully, especially in miserable times.

The last sentence recalls the legend of the 36 righteous people who sustain the world, who make the world worthy of being sustained. They are said to be quiet and unassuming, but manifesting an integrity and piety that balances the evil that so pervades our world.

Historians often remark that the persecution of the Jews in Polish ghettos in the years leading up to concentration camp was uneven. I have written that there were three stages: 1939 and early 1940, when people were moving into the ghetto, adjusting to life in confinement, and still had material possessions they could barter with and thus feed their families; the period of 1940 and 1941 when it seemed that the ghetto was to be their home for an indefinite period of time, and one could imagine life continuing on; and then the period in which the deportations started and danger lurked, when rumors swirled and everyone was desperate. Only in retrospect did German policies appear to be one seemingly unending assault without letup. Those who lived through the persecutions experienced them unevenly: periods of great tension were followed a time of calm, and then once again more difficulties followed by an even greater assault. The first period, of moving in to the ghetto, was a time of difficult and tense adjustments, and then life there became "the new normal." Golda's recollection of the ghetto gives voice to this tension: "We were hungry and cold, and yet we were very happy that we were still together."

The Finkler family remained observant even in conditions of oppression. Kaja's father would not eat any forbidden food, even when food was in short supply and religious authorities would have permitted non-kosher food under the principle that "one may violate Sabbath to save a human life." He might have permitted others to eat food that he denied himself, but he held himself to a higher standard, what in Hebrew is termed *lefnim mushurat hadin*, beyond the letter of the law.

Saturday was *Shabbos* even in the ghetto: Kaja was sent on Friday to get raisins in order to make the Sabbath wine. En route she ate half of them. A child remained a child, even on the eve of *Shabbos*, even though at moments of crisis she had to have the cunning of an adult in order to survive.

Most difficult was the uncertainty and the fear: Golda comments, "Nobody knew. But putting us into a situation of fear and unknowing was a Germans strategy to demoralize us."

The distinguished literary critic Lawrence Langer introduced a term to describe the decisions that ghetto inhabitants had to make: "choiceless choices." As ghetto life deteriorated and word of mass murder filtered in, ghetto residents had to make fateful decisions. Do we give our children away to non-Jews, and perhaps they will have a chance to live but they may also be lost to the Jewish people, or do we keep them with us no matter what and experience our fates together? "Crucial decisions," Langer wrote, "did not reflect options between life and death but between one form of abnormal response and another, both imposed by the situation that was in no way of the victims' own choosing."

There is one moment in Golda's narration where she and her husband are paralyzed by a choice they could not make. When Golda was being sent off to a slave labor camp, she and her husband had to decide whether Kaja was to stay with her father—who was to remain in the ghetto—or go with her mother to a place unknown and unnamed. They could not decide, and asked Kaja whether she wanted to stay or to go? Father or mother?

Woe to the parent who is forced to make such a decision. Kaja writes:

> Only a memoir can reveal the unique personal dramas and moral dilemmas each individual must confront at a time of historical calamity, conundrums like whether to "sacrifice" a child's life or to save it, even if it may eventually live a life alien to one's own being, as my parents had to decide; or whether to "sacrifice" a child's life to protect the larger group, as in the situation that presented itself in the hiding place; or the bewilder-

ment I faced, as a young child, having to decide with which parent I should go, each tugging me in a different direction.

She is clearly not recalling the moment of sheer terror, but reflecting on the moment.

Similarly, both Golda and Kaja recount a moment when the family was in hiding and Germans were nearby just as young Kaja began to cry. The sound of her voice would have revealed the hideout. Her cousin came up to her with a pillow and placed it over her mouth. Her mother and father could not move. Fortunately, the pressure was adequate to stifle her cries but not quite strong enough to smoother her. Her cousin too faced a choiceless choice, and had the deed been carried out he might have been both a "savior and a murderer" and forced to live with the consequences.

As a religious Jew, Golda stresses not only the physical aspects of survival, but its spiritual dimension as well. Time and again she reiterates with pride: "We did not permit the Germans to destroy us spiritually or morally…, physically they succeeded in breaking those who were ill and couldn't withstand the ghettos and camps… The healthier remained thanks to their stronger constitutions. But spiritually the Germans did not succeed at all." We must add, at least not with Golda. Elsewhere she writes: "The Germans have ruined us in many ways but spiritually they did not break us. They will not take from us our humanity." Her reiteration of this theme indicates just how important spiritual survival was to Golda.

Much attention has been given to armed resistance, properly so, but too little attention has been paid to spiritual resistance, which was integral to preserving the dignity of the destroyed.

We know that dehumanization was an essential part of the German plan. When asked, "Why do you bother to dehumanize the Jews if you are going to kill them anyway?," the Kommandant of Treblinka Franz Stangl answered: "It makes it easier." A dehumanized victim does not inhabit a common universe with his tormentor, at least not in the eyes of the killer.

Golda takes pride in the fact that her step-father, the father she loved so deeply, died in prayer, wearing his tallit and teffilin—prayer shawl and phylacteries—just as the Germans were coming to deport him. His body was destroyed, but he chose his moment of death. Others were not quite as fortunate.

From the ghetto of Warsaw and Piotrków, Golda takes us into the slave labor camp of Skarżysko-Kamienna. Golda brought the same attitudes that she had in the ghetto into the camps. She continued to observe tradition as much as possible, and gives us important historical information. Her brother-in-law read Megillat Esther in the camp on Purim, with Golda attending. This text, the Scroll of Esther, tells the story of a failed genocide against the Jews. The wicked Haman is foiled by the beautiful Queen Esther, and Mordecai and the Jews defend themselves and triumph. Were Golda still alive, I would have loved to ask how that story "played" in Skarżysko-Kamienna. It takes no imagination to understand who appeared in the mind of the listener when the name of Haman was read, but who were Mordecai and Esther, and what did Golda think of when retelling the story of rescue from would-be genocide in the camps, from which there seemed to be no rescue.

Golda's brother-in-law also blew the shofar on Rosh Hashanah, the Jewish New Year. Tradition tells us that the Shofar blasts reflect the world and its brokenness: *Tekiyah* is whole, one complete note; *Shevarim* is broken, three short notes; and then *Teruah* is a shattered world of 9 short staccato notes. The Shofar blower is then called upon to blow the final blast, the *Tekiyah Gedolah*, when the world is whole again—restored, renewed, cleansed and healed.

Golda lit candles each Friday night. She composed a Jewish calendar by memory, so that she would know when the holidays were to occur. She wrote prayers of her own and wrote down the Psalms she recalled, all of which nourished her soul precisely as her body was being brutalized. One must admire such faith and the strength that such faith offers the believer. This material is so valuable that it is among the collections of the Museum of Jewish Heritage: A Living Memorial to the Holocaust, in New York.

On Yom Kippur eve, she and her fellow prisoners refused the water that was offered them. In a heroic act of spiritual resistance, they insisted on fasting in a camp where starvation was routine and fasting imposed daily upon the prisoners by their tormentors.

The next year, 1944, she was in Hasag-Leipzig on Yom Kippur eve. She writes:

> We did not take the coffee. The same SS woman who guarded us and also conducted us to and from the factory could not understand what was happening, why we did not come. Luckily, she did not do anything. It was our great delight to openly demonstrate that we were Jewish people and that we followed our traditions; they could not make us inhuman. I still don't understand why they did not do anything to those of us who refused the "coffee" on that evening.

Golda had two strategies of survival. One required enormous discipline and the other great courage. Bread was distributed once a day. Some prisoners divided their bread so they could eat just a little several times a day and use it to reward themselves and to endure. Since they would never have enough to satisfy their appetites, they ate just enough to momentarily relieve their hunger. Golda tried a different tack:

> I ate it all up and knew I would not have any more until the next day, so I didn't think about it and I could think about other things… I was sated for a half an hour, but later I was not bothered because my thoughts were occupied with completely different things. I thought about a book I had read, I thought about many other things, just so as not to think about bread.

Who is a "hero," the Talmud asks? One who masters their will.
Golda refused all entreaties from her masters. One day a nurse offered her two cookies, a veritable treasure in the camp:

> The nurse had a small bag of cookies; she opened the bag and offered me two cookies. I thanked her and I said that I wouldn't take anything from Germans. She looked at me. Here I had this great opportunity to get something without even begging, and I refused. The overseer, the SS woman, and the nurse all looked at me as if I were a very strange, crazy, woman to decline an offer like this. The nurse finally understood that I was a

person who could not be crushed. She took the cookies back.

I am not sure what the nurse understood, but I am certain that Golda's gesture strengthened her resolve and enabled her not to be crushed.

Elsewhere she writes:

> I generally refused to accept anything from the administrators. One "bonus" I did accept, however, was when I stood in front of the machines by myself and needed some rags to polish the machine. A temporary foreman, a decent Pole, not the regular one who was very nasty, told me that his child was sick and asked whether I knew of any remedies. He described the child's symptoms, and I told him what I knew, based on his description, from my experience. He was very grateful for that. He went with me to a storage room and selected a few rags that I could take with me to the camp and maybe find a use for. I got a few rags for the machines, and a piece of a serviette ,and some black silk cloth. Later these few rags were useful. I had a serviette to put on the table, to pretend that I had a table with a cloth. I managed to piece together something like a skirt from the black silk. The one skirt I wore was falling apart, so it was a relief to have a "fresh" skirt.

The fact that he was a decent Pole permitted her to accept the rare gesture of human decency.

Primo Levi wrote: "Survival without renunciation of any part of one's moral world… was conceded to very few superior individuals, made of the stuff of martyrs and saints." And Wiesel would add that "saints died before the end of the story." But Golda retained her decency in a world where indecency was the norm.

Consider Golda's counter-testimony to Levi and Wiesel's statements in her story about finding 20 zloty:

> I didn't want to use the money until I knew if anybody

from the camp had lost it. But this was a test for me (*nisoyen*). I held on to the 20 zlotys for about a month; then, since nobody came to claim it, I decided to spend it. Not much could be bought with 20 zlotys; whole bread cost 100 zlotys. I could buy two or three saccharin tablets to sweeten the water they gave us. As I recall this episode now, it seems that I was more bothered by the fact that I could not return the 20 zlotys than happy that I had this money. I didn't want to use it. I wouldn't tell this story to anyone because people would laugh at me.

Every beginning Talmud student would recognize her dilemma. Young students are introduced to the intricacies of the Talmudic universe by studying the section dealing with returning lost objects.

Self reflective, Golda wrote of her own behavior:

As in Skarżysko-Kamienna, I acted in Hasag-Leipzig with *chutzpah*. When they handed out the bonuses, I told the German overseer in a sarcastic tone to keep his "money" so that they could make more ammunition. I turned around and walked away and returned to the machines. I was scolded by the people around me. People said, "What are you doing? You said something to him. It smells like sabotage." I said it made no difference to me. I believed we had already been condemned; the question simply was when the execution would take place. Therefore, let me have the satisfaction of saying a few words to the German.

It could have cost her her life. Since it did not, it sustained her, empowered her.

One of the items that Golda found was a notebook in which she recreated a Jewish calendar and a prayerbook. What she did was of historic note:

This notebook was a big find for me because I could write in it. I reconstructed a religious calendar based on the dates I remembered. I knew when Shabbat was but

> not when the holidays, like Rosh Hashanah and Passover, were. They did not tell us when Saturday or Sunday was, but those days were easily calculated because of the work schedule. However, I had no similar clues about the Jewish holidays. I guessed the dates as best I could. There were a few women who knew when the month of January occurred in the Jewish calendar, and based on that I created a calendar of all the Jewish holidays, recording them in the notebook. I wrote out the days, Sunday, Monday, and on to Friday, following the dates. After liberation, when I returned to Lodz, Poland, I checked the accuracy of the dates I constructed from memory. I showed people my calendar, and they found that it was very accurate, and there were no mistakes about any of the dates of the holidays.

Many survivors testify that they had reached the end just before liberation. Had it come even a little bit later, they would not have had enough within them to survive. Indeed, the death marches that Golda experienced forced the victims to go beyond the limits of their endurance, to confront the choice between struggling for life and just givimg up with virtually each step. In the end, at the moment of liberation, Golda was numb. Characteristically, she was self-reflectice.

> In the Warsaw ghetto, during the bombing, and even later in Piotrków, I was very active and energetic. As I recounted before, when the bombs started falling the first days, many people gathered in our house, and we packed them all in. I took care of and fed everybody. I was very enterprising in the ghetto. But here, from the time they took us from the Hasag-Leipzig camp, I was totally brutalized and numb, like a stone, totally ineffectual. I wouldn't even say weak, just immobilized, like a hand that has fallen asleep, numb, and cannot be moved. So was I: my head and my entire body were like that.

Liberation was anything but joyous. It was a relief. Naturally she wanted to find out if her daughter, from whom she had been separated three years before, had survived; naturally she wanted to know the fate of her family and loved ones. But first, she had to overcome depression.

> Now, after the war, I was overtaken by depression. This was not the same as when I struggled with death in the camps. I had foreseen in the camps that the real tragedy would begin when, with God's help, we survived. The nerves had been strung out for so long; now that we had arrived on the shore, they broke, and there were no arms with which to raise myself from the spiritual (geystlekhe) depression. But I should not digress.

As the reader now knows, both the co-authors of the book, mother and daughter, survived. They were reunited in Sweden, where Kaja found refuge as one of the youngest survivors of Bergen Belsen when she was taken there for rehabilitation. They established contact through Golda's estranged biological father, who had immigrated to the United States during the war and who reappeared briefly in her life, arranging for a visa to America.

The Holocaust had taken its toll on Golda. Still biologically a young woman, she was expected to remarry and to recreate life in the aftermath of destruction. One could have imagined that a woman who had graduated from a prestigious Polish law school would have thrived in post-war America economically and socially. Many survivors with much less education and erudition did. Many remarried and brought new children into the world. But her experience of America was not a story of rags to riches, but the basic struggle to survive and to live with dignity. After surviving Bergen Belsen, Kaja began her education and resumed her life. She went on to professional success and academic productivity, and her mother, who had done so much and withstood so much, managed to live alone with her daughter and to eke out a living. The more Kaja achieved, the more her world diverged from her mother's, the greater the distance between them. Still the bond forged between mother and daughter could never be severed. This joint memoir reunited mother and daughter, and they overcame even the separation of death.

Kaja comments:

> This trauma cannot be healed by forgetting but by remembering. Only individual narratives can bring back to life the violation perpetrated against an entire people. Time does not heal these wounds; to forget is to betray all those who were murdered, a desecration of all those who were slaughtered. As my mother states so wisely, her memory is their tombstone.

A magnificent tombstone, it surely is.

Michael Berenbaum
Los Angeles, California

Prologue

I often think about where I would be today—and what kind of person I would be—if World War II had not happened. I reflect on how history has intruded on my and my family's existence, taking our lives in a direction we did not choose, but were profoundly shaped by. Undoubtedly, I would still be living in Poland, most likely in Warsaw, where we resided on the eve of World War II. I would have grown up in the home of my mother's stepfather, a well-known Hasidic rabbi with numerous followers in his rabbinical court, and I would have been nurtured and loved by a very large extended family, particularly because of my mother's position in that family. I would have had a strict Orthodox upbringing and conducted a traditional religious life, but like my mother I would have negotiated two worlds, seeking ways to gain a foothold in the western scholarly and literary traditions while remaining in the embrace of traditional Hasidic religious life.

I would not have left Poland and spent my life in the United States, nor would English be my primary language, among the many I speak. Rather, I would be bilingual in Polish and Yiddish, as my mother was; while I am still fluent in Yiddish, I can no longer communicate in Polish. I would most assuredly not have become a professional anthropologist, a professor of anthropology, as I have been for over 40 years; I would not have become a secular Jew, albeit with a strong attachment to my Jewish—Hasidic—roots and traditions; and I would likely have had many children. I would have stayed in Poland, because dynastic rabbinical families such as ours were not in a dire economic situation, impelled to migrate in search of a better livelihood, as were many Jews in the nineteenth and early twentieth centuries. In rabbinical circles, going to America (if there had been no Holocaust) would have been considered unacceptable, despite Poland's history of rabid anti-Semitism. Our family had lived in Eastern Europe for hundreds of years. My ancestors were leaders in their communities, with numerous followers whom they would not have left behind for any reason.

All of that is in the world of "if"—speculation. The reality was that only one small branch of my family left Poland on the eve of World War

II. Most remained even then, despite the ominous clouds visible on the horizon, threatening our very lives. Only a few of those of us who stayed, including my mother and me, managed to survive World War II. In preparation for this account, I returned to Poland for a visit to the towns where different branches of my family had resided. I found it to be a lovely country. Alas, its history marred my enjoyment, as I remembered the persecutions of Jews even before the Second World War. I couldn't identify with the Polish people, but the names of the towns were full of meaning. In the pre-war Polish Jewish community, people were often referred to by their town of origin rather than by surnames, and as we drove on the highways it gave me comfort to read road signs with familiar town names. I saw signs for Piotrków, where my father was born and is still buried; for Lublin, where my mother was born, and which I had heard so much about all my life; and, of course, Warsaw, where I was born. Ironically, I was able to relate to the names of these and other towns but, to my regret, not to their people.

The initial impetus to write this book, based very closely on my mother's recorded memories, emerged from my desire to honor her, a woman way ahead of her time. But as I thought about her—her small frame, her beautiful legs, roundish face, athletic posture, her quick footsteps when I heard her enter the apartment—and thought about her life and memories, I realized that our lives were very closely intertwined, even though we lived, as adults, in very different worlds. Transcribing, translating and editing her narrative led me to formally edit my own memories that I had previously written down. And because all lives, including mine and my mother's, are shaped and molded by the broader contexts of family, society, culture and history, I needed to understand these contexts to make sense of our lives, if any sense can be found in the events we experienced.

I was an academic from the beginning of my graduate student days until I retired in 2009, working as a university professor, researcher, and writer in my field since the early 1970s, yet I do not intend this book to be solely an academic tract. Nor do I wish it to be a purely subjective narrative. I have tried to depict our lives against the background of wider events and history, realizing as an anthropologist that an individual life makes sense only in the larger context that shapes and informs it. Although this is a personal record of two lives, the narratives open a window to many aspects of the twentieth century Jewish existence, especially during World War II, as well as to facets of East European Jewish life, including religious life before and during the horrors of the Holocaust, and the experiences of refugees in America. In short, the book is also a history and ethnography of how people lived, their beliefs, and their experiences in a particular period in time.

This book stands at the intersection of biography, autobiography, memory, and history. It is made up of my own and my mother's memories of our experiences, supplemented by my mother's letters written immediately following the war and by documents found in memory (*Yizkor*) books, German archives, and scholarly historical sources. But ultimately, it is about memory, a certain kind of memory that brings into bold relief the events and thoughts that most touched our lives and that also breathe life into archival documents (cf. Bartov 2011, Bartov in press; Browning 2003).

There are important reasons for writing this account, both personal and otherwise. I wish to commemorate and preserve the memory of my mother, a remarkable woman, and my father, who was murdered in World War II when I was a young child. It was most important to my mother to leave a legacy of her stellar reputation, especially during the war years—a reputation her narrative supports. It is my hope that this work vindicates her valor and her decency. I wish to celebrate my mother with this work, and to honor those she loved and lost during the war. I also think it possible, as she noted in her narrative, that others could learn from her story and from her character as well.

One might still ask why I needed to write this book, since there is now a plethora of books dealing with the Jewish experience in Europe during World War II. There is no complete answer to that, but what comes to me is a question I have asked myself subconsciously my entire life. How did I manage to survive by myself during the German persecutions, separated from my parents from an early age, in ghettos and concentration camps? How did I manage to avoid being sent to Treblinka—where the overwhelming majority of people from the town in which I had lived ended up—especially given my age and size? Was it the smarts of an unusual child or just dumb luck? I hoped that by recording this account I might find an answer. Writing this narrative allowed me to meditate on such questions and set them down on paper, although I'm still not certain that I found the explanation for my survival. Perhaps the reader may have more insight into this from my telling.

Indeed, this work may be adding one more brick to a house built many times over, but unlike bricks, every person's experience in the war was not alike, a point my mother underscores when she speaks, for example, about the death march she was on. She observes, "The situation was not the same from one minute to the next, from one place to the next. The thinking of one person was not the same of another. And the horrible experiences one lived through were not the same for everybody; there were so many different ways of living through these horrors." The Talmud tells us that each human experience is unique, but also speaks for all. The life of an individual gives clarity and meaning to recorded historical processes. What is more, when I place my family history, my life, and my mother's life against the panorama of European history, I realize how one individual life cannot be separated from these far-reaching forces. It is my hope that by writing this book I will contribute one further speck to that which can be deciphered and made into sense, and to that which does not and cannot ever make sense; to the telling of a time seemingly far away yet near us all.

Although I come from a subculture of a larger subculture of a minority, from a profoundly religious Hasidic family—the men who wear black hats, beards, and curls on the side of their faces, and may seem funny to a contemporary outsider; women who wear wigs after marriage—I have moved away from that life. I wished to become part of the larger world, and when I broke away from my family's beliefs, I dimly realized there would be a trade-off. I dreamed of traveling, of being among what I thought were "sophisticated" people—writers, artists, intellectuals. I subsequently discovered that these people weren't as interesting or exciting as my daydreams painted them, but I didn't know that at the time. By breaking away, my life moved away from my roots, even though my roots never left me. I didn't study the Jewish texts; I studied texts of intellectual history, and texts of my discipline. I did extensive fieldwork in foreign places, distant from my ancestry, which brought me close to the Other, but I failed to realize until much later that I myself was an Other. I became an Other to my own family; I was an Other to the outside world in which I immersed myself after I started college at age 17. I remained an outsider throughout my life. I became an unbeliever, but didn't reject the Jewish rituals and traditions that were part of my heritage. Rather, I grew to embrace them even more after having done fieldwork among Mexican Spiritualists. In my role as an anthropologist, a participant and observer, I witnessed and took part in Spiritualist rituals, about which I have written a great deal in my professional life. In doing so, I gained a deep appreciation of the power of religious life, of the meaning it gives to its practitioners. While I deeply respected the people I studied, I could not share their religious beliefs because such beliefs were, in the end, alien to me. Ironically, the two years I spent doing research on Spiritualism and its healing practices brought me closer to appreciating the religious traditions in which I was brought up. I still do not follow precisely my family's religious rituals, but I now feel close to these practices and even get goose-pimples when I hear certain Hebrew prayers that echo my father's and grandfathers' depth of feeling and religious devotion.

After my mother passed away, I desired to know the sources of the religious beliefs I was raised with. I wished to understand what kept my family: my ancestors, my grandfathers, my father, and my mother, adhering to beliefs and activities that imperiled them even more than secular Jews were imperiled. What was it about their faith that made them cling to it? I hasten to emphasize that during World War II, because of the racial venom spewed by Germany, it did not matter whether one was or was not a believing Jew; Jewish ancestry was enough to condemn. But the Germans had an especial animus for religious Jews with their "funny" garb, with the beards that they forced men to cut. I wanted to know what kept people holding fast to these observances. My mother went to extraordinary lengths to light candles in the camps for Hanukah, and refused to take even water on Yom Kippur when she was starving; and there were other such acts that endangered her life, as she recounts in her narrative. In secret, she constructed a calendar of Jewish holidays from memory; this gave her an anchor in time, the sense of which people had otherwise lost. She also wrote a prayer "book" that, we see from her narrative, revealed her feminist inclinations, which were well ahead of her time.

I ask myself why these beliefs were so powerful that my father was willing to "sacrifice" me by refusing to even consider giving me away to non-Jews who might have been able to save my life. He would rather have seen me perish than be turned over to the Other and lose my Jewish heritage. (As I heard my mother recount this tragic dilemma, I thought of the *Akedat Yitzhak*—when God asked Abraham to sacrifice his son Isaac—and wondered whether my father was committing an act of greatness, a sacrifice, or a crime.) But in the end this was a false choice, because there was no choice, as my mother relates it, even though there were moments when that choice seemed real. Each individual was forced to face unspeakable conundrums on different occasions. Though all such experiences, and trials of this and other kinds, form part of my mother's narrative and my autobiography, I must add here that I am not certain I found the answer to the questions that initially propelled me to attempt to gain an understanding of the power of religious beliefs.

Only after I began writing this book and learned from my mother's narrative about the dilemma my parents faced—whether to turn me over to a Polish family during the war—and their subsequent decision, which was informed by a fear that I would not remain in my faith, did I realize how deeply my mother desired for me to remain observant. This had been the sole source of conflict between us. She was deeply pained during the years I was building my career, when she saw me drift away from her community and disassociate myself from its religious practices—although not from her, nor from my Hasidic relatives. While I could no longer return completely to my ancestral way of life, I slid into it comfortably on family visits, even relishing it. I lived in two very distinct worlds simultaneously, recognizing that the price was the loss of a sense of community.

This book enabled me to reflect on various such issues and also to speak of my experiences, which I have not been able to do till now without crying. The experiences I write about shaped my life and my mother's. Until the present, I have carried my memories in my head. During my anthropological field research in Mexico and the United States, I needed to record all my verbal interactions with every person I spoke to. When I was unable to do so immediately, I kept all that I saw and heard in my memory verbatim; my head felt very heavy until I was able to write everything down. Once all was down on paper my thoughts would feel airy. I didn't realize until writing this book that keeping my personal memories in my head for most of my life, until at last setting them down now, was excellent preparation for doing anthropological fieldwork. I kept all my memories of the past in my head, and now my early life has bubbled up in me as I write about it, rendering my head lighter. Similarly, Mother mentions that in some measure it was liberating for her to speak about all that she kept to herself until she began recording her narrative.

The source for what I write here is first and foremost the audiotapes, numbering over one hundred, that my mother recorded in Yiddish beginning in 1970, discussing our family history, her life, her childhood and youth, her experiences during the war, and her life in the United States after the war, as well as about me during the war. She retired around 1968, just as I began my graduate studies, and she was left with a bit of a void. I suggested that she begin to record her life story and, with some hesitation, she did so. I would tease her every time we spoke, asking her whether she was "working." She continued recording until the end of her life; she also entered into extensive tape-recorded exchanges with her brother in Israel, in which both reminisced about the past and also reported to one another their daily activities. It took me many years, until I retired from my professional life, to transcribe and translate all these tapes and begin this project. As I did, I realized, as I had in my anthropological field research, how difficult it was to translate from one language to another without losing the nuances of meaning. For this reason, I insert in some instances the original Yiddish words my mother used. These tapes are the foundation of this book and also provided the impetus for writing it.

I might add that for many years I feared my own painful reactions to these cassette tapes, until I actually sat down to listen to and transcribe them. To my own amazement, I had the opposite response: I found hearing the tapes soothing, and each day during the course of three years I eagerly turned to my mother's narrative. I found hearing it exciting, especially since I discovered that she was an excellent narrator. I listened with anticipation—so then what happened? I have attempted to retain her words, in translation, of course. With some exceptions (such as when she weeps recounting some of the dilemmas she and the family faced), she spoke dispassionately; her voice is matter of fact, without anger, unlike my own. Not infrequently the voice conveys a feeling of surprise at the life she is recounting, which seemed to her to be "the world of another planet," and she now an explorer of that world.

Listening to each period of my mother's life brought out different reactions in me. As I heard her speak about her childhood, I was overjoyed to learn how happy she was; I was enchanted by the world she had lived in as a child and that I had missed. But when I began transcribing her narrative about the war years, beginning with the Warsaw ghetto—even though I too have vivid memories of it, perhaps now more than ever—I came to realize the enormity of the tragedy and the loss that we all suffered. This unleashed pain in me I have carried, and suppressed, all my life. Not until then did I cry not out of sorrow but out of great anger: how dare they! How dare they destroy these lives? How dare they? The horror of knowing; this horror did not fully strike me until I heard it in totality, during the course of transcribing the tapes. And as I went on listening to my mother, and afterwards read further about the war years, I came to realize more than ever that there never had existed before, in human history, such deliberate, systematic and sadistic genocide. I read a speech given by Heinrich Himmler to the troops on October 4, 1943, ordering the deliberate extermination of the Jews, instructing his troops not to be affected by what they must do. There were genocides in the past, and there have been more in recent years, unfortunately all too many; but there never had been an extermination of a people carried out so systematically and with such deliberate shrewdness, such precision, such purposeful cruelty, with the desire to humiliate not only individuals but an entire people simply because it existed. There were no conflicts over land, or struggles for power, no threatening ideologies or any other sorts of competition, which, arguably, is what most often leads to genocide. This story cannot be told enough. It must be told and retold, perhaps in the tradition of the Passover *Haggadah*. But this story also recounts the history of a particularly convulsive time: mid-twentieth-century Europe.

Human beings may experience natural calamities such as earthquakes, tsunamis, and hurricanes, but nature has no intentions. The human destruction of other human beings is done purposefully, with evil intent. More frequently than they suffer natural disasters, human beings experience ordinary adversity in their lives, be it through sickness, loss of loved ones, poverty, painful marital relations, or combat. I have seen all of this in my own life, and during my research among people in developing nations. Some adversities are the result of the intentions and actions of others, and some are inflicted on oneself by oneself. But being a Jew in a German concentration camp during World War II was an overwhelming and unparalleled experience, when each day equaled a hundred—or even more—because the horrors perpetrated against the victims conflated the individual and the collective. While all people experience pain at times on a personal level, existing in the concentration, work, slave labor or death camps was an ongoing, unrelenting experience from which one could not escape. There was nothing you could do but submit or be shot on the spot. I have heard some people ask why the victims didn't stand up to the Germans. Some Jews did, including my mother in her singular way, as she narrates. Even I, a child, resisted with some small actions. But if people understood the conditions under which we stayed alive in ghettos and camps, this question would not even be posed. This kind of systematic assault on each and every human being and on the Jewish collectivity for just existing is unique in human history.

Immediately after the war, when my mother returned to Poland, she wrote a 16-page letter recounting her experiences during the war to her brother in Israel, followed by a series of other letters. This extraordinary document remains yet another source for this book. My mother hadn't read any personal memoirs of that period before making her tapes. Nor did I consult such documents, movies, or other sources until I recorded my own remembrances, because I feared my memories might become "contaminated" by other people's narratives. Only after having set down my own experiences in preparation for this book did I search out people who had lived through the war in the same ghettos and camps in order to compare our memories. The personal experiences I present here are as I remember them, vividly and clearly, before having discussed them with anyone else; in general, almost all the events I recall coincide with those of others who have been in the same places.

Ingrid Bergman is quoted as having said that to achieve happiness one needs good health and a bad memory. My mother wished she could follow Bergman's adage; she wished she could have managed to "break with the past," and regarded those able to do so as lucky. In truth, she regarded such "breaking with the past" as a betrayal toward all those who are gone. My mother's commitment was to keeping her memories vibrant in their various dimensions. Throughout her narrative she is particularly concerned about the accuracy of her memory; she was acutely aware that there have been distortions in people's presentations of the Jewish World War II experience. She continuously reexamined her facts to avoid any possible distortions. Fortunately, she had a phenomenal memory until the last days of her life (she passed away at age 88), which never ceased to amaze me. This was often to her detriment, because she could not always accept it when somebody told her, "I don't remember". She does note that while the facts she presents are accurate, she doesn't always recall the exact dates of a particular event other than by seasons of the year and the Jewish holiday calendar she constructed from memory, currently displayed in a museum.

Prologue

My mother was not a mover and shaker in the common meaning of the phrase. Her acts were not recorded in history books. Her heroism rested not only in surviving the war but—what was most essential to her—surviving it honorably, and more so, recording her memories accurately. The world depends on unknown figures who live their lives gallantly and respectfully, especially in miserable times.

One may not recall day-to-day ordinary events, but one does remember extraordinary events with great clarity, even though the exact time when an event took place may not be recalled. Forgetting is not a choice. Finally, Mother states, "I will also say that I am 100 percent responsible for what I say; I say what I know and what I remember. And if I am not a hundred percent sure that what I say is correct I will not say it at all."

Remarkably too, my mother recalled an endless number of people and their children from before the war, and where they had lived, as if they were now living next door to her. Not all such details lend themselves to presentation here, but by recalling them she memorialized them. The book is thus also a narrative of love, loss, and longing for family engulfed by war. To assure the accuracy of her account, she would always preface an event by saying, "I remember." She emphasized that when she stated "I remember" she had no doubt that the event had occurred in that way. In her own words, "I am using the words 'I remember' all the time, because I make these memoirs for you, my child. Since it is specially for you I must use the word 'I remember' because I want you to be sure that I am telling not just a story but am speaking about things that I myself recall, that I lived, that I saw with my own eyes, and heard with my ears; if this is not the case, I will not say 'I remember.'" My memory is not as good as hers, but it too reflects the events of my life as they happened, especially when my mother was taken away from me, as was my father; there are experiences that cannot be forgotten and must not be forgotten.

My memories, like my mother's, do not include dates, or how much time was spent in a particular place; the exact dates I spent in ghettos and camps I learned through my research and communications with others who had remembered me as a child. But while I did not have any knowledge of the Jewish holiday calendar at the time, and I did not remember any specific dates, I remember vividly events by the seasons when they occurred: whether it was cold, warm, or hot. My body remembers each of the places where I have been. I also remember the sequence of scenes, and I remember conundrums in which I found myself, including life-and-death decisions I needed to make, with corresponding sense-memories of the seasons. Perhaps that is the nature of memory—to record time through one's physical experience of the seasons, rather than though human constructions of time. All the events I report here have formed me; they feel distant and yet close at hand; I feel them intensely.

While I had previously avoided reading other people's narratives, after I finished writing up my own life experiences I turned to reading histories of Jewish life in Poland; of the rise of Hasidism and Hasidic life; of events leading up to World War II; and of the separate camps in which my mother and I were incarcerated, in order to gain a broader view of our personal experience

In March to April 2007 I visited Yad Vashem to obtain materials for this book. I met with people there and gathered some valuable information, including a testament left by one of my now-deceased cousins, who described our shared experiences in Piotrków, in our hiding place, and in the Great Synagogue exactly the same way I remembered and recorded them earlier. During this trip I interviewed a scholar of the Ravensbrück camp, Judith Buber Agassi, and my experiences as I remembered them corresponded to her findings; she showed me my name and number on a list of women who were brought from Piotrków to Ravensbrück, a list that she had published in her book. I also consulted with other professional historians of the Holocaust, including Daniel Blatman, as I have with scholars of the period in my university in the United States, specifically Christopher Browning and Gerhard Weinberg.

I traveled to Poland to see if I could recapture something about my mother's life before the War, when she experienced a happy childhood, or remember anything about my first years of life in Warsaw and in Piotrków, in the ghetto and camp. To my dismay, I found that the house in Lublin that my mother loved, where she was born and grew up, was completely demolished along with the entire Jewish section of this famous center of Jewish learning. Actually, the Lublin ghetto was the first one in Poland to be totally demolished, in November 1942. I almost felt that my trip was for naught, notwithstanding the attractiveness of the city, but I did gain something from walking on streets my mother had walked on as a young woman, and I visited Piotrków, which brought me back to my war experiences. I was even able to visit the attic where my family and I were hidden for several weeks in the hope of escaping deportation, until we were discovered by the Germans.

While in Poland I met with several Polish historians who have made it their life's work to recapture Jewish life prior to the War, and it was especially gratifying to meet with Robert Kuwalek, a scholar who had studied the history of my family in Lublin. I learned some facts I didn't know about my ancestors, including the prominence they had outside the Jewish community, because they had represented the community to Russian and later Polish authorities.

I solicited information from Bad Arolsen, a repository of the records the German regime meticulously kept of all the people in the camps, to obtain their accounts of my own and my mother's incarcerations in each camp. (These records are currently also housed in the United States Holocaust Memorial Museum.)

Since I was taken to Sweden shortly after the liberation of Bergen Belsen, I visited Sweden in recent years, and found in a Stockholm archive my name on the list of children who were brought there—brought back to life. I never cease to be amazed each time I find my name and designated number on such lists; it leads me to cry out because such lists concretize even more the reality of my experiences.

As a professional anthropologist I have written a handful of books and numerous articles; writing is thus not a strange experience to me. My anthropological research entailed living with people who existed under harsh economic and social conditions, and who had experienced great hardships in their private lives; writing up my field notes was saddening because my heart went out to them. I deeply respected their resilience and empathized with them, but their pains were not my own personal anguish. Writing this book was different.

The Organization of This Book

The book is divided in three broad sections, each comprising separate chapters. In the first section my mother narrates her life before, during and after World War II; her description of her childhood before the war also depicts Hasidic life at the beginning of the twentieth century in all its minutiae, including familial relations, preparations for holidays and their celebrations, marriage arrangements, and dealings with sickness, all from the point of view of a young girl. She speaks about her youth, her study of Law at the university, and her marriage, and we view

Prologue

a depiction of women's and Jews' accessibility to higher education at the time. Her narrative continues with a description of the beginning of World War II and her life in the Warsaw ghetto, as well as people's perceptions of the German onslaught. She describes the attic where we hid and her subsequent capture and relocation to two different ammunition factory slave labor camps, about which very little has been written and there is very little knowledge even now. This part also offers an ethnography of these ghettos and concentration camps; the section concludes with her account of the death march, liberation, and return to Poland immediately after liberation. The challenge of this narrative provides the urgency of the story and the richness of the historical record.

Listening to and writing down my mother's narrative brought out various responses in me that I will have occasion to note in a different script. In general terms, and perhaps because of my anthropological eye, as I contemplate at a distance my mother's childhood, I realize how much the world in which she grew up differed from my own and, needless to say, how much that life changed. Sometimes, as I wrote about her childhood, I felt that she had lived in another universe than I did.

My mother relished and marveled at the transformations of the world of her youth, a new world of which she wished to be part—a world stolen from her when World War II began. She lamented, however, the alien surroundings she experienced upon arrival as a refugee in the United States, and she never recovered from the losses she suffered during the war.

In Section II my mother narrates her life and thoughts about America, how it felt being a stateless refugee in a strange land. Unlike those who immigrate to the United States of their own volition, to improve their economic position or to seek religious freedom, stateless refugees often have no choice but to seek refuge wherever they are admitted. The hardships she experienced being a refugee in the United States took a toll, despite her valiant efforts.

Much has been written by and about being an immigrant in an alien, if welcoming, country: the inherent difficulties with learning the culture, the language, and living in two worlds—the world of one's family and past, and the world of the present. But for those who had survived World War II, it may have been especially troubling to be confronted by a society ignorant of or naïve about the depth of evil and suffering that had been inflicted on them by strangers. People had, like me, lost their childhood, which cannot be brought back; people lived, like my mother and me, in several worlds—the world of the past we could not relinquish, as we couldn't let go of the longing for those who were murdered and could never be revived, and the world of the ongoing present we had to learn to navigate during different periods of our lives—and struggled with special hardships. From the time my mother and I arrived in the United States, our lives once again converged, after a lengthy separation, as she describes in her narration of her life in the United States. But I will leave sketchy, to some degree, my own existence after my life diverged from my mother's.

Several themes repeatedly flow through Mother's narrative as she portrays her war experiences. She consciously repeats for emphasis; one of the most persistent is how the Germans could not rob her or the Jews of their humanity, which she and some of the other women in the camps demonstrated by practicing Jewish rituals. With great pride in her voice she asserts that the Germans failed to meet their goal of "breaking us not only physically but even more spiritually" so that people would behave like animals. She constantly underscores the nobility of camp inmates, rather than some of their untoward acts.

Another theme is the unbearable conundrums associated with the constant uncertainty the Germans deliberately created for people. In today's world, in the United States, we often are indecisive because of the uncertain outcomes of our actions. We are constantly reminded about economic risks, health risks, and many other types of risks we must confront. During the war, the outcomes of so many decisions were life-threatening, yet people were deliberately left in the dark about what might happen to them. The uncertainties were a result of an intentional German policy of leaving people in a perpetual state of unknowing, an ignorance of their fate that was disorienting, disconcerting and demoralizing.

In Part III, I turn to my life, also before, during, and after World War II. Since I am part of the very last generation of people who survived the horrific events of the Second World War, my memories give an eyewitness account of the experience from the perspective of the very youngest survivors. I depict my life in the ghettos before and after my father's passing, and in two concentration camps where I spent the war years, separated from my mother. Here there is some overlap between my and my mother's experiences and memories, especially from the beginning of the war and later in the ghetto in Piotrków, even though I had not heard my mother's memories before recording my own. My own memories lack the minute details that my mother furnishes about her life, and thus my descriptions are much briefer, and they are those of a child. I do not write about my father separately because he did not leave me any audiotapes; he was beaten and perished in the small ghetto of Piotrków when I was a young child. I have little information about his childhood and early life.

At the end of the book I include Appendix 1, which briefly places my mother's life in the context of the history of different branches of our family, and against the background of the history of Polish-Jewish relations, based on my research. Similarly, in Appendix 2 I provide a very brief history of Hasidism and Hasidic life, which represented a small, but unique and influential segment of a very large Jewish population in pre-World War II Poland. Appendix 3 presents a genealogy of our family; Appendix 4 displays a copy of the calendar and prayer book Mother constructed in the camp, showing the names of each prayer.

This book deals with unhappy events and need not be enhanced to make it dramatic: the drama rests in the horror of the situations it describes. It is exhilarating to realize how my mother, and others, could rejoice in the most trying moments and how human beings survive under deadly conditions; but my mother's life has a bittersweet ending. The book thus creates a mirror in which people can recognize their own humanity.

This book will be rewarding for those interested in the history and ethnography of the Jews of Poland and their religious life, for those who attempt to make sense of people's existence during senseless persecution, for those seeking to comprehend what it means to be an immigrant, for all those who feel themselves to be outsiders. It is for those interested in the lives of women and children—mothers and daughters—and the epoch before and during a transformative period of European history. Lastly, it was particularly important to my mother that her memories be useful. Certainly they have been to me; it is my hope that they will be to the readers of this book as well, and to future generations unfamiliar with the life and history of that period.

PART I
IN MY MOTHER'S VOICE

CHAPTER 1
My Childhood and Youth: In the House of My Grandparents

My entire past, before coming to America, lives in me; I cannot separate myself from it, nor do I want to. I say this not with regret. It gives me something to live for now. I can remember and take pleasure in the past, before the war began.

I cannot present my earliest memories of my grandparents, my great grandmother and my very early childhood in chronological order. I don't remember what came first and what came later. But that is not important. The facts and episodes that I have carried with me all my life are what matter. My memories remain like painted pictures.

On both my mother's and father's sides, I was born into a family of rabbis and rabbinical courts that had different *shites*, or ways of being. Each rabbi, in Hasidic society known as a *rebbe*, advanced a particular way of practicing Judaism, which gave each court with all its followers, or Hasidim, a unique character. Different courts would serve God in various manners, one with prayer; another with charity and goodness; another with study, scholarship and learning; another with spirituality; and another with song and music. There were courts that were known for thinking of others first and there were courts that were known for thinking first of themselves. This did not mean, of course, that every child born into a rabbinical court followed the ways of that court.

The ways of the Lublin court (my mother's side of the family, going back for generations) was to serve God by complete devotion to talmudic and scriptural studies. My mother was four generations removed from Rabbi Akiva Eiger (1761-1837), who was considered by some as second only to the Gaon of Vilna as a genius in the learning of scripture and Talmud; nonetheless, he was renowned for his great humility. Akiva Eiger's descendents were also recognized for their scholarship and saintliness. Several of his offspring were referred to by the names of the tracts they wrote. His son Shlomo was famous for his erudition; his grandson Yehuda Leib (Leibl), even more renowned, went by the name *Torat Emet*. Akiva Eiger's great-grandson Abraham, known by the name of his book, *Shevet mi Yehudah* (The Scepter of Judah), was my mother's father **(see Appendix 1 and 3)**. I grew up in his house. All these men, deemed saintly by their community, were famous for serving God by devoting their entire lives to the learning of the Talmud and scripture. My birth father's court, the Modzitze court, while also committed to learning, was principally dedicated to serving God through song, music, and mysticism.

My mother, then, originated from a dynasty known as *talmidim khakhomim* (brilliant students), also known as *lomdim* (great scholars), which had numerous followers who were well situated economically. The family was regarded as spiritual (*geystlekh*) and had been financial aristocrats for many generations.

My mother was the only daughter—out of six surviving children—of the celebrated *Shevet mi Yehuda*. She was an exceptionally accomplished child: beautiful, smart, honest and truthful. Her parents arranged a marriage for her, as was the custom, with a man they considered a worthy person, the son of the Modzitze rebbe. His father, Yisrael, composed great melodies and songs, but my father expanded the musical repertoire and gave them more depth. He composed religious music and also sang his compositions in a beautiful voice. My younger brother, Shmuel Eliahu (Shmilele), who passed away in 1984, inherited my father's musical talents.

The Modzitze dynasty began with Yeheskel of Kusme, who was followed by my grandfather Yisrael Taub, my father's father. My grandfather was the first to begin composing and singing his own melodies, and these talents were transmitted to his descendents, who are known in the Hasidic community to this day **(see Appendix 1 and 3)**.

There could not have been a more suitable arranged match than that of these two children, and I say "children" because in early 1902, when they married, my father was only 15 years old and my mother was not quite 17. I was born a year later, in 1903, and my brother followed less than two years after that.

It was believed that a child mirrored its natal home: children inherited not only economic goods but also the good and bad traits of their families. At that time people did not delve into psychology, nor did they take into consideration the emotional and personal preferences of a marriageable young person.

My mother and father each brought with them the characteristics and mentalities of their respective family courts. They had very different personalities, bred through generations, and each brought to the marriage a distinctive upbringing and education. There were both small and large differences between them—sufficiently disruptive that they could not continue living together, and divorced when my mother was twenty-one years old and I was three and a half.

The Lublin and Modzitze courts were opposite in character, which first became apparent in small things (so I was told), and later in big things. It is difficult for me to say much about the Modzitze court because I wasn't there. I know only what I heard from uncles and aunts, but every court had its reputation.

I never learned about the "small things"—possibly their different dispositions—but the "large things" were certainly what I had heard about all my life: that the followers from the two different courts did not get along with one another. The followers of the Lublin court criticized the Modzitze followers for not being sufficiently scholarly or even serious students of the Talmud; they were interested in music and dancing, considered by the followers of the Lublin court, as well as by the Eiger family, to be frivolous ways of serving God. The gossip was that while my mother's father, Abraham, and my mother's brothers had not favored a divorce, the Hasidim on both sides wished to see the marriage dissolve. The clash between the approaches of the two Hasidic courts was sufficiently great to affect the couple's existence, resulting in the divorce. My parents' divorce reverberates on my life to this day.

The Lublin family was aristocratic, whereas Modzitz were folk (*amkhu*). My mother's mother, my grandmother Hana, stemmed from a Hasidic family whose patriarch, Yehuda Zylberberg, was considered to be extremely rich. She came from a small town (Sadochow), where her father was a forest merchant; he exported timber through Danzig to Central Europe, to France, Germany and other countries. There was a weekly and monthly market in the town where my grandmother's family lived. On market days people came from different towns to exchange goods. Peasants came to sell their wares and Jews came to buy from them. On the days of the market, and especially during the winter, the Zylberberg family would prepare large pots of soup, tea and coffee in their home for the Jews who came to the markets from all over the area. In the summer the Zylberberg family distributed cold drinks for the merchants coming to the town. Their large house was open to all Jews who came to the markets.

I once heard my father's mother, Dobre Brandel, recall that when she was 12 years old, she was engaged to my grandfather Yisrael of Modzitz, and they married around the age of 13 or 14. Her father was a fabrics merchant; he used to travel from one weekly market to another to improve his business. When he would arrive in my maternal grandmother's town on market day, he would be invited by Hana's father to their house for a warm drink. On one such visit he brought his daughter with him. Grandmother Hana was engaged to my grandfather, Abraham, at that time. Hana's father had ordered for his daughter a wedding dress from Paris, which was considered even then a sophisticated fashion city. The dress made an extraordinary impression in the small town where they lived, and Dobre Brandel supposedly said to her father that she too wished for such a dress, but her father told her that she must not compare herself to Yehuda Zilberberg's daughter, stressing the difference in background between the two families. My two grandmothers originated from dissimilar environments, different kinds of homes, and had different upbringings and education. My paternal Modzitze grandmother, Dobre Brandel, recognized the difference herself.

The economic differences between the two courts could also be seen in the ways in which the two grandmothers were dealt with in their last years of life. Both became widows, but my maternal grandmother, Hana, was well taken care of, surrounded by her children, living in her own large house, with her own staff. My paternal grandmother lived with one or another of her daughters—none of them having much money. She had to move from place to place. She couldn't live with my father, probably because he had a second wife with whom she had a tense relationship.

Out of respect for my parents I never asked why there was a divorce; I didn't wish to touch on their personal lives. I know my mother had to divorce my father even though to have to take such a step was a huge tragedy in her life. During the divorce there was a great deal of conflict concerning who should have the children. Both my mother and father wanted both children. Finally a rabbinic court decided the girl would stay with the mother and the boy with the father.

I remember clearly the moment my brother was removed from our house, when he was a year and a half old, but I don't recall who took him. We were in my grandfather's house, in the big dining room with four large windows. My brother wore a dress and he stood on the very large table where there was a whole mountain of caramels and other candies wrapped in paper. He played with the caramels. I stood next to the table that came up to my chin. He couldn't speak, but I talked to him, standing on my tiptoes because I was too small to reach him at the table. I don't know if I understood about the separation from my brother. My mother wasn't present, and I don't know how she felt at the time. They took my brother to Modzitz, to my father's house. From then on I didn't see my little brother till 1915 when we were in Warsaw, when I also met my father for the first time after the divorce.

The separation from her brother was a significant moment in my mother's life: when she recounted the scene she described here, I could hear her cry into the audiotape. Even though she was cut off from her brother physically for most of her life, she still retained deep-seated feelings for him.

At this time in the Hasidic world, if there was a divorce, it was not uncommon for there to be a total break between the two parties, and neither parent was able to have any contact with the child he or she had surrendered to the other. In effect, my little brother was lost to my mother until he became an adult.

My brother was brought up in the house of my paternal grandfather, Yisrael Taub, in the spirit of Modzitz, with their emphasis on music and song. He, like my father, composed many melodies that became well known in the Hasidic world. I was brought up in the spirit of Lublin, which emphasized learning and scholarship, and I was greatly influenced by my beloved stepfather, who was a well known scholar and also a mystic. Consequently, the two of us had very different orientations to the world.

It was in 1909. My mother attempted to see her son when he celebrated his fifth birthday, when a party is made (*khimesh side*) to celebrate a boy's first day of study of the Torah, the scripture. My mother was dressed very elegantly and opulently when we went to visit my brother on this important occasion. It was fall, and she wore a three-quarters length Persian lamb coat with a silk scarf on top of the elegantly styled wig that covered her hair. She wore only a scarf to cover her entire head later, when she married my stepfather. **(In Hasidic circles a wig was regarded as more modern than a scarf or bonnet.)** My brother's teacher in his yeshiva was a follower of her father's, and my mother arranged with him in advance to come to the yeshiva to see my brother on his fifth birthday. Her brother's oldest son came with us to Modzitz (known officially as Dęmblin), and we arrived in a coach. Mother brought many gifts, including silk fabric to make a special suit for my brother, many sweets, and various other things.

We arrived in this very small town in a coach; my mother dressed in her Persian lamb coat. Everybody in the town knew who she was. When my grandfather's people heard that we had arrived in town they quickly went to the school and whisked my brother away. When we reached the yeshiva, my brother wasn't there, and we had to leave town without seeing him. My father wasn't there at the time either: he had remarried and lived in his wife's town (Stopnice). I don't know who conducted the rabbinical politics and decided to grab my brother away from the school when we came. My mother took all the things back with her, and I played with the toys she had brought for my brother as we waited at the train station for the train to take us back to Lublin.

My mother didn't give up on the idea of seeing her son. In 1910, she went a second time, alone. She once again arranged with the same teacher to meet him in the school. This time she went in a simple coat, wrapped around with a big scarf, and looked like a peasant woman. She arrived in a wagon rather than a coach and nobody noticed her. This time my brother was present at the school. He was in a very bad state, dirty and neglected. The teacher brought in a bucket of water with soap; my mother gave him a bath and dressed him with outfits she brought for him. She returned home heartbroken at having seen him in such a neglected state. Later I was told by one of my mother's brothers' wives that my mother never forgave herself for allowing her son to be taken from her. She never spoke about it to me. He only started visiting my mother as an adult, after he got married. But then, such were often the arrangements after a divorce, separating the children from one parent or the other. I believe that it was to assuage her guilt for allowing my brother to be removed from her that she tried everything in her power to make it up to him, showering him with gifts at his wedding and whenever she had the opportunity.

Notwithstanding the divorce, my childhood years were extremely happy, and I was a joyful child. I didn't miss having a father when I was little. I never asked about a father, probably because the entire family

I. In My Mother's Voice

took care of me—my great-grandmother (Bubbe Basia), my grandfather and grandmother, my mother's brothers and my aunts. I was at the center of this very large extended family, surrounded by a bounty of love and warmth. The entire family embraced me. My grandfather and grandmother treated me as their child; I felt very strongly their love and devotion. It is not surprising that I am so tied to my family to this day, despite the fact that everybody is now gone, most of them lost during the Second World War.

Until my mother remarried when I was between six and seven years old, I lived with my mother and grandparents in the home of my birth in Lublin. When my mother had been married to my father, they had lived in my grandfather's home in Lublin, as was the custom. They were "eating *kest*": that is, a woman's husband comes to reside with her parents and the couple is supported by them for an extended period of time. My grandfather had a very large apartment situated in one of two mutually-adjacent buildings divided into eight apartments. Two of my mother's brothers lived in two separate apartments in the same building complex. Until their divorce the young couple lived in the same building. After the divorce, my mother remained there.

The complex was comprised of two three-floor adjacent houses (Sheroka 40 and 42). Two apartments and the sanctuary were located on the ground floor as one walked in from the courtyard. At one time there was also a bakery on the ground floor. From the time I was born, at the beginning of the twentieth century, we had electric lights, even colored electric lights in the courtyards for the weddings that were usually held at home; at such times, the first floor of the Lublin house was reserved for women and the second for men.

My great-grandmother's apartment was up the stairs on one side of the house, the other side housed a very large kitchen with a brick stove and oven. The kitchen led to a large veranda that served for making a *sukkah* **(see Glossary)** built for the *Sukkot* holiday, celebrated separately by women and men. My grandfather had two well-furnished and immense sukkahs where he spent the seven days of the holiday: one for sleeping, with a bed, table and chairs; the other for eating and for receiving his followers.

It was my grandfather's custom to give his grandchildren money for this holiday. Two of my cousins and I went down to his sukkah for money and nuts. I got double the amount of money my cousins received, and they used to say, "You are grandfather's child." They were a bit jealous of me because they thought that I was the apple of my grandparents' eyes.

During the rest of the year the veranda served as a storage room. Every Thursday my grandmother baked a variety of cakes and cookies for the Sabbath and sent them to all of her children who lived in the building, and to the other two sons who lived nearby in Lublin. One of her sons left Lublin after his marriage to live with his wife's family in another town, but the family returned to Lublin at my grandmother's insistence when World War I began. I always grabbed the packages of cakes she prepared to bring to my uncles who lived in the house.

There are no photographs of my grandfather. He was of middle height, not heavy, not thin, with a beautiful long white beard and a very light-skinned face that usually had a slight smile. I will always remember his smile. His face expressed his generosity, his goodness, his sanctity. He was known to his followers as a *tzaddik*, a holy man, a rebbe, a scholar. A Hasid who attended one of his Saturday tables at dusk, known to Hasidim as a *se'udah shelishit* **(the third meal on the Sabbath: see Glossary)** wrote about it by saying, "It looked to me as if the table sung," revealing my grandfather's intense spirituality to the extent that the "table itself could rejoice."

But for me, I can only describe him as my grandfather with the beautiful smile. From the time I remember him, he must have already been afflicted by some illness of the leg, because he didn't walk straight. He shuffled his feet and went up the stairs slowly. But he was a majestic figure with an aristocratic bearing. He was extraordinarily happy man, and as a result the mood in the house was always very cheerful.

Grandfather was also a tolerant person. I don't know whether one can describe Hasidim and rebbes, in general, as tolerant people; but I will use the word to describe my grandfather. In Lublin there was a synagogue frequented by butchers, and it burned down. When the congregation built a new synagogue, they asked my grandfather to give a sermon on how women should dress modestly. My grandfather declined the invitation, because he said that one should look to oneself before telling others how to behave. Well, this is an extraordinary thing; he always guarded against telling others how to conduct themselves or teaching morality, even though he may have made certain that his own children were dressed modestly.

My grandfather had thousands of Hasidim. He helped them with

I. In My Mother's Voice

advice; he sustained them. Today people go to psychiatrists and pay a hundred dollars an hour, and the doctor forgets the person as soon as he leaves. At one time the psychiatrists were the rebbes. A man went to see the rebbe to unburden his heart; he told him his troubles, what gnawed at him, and the rebbe gave him guidance. When the man left, the rebbe still had him in mind.

All my grandfather's *shamusim*, his trusted servants/ assistants, lived and ate in our house. They lived to serve him. Many of them liked to play with me. I recall each by a special characteristic. One would only drink dark cacao. The house servants knew to prepare for him his favored drink. Another one drank only tea, and the servants knew that a big tea kettle must be ready with tea. In Poland, the ovens were made of tiles. In the dining room there was a big stove on the bottom of which there was a door opening to the fuel burner and a small oven; on top of the stove one could place pots to warm up food or water. There was an earthen gray tea-kettle that was placed inside the little oven, so that this man could have his tea all day.

At that time there were no children's shows, but there were Purim shows in my grandfather's house. One show dealt with *Mechirat Yosef*, the story of how Joseph was sold by his brothers. Another dealt with Hana and her seven sons. On Purim children were disguised in the manner of that time.

My grandmother had a footstool on which I used to sit while she would read to me the Joseph story translated into Yiddish, and the *tzene rene*, which was a Yiddish translation of the Torah especially for women. When I can't fall asleep, sometimes my thoughts lead me to wonder when I acquired my love for Israel. I believe the love was instilled in me from my earliest youth, when my grandmother read me these biblical stories.

I used to pray when I was five years old. One time, as I prayed the *Shimenesre* **(core prayer, see Glossary)**, in my grandmother's room, my grandfather paused in the door to listen to me. It must have been a day prayer. He called to my grandmother, "Listen how she prays; she prays and knows Hebrew better than a man." My grandparents put a lot of effort teaching me; they were proud of me, they had *nakhes*, joy **(see Glossary)**.

My grandfather was the first one I would call when I was hurt. As a very active and curious child, I always ran. I recall running out of the kitchen with some baked goods my grandmother had prepared for the

Sabbath, to bring them to one of my uncles who lived on the top floor of the house. I ran so fast that I fell, and a nail pierced my forehead. I started screaming for my grandfather, who came out of his room; I grabbed him around his legs and then I called for Refuel the *Feldscher* **(Feldschers were lay physicians, with no formal medical training: see Glossary)**. The first person I called for was my grandfather—not my mother, but my grandfather—who was to me like my father.

I usually slept with my mother in her room, but when I was sick I stayed in my grandmother's very large room. When I was seven years old, I had typhoid fever and lost my curly hair, which never grew back as thick as it had been before. Aron the *meshamesh*, grandfather's assistant, and a lot of other people surrounded me. They treated me with *babske*—an old wives' remedy involving putting herring in a cloth and wrapping it around my feet, which made a big impression on me at the time. They didn't resort to such remedies in later years. There was a time when they used cupping for colds; when I came to the U.S. there were no such remedies. I had a bad cold one time and asked to be treated by cupping; nobody knew what I meant.

During the summers, our entire household moved to Otwock, a town known for its beautiful pine trees and fresh air. Grandfather rented the same villa every year from the Moskowitz family. It was located in a very beautiful area of the town. Each villa included several houses and we always had the same one-story house with very large glass verandas all around. My grandfather's assistants and servants and regular Hasidim lived with us there too. The family lived downstairs, including the grandchildren when they came for a few weeks. One summer the only children around my age were boys.

I was about five or six years old. At one point that year, I remember sitting on the middle of my swing, and two of the boys were standing on either side, pushing me on it. It was a very pleasant game for us all. Suddenly my grandfather appeared, walking in our direction. The boys became terribly embarrassed and ran away, and I was the only one remaining on the swing when grandfather came closer. He laughed at the boys for running, afraid that he would scold them. Grandfather greatly enjoyed seeing us play, and also the boys' embarrassment that they were playing with a girl. Later, grandfather asked us why we were afraid of him; it seemed to me even then that for him it was perfectly natural that we played together on the swing.

I did experience some little traumas in my childhood. I had a nanny in Lublin, and one time she looked away when we were sitting outside. A Polish woman took my hand and started walking with me. A neighbor noticed and asked if it could be possible that the rebbe's daughter (my mother) would have hired a Polish woman to take care of me. When the neighbor asked the woman whose child this was, the woman told her it was hers. The neighbor started screaming and I was quickly taken from the woman, who wanted to kidnap me. It all happened within a few minutes—it was a miracle that I was saved.

And then, when I was two years old in 1905, there was a revolution in Russia. I was outside when Cossacks came into our courtyard, and one of them jumped over me with his horse. It was extraordinary lucky that I wasn't crushed by the horse. This story was told very often.

I speak about my childhood, but I have not mentioned my mother's relationship to me as of yet. One thing I loved was how my mother sang me songs at bed time. I still recall the songs *Ofen Pripichik* (this is a very famous Yiddish song). Another was "Sleep, My Child." In 1905, when this song was popular, a lot of men had left for the United States. With the revolution in Russia and Poland that year, there were songs about Russia, with lines like "Yesterday they dragged coal, now we rule Poland." She also sang *Rozinkis mit Mandlen* (Raisins with Almonds) in Yiddish, as well as Hebrew songs.

As I grew older she was a friend to me. She trusted me; she would seek my advice and confide in me. For example, when we were among Jews and Poles in the park in one spa town, we saw a hunchbacked woman walking with a very handsome man. All the guests would talk about this couple. They asked how such a good-looking man could be with a deformed woman. This woman was very rich, and the talk was that this man sold himself to this very rich woman. My mother must have told me about this couple and what was said about them, because I could not have known it otherwise. It was typical that my mother spoke to me as she would speak to a friend, not like a mother speaks to a 5- or 6-year-old child. She entrusted me with her impressions and her opinions.

I imagine that after her divorce my mother was being introduced to various men. One time she was sitting outside on a big veranda. I played at a distance. She called me. I saw a man walking away from her. She told me to run and take a look at the man and see if I liked him. She seemed to value my opinion, and wanted me to like the person whom she would marry.

I can still vividly picture many of my mother's outfits. She was always dressed very elegantly and she liked beautiful clothes. Until she married my stepfather, she wore a stunning black wig, arranged in a chignon. (My grandmother was upset when my mother made the change to wearing a scarf, since all her daughters-in-law wore wigs.) My mother said that since she married into a family where everybody wore scarves she would also.

I especially recall one of her outfits, a lovely lilac woolen jumper cut in a princess line, fitted at the waist with a long, wide skirt. She wore it with a blouse buttoned with hooks, a bow, and French cuffs. This was in 1908 or 1909, when long dresses were still worn. She looked striking in this dress. She was still very young then, and a beautiful woman.

After my grandfather passed away in 1914, I became my grandmother's favorite, as was often remarked by my girl cousins. I accompanied her wherever she went in and out of Lublin, even when she travelled to Opole to look for a house for my mother after she remarried. One time she took me to visit her son, my uncle Shlomo, who lived in Krushnik. My grandmother loved all her grandchildren, but all had the feeling that only I was grandmother's favored grandchild. I will not go into a superficial psychological analysis of why I was favored, but probably the family believed that I was disadvantaged (*baavlet*), that I was dealt a bad hand by fate because of my parent's divorce.

When my mother remarried and moved to Opole with her new husband, whom I called *Fete*, meaning uncle, I continued to reside with my grandparents. But even if the divorce had not happened, I would still have been spoiled by my grandparents: my mother was their only daughter and they had special feelings for her.

I felt I belonged to the whole extended family, perhaps because of my mother's divorce or perhaps because her five brothers loved their only sister. When my mother's brothers went to Carlsbad in 1913, they brought back presents for me but not for the other children in the family. I particularly remember six very expensive bed sheets made of cotton, fashionably embroidered in Richelieu style from this famous spa town. I put the sheets away for my wedding.

I used to dance on top of the long tables that stood in the sanctuary of my grandfather's synagogue, and study hall, the *Besmedresh*. The followers—Hasidim—who sat around these tables never said anything. I can't believe I did that, but I was a joker. One time I took a cup of water and poured it down a person's neck. People laughed. I was 5 years old. The old Besmedresh was located in the same house where we lived, but two steps below the ground floor. One came in from the courtyard and went down the stairs. The new study hall was located in the same house; it was completed at the beginning of World War I, after my grandfather passed away. It was very big.

I laugh now because here in the United States, a Besmedresh is built the same size for men and women, so that on holidays as many seats as possible can be sold. At that time, there was only a very small sanctuary with one window, which was used only by the family and a few women; we did not rent or sell the seats. The Besmedresh for the Hasidim was very large with windows along three walls.

Before Passover the boys (my grandfather's students) removed all the books from the study hall to air them out. I used to dance around the books, and go up and down the ladders that were placed to reach them.

Passovers in my grandfather's house were very special. It was my favorite holiday, because different dishes were taken out of the closets; everything was new, clean and fresh. A few weeks before Passover the tables were already scrubbed and covered. The matzos were prepared in the matzo baker's house a few days before the beginning of the holiday. A mortar and pestle was used to make the matzo. Some of the matzo meal was set aside to be used on the last day of Passover for making farfel and *kneidlech* (matzo balls), which were only eaten on the last day of the holiday. I used to run back and forth to watch how they baked the matzos by hand and I danced around when they were baking them. I was everywhere.

Special matzos were eaten the day before Passover (*erev pessah*), and these were baked several weeks in advance. We began getting ready for Passover in the winter, around Hanukah, when we prepared beets for Passover borsht. Grandmother's women helpers peeled pounds and pounds of beets, which were then soaked in immense barrels and placed on the huge glass veranda until Passover.

Around Purim, about a month before Passover, we prepared schmaltz made from goose fat; the *shoykhet* (ritual slaughterer) came to the house to slaughter the geese. When I was two and a half years old I became frightened by the screeching of the geese, and somebody suggested that we perform a wax ceremony to rid me of the fright. They took a pan of hot water, which they placed on my head, and let wax melt into the hot water. When the wax melted it turned into a goose, establishing that the geese had frightened me. I don't know whether we got this custom from the Poles, or they got it from us, but many years later I heard about a book written by a Polish peasant who described this ceremony. I suppose Jews must have gotten some of these customs from the Polish peasants. The practice was given up some years later.

The wax cure was a type of divination ceremony that Poles used; in 1905 this was a popular mode of curing various illnesses. Ever the rationalist, my mother did not have any confidence in such "old wives'" practices in her adult life.

Central to the preparations were the special procedures we followed to make the stove kosher for Passover. Normally, my grandmother baked *challah* in the wood-fueled oven to send to all her children for Shabbat. But on Passover the oven was not used, and it had to be specifically prepared for the holiday.

The stove in the kitchen had burners. For Passover, bricks were put on top of each burner, and on top of each brick three-pronged iron burners were placed, to be fueled by either coal or wood. The fuel went on the brick, below the burner, and the pot was placed on the burner. For some reason the Passover pots were made of earthenware, not iron like our regular ones.

Let me describe the first Seder that I remember. Unfortunately, I am not a painter or poet, so I cannot really portray how beautiful it was. If I could paint, I would paint the vivid colors I see in my mind. My great-grandmother, Bubbe Basia, was still alive then. She was the wife of the first Hasidic rabbi of the Eiger dynasty (Yehuda Leib Eiger, known as Leibl), and a very feisty lady **(see Appendix 1)**. For the Seder, Bubbe Basia wore a light-colored dress, and her head covering was different from my grandmother's. My grandmother (Bubbe Hana) wore a *haybl* or *habu*; it was a tall scarf, or bonnet, with points on top. Bubbe Basia wore what was called a *kapturek*, tight around the head and tied with bands in the back of the neck. Such head covers may now exist only in museums.

The Seder was conducted in my grandmother and grandfather's rooms, which was rearranged for the two Seder nights. Grandfather's room was large and square, with two windows facing the street. There was a very large table, at the head of which stood a black leather fauteuil, a type of wide lounge chair. The room was painted white and light blue, but what intrigued me as a child was that above the doors of this room there was a whitewashed square. I had seen similar squares elsewhere, and they puzzled me. I was told later that they were made in commemoration of the destruction of the Temple .

The second room belonged to my grandmother, Bubbe Hana; the two rooms were separated by French doors. My grandmother's room was the larger of the two, and the Seder was conducted there. The French doors were opened for the Seder, and the women sat in one room and the men in the other. Grandfather could see the women and Grandmother the men.

This was the first and only Seder I remember with Bubbe Basia, who sat at the head of the table on the fauteuil, in my grandfather's room. The women—the daughters-in-law and my mother—and the grandchildren sat on either side of the long table. There was a smaller table with chairs on the side where the servants, cooks, and cleaners sat, along with a nanny for the infants and another one for the children.

The Seder was an event exclusively for the family. The Hasidim were not invited to it, except those who lived in the house, those who came specifically for the Seder, or people who had nowhere else to go. Other than these men, there were no outsiders. I remember well the names of the Hasidim and my grandfather's assistants who remained in the house for Passover.

Hanukah was also a joyous holiday. My grandfather had several Hanukah lamps he would light; one looked like a covered box, out of which protruded the wick and the fire. It burned natural oil. He also had a very large one, with all kinds of decorations that had belonged to Akiva Eiger. Bubbe Basia had given it to him, but, alas, it was lost during the war.

I took great pride in possessing a copy of Akiva Eiger's mother's will and some other memorabilia until the Second World War. It came into my possession in an unusual way. In around 1914, when two of my uncles went to Carlsbad on their return they got caught up in World War I. They could not return directly home and had to travel via small towns in Russia. In one of these towns they met a man whose name was also Akiva Eiger. He was also a descendant of our ancestor, and he possessed the will of Akiva Eiger's mother, Gitel. This man gave the will to my uncle at that time, and a few years later, being very close to my mother, my uncle gave it to her, and she then passed it on to me. My uncle thought that I would appreciate it most. My grandmother also gave me a desk that had belonged to Akiva Eiger, which was in my possession until the Second World War.

Bubbe Basia was a legendary figure in the family. I remember her cracking open nuts with her own teeth when she was in her late 90's. She used reading glasses, but had her full hearing. She was a woman of extraordinarily strong will. She married my great-grandfather Leibl when she was around 13 or 14 years old and he was 19. Like his grandfather, Rabbi Akiva Eiger, my great-grandfather was known for being a *misnaged*—a person who vehemently opposed Hasidism. Bubbe Basia was the daughter of a very wealthy man, and when the marriage was arranged, he believed that his son-in-law would also be a misnaged, as indeed he was at the time. To his regret, however, Leibl became a Hasid after the marriage. When her father learned of this, he instructed Bubbe Basia to divorce him. She refused, and even encouraged her husband to go off to the rebbe of Kotzk and become his disciple, and to the rebbe of Izbica and study with him as well. When Bubbe Basia's father failed to convince her to divorce Leibl, he attempted to kill him by pushing him out of a window. Fortunately, Leibl survived the fall and became a renowned Hasidic rebbe, establishing the Lublin dynasty and court.

Bubbe Basia also directed her son's Hasidic career. After her husband died, her son, my grandfather Abraham, was naturally supposed to inherit his father's position and become rebbe and head of what had become known as the Lublin court. He was reluctant to do so, because he did not feel he merited the position. Abraham wished instead to become a disciple of another brilliant rebbe and close friend, Tzadok HaKohen, but his mother would not permit it. She insisted that it would be disrespectful to his father for him not to assume the rebbe's position and lead the court. He accepted his mother's judgment. When Tzadok HaKohen passed away, his Hasidim accepted my grandfather as their rebbe as well.

I have vivid memories of scenes in which Bubbe Basia was present. She had a huge apartment within my grandfather's house. One room had a balcony that was beautifully furnished, with a red velvet fauteuil and antique furniture which she must have brought with her after her wedding. She also had a large kitchen, and from the kitchen was a door

I. In My Mother's Voice

that led to a salon. She usually sat in the front room with the balcony: that was her dining room.

She had a china closet where she kept silver and glass things, gifts people brought her from foreign countries. She drank coffee every day at noon out of a special porcelain cup. No matter what I was doing, I was always brought in to her room at that hour; I sat across from her, and she took out a matching cup and saucer and gave me coffee, milk or tea. It was a tradition.

I had a similar tradition with my grandfather. My grandfather fasted all day, and ate one main meal at night at around 9 or 10 p.m. Even if I was already asleep at that hour, I was awakened for his evening meal and brought to his room; he sat on his high fauteuil, and I on the nearby sofa. He was always in a good mood and full of laughter at these meals.

I was eight years old when Bubbe Basia passed away in 1911. I didn't go to the funeral; children weren't taken to funerals. I sat at the window in the large kitchen, mourning. Her death had a powerful impact on me.

My grandfather passed away three years later, while I was in Lublin. He'd been very sick, and my grandmother and uncles were all gathered in his large room. My mother learned about her father's death at the circumcision ceremony of my brother Avrumce. She had been in her ninth month of the pregnancy with him when grandfather had died, and would have been unable to travel to Lublin from Opole, where she lived after she had remarried, to attend the funeral, and so she was not even told. Her husband did attend the funeral, along with a huge crowd, even though a heavy snow fell that day. I remember my grandfather's passing as if it were a dream; he was stretched out on the floor. I think somebody took me to his room to sit with him. I don't know what happened later, or what it was like when grandmother and all of his children sat *shiva* **(the usually seven-day requisite time of mourning, requiring the bereaved to remain in the home)**. What I clearly remember is that I, as a child, thought that as long as my great grandmother and my grandfather were alive, the world remained in one place; until their death it seemed to me that time stood still. I was shocked when a new year rolled in. From the moment of their passing, everything shook and everything moved.

My grandfather's will stated that he knew that according to Jewish law, daughters were not entitled to any inheritance; nevertheless, he asked that his sons would give their sister (my mother) her inheritance, and hoped they would do so. In order not to transgress Jewish law, the brothers had to give their sister her inheritance as a "present," and they must give it to her "with all their hearts." This "present" was to come from the money garnered from grandfather's properties, including the houses where they all lived, and from the remaining available cash. When I became engaged, my groom, Haim, came to Lublin to sign the papers allowing my mother's share of these properties to be transferred to me and him as my dowry. The transfer was not that easily resolved, however.

Traditionally the oldest son succeeded to the position of rebbe. All the followers understood that and wished it. But my grandfather's oldest son did not wish to become rebbe, believing to his sorrow that only his sister, my mother, merited that position, but she was a woman. Later, a conflict over succession emerged between the oldest and the second son, which was unsatisfactorily resolved by a split among the followers with some recognizing the oldest son and some the second son.

The succession conflict between the brothers lasted for many years and had many ramifications for my grandfather's followers, and especially for me and my possibility to marry. My mother's oldest brother, Shlomo, had married into a very wealthy family, and his father-in-law owned an iron works in a small town not far from Lublin (Krushnik); he moved there after his marriage. The next-oldest brother, Esriel Mayer, had remained living in Lublin, close to his parents, after his marriage. Although he was a businessman, he was also learned and seemed spiritually prepared to be the inheritor of his father's court. After World War I, the situation had changed and, as I mentioned earlier, Shlomo, the eldest, returned to live in Lublin at the urging of my grandmother because she felt it was dangerous to live in a small town during a time of war. The conflict, then, was who of these two sons should inherit my grandfather's position as the Lublin rebbe, both spiritually and materially, since the position came with a considerable income. Shlomo was the oldest ,but Esriel Mayer was the more spiritual and closer to his father. The conflict finally ended in a religious court and judgment **(a din Torah, see Glossary)**.

Until the inheritance issue was resolved, my mother lacked a dowry for me, which made it difficult for me to marry. No matter how accomplished or beautiful a woman was, if she lacked a dowry she could not marry. Finally, one brother bought out the shares of the others in our house, and my mother remained owner of part of it, which she transferred to me and my future husband as my dowry.

I speak about deaths in our family, not births. In rabbinic families the dead are forever remembered by commemorations of their death, their *yahrzeit*, marked by a feast. Birthdays were not noted or celebrated. I don't even know my mother's birthday, nor do I remember exactly my siblings' birthdays, only the places where they were born and the season of the year.

I always light candles on the days of my forebears' passing: my grandfather, great-grandfather, great-grandmother, grandmother. I believe I am the only grandchild that remembers to light candles for the grandmothers; for the grandfathers there usually is a celebration on the day of their passing.

My education in childhood was uneven. Boys began their Hebrew education at age 5, but girls just learned to read and pray informally. I learned to pray when I was 5 years old. My mother must have taught me, because I knew Hebrew well by that age. I learned arithmetic and Russian. Mother gave me children's books in Russian.

I was six years old when my mother took me to my first school. There were no official schools at that time as far as I know. Perhaps later, in the 1920's, elementary schooling was made obligatory by the Polish government and some schools were established for Jewish girls. But when I was a child, such schools did not exist. There was a girls' private school not far from where we lived where they taught a little writing and arithmetic. Mother made a special dress for me, a *marinash*, or marine-type outfit, fashionable at that time, with a pleated skirt and a blouse with a marine collar, to wear when she took me to my first day of school in Lublin. She also made me a special black apron, like every child in our family had. There were no school uniforms, only these outfits.

The teacher had a ruler, which he would whack on the desk to keep the children quiet. I got frightened when he banged on the table, and I got up and ran back home. I didn't return. There was another private school in Lublin where I remained a little longer. I had a little girlfriend; she would come to the house and we would do our arithmetic homework together.

I don't know where I studied in Lublin later. After my mother remarried and we moved to Opole, I went to school there for awhile. The teacher was a man with a white beard, and I didn't like him. I used to always hold my index finger bent and the teacher kept straightening it out, because he was teaching us calligraphy.

I didn't go to any school for long, because I would spend a few months in Lublin with my grandparents and a few months in Opole with my mother and stepfather. In Opole all I remember is the episode of the teacher wanting to straighten out my finger. Considering all this, how I learned anything at all is a mystery. My mother must have taught me.

Later, I studied with private teachers in Lublin and Opole. My mother hired teachers to teach me French, and I even briefly had a Polish teacher who came to our house. I was struck by her eating habits: she drank tea and ate dry dark bread. I was not used to seeing people eating dry bread. I also learned by myself. I loved to read, and I read a lot of Yiddish stories about rebbes. Later, I read more serious things, like books by the great Russian and Polish writers.

My mother had a hand sewing machine in Opole; she liked to sew, and I stood next to her watching her, and that is how I learned to sew. I always sewed for myself when I was older. During my childhood years, mother also taught me how to knit and do many different types of embroidery, and how to paint on glass and create pictures using plaster.

I was a child who was interested in everything. I needed to know about everything going on around me, whether it was sewing, cooking, or baking. My mother would say, "You should know everything and need to use little of it." **(In Yiddish it rhymes: Solst altz visen and vainick banitzen.)** By that, she meant that I shouldn't be in a position where I needed to do everything myself. In the end, I did have to use everything. In the very difficult first years in America, all that I learned from my mother in my childhood was very useful, especially the knowledge of sewing. My mother used to say, "My child, you should always look down, not up (*inte ziyech, nicht ibe ziyech*). This way you will always be content. If you look down you will see there is worse than what you have, whether in health or anything else." She had a saying for everything.

My grandmother wished me to study in a gymnasium. She had a close friend who was enlightened about secular education, and whose grandchildren had studied in a religious gymnasium built by Jewish people in Lublin in 1915. They advised her to send me to this gymnasium. But there was a concern that everybody would oppose it, and I was not sent there. **(There was an ongoing fear in the Hasidic community that a youth's exposure to a gymnasium might alienate him or her from religion or Orthodoxy; not until the 1930s were girls from the family**

I. In My Mother's Voice

sent to secondary schools or gymnasium.)

I was raised among adults. There were no children, and certainly no girls of my age, living with my grandparents until 1914, when my mother's brother and his family came to live with us. All the other cousins in Lublin were much younger than I was. I only heard about what adults were interested in, such as world events and Jewish events. I listened to what everybody was saying.

In 1912 there was a great deal of talk about the Beilis affair, and I was very interested in it. **(Mendel Beilis was a Ukrainian Jew accused of the ritual murder of a 13-year-old Christian boy in Kiev in 1911 in one of many historical examples of the "blood libel"; his arrest and conviction spurred an outcry against anti-Semitism.)** I was in grandfather's room in 1912 when a man came in and announced that Beilis was freed from jail. I ran to grandfather, shouting, "grandfather, grandfather, Beilis was freed, Beilis is free!" Everyone in the house was extraordinarily happy, as all Jews were. I remember dancing and jumping with joy that this falsely-accused man was freed. It is difficult to describe how happy grandfather was that God had helped us emerge from the danger that the libel demonstrated. The mood in the house was thrilling.

I often accompanied my grandmother and my mother on their travels, particularly when they attended weddings. For one such trip around 1916 or 1917, mother made me a gorgeous electric blue silk dress to wear at the wedding at our destination. I saw the bride, a cousin, when her hair was being cut on the day of the wedding, as was the custom. As I watched, the groom's sister, whose family was a bit more modern, observed sadly that it was beautiful hair to be cut so short. I don't recall the wedding, but I do remember the hair-cutting scene very clearly.

On another occasion when I was a young girl, my mother took me to Warsaw to attend a wedding. Someone in the family organized a trip for several cousins to the Tlomackie synagogue, the Great Synagogue on Tlomackie Street in Warsaw, built in the nineteenth century. One of my mother's brothers heard about our excursion and created a terrible uproar about our visiting that synagogue, where they played an organ at all services. **(Instruments were never played in a Hasidic sanctuary.)**

My mother often refers to weddings she attended throughout her childhood and youth, and how elegantly and fashionably the

women were dressed, in contrast to the men's dark garb. She went into great detail about the style and fabrics of the dresses, such as taffeta, which seems to have looked especially elegant on the dance floor. In Hasidic circles, marriage is the single most important event in a person's life, because marrying is commanded by God (it is a mitzvah, a sacred deed). On the day of her wedding, a bride is considered to be in a sacred state, and guests may even give her notes with petitions for God, in much the same way that a person may place a note in the Wailing Wall. Weddings were also occasions that brought families together from all over the country and abroad, because the marriage was a union between families rather than individuals. Festivities usually lasted a week.

I had a complicated relationship with my father. After the divorce, my father made no attempt to see me, but my mother wanted me to see him. He once visited Lublin when I was five or six years old, but didn't make any effort to see me. When by chance my mother learned about his visit, she walked with me to a place she knew he would be passing and pointed to a man across the street, saying that man was my father. I answered a bit brazenly (I was sometimes *chutzpadik*), "You can tell me that any man is my father." My mother had never mentioned my father until that time. I imagine now that she was hurt by my answer. I believe that my father took out his anger towards my mother on me; for this reason he did not want to see me, and would not let her see my brother.

I had little contact with my father's family. Once I saw my paternal grandfather, but not my father, when my mother and I travelled to a wedding and changed trains in the town where he lived. I visited him then, and it had a great impact on me because my grandfather had a medical problem that had required one leg to be removed. (During the operation, incidentally, he had composed a very beautiful and now famous musical composition). When I was brought into his room, his wife told me to go over to him and kiss his hand. This was an extraordinary event for me. In Lublin, we did not have a custom of kissing anyone's hands. I can still picture the scene. His healthy foot was hanging down from the chair; he smiled. I don't know what he said; all I remember is walking over to him and giving him a kiss on the hand.

I saw my father for the first time since the divorce in 1915, when I happened to be in Warsaw at the same time that my father was visit-

I. In My Mother's Voice

ing his parents. They had come to live in the capital to seek safety from the Russians who arrested Jews in the small towns during those years. It was in the summer at the beginning of World War I when Russians began taking such hostages (*Zakwadnikis*).

My father lived in a town called Raków, where he was the chief rabbi, and occasionally he came to visit his parents for a Sabbath. I visited him without an invitation, at the suggestion of a follower of my paternal grandfather, who also accompanied me to the meeting. It was late afternoon around the time of se'udah shelishit. My father's mother set a table, and my father's youngest sister, Malka, was there. My grandmother received me quite coldly. Malka talked to me and smiled. I sat and waited till they called father out from the se'udah shelishit. My father's sister escorted me to the door and my father came over. I don't remember if we spoke. It was evening; it was dark. He stood in the doorway and I couldn't even see him, or my brother. He gave me a kiss on the forehead. The whole thing took a minute. Then I was taken back to his mother; Malka gave me a silver charm bracelet and a small box of marmalades, and I was sent home. When I got home I sat down on a sofa and hung my head down in silence. Nobody asked me anything, because they saw how unhappy I was.

As I was transcribing this episode in my mother's life, tears came to my eyes. Her relationship with her father was very painful to her, and she "bled" all her life as a result of her father's apparent rejection.

There may have been a general insensitivity to children's feelings in those days (to everybody's feelings, really). Additionally, my mother's birth father at the time of this first visit was only about twenty-eight years old. He may not have realized how deeply he had hurt her, leaving a mark on her entire life.

His subsequent lack of acknowledgement of her existence during her childhood also had lasting consequences on her life.

My second encounter with my father was when I visited him after I became engaged for the first time, when I was 15 and half years old, between Hanukah and Purim. We lived in Opole, and my mother, stepfather and I came to Lublin to my grandmother's house for the betrothal. My mother and stepfather then returned to Opole and I remained in Lublin. I don't know whose idea it was, grandmother's or one of my uncle's, to send a telegram to my father telling him that I'd become engaged. At that time I was so involved in reading and studying that I didn't think about such things.

The telegram was sent to him in Raków, where he lived with his third wife. In response, I received a letter from his wife congratulating me and inviting me to visit them; my father added a few words. His second wife had died during the great typhus epidemic of 1918. My grandmother, Hana, was pleased by the invitation; my mother, hearing about this plan in her home in Opole, prepared me to visit after Passover in 1919. My mother made me new dresses so that I would look like a wealthy daughter of the Lublin court. My grandmother gave me a 500-mark bill, a large sum of money at the time, (there were no zlotys at that time, since Poland had just become an independent country), to buy anything I wished. She also gave me smaller change for the ticket and for a carriage.

I left for Raków soon after the invitation came. I went by myself, since I was already accustomed to traveling from Opole to Lublin alone. To get to Raków I had to change trains several times in very tiny towns. At this time there was a lot of unrest and *halerchikis*—thuggish hoodlums known to be anti-Semitic—roamed around the countryside attacking Jews. But I went anyway. There was a young Jewish man traveling on the train at the same time, and he kept an eye on me. He told me where to get off and helped me with my things. In Raków they were waiting for me at the station. I remember going in a horse and carriage, a *brichka*, to the house.

When my father quickly remarried after my parents' divorce, his new 18-year-old wife, who had never been married before, was promised that she would not have to take care of his two children. I, of course, had remained with my maternal grandparents; my little brother, when he was taken away from my mother, was sent to my father's parents' home, where he was raised until he married. When his second wife died, my father was left a widower, now with four more children by his second wife. He remarried, this time to a woman who had been married before who had no children. She agreed to care for the four children from the previous marriage, but was never told about the existence of the two children from the first one. She learned about our existence when my father was ill with typhus; he was delirious with a high fever and he called out my name and my brother's. The wife asked who these two people were, at which time she found out about us.

I was ecstatic to be able see my father, but three or four days after I arrived, he said that since it was shortly after his wedding to his third wife, and she had not seen her parents in some time, they would like to go for ten days to visit them. They asked me to remain with the children, who were a few years younger than me. I hadn't known about my two sisters and two brothers when I traveled to Raków, so I hadn't brought any gifts for them. Of the four children from the second marriage three were living in the house; the oldest had gone to live with my father's parents. The youngest, a boy of three, needed to take medication, and I was frightened by the responsibility. A servant stayed in the house to help me with the chores. I remember going with the two girls to pick berries in a beautiful forest.

I was 15 and a half years old, and I was not interested how they lived, or whether they had ample food. But looking back on it, I don't think they did; I also realize that they had very little income. It was at the end of the First World War, and a Jewish organization from abroad would send flour, sugar, potatoes, and the like to these small towns to help people. When I arrived in the house there were sacks of flour and other food supplies, and my father's wife cooked big pots of soup to distribute among the poor people who came for it with their bowls. To me it seemed strange that my father's wife would cook and distribute the soup. Why did she need to do this? Later I grasped that she was paid for this work. My father even borrowed from me the 500 marks I had brought along, to take on the trip with his wife. I was glad I could help him, for it meant that I was not a stranger after all.

But I wanted to leave quickly, because it was said that the Bolsheviks were about to attack Poland. I became frightened and wanted to return to Lublin. All told, I remained in Raków for about three weeks.

Poland became an independent state in 1918 with the signing of the Treaty of Versailles, but the treaty failed to clearly define the borders between Russia and Poland. Both countries sought to regain some territories they had lost in the partition, and a war ensued between Russia and Poland in February 1919. The conflict ended with a cease-fire in 1920, and a peace treaty was signed in 1921. During my mother's visit there were already rumors about the impending war, which frightened her badly.

The entire trip was an extraordinary experience for me. Because I was a happy child, I did not feel so bad at the time but, as I begin recollecting this and other happenings, they are very painful, particularly the matter of my surname. When the Russians ruled Poland, it was not customary to register a child at birth, at least among Hasidic families. Neither my brother nor I was registered at our birth. Later, at the time of the divorce, my father, or his father, didn't wish to have me registered in his name. Despite the arguments over this issue among my mother's and father's representatives, it was never resolved. So I remained registered in my mother's name until I got married. My mother later told me that my paternal grandfather sort of apologized, by saying what my grandmother had also said, that a girl will get married, so she will take on another name anyway.

The issue of my name became a problem for me as I grew older, and it was very unpleasant for me to present myself everywhere by the name of Eiger, my mother's maiden name. In 1903 when I was born, or in 1907 when my parents were divorced, they didn't expect that I would want go to a library, or register in a library, or register in a school or university. Nobody had thought about such things. Of all the things that happened later, I suffered most from not carrying my father's name, and from not knowing him at all until I was grown.

I had several unpleasant incidents relating to the name problem. Just before my wedding, there was a whole upheaval. My future husband did not know that I was officially registered as Eiger; he assumed my maiden name was Taub, my birth father's surname. We never discussed it. When he filled out the marriage documents, he wrote Taub. Once I corrected the error, the documents had to be changed to be fully recognized. When I was married it showed that Golda Eiger married Haim Finkler. But the invitations to the wedding had already been printed, stating Golda Taub. My mother-in-law had to reprint all the invitations and replace Taub with Eiger. In my Polish passport there were two Ns, meaning "father unknown." (I needed a passport when travelling between Warsaw and Lublin, because until Poland became a unified country the two cities were occupied by separate countries.) That hurt me a great deal, but I couldn't do anything about it, no matter how I tried.

I would have regretted giving up my Eiger name, because it was so well known and respected. But the Ns in my passport were very hurtful.

I. In My Mother's Voice

Also, I needed documents in various places, including the Wszechnica, the university I attended later, and in Lublin where there was only one library, in the Catholic University, from which I borrowed books. It was very unpleasant to present a document with NN on it.

The fact that my mother went by her mother's maiden name until her marriage was so painful to her that she dwells on the subject in even the most tragic contexts, as we will see from her narrative when she returns to Poland from the camps after the long death march. I profoundly regret that I did not know about this episode of her life until I heard her tapes. Perhaps I could have eased her pain.

As I listened to my mother recounting the very painful subject of her name, it is difficult to understand why her birth father, or paternal grandfather, who at the time was a famous rebbe, refused to have my mother registered in his name. All I can do is speculate that it was indeed a reprisal against my mother's mother for the divorce, or perhaps my mother's father's family wished to keep the children, or at least this one child, a secret because it was not honorable, as my grandfather's wife said, for a rebbe to register a child years after its birth.

As I write about my mother's interactions with her father, I realize for the first time what a tragedy it was for my mother not to have had contact with him until her mid teens, and the damage brought upon by the divorce, which still echoes in me to this day. My mother's parents' divorce, and later her perceived rejection by her father, had a devastating effect that had not left her even by the last days of her life. Indeed, in her descriptions of her interactions with her father prior to World War II, there may not be "his side of the story," for the insensitivity and, one can even say, cruelty toward her seems heartless. As I was listening to her narrative, I was almost as pained by it as she was. One can only say that my mother's birth father may not have been aware of the effect his actions and indifference had on his daughter, and in his way may have even loved her. My only consolation is that the love her stepfather and the rest of the family lavished on her possibly compensated in some measure for the pain he caused.

I drew closer to my father after my marriage, when he moved to Otwock. I was able to accommodate myself to the ways of Modzitz, and at this time I also began seeing my younger brother. He had an exquisite voice, and people would stand in the street to hear him sing. He came on occasion to visit us in Lublin, and later came to see us in Warsaw quite often, especially after he married.

My mother's remarriage occurred when she was 27 years old, in March of 1910, approximately three years after her divorce from my father. She and her husband moved after the first year and a half to Opole, where they resided until 1922, except for the period during the First World War when we moved temporarily to Warsaw. My stepfather, who was 37 years old at the time of the marriage, had also been divorced, chiefly because his first wife was more secular than he was. His divorce had been much more amicable than my parents'; his first wife was not totally estranged from my stepfather, and neither was estranged from his or her children as I was from my father.

Immediately after their marriage, the couple lived in Lublin for over a year in a rented apartment on the same street as my grandfather. I remember that this apartment had what was called a "heaven bed" for the servant, because one had to climb a ladder to get to the upstairs room above the kitchen.

I don't remember my stepfather from Lublin, but I remember him well from the time we arrived in Opole in mid-winter of 1911, when I was 8 years old. From the time we moved to Opole, my stepfather assumed all the responsibility for me, and he was a most devoted father. Actually, many people thought that I was his birth daughter. I adored him.

I struggle with how best to honor my stepfather because I don't know whether I can mention him on my tombstone—it is customary to list the birth parents of the deceased on a person's tombstone. I don't know how to solve this problem, because I would like him to be inscribed on it. I ask myself whether it is right that my father's name, the biological father as they now say, should be engraved on my tombstone, but not the name of my stepfather, who was my real father. He was the one who worried about me; he was the one who put his energies in raising me. He was my true father.[*]

We moved to Opole because my stepfather obtained a rabbinical post

---

[*] My mother is buried in Jerusalem; we placed on the tombstone her birth father's and mother's names and ancestries, and on the side her stepfather's (fete's) name and ancestry.

there after he married my mother. He was known throughout the Jewish world as a holy man; Jews and non-Jews alike came to ask for his blessing. The story was told that a member of the ruling family of Opole once came to ask for his blessing and prayer on behalf of a sick person. Later the person returned to say that the sick man recovered, and he brought my stepfather antique silver candlesticks.

Opole was a typical small town in Poland where Jews had lived for over six hundred years. The town was established as the private property awarded by the King of Poland to a noble, who thus became its ruler. Such towns tended to develop and grow once Jews came to live there. The Jews of the towns were usually artisans, merchants, or engaged in commerce. Like in many other small towns in Poland, in Opole more than half (66.5 percent) of the population was Jewish at the beginning of the twentieth century.

Shortly after the family arrived in Opole, a conflict ensued between two factions in this Jewish community. My stepfather's position was as the official rabbi of the community, and that had been arranged as follows: small communities such as Opole were under the rabbinical auspices of larger ones, and Opole's official rabbinical positions were controlled by my mother's father for years. My grandfather handed over the Opole rabbinate to his new son-in-law to lead, with other rabbis serving various areas of the community. Those who were opposed to my stepfather assuming the post were followers of other courts; they didn't wish to receive a member of my grandfather's Lublin court, and they opposed my stepfather's appointment to this central position in the Jewish community. The fighting was such that I even saw a man returning from the synagogue with blood on his head.

One of my stepfather's opponents was the ritual slaughterer (shoykhet) for the community, who was concerned that he would be supplanted. The conflict was settled by a ritual court (*beit din*) several years later. Before the dispute was settled, it had to be established who the legitimate ritual slaughterer was. This position was important both because it provided the assigned person a livelihood and because it was highly prestigious. My stepfather had three such slaughterers under his supervision, but the local rabbi refused to recognize them because he had his own slaughterer.

To avoid further conflict, the dispute was settled with all four ritual slaughterers functioning in the community. My stepfather agreed not to officiate at weddings or funerals or adjudicate divorces; all such matters he would refer to his opponent. Such conflicts were so potent that even after the tragedy of World War II they were not forgotten. I visited some people in New York after the war, and saw the son of my stepfather's opponent there, but he refused to speak to me.

A month after the First World War began, my stepfather was arrested; he spent the High Holidays in a Lublin prison and remained in prison for 11 or 12 weeks, while my mother was pregnant with Binim, her third son with my stepfather. Until the end of the First World War in 1918, the country of Poland was divided among the Russians, the Germans, and the Austro Hungarians. The Lublin district was held by Russia till 1915, and then it was occupied by German and Austro Hungarian armies. Warsaw was occupied by German forces in 1915. The Russians wanted the Austrian sector, which included then Lublin and its surroundings. Nicolas II began to attack Austria, but the Russians lost the battle in the Lublin district. All this I know very well, because the Austrians arrived on the Lublin-Opole line. The Russians blamed the Jews for their loss in battle, accusing them of spying for Austria; they arrested all the rabbis and important Jewish people in small towns, among those my stepfather. Many of the rabbis, including my birth father's father but not my stepfather, went to Warsaw, which by then was occupied by Germany; our family also came from Lublin to Warsaw when it was already occupied by Germany.

My stepfather was freed from prison as a result of my mother's incessant efforts to have him released; many other rabbis were shot. She succeeded through the intervention of one of our assimilated Eiger relatives, who was at the time a high official in the diplomatic corps. Mother also gave a lot of her jewelry to the governor and governor's wife so that my stepfather would have some comforts in prison.

It can be said with some irony that during the First World War, except for incarcerations, daily life was not really disrupted for most people. My mother gave birth to three of her four children with my stepfather during those years, while we lived in Opole. While we still lived there she fell ill just around the High Holidays; I had to assume the responsibilities of the household and also take care of my siblings during her illness. She was taken to Vienna, via Lublin and Warsaw, to have a gall bladder operation, and when she returned to Warsaw she developed pneumonia.

I was put in charge of the household when my mother was ill and away, and I was still a young girl. That year two male guests came for Rosh Hashanah, and I was responsible for preparing everything for the holiday (with the help of several servants). I recall a silly thing that happened to me, which was not important to anyone but to me. I prepared everything for the holiday but forgot to buy a sheep's head, which would normally have been part of the feast. When I realized that I had forgotten it, I cried. My stepfather asked why I was crying, and when I answered him he laughed. This silly story has remained in my memory all these years.

When my mother was well (she was sickly in her later years), she was always involved in charity work to help the less fortunate; she founded a kitchen to feed yeshiva boys and organized women to distribute the food. When we lived in Warsaw and somebody arrived from a small town needing a doctor or requiring a specialist, she and my stepfather would refer people to the appropriate physician, who would always receive them whether or not they could pay. But people then did not speak about their good deeds. Whatever she did, nobody heard about it.

In 1922, my stepfather was invited to become the rebbe and leader of the Opole Hasidic court in Warsaw, and we moved there permanently. My stepfather was respected by everyone who knew him. One of the many tasks of a Hasidic rebbe was recommending medical specialists to his followers. My stepfather and our whole family had a close relationship with various doctors, who were also devoted friends. They assisted us above and beyond their medical expertise. Medicine may not have been as advanced as it is today, but the doctors were rich in spirit (*geist*).

As I mentioned earlier, I became betrothed at the age of 15. My mother gave a great deal of thought to the marriage matches (*shidikhim*) proposed for me. The marriages in our family were usually arranged between families that were wealthy or considered prestigious, having *yikhes*—pedigree **(see Glossary and Appendix 1)**.

When I was 15 years old, a boy from Lublin was proposed, the 17-year-old son of a businessman. He was tall and slender and already had the reputation of being an excellent businessman, with much talent. When we became engaged, I lived in Opole; my mother, my stepfather, and I came to Lublin for the engagement. It was not an official betrothal (*tnoyim*), but rather an informal ceremony in my grandmother's house when the family of the bride and groom give their "word," or promise that the couple will marry. Usually, people seal the arrangement by drinking *l'chaim*, or a toast, with a bit of whisky, and eating sweets. My mother and stepfather returned to Opole and I remained in Lublin after the engagement.

It was customary in an arranged marriage for the pair not to meet before the wedding. In my case my mother strongly insisted that I see the boy first, to decide whether I wanted him or not. She arranged for us to meet—"a seeing" as it was called—and my mother, the matchmaker (who was one of my grandfather's followers), and I met the boy in a non-Jewish neighborhood where there weren't any people who would recognize us. The boy and I liked one another and my mother felt good about the match. After this meeting we became formally engaged.

We met several more times. He had a female cousin, who was our age, and she would mention that my betrothed wanted to meet with me and that we could get together in the street behind the university, where there were not many people. This was exceptionally daring on my part, because I did not wish to cause my grandmother any grief. But since he asked to meet, I agreed. I was very pleased that I went. When we met we spoke only about politics. That was shortly after the Balfour declaration of 1917, when England proclaimed itself in favor of establishing a Jewish state in Palestine. There was a lot of discussion about this momentous event. He said, and I remember this clearly, that it was in Balfour's interest, not in the interest of helping the Jewish people. That was the thought that probably circulated at the time in the Jewish communities. He had a wide perspective on many things.

In that era, as I said, a betrothed girl like me never saw a prospective groom before marriage, so our behavior was quite unusual. It was a topsy-turvy act. What's more, I was a girl whose head was immersed in books. I didn't have any interest in boys—and yet suddenly I began seeing a boy. He was very respectful. Even though I didn't want to distress my grandmother, she did want the children to go along a bit with the times. She was actually very liberal and she may have known about these meetings. I know that she gave money to a cousin to go to the movies, which normally was not acceptable.

One time my fiancé hid in our house on the third floor, in the attic, where his teacher also lived, because 18-year-old boys were being conscripted by the authorities to dig ditches, or worse, were drafted into the Polish army to fight the Russians. The door was hidden by a commode and the boys were safe there. At 11 p.m. when the gates of the house were closed, the boys came down to get some fresh air. They sat in the courtyard and then returned upstairs. A cousin proposed that I come down to meet my fiancé one night. I said I would not do that because there were other boys present; if my grandmother found out she might have been distressed.

While he was hiding in the attic he once sent me a message asking if I could get him a book to read. I remember exactly what the book was. There was a nineteenth-century Polish writer named Eliza Orzeszkowa who belonged to the Polish Positivists movement, which was very favorably disposed to Jews—one could call them philo-semites—but who also wished Jews to assimilate into Polish society. She wrote several books about Jews in Poland. One of her books was *The Forsaken One* or *Meir Ezofowicz*. I sent him that book. A few days later he returned it and he wrote me a few words.

The Positivist school in nineteenth-century Polish literature was a movement in response to the romantics. The Positivists were interested in restructuring society and working for social justice, religious tolerance, and improvement of the Polish peasants' conditions. Orzeszkowa, a Pole, was at the forefront of this literary movement and well-disposed toward Jews. What is most extraordinary about this particular little episode is how my mother was able to bridge two worlds. She transcended her home life, which she never left, and also immersed herself in what was essentially a foreign literature that she loved (see further discussion of the Polish Positivist movement in Appendix 1).

The engagement was broken in 1921, for reasons that have never been clear to me. I was told later that after the dissolution of our engagement there were various other matches proposed to him. He broke different engagements two or three times because, I later learned, they were "not Golda." He did marry at last.

It was customary when an engagement was dissolved for the aggrieved party to write a note of forgiveness known as a *ktav mehila*. Such a note states that he or she forgives the other person for ending the engagement. A lot of emphasis was placed on it. In Hasidic circles, an engagement carried a great deal of weight; in certain parts of the country, it was preferable for an engaged couple to marry and then divorce rather than break the engagement. In my case, the boy never sent me this communication, suggesting that he never forgave me. Being a bit superstitious, sometimes I believed that his refusal was a bad omen, but my mother did not believe in omens and disregarded the whole issue.

My mother kept this engagement a secret from me. She associated the break-up of the engagement with her father's family and did not wish my relationship with my paternal grandfather to be affected. I only learned about it through hearing her tapes. She mentioned that she had told me something about it but I do not recall it. The breaking of her first engagement was a significant event in her life, especially because the reasons for it were baffling to her. It never became apparent to me whether the dissolution of the engagement was a mutual decision by the two families or the decision of one side, possibly on her side because she felt he should have sent her the "forgiveness note." She devoted a lot of space in her narrative attempting to make sense of the break-up, speculating on how and why it happened. These kinds of personal tragedies are never easy even for contemporary couples; in those times, marriages were made between two families, involving many people, rather than between two individuals; reputations were at stake, involving honor and shame for the entire group.

Between my first engagement and the second one, in 1929, to my eventual husband, Haim, my mother received numerous proposals for a potential match. I didn't meet all the boys suggested for me, but one boy, whom I met in the lobby of a hotel in our neighborhood, was actually a distant relative and also Haim's relative. We were both accompanied by someone. I have a vivid memory of him because I judged him to be a blowhard and showoff. Within the half hour of our encounter, he took out three different cigarette filters. He praised himself, and he kept on praising himself. I disliked him immediately.

It was difficult finding the right match for me: somebody who was from a Hasidic family, wealthy and also a bit worldly.

I. In My Mother's Voice

My mother's brother who resided in Israel also recalled this situation. When talking about my mother's dilemma in finding a suitable match, he recalled that one matchmaker, her grandfather's follower, upon proposing my father to her, had said, "She will not be able to speak to him about Spinoza." Initially, my mother rejected this proposal.

There was also the problem of the dowry. As I mentioned before, irrespective of how gifted or attractive a girl was, in this society she could not marry without a dowry.

I became engaged to my husband when I was 26, and we were married three years later. My husband was related to my birth father's family. My mother-in-law was my paternal grandfather's half sister **(see genealogy, Appendix 3)**. She was raised in her husband's family in Radoczyce, and didn't know her Moditze family. After the subject of the dowry was settled, my husband came to Lublin and, as I mentioned before, my mother's part of the house was signed over to us in both our names. We were married on Purim (spring) in 1932. I am not sure why we were engaged for so long. It was, of course, an arranged marriage, promoted by one of my father's relatives.

The wedding took place in my home in Warsaw, which was not unusual since weddings were often held in private homes, especially if the house had a courtyard and was large enough to accommodate many people. I had a beautiful trousseau. It was a huge wedding. I received many gifts, including 300 silver chalices. Several neighbors made their apartments available to us for men and women separately.

The breakup of her first engagement set my mother on a maverick course for a woman in her society: as she will now discuss, she entered the university, a step never taken and unheard-of for women at the time, especially from rabbinical Hasidic families. Far from cutting her close ties to her family or her religion, she nonetheless pursued a very independent path, for which I have admired her immensely all my life.

Between the time of my first engagement and my second engagement and marriage, I took another daring step that had never been taken before in my family or by anyone in our Hasidic society. I registered at the university—the Wolna Wszechnica Polska (Polish Free University)—to study law. It was the only university in Poland at the time where Jews were freely admitted.

My mother encouraged this move, and my beloved stepfather knew about it, but it had to be done completely in secret. Nobody in our community could know that I was attending a university, chiefly because that would serve as a dangerous precedent to other young people in our society, in the same way that I needed to hide my face-to-face meetings with the boy to whom I had been engaged years before. Not only the rebbe's conduct but also his family's had far-reaching consequences, including setting an example for others in the Hasidic communities. Attendance at the university did not, of course, violate any religious strictures, it was only that the possibility existed of my being exposed to outside influences that were considered dangerous both to me and to any young women who might emulate me.

In contemporary times, women often comprise the majority of a university's student body, but it cannot be emphasized enough what a nonconformist move my mother's attendance at the university was then. As a Jew in Poland, as a woman, and as a daughter of several rabbinic dynasties, attendance at university was unprecedented.

There were also other hurdles to overcome. Exams were often given on a Saturday, and since I did not wish to break the Sabbath laws, I had to get permission from professors to take an exam orally. At such times I walked from my home to the University. But since I only had my allowance to pay for my studies, I often had to walk even on a weekday. The administration building of the University was located on Marszalkowska Boulevard, a major avenue in Warsaw, far away from my house on Pavia Street, but it was a nice several-kilometer walk. When my allowance ran out and I still needed some money for school, I asked my stepfather, and he always gave me money without question. Nobody except the immediate family knew that I was attending the university.

It was fascinating to me to learn that my mother's stepfather, this holy man, gave her money to pursue a secular education that in principle he most likely opposed, even though she attended the school in secret.

I. In My Mother's Voice

I began my studies at the Wolna Wszechnica Polska in 1927. I was registered in the name of Golda Roise Eiger. To become a matriculated student one needed to have received a *matura*, or a matriculation degree, equivalent to high school and two years of college, or one needed to take an entrance examination. Since I lacked the matriculation certificate, I was required to take the entrance examination. Until I was admitted officially I audited classes for less than two years. Then I decided to prepare for the entrance exam. The exams were given orally, but I don't recall which were the most important subjects. In all likelihood, history was required, and I remember one written paper which the students had to write at the University. As students were writing, the professors walked around watching over them. There were three subjects, from which we had to choose one to write about. Of the three topics, I selected Polish classic poetry; I don't remember the others. The professors told me that I did extremely well on the exams. After I completed the tests I was admitted as a regular matriculated student. Later, I became an officially matriculated student in Law, finishing my studies and exams in 1932.

At the time it was almost impossible for Jews and women to be admitted to the Warsaw University because of stringent quotas. The Wolna Wszechnica Polska was established as a private free academy in 1919 to counteract these quotas; it was open to all, irrespective of an applicant's religion or gender; admission was democratic and the professors were liberal. While there were fights and protests and upheavals at the University of Warsaw during the time I was a student, at the Wszechnica the atmosphere was peaceful, and the professors were pleasant people.

I saved whatever I could for tuition but it was not costly. Initially, I took courses in sociology, philosophy, and art—what is called in the United States liberal arts courses. I benefited greatly from these studies. Then I entered the Faculty of Economics, Laws and Jurisprudence. I attended this division for four years, taking all the Law courses. At the time there were 100 students in the school of law, and of those five were women. Two of the women were non-Jews. All five knew each other. The fourth year I took all the final examinations, except one because it was when I became engaged, and then there were the wedding preparations. I had excellent grades, all Fives, **(equivalent here to 100)** except statistics, where I received a Three **(equivalent to 70)** because I did not like studying statistics.

I still recall the names of some of the professors and the subjects they taught, especially at the school of Law. When Poland became independent, it had three kinds of laws: Russian, Napoleonic, and Austrian-German. Every section of Poland, depending upon under whose rule it was, had a different legal system. After Independence, the government established a Codification Commission to unify and codify all three legal structures .When I began studying at the Wszechnica there were seminars dealing with the Codification Commission and among the various topics we discussed was abortion. I don't recollect how each of these three legal systems treated this topic, but I recall well that Professor Szymakowski, one of the great jurists at the time associated with the Commission, who was professor at the Wszychnica and the University of Warsaw, analyzed the matter of abortion. I cannot say now how exactly the question of abortion was resolved in the code, but I believe that it was established as permissible during the first three months of pregnancy, and that the government may have had to pay for it.

One of the most interesting professors on the Law faculty was Professor Rappaport, who taught Prison Law and was internationally known for his work on prisons. I don't know where he spent the war years, but immediately after the war, in 1945, he published a short book about Hitler, titled "Criminal Nation" (*Narud Zbrodniarz*), which I bought in Poland and brought with me to the United States. I took a seminar with Professor Rappaport, who had many hopes for me. He once took us to the highest court to show us what it looked like, and he said to me, "You will one day be here in this court."

Professor Rappaport's assistant was Rafael Lemkin, who later came to the United States: Professor Lemkin conceived of and advanced the law regarding genocide. He proposed it after the war to the United Nations, and it was formally enacted and accepted. **(Rafael Lemkin coined the word "genocide" and was the principal author of the Convention on the Prevention and Punishment of the Crime of Genocide adopted by the United Nations in 1948.)**

The Professor of Criminal Law knew a great deal about Jewish Laws from the *Hoshen Mishpat*, although he was not a Jew. **(Hoshen Mishpat is one of the four books of the Shulchan Aruch, which is a written manual codifying Jewish Law. Each deals with a different aspect of life. Hoshen Mishpat deals specifically with torts and criminal law.)** He cited many examples from this tractate. Once he gave the example about the role of a witness. If a person is murdered, one must have two witnesses who actually saw the killer in order to condemn him to death. The example he gave from the tractate was this: if there was only one house in the middle of a field, and a man ran out from it with a bloody knife, and a dead person was found in the house, but there were no two witnesses who saw the man kill the person, the man could not be sentenced to death. This made an enormous impression on me. This professor's lectures were always fascinating, and I never missed even one of them, taking copious notes. At the end of the semester, when I asked him to sign my grade book, he gave me a five and marked it "outstanding." He did not ask me to take the last examination because he said, "I think you already know this subject better than I do."

I had another professor who gave classes in history, economics of law, sociology of law and other related subjects; he was very strict. He was the only one with whom I had a problem. This man gave his exams on Saturday, so I had a terrible conflict. It was a subject I had to take, whereas others were not required. I thought I would risk it; I went over to him to tell him that I was a rabbi's daughter, was religious, and could not come on Saturday. I asked if he could give me the exam in the middle of the week. One time I had to come on Saturday but he gave me an oral rather than a written exam; another time he did give me the exam during the following week, to everybody's astonishment. I was told that I was very lucky, because he had never postponed an exam before; I felt great satisfaction. I think I can say that I was his best student at the time. In fact, there was a non-Jewish official from one of the ministries who took the same courses, and she always asked me to help her with the material; there was also a Jewish woman who usually sought my help. I had prepared for the exams very thoroughly and I devoted myself only to my studies.

There were various organizations on campus, including a Zionist organization called, I believe, Yardeni. There were political organizations, democrats, socialists, and various others. They all wanted me to join, but I told them that I would not be involved in any political organization. I did go to B'nos, an organization of Orthodox Jewish women, though, of course, that was not an organization associated with the University. But I did not go there much either; I was totally immersed in my academic work, and it was for this reason that I did so well. I was very happy being at the University.

She does not mention that she had a phenomenal memory and a profound understanding of the material, just that she loved being at the university, a point she kept repeating throughout the narrative of her university experience, though I have eliminated some other references to it here. She entered the University for the love of learning, rather than with the intention of entering the legal profession, knowing that given her family position it would be inappropriate for her to seek employment in the profession.

After we married, my husband and I lived in Warsaw until about 1937, when we moved to Otwock, where the weather was better. We rented an apartment there, and my husband devoted himself to talmudic scholarship and minor business; he also had his followers, because he too was considered a holy man. I remained at home, as was customary for women to do, irrespective of their educational level. Certainly for the daughter of a rebbe to work at any job was unheard of. It would have damaged the social position of the family, although I should say that women, including my great-grandmother, conducted commerce. In Hasidic families, it was not unusual for a woman to run a business, but she could not be employed by others. In my case, my husband would not hear of my doing any kind of work, especially legal work that would have taken me out of the Jewish community.

When we lived in Warsaw, my friends and I—my friends were mostly my cousins—would go to the theater very often, and we participated in the cultural life of Warsaw. My hair was never cut off, as my mother's was. I put a wig over it, and it looked very much like natural hair. It was so striking, in fact, that at one wedding in 1933, the last one I attended in Lublin before World War II, people gossiped that the rebbe's daughter did not wear a wig; that her head was uncovered. Hearing the gossip, my mother came over to me and removed the wig to show people that indeed I was wearing it. Needless to say, this was a bit embarrassing to me, but now I laugh about it. My husband may have quietly complained to my stepfather that I was a bit modern, but my stepfather raised objections to his dissatisfactions, and I was never reproached on this matter.

My mother died at the age of 52. Her death was very traumatic for me; she had been ill for some years, and before I had married I had taken care of my three brothers and sister. I doted on them. I prepared them

I. In My Mother's Voice

all for their important transitions, beginning with the boys' hair-cutting ceremony at age three and the celebration of the first reading of words in the *Humash* **(Five Books of Moses)** at age five, and I prodded them when they forgot what they were learning. Later I oversaw the boys' bar mitzvahs, and two of my brothers' marriages. The oldest of the four children married our cousin, my mother's brother's daughter and I organized the entire wedding. They left shortly after the wedding, in 1935, for Palestine. The second brother married a woman from Galicia. The two youngest of these four siblings, the children of my mother and stepfather, were still unmarried when World War II broke out.

Because I acted as their mother, my siblings from my mother's side, unlike those from my father's side, were strongly attached to me, as I was to them, all of their lives. My father had nine children with his three other wives after he and my mother were divorced **(see Appendix 3)**. As I mentioned earlier, two of these wives died due to illness before the Second World War, and his last wife outlived him by several years.

My mother passed away a few months before the birth of my only child. I was in Piotrków, my husband's town, for Passover, and two weeks after my return she died. I was devastated by the loss, and it may even have affected my pregnancy and labor with my daughter. Unlike my mother, who gave birth at home on her bed, with privacy given her by hanging sheets, I gave birth in a special birthing clinic. I was in labor for more than a day, and at some point the doctors at the birthing clinic asked my stepfather as the patriarch of the family to decide whether to save the child or the mother. He ruled with no hesitation and in no uncertain terms, I was later told, that I, the mother, must be saved first and foremost. Fortunately, my child was at last born healthy.* As was customary, I named her after my mother, but since my mother had passed away at a relatively young age, my husband insisted on adding the name of a much longer-lived grandmother. It was a common belief that the age of the person whose name one carried would grant one the same length of life. My husband firmly believed this.

After my child was born I completely devoted myself to her. I followed all the pediatrician's instructions: I breastfed her and fed her especially

---

* My mother had a habit of not using my name when speaking of me. Throughout her memories, I am referred to affectionately as "my child" and "my daughter." While it may sound odd or even cold to English speakers, I chose to preserve her usage here, and ask that the reader understand that her references to me are anything but cold.

healthy foods, as the doctor instructed. He indicated that it was very good to bathe a baby outdoors in the sun at noon, weather permitting, and to feed her raw ground carrots, so I bathed her at noon and fed her ground carrots. I fed her mashed spinach and raw carrots from a very early age. After breastfeeding her, if she needed more milk I fed her with a spoon, because the doctor told me that when an infant is fed with a spoon it will have a beautiful mouth and lips. When I walked with her in the park, people stopped me to remark what a gorgeous baby she was. I read books to her from her very earliest days.

My father lived in Otwock in the years before the war with his fourth wife, who was also his niece. He and I became more familiar. He would come visit us and bring presents for my daughter. My daughter still remembers him from that period and speaks about him with fondness. He would arrive with one or two of my siblings from his third wife; they were many years younger than I. My siblings from his second wife had already married and no longer lived with him. Regrettably, I never had the opportunity to get to know most of my siblings on my father's side, and we never developed close ties, with the exception of one of my married sisters with whom I became close when we were both in the Warsaw ghetto. She and one of her two sons unfortunately were murdered there in the ghetto.

My life until 1939 had its pains, but it also had coherence, joy, love, and dignity. When the bombs began falling on Warsaw on September 1, 1939, my world lost its logic, its unity; it collapsed, and my life entered a new phase, a chapter of unimaginable chaos, horror, and suffering.

CHAPTER 2
The War Begins

> Don't worry about me. I am OK. I am OK. There is a mythological bird that always got up from the ashes. It always came back. I can tell you about me that every time with every throwback I get up and I go on. I fall, fall and I get up and I go on. Do not worry about me. I can also say that from the first day of the war the emphasis was on being strong. One must not fall in one's own eyes.
>
> *Excerpt from an audiotape Golda sent to her brother*

Officially the war years began with the bombs dropping on Warsaw, but the summer before the war broke out was already a bewildering time. All summer we spoke about the war, although we didn't believe it; subconsciously we thought about it, but still people did not believe that there would be a war. We were all in turmoil (*tzeridert*), and because of all the tumult, it was not clear to me until now what happened that year. Jews with Polish citizenship living in Germany were chased out of Germany and began returning to Warsaw. They were brought to Będzin, a border town between Poland and Germany, suitcases and all. There was talk about the Będzin refugees, and it was felt that something was happening; the atmosphere was grim but we still did not believe there would be a war. Nevertheless, the Jewish expulsion from Germany began to be recognized as a serious issue. These Jews and their parents had lived in Germany for fifty or sixty years, but they were Polish citizens. Even so, at this time people still joked about how patriotic German Jews were. We were still in the mood to mock German Jews whose feelings toward Germany were *Deutschland Uber Ales*, Germany above all. A joke circulated in Warsaw about these Jews, saying that when Germans came in to search their homes, they gave them everything they had; they hid nothing. When the Germans left one of these Jews yelled, "Herr Meister, you forgot the watch I have to give you." We laughed at what patriots the German Jews were, even as they were being deported from Germany. The Będzin Jews may have been placed in a synagogue, or in private homes, even though it was still before the war.

One of my brother's friends, interested in the foreign press, knew English and German; he could read all the newspapers that we couldn't. He told us about all the terrible predictions of what could happen. He began to tell us that there would be a war with Germany, but we didn't believe any of the horrible stories we were hearing. We supposed that these reports were just trying to frighten people. No, I know now that everything he said was in the press, it was not his fantasy, but we did not think that such things could happen. We did not believe! It was not believed that a world war could happen again; it was not believed what was said by those who had read *Mein Kampf*. People just laughed at it. Everything bad that could happen was laughed at. There were no visible preparations being made in the country; people's lives went on in a normal course. In fact, my husband's brother married off his oldest daughter, Sara, in Piotrków; the wedding was set for August 29 or 30, three days before the war started. My husband went to Piotrków just before the war broke out.

Life seemed to go on normally, but however it seemed, a great deal had already changed. My child and I returned from Otwock to live with my stepfather and my younger brothers in Warsaw when my husband went to Piotrków. The lack of seriousness about the war went on like this in July and mostly in August, but in August there was more apprehension than before. Already there were government officials instructing the public to prepare provisions for two weeks. At the beginning of the war there were enough products of all kinds, even luxury items such as sardines and cacao, and people got ready according to their means.

People began preparing provisions not for two weeks but for two years. Why, I don't know. There was no certainty about anything. My stepfather did not believe in special preparations, but he did allow us to buy some food supplies. My brothers proposed that we get sacks of potatoes, flour, sugar, and various other provisions. My stepfather did not permit it. Nobody asked him why we should not prepare food while everyone else was getting ready. We gathered some supplies nevertheless, including chocolates, various dried fruits, and other edibles.

We had a servant, a girl who was very practical; she did not pay attention to what was said, and bought some of this and some of that. There was also a sister-in-law in the house, the wife of my stepfather's son, visiting at the time. She said, "Children, let's prepare something. Don't listen to what my father-in-law says, we will prepare something." We bought eggs and placed them in barrels of salt, because it was said that if eggs were placed in salt, they would last for a long time. We prepared sprats. We didn't bake anything, but we had a small supply of items for two days—not for two weeks. When the bombing began, we were quickly left with nothing. But my stepfather's followers sent food when they heard that the rebbe did not prepare much. One sent sacks of flour, others sacks of potatoes, a third beets. When they heard that the rebbe did not permit us to prepare, they prepared for us and they sent what they could to the house, so there was food till the day of the bombing.

Once the bombing began it was no longer possible to go into the streets or buy anything. But the Hasidim continued to see that we were not left without food. We cooked soups, and whatever food was in the house—potatoes, bread—we shared with all the people who were there. During the first three weeks of the war, during the siege, we had some sprats left. My stepfather insisted that my child be the first one to be fed with the available food, but she never actually complained. She behaved during this period, and all the time afterwards, like a mature adult. She did everything that she was told to do.

Our neighbors and very close friends, who were wealthy businesspeople trading in piece goods, had merchandise at home, and also had prepared provisions for an entire year. They left on the seventh of September and did not even lock their doors. After the bombardment, a not very nice man who lived in the basement attempted to steal all that was in these people's house during the chaos. When my brother noticed it, he stopped him and took their belongings into our apartment. My brother saved much of the fortune of these people.

The Poles believed that the war would not last more than two weeks. Poland had an agreement, or a promise, from England and France that they would come to help if needed. So we were told to prepare food for two weeks. The Polish government began to mobilize its army by calling up its reservists to report here and there on a given date. This was 8 days before the first of September.

It was late at night, and people were on the balcony when suddenly other people began congregating at the gate to the buildings where we lived. They spoke loudly. I asked, "What has happened?" and learned that the concierge had received an order that he must present himself to his platoon commander. He was young enough, in his 30s or 40s.

After we heard this news we knew that our fate was sealed; that war was inevitable any day. I have an exact picture of that day in my mind: my two brothers, Avrumce and Binim, and I stood on the balcony and listened to what people were saying.

When I heard the story about the concierge's conscription, I went into the house and said to the others, "Children, we are lost." These words came out of my mouth, and this was really frightening. They asked me what had happened, and I reported what happened to the concierge, but nobody gave it much importance. Nobody believed that the war was imminent but me.

Even before the actual bombardment began, the mayor of the city had made an announcement on the radio, instructing people to store water in as many utensils as they had available and in their bathtubs. They anticipated that the water pipes would be destroyed, so the population was urged to collect water and to place sacks filled with sand on the roofs because there would not be enough water to extinguish fires. By the time of these last announcements the first bombs were already falling.

It was said, although I did not verify it, that the newspapers did report that the population would be bombed, but once the bombing began there were no more newspapers. We heard at the time that Poland had airplanes standing at the airports to protect herself; there were also a lot of disassembled airplanes when the bombing began. Rumors abounded: that in the Polish Seim (parliament) there was one delegate who was a German spy. When there was talk about defense, she proclaimed that we should laugh at such talk; nobody would attack, it was not necessary. Nothing needed to be done. The truth is that it was difficult to know from these rumors what was really happening. There were just many, many different reports. Another rumor was that three or four weeks earlier a general disappeared; his name may have been Galecki. Nobody knew where he was; only that he had disappeared. So it was said that perhaps he too was a German spy. Maybe the Poles arrested him, or killed him. All this was gossip.

As I mentioned earlier, those who read the foreign press had a great deal more information than we did; even in Palestine they seemed to have known much more than we what was going on in Poland. Leibl, the oldest of my mother's children with my stepfather, who lived in Palestine, began flooding us with letters in June and July of 1939 beseeching his wife, who had come to visit us in 1938 for a year with their two small children, to return home immediately. She did not wish to leave, because her one–and-a-half-year-old daughter was sick, and she hoped to have her treated in Poland. She was not in a great hurry to go back to Palestine, but when she began getting these pleading letters, she thought about leaving.

She asked her father-in-law, my stepfather, what to do. He seems to have told her that if her husband wished her to return she must do so. At first she considered remaining, because it was believed that it was too dangerous to travel so far away at such a time. But her husband continued to urge her to return immediately. She had a return ticket; she left by train to Trieste, having to cross Rumania—an ally of Germany—on August 29, two days before the bombs began falling. My two younger brothers, Avrumce and Binim, who were 28 and 27 years old but whom I call "the children," saw her off at the train and there too it was chaos. People were throwing their suitcases onto the train through the windows; there was a great deal of pushing and my sister-in-law lost her suitcase in all the pandemonium. She reached Trieste before the bombs started falling in Warsaw and managed to catch a boat, passing through Turkey. She arrived in Palestine much later than was expected, but she did arrive.

During the first days of the bombardment of Warsaw I was very active and good at managing everything that was needed. When the bombs began falling, people ran and nobody knew where to go. We looked for places such as basements, or the middle of a house, in rooms with no windows facing a courtyard; we had a few such rooms, in addition to two rooms in the front of the house with big windows. Because our apartment was closed in, a lot of people congregated there; it was regarded as a safe place. The inner rooms were filled with people. I showed people where to sit and where to stand and I distributed whatever food was available. In general, I was very involved and enterprising, unlike by the end of the war, when I was totally immobilized.

On the Friday before the war began, after we lit candles, a young man came, a relative of ours, who was in the military, to tell us that the Polish soldiers were deserting. His entire company ran back to Warsaw from the German border, where they were stationed at the front. He came to Warsaw; he wanted to be with us on Shabbat. We gave him a big challah. On that Friday we still had one—a week later, when the bombs were falling, there was none to give away.

After hearing that the army was disbanding, we realized the situation must be very dire and became very frightened. Bombs were not yet falling in the city, only around its environs. The city began to be bombarded when the Polish government escaped on the seventh of September. Warsaw surrendered to the Germans on September 27, 1939.

The Bombing of Warsaw

On Friday, September 1, at 9 a.m., although people were still walking in the streets, it was already known that a bomb had fallen on a children's sanatorium in Otwock, about 16 miles from Warsaw. But even then people didn't believe there was a war, because they didn't see or hear the bombs. I went down into the very crowded street with my child to buy something, and we walked around Pavia Street and Zamenhof Street where we lived; a lot of people were there. We returned to the house and stood on the balcony, watching passing airplanes, flying out over the countryside and seeing smoke rise as they flew. There was nothing seen in the city as yet.

We all went out onto the balcony when we heard loud airplane noises, but we still didn't believe we were hearing real bombs falling. We persuaded ourselves that we were hearing Polish airplanes, and that the Polish army was doing its maneuvers. In the afternoon, at around 2 p.m., the radio announcer told us, "Citizens, what you are hearing are not exercises, and these are real bombs falling." By then, the streets were full of people, and all watched. I went down with my daughter into the street, and still nobody believed that the Polish army was not doing its exercises. Ignacy Mosciski, the president of Poland, spoke on the radio; he gave a short speech and said a few moving words: "I take God as my witness that we did not wish a war; we don't want a war, but the Germans attacked us without any explanation. We did everything we could to avoid it." Then we believed that the bombs were real bombs. We could hear the despair in his voice. We were instructed not to walk outdoors but to go into shelters, into the houses. After the president's speech, we accepted that there was no hope; the bombs were falling and there was a real war.

With this began the siege of Warsaw. In the afternoon the bombs began falling in the city proper. On Friday evening people came to our house through doors we rarely used. The courtyard of our buildings was connected with the courtyard of another street, Gensia Street. My brother's friend came with his whole family through this passage, because on Gensia Street there was a tower that could be used as a defense point, and therefore it might be a more dangerous street than ours. People ran from Gensia Street to Pavia Street. People came also from the provinces.

When incendiary bombs began falling, my brothers insisted that we go over to our neighbors who lived across the street, because their apartment was on the ground floor facing the courtyard and it was still considered safer than ours. It was in the middle of the night. I looked around to see what I could take with me and saw one silver candlestick standing on the table. I don't know why there was only one candlestick, but I grabbed it. It was a silly thing to do, rather than take some food, but I simply did not have time to think about what was better and what was worse. One took what was in front of one's eyes. The servant girl was smart; she saw immediately that we had to have something to eat. She was very good in this stressful moment and took some food. My brothers grabbed the two *Sifrei Torahs* **(scrolls of the Torah)**. We sat in this neighboring apartment until it calmed down a little, and returned to our house a few hours later.

My brothers Avrumce and Binim, and three of my stepfather's children from his first marriage, along with their grandchildren, none of whom regularly lived with us, came to our house during the bombardment because their house was immediately destroyed. Other people who had nowhere to go also came to stay with us.

Parenthetically, I must mention that just before the war began, it was said that the Germans would either shoot us, use chemical bombs, or conduct bacteriological warfare. We were prepared for these things. We did not consider bombs. Everybody was prepared with masks to be worn on the nose and mouth made of various materials, including pillows. We wore such masks, which we had prepared; we knew that we should stay high up in the house when there were bacteriological bombs falling. Shelters were made in basements for simpler types of bombs, but we were expecting chemical materials to come at us at any time.

As I heard this portion of my mother's audiotape, I could feel the confusion people must have felt from not knowing what kind of

bombs would be falling. I do not remember the confusion, but I do remember vividly the bombs falling.

In fact, the masks were never needed, and it was not safer at all to be on a higher floor of a building. If one stood on the fifth or sixth floor, the bombs fell straight on one's head. If one was in the basement, a bomb could fall on top of the house, or half a house could collapse, but there would still be the possibility of remaining alive and uninjured. Because of this, my brother and the family went first to the basement. But I told my brother that I didn't believe it was better to stay in the basement, because if a bomb hit us, we would be covered by the debris and wouldn't be able to crawl out from under it. If we were on the ground floor, or even the first floor, and the roof was torn away we'd have a better chance of surviving than if we were in the basement and covered by rubble. He listened to me, and we didn't stay in the basement. We remained in the apartment the entire time, or we stood at the gate, which was closed but was a good hiding place.

The next day, as the bombs continued to fall, one neighbor who lived on the second floor came to our house because, she said, she would be safe only in the rebbe's home, even though she was not especially religious. She believed that in my stepfather's house nothing would happen. In fact, in our house nothing did happen. We stood in the corridors leading to the front room. The incendiary bombs we watched through the window landed on the roof, but were immediately extinguished with sand prepared by a previously organized committee that included my brothers, who were standing there. **(I remember standing there too, watching the flames.)** Others also felt that the rabbi's house would be the safest. A neighbor, whose apartment was one we had used during my wedding, came to stand with us in the corridors, as did various other people, especially neighbors, who wanted to be with the rebbe. Some came who didn't have anywhere else to go because their houses were damaged or destroyed, and some family members stayed with us until the bombardment ended.

Much of the bombardment took place during Rosh Hashanah and Yom Kippur **(September 14 and September 23 of that year)**. We heard that the Germans intentionally bombed the Jewish neighborhoods forcefully on Rosh Hashanah, to punish us for observing our holiday. On Rosh Hashanah Eve, the bombardment was terrible, but we still said the prayers for the first night of the holiday. The apartment was always packed with people—neighbors and any others who could reach us—but especially on that night.

It is difficult to reconstruct and picture what was happening during the first days when the bombs began falling, when everything changed. We now realized that there was a war coming, a war on the Jews, and we learned about Hitler's ideas in *Mein Kampf*, but we still did not believe that what he had forecasted would actually happen. We didn't take his words seriously; we thought he was just saying that he wished to annihilate the Jews.

And actually, I feel that is why most people did not run away at that time. They could have escaped to foreign countries, with or without a visa, but like us many could not imagine how bad it would get. Between the initial day of invasion on September 1 and the day of Poland's surrender, there was a brief opportunity to escape, when it was reported that all who wished to leave could do so on September 7, when the Polish army began retreating and the military left Warsaw. There was only one opening in Warsaw through which people could leave, going east in the direction of Russia; otherwise Poland was surrounded.

On that day the diplomatic corps of the nations of the world all departed, as did the officials of the Polish government. Polish citizens could leave with the military. My beloved younger brother Avrumce considered going to Russia. He asked his father, my stepfather, what to do, whether to go or not; his father told him that he must do what his heart told him. He said, "In this instance I cannot tell you what to do, even my own child; whatever you feel you should do, do." He put on his coat, said his goodbyes, and left. Within half an hour, he came back. He said, "No, no, I can't leave my father and siblings, I won't go." He decided not to go to Russia, but our sister went. She set out on September 7 with all of those who left at that time. Other people came to my stepfather to ask him whether to leave with the Polish army and go toward Russia, or to remain in Warsaw. The rebbe answered them all in the same way: "I can tell you what I told my child, to do what your hearts dictate." Many wished that my stepfather and his son would go, but he said he would not leave the other Jews here, leave his friends, his other children. In the early months of the war—September, October, and November—people were still running to the borders; the borders were not completely closed yet. They smuggled themselves through different roads and towns. The Germans did not enter Warsaw until the army, by then long gone from Warsaw, at last capitulated. At that time we began going outside again, for there was no fear of bombardments anymore. We saw terrible things: houses were destroyed, and I don't know how many dead were found and removed from the city.

At the urging of one of his sons-in-law, my birth father also left on September 7, with two of his older sons and his son-in-law. They walked for about 400 kilometers **(240 miles)** to Vilna, in Lithuania, where my father remained for 11 months until he received a visa for the United States from his brother who lived in New York. He arrived in the United States in 1941 with his children, whereas his son-in-law and grandson moved to Australia.

While my birth father was in Vilna, two months after he left Poland, he sent two Polish couriers to us to gather and smuggle his remaining children out of the ghetto before the ghetto would be completely sealed off. The first messenger came to collect his fourth wife and the younger children, and brought them to Vilna. The second one came for the married daughters. Neither I nor my birth father's other two daughters, my sisters, could leave. One of them didn't wish to go because she was expecting an inheritance from her father-in-law, who had left a great fortune. The second sister was away in a small town and could not be reached. Both these sisters were murdered.

I could not leave, for my husband was in another town (Piotrków) and couldn't return to Warsaw. I didn't wish to leave him behind, nor did I wish to leave my other brothers and my stepfather. But actually, a few weeks after the bombing stopped, and things calmed down a little, I managed to travel to Piotrków to see if Haim could come back with me to Warsaw; my child and family remained in Warsaw. I thought we should perhaps go with the courier to Vilna. I remained in Piotrków for about two weeks; we could not decide what to do. My husband didn't wish to leave Piotrków for various reasons. He did not want to leave his aged mother; he was afraid to travel because when the Germans saw a Jew with a beard they tore it off, and my husband did not wish to cut his beard off. Before the actual ghettos were established and separated by walls, it was still possible to travel within Poland, but it was much simpler for women to do so than for men. At this time, before one realized how murderous the German plans were, it was extraordinarily difficult to know what would be best: to stay in Warsaw or to try and go elsewhere.

Strange things happened during the bombardment panic. As I mentioned before, throughout the actual bombing we spent most of our time in the house, or around the courtyard and at the gate to the buildings. Thank God nothing happened at the gate, or in the buildings where we lived on Pavia 16. The house did not burn during the bombardment, nor was it greatly damaged. The great danger was of being hit by shrapnel. But when the bombs started falling on our street and hitting people, the neighbors started running away, and one man ran with a box containing money, jewelry and other valuables. The first thing he grabbed was a box with his treasures; he ran somewhere, leaving his wife and child behind. I don't remember what happened to the wife, but a Polish woman grabbed the child and ran out into the street. My brother saw how she grabbed the baby and ran after her; he got the child away from her, bringing it into our courtyard. Later, the man returned and saw my brother holding his baby. My brother asked him why he seized the box and not the child. There was a lot of talk about this man who thought about the money first and not the child. Maybe he had two children.

Immediately after the bombing subsided, defense committees were organized. Every house had such a committee, and my two brothers were members of ours. We brought sand that we had prepared earlier up to the attic, and, as I said earlier, the members of the committee extinguished the incendiary bombs with the sand. As a result, our house was not damaged; nothing burned there. It was very well defended by the simple pouring of sand when an incendiary bomb fell on it. I don't know what happened to the house later, during the Jewish uprising in 1943 when the Germans attacked the ghetto, but during the bombardment of the city we were protected. One bomb fell on the house when my daughter and I stood in a corridor in front of the apartment, but we were not hurt.

When the city surrendered and the bombing quieted down, the commissar in charge of our neighborhood came to thank my brother and tell him that he deserved a prize for the excellent defense he, and the members of our committee, had mounted. **(Pavia 16, where the family had lived, formed part of a huge apartment complex, comprising several large buildings surrounding a courtyard that was closed off by a gate, usually locked at night. When I returned to Poland there were no remains of this or any other buildings from that period.)**

Fortunately for us, our street was saved from destruction; even the pavements remained in good condition. I should mention that others, especially wealthier people, were also very active and distributed soups to everyone. People helped one another as best they could.

At first, while the bombs were falling, we had little contact with people outside of our house, but when Warsaw surrendered and things calmed down a bit, we got together with people; we thought from the first moment that when the Germans reached Warsaw they would walk through the houses with knives and slaughter people. We did two things. We removed the *mezizes (mezuzot)* from all the doors in all of our rooms, deceiving ourselves that the Germans wouldn't know where Jews lived if there were no mezizes on the doors. Secondly, it was thought that the men must not remain in their homes, especially my stepfather, a famous rebbe, and other such well-known people. We moved him to a Hasid's home a few blocks away. This Hasid owned a grocery store where he still had milk, cheese and other foods, so my stepfather would be comfortable, and it was believed that the Germans would not find him there. He stayed for two weeks and then returned home. Nobody knew what ought to be done, or how to conduct oneself; no one had any idea what would be the best course of action.

After the offensive ended, we were able to go out of the house to get whatever food was available for sale. There was no electricity, no gas, and most important, no water. To get water we walked to the Vistula River, and my child and I went there alone, without the servant girl. **(I remember such trips well.)** Only the women went out: the men could not, because there was fear that they would be attacked on the streets. My little girl carried bottles of water.

A curfew was imposed on the city, and we didn't go out unless it was necessary. But mostly we were afraid for the men.

There were people who wished to run somewhere, but among the many rumors one was that the Germans poured benzene on the pavements of many streets, so that the streets would catch fire and people could not run away. Whether that was an invented tale or whether there was some truth to it, I am not sure, but on those rare occasions that my brother went out, he said when he returned that many streets were indeed slippery. He attributed the slipperiness to the benzene.

More rumors flourished. One story travelling around was that there were spies in houses and that these spies reported to the Germans what was said, where people were, how they planned to defend themselves, and everything else that was happening. Instructions came by radio that one shouldn't speak to any stranger. This was a terrible thing, because people were afraid to speak in general to anybody. We were even cautious about speaking with a person we knew in passing. We felt terribly constricted. Any time we spoke with somebody, we thought we were divulging something. This stricture added to the chaos and panic that was brought on by the Germans, this terrible panic.

As I write this, I feel the panic swell in me as well. My mother's reference to the instructions transmitted by the Poles to avoid strangers was oppressive. To stifle people from communicating what may have been valuable information was a powerful tool of repression—or perhaps it did indeed protect them against betrayal. One doesn't usually learn about such tools of oppression when reading about the events of that time.

All these happenings occurred in the first three to four weeks after the first bomb fell on Poland. Warsaw was under siege and chaos ruled. When the Germans marched in, immediately after Poland surrendered, everything stopped; everything was destroyed—schools, libraries, theaters, newspapers. All cultural life stopped. The Germans appointed a Jewish Council (*Judenrat*), with Adam Czerniakow as its chairperson. The Germans did not lose any time. Czerniakow was appointed head of the 24-member Judenrat on October 4, 1939. They also designated a Jewish police, whose duties included sanitation and snow collection as well as tax collection and rounding up people for work and, ultimately, for extermination. To anticipate Czerniakow's story, tragically on July 23, 1942, three days before the liquidation of the Warsaw ghetto, he committed suicide by poison, because he refused to deliver people for extermination and work anymore. As long as he could lead the ghetto and offer a possibility that people would survive, he continued to work. But when the moment came that the Germans demanded that he hand over children for deportation, he could no longer continue. He did not wish to be instrumental in sending Jews, especially children, into the ovens. There were other individuals who committed suicide during this time, but there was no mass suicide. The Germans may have expected the Jews to simply kill themselves or one another, but these expectations were not fulfilled. People held it against Czerniakow that he committed suicide. They thought he should have gone with all the Jews to be murdered instead, but he did not want to surrender to the Germans.

After the siege and before the ghetto was established, we did not give up. We were left with a lot of hope and a lot of faith. We did not permit the Germans to destroy us spiritually or morally—we simply did not allow it, ever. Physically they did succeed, breaking those who were ill and couldn't withstand the abominable conditions in the ghetto and the camps. They fell quickly. The healthier remained living longer, thanks to their stronger constitutions. But spiritually the Germans failed to accomplish their aims. I am reminded of an incident in the Warsaw ghetto when I went to see some relatives, middle-aged people, and the husband offered me two apples. I said, "Why are you offering the apples to me? Keep them for yourself!" He said, "The Germans have ruined us in many ways, but spiritually they will not break us. They will not take from us our humanity."

Life in the Warsaw Ghetto

During the days of the Warsaw ghetto, there were many opinions about how to handle the horrific events occurring daily. People thought that we were allowing ourselves to be brought to the slaughter like sheep, because we didn't fight the Germans or stand up to them. Others questioned why we didn't commit suicide. Still others argued about hiding their children with Polish families for money, with some fearing that if they did so the children would be lost forever, or even murdered, which in fact was known to happen. Another disaster that was not predicted was that after the war there were children who did not want to return to their parents. The truth is that no one who wasn't there can judge anyone's response. In short, there was a complete paralysis regarding the actions we should take. Nobody knew. But putting us into a situation of fear and unknowing was one of the many German strategies to demoralize us.

Immediately after the occupation of Poland, the Germans systematically developed their ghettoization program. By the first two months of 1940, a ghetto policy was enacted and organizations to implement it were established.

I. In My Mother's Voice

But the first winter was not tragic compared to what followed. The city was open until the ghetto was established in October 1940, with the Germans setting its boundaries. It was sealed off by a 10-foot wall covered by barbed wire and glass; about half a million people were crowded into the enclosed space. There were actually two Jewish neighborhoods that comprised the ghetto. In effect, it was divided into two separate sections: the ghetto of the Nalefkis Street and the ghetto of the Grzybowski Street. One wall went around one ghetto and one around the other. The Germans constructed a wooden bridge in between, which enabled people to pass from one ghetto into the next.

To create the ghettos, Jews were chased out of all the other neighborhoods where they had previously resided, such as the Marszałkowska Street area. When they put up the wires around the ghettos, they wrote at the gate "Entrance forbidden," because of the typhus epidemic. The stomach typhus epidemic **(transmitted by lice)** erupted in the winter of 1940-1941, and was due to the appalling sanitary conditions. About ten percent of the population was wiped out by the disease during that time alone, including my uncle and many other relatives. My uncle's children were sent to us. Whenever the disease afflicted a house, the children were immediately removed and sent to a house not affected by the disease. **(This house had to be within the ghetto as well; sealing off the ghetto cut the people off from social contact, as well as employment and business, with the outside, pushing them into a black market economy).**

As I have said, and I cannot emphasize it enough, the Germans did not manage to crush our humanity. As soon as the bombs stopped and things calmed down, we tried to normalize our lives. Even as they created the ghetto and surrounded us with walls and wire, volunteers started organizing schools for children in different venues; in private homes for little children and in a gymnasium for older children in the winter of 1939- 1940.

My daughter attended one of the home-based kindergartens, which a teacher organized in her house that first year for a few hours a day. The children would sing, play, and learn to write; I think one paid for that. **(I remember going to this kindergarten during that first year of the war.)**

In the spring and summer of 1940, the children were taken to play in a big courtyard at the Paviak (a jail, believe it or not), where there was a big tower surrounded by a wall, but also trees and a few benches in the courtyard. During the winter the kindergarten was in the teacher's home, but in the spring she transferred it to this courtyard. At the time that my daughter attended this kindergarten, we changed her name from Kaila to Kaja, because the teacher did not like the way it sounded phonetically in Polish. We thought about what we should do. I did not want to change the name, but on consideration I decided that we should call her Kaja (a Scandinavian name I read in Ibsen) instead of Kaila, and so we did. The one positive moment I recall during that time is that I could take my daughter to a school. I brought her the first and second breakfast, a roll with a little butter and an egg, which was all we could get; it is a very poor lunch by today's standards, but by the standards of that time it was a very luxurious one.

Under normal conditions, people usually had five meals a day. A first breakfast consisted of a warm beverage and light snack eaten early in the morning, followed by a second breakfast around 11 a.m., which was more substantial, equivalent to a lunch. The main meal was eaten at around 2 p.m.; tea and sweets or fruit were had at 5 p.m.; finally in late evening a small meal was served.

During the first winter, my stepfather's daughter by his first marriage and her daughter came to stay with us, because her house was bombed out. She used to take my daughter for walks and teach her various Hebrew songs. My daughter was dressed beautifully, even at that time; she still had her little fur coat, with fur inside and out. One day they returned home, and she recounted how people had stopped her to tell her how beautiful the little girl was.

The first winter of the war life went on; people traveled back and forth and conducted commerce; whatever one possessed was traded in and out of the ghetto. At the time, everything was still accessible; one of our cousins came to Warsaw to buy things, which she sold elsewhere. We even put up a sukkah for the holiday of Sukkot for my stepfather, where he could eat something.

There were poor people in Warsaw before the war, but during that first winter the hunger was terrible, and as more people were brought from the small towns the famine worsened. The hunger in the city was unbearable, and the conditions of life in the ghetto I will not describe here. They are well known. But even though there were hungry and poor people, one day I came into the house, and I said, "I cannot understand that people are starving, yet I can walk in the street and it does not occur to anybody to tear off my coat, or to tear off the fur." In contrast to today, such thefts were not common, or happened to anybody I knew then; nobody was bothered at that time, nobody had their pocket books torn away from them. If they tore away anything it was a bag with a roll, a bag of potatoes.

Children would sometimes grab a package with a piece of bread out of a person's hand. One time I walked with my daughter with a package of food in my hand and a child grabbed it away. When somebody did something like that I was not unhappy, because we were not in such a terrible situation as many others; it was unnecessary to get too upset about the loss of the lunch. That was the last winter that I still had my fur coat–by the second winter we had to surrender all furs to the Germans. That decree came in the summer of 1940.

When I think about the ghetto period I recall extraordinary scenes, and it leads me to wonder how my child, at her very young age, had such understanding and diligence under these conditions, and in such trying situations. In 1940, after the ghetto was established, the Germans charged the Jewish police to catch men for work wherever they found them. They entered a building, came up the stairs, and snatched away whomever they met to place them in a group to transport to work. Nobody knew where these people were taken. There were all kinds of rumors; it may have been work in the city, but nobody knew.

We were at home, me, my child, and my younger brother Binim. A Jewish policeman came into the apartment, walked around, and took my brother into the courtyard. I ran down and began speaking to the policeman, holding my daughter by her hand. At that moment she began crying terribly, yelling, "Don't take my father; don't take my father." She screamed and yelled. Thanks to the fuss she made, the policeman said, "Go upstairs with your father, back to the apartment." This was an extraordinary occurrence. My daughter grasped on the spot what she should say. Whoever heard about this scene admired how quickly she oriented herself and knew to claim that my brother was her father. Had she said he was her uncle, her protests wouldn't have carried any weight. It made such an impression on the policeman that a five-year-old would scream so he did not take my brother. It was a miracle. Later she accomplished other, similarly amazing feats. **(I remember this incident very clearly and I can still hear myself screaming and crying.)**

By the second winter, libraries began springing up, stocked with Polish books and children's books. The libraries were secret, but they began lending books out. Later a theater was organized. All the artists who had performed in the Polish theater now performed here, and all of a sudden we learned who was a Jew. The actors usually had Polish names, and generally they did not present themselves as Jews; it was not always known that they were Jews until they were moved to the ghetto. By the second winter, there was a review theater on Leszne Street. There was a large café and the review consisted of various short skits. In one of them the actors portrayed how packages of food were grabbed from people, and how one woman walked with a package of food wrapped with a chain, and carried the chain on her back so that nobody could steal it from her. I took my daughter to all the performances in the Leszne Street Theater. I will add that my daughter was a very happy and content child, even though the situation was so terrible and so different from before the war began; we did not allow her to feel it, so she was a joyful child.

As I listened to my mother describing those early days of the war, I too remembered them, and also recalled that I was surrounded by the people I loved most: my mother, my mother's two brothers, and my mother's stepfather, people whom I long for to this day and whose loss I still mourn.

There were no particular happy moments at that time, except that my daughter brought a happy mood to all in the house. She was adored by my two brothers, and by all our friends who were with us. Our love for her created a happy mood in the house that brought joy and light into the apartment. We used to joke, play, and learn with her, even more so when she and I moved from my stepfather's house to a little furnished one-room apartment my brother Avrumce rented for us from a local family. Avrumce and Binim would work there during the day and sometimes would go back to my stepfather's house before 8 p.m., when the curfew began, and we were locked-up in our houses. We rented the room because toward the end of the first Passover my brothers began conducting some business, and they feared they might be caught by the Jewish police or betrayed, for the Germans prohibited Jews from conducting any kind of legitimate commerce. The owner of our apartment was an accountant or bookkeeper before the war, and my brothers and I developed a friendship with him. We asked him to teach us bookkeeping in the early evenings, since there was nothing else to do. My daughter pretended she was asleep, but an hour after we finished she would get up and repeat to us all that we were learning.

Because of the typhus epidemic that was decimating the ghetto in the summer of 1941, I sent my child away to stay with her father in Piotrków, smuggling her out with a Polish courier. The typhus epidemic did not bypass any family, and ours was no exception. The first one to fall ill in our household was the servant girl. She survived. Then the younger of my two brothers, Binim, was afflicted, and when he became sick we sent my daughter to a relative in another house. After Binim recovered, Avrumce got sick, and we sent her away to yet another relative. After he recovered, I was afflicted with the disease, and at that point there was nowhere to place her in Warsaw, so we decided to send her to my husband in Piotrków. This was a time when a lot of people smuggled their children out of Warsaw and sent them to relatives outside the city. It was already after the holidays, in the fall. It was believed that in the Piotrków ghetto there was still food, because it was not closed off by a wall as the Warsaw ghetto was. By now there was very little food in the Warsaw ghetto, and disease, as I've said, was rampant. Instead of moving her from one place to another in Warsaw, we decided to send her to Piotrków where the situation was, we hoped, better.

It was extraordinary how my daughter was smuggled out of the Warsaw ghetto. There was no mode of transportation except a rickshaw-type vehicle, which was made out of bicycle parts that were converted to form a cart pulled by a person. We arranged with a Jewish man, who passed as a non-Jew, to transfer her. As a non-Jew he could travel back and forth. We paid him a lot of money to take her out of Warsaw and get her to Piotrków. As a non-Jew he couldn't enter the ghetto; we arranged that he would wait for her on the other side of the wall. She had to climb a ladder and cross over the 10-foot wall with my brother pushing her over to the other side, where the man was waiting with a non-Jewish woman who would put her on the train. There were empty houses on the other side; it was a good place to smuggle people out. My brother Binim, who took her to the wall, told me of her exemplary conduct at the time.

She looked beautiful even then. She was well dressed and had a little coat with Persian lamb on the inside and velvet on the outside. There was also some fur on the collar, on the hood and muff; it was fashionable at the time. My brother Avrumce had a seamstress make it for her the first winter we lived in the ghetto. Separating myself from my child at that time, the first time, was excruciatingly difficult. But we thought it was necessary, so she could avoid all the diseases. She cried quietly but did not say she didn't want to go. My brothers stood there in great pain watching her crying inaudibly. After all, we were taking a terrible risk smuggling her out of the ghetto and getting her to Piotrków. All we could think of was that there would be more food and less disease. She would not get sick there.

I recall this entire episode with great clarity: the separation from the four people I loved most in this world, the climbing over the wall, the train trip, and being brought to my father's house. This was a separation from which I do not believe I have even now recovered.

As soon as I got well, all I wanted to do was be reunited with my child and husband in Piotrków. The last few weeks before I left, people were arriving from the smaller towns, including Lublin, where the liquidation of the ghetto began in March and April of 1942. My brother searched for ways to get me to Piotrków. A cousin who had just arrived from Lublin warned that I was putting myself in great danger. He said, "Don't be crazy, don't run, you will go into a fire. You will be going into the mouth of a lion." I said, "Let it be so; I want to be with my child and my husband." That was my argument. We believed that our end was coming; I wanted to be together with my child; I wanted for all of us to be together, whatever happened. That was our decision from the first moment of the war. At first I had wanted to bring my husband back from Piotrków to Warsaw, but that had failed. Against my will and reason, I now had to risk my life and steal into Piotrków in order to bring them back to Warsaw because we were sure that the Germans would first destroy everything in the provinces. Warsaw would be the last to be annihilated, or so it was believed.

I was smuggled out from Warsaw in much the same manner as my daughter had been, with a male courier, on May 10, 1942, two months before the beginning of the liquidation of the Warsaw ghetto. My brother accompanied me to the wall and helped me climb over it. The courier placed me into the droshky, and I noticed, interestingly, that there had to be many Poles dead, for as I came to the other side of the ghetto wall, I saw almost every women wearing a special black mourning outfit, commonly worn by women in Catholic Poland. The mourning costume worn by women included a very thick black veil over the face, and a black armband. I, too, wore a black suit, with a black hat and huge veil to cover my face. If one was caught without wearing a Mogen David—the infamous yellow star—on the Polish side, the punishment was even greater than usual. I wore the Mogen David star, I didn't remove it. But I carried a coat over my hand, and that is how I dressed to travel to Piotrków.

The droshky came out from one street (Krulewska) onto the main boulevard to the Marszałkowska Street, and another droshky came up next to ours. The driver yelled to our driver, "You think I don't know that you are carrying Jews; I know." When our driver heard this he began to drive the horse even harder, and we rode furiously on the Marszałkowska Street until we reached the train station. When we arrived at the station another man met me; I sat down in a corner so that I would not be seen, and he walked away. When it got dark we walked into the train, which was also dark. There were no candles. The train was packed, and I sat down on a bench with the man next to me. Nobody looked at me or bothered me. When the conductor came for the tickets I gave him mine and the man gave him his; the conductor looked at me but did not say anything—he just went on. We travelled, I believe, the whole night. The train stopped for a long time at various points. We arrived in Piotrków before dawn, just before sunrise. The train station was outside the ghetto; we walked together toward the ghetto. The man knew that nobody would bother us there. I don't know how I reacted when we finally walked into the ghetto—whether I gave a sigh of relief that I was no longer in immediate danger, whether I was happy that I would see my child. I don't remember what feelings I had. I do know the man brought me up into the house, but I don't remember whether my husband, who was living with my mother-in-law, knew in advance that I was coming, or whether it was a total surprise. All told, this trip was extraordinarily dangerous. Had the driver of that droshky, who yelled at us, managed to stop us, my courier and I would have been taken directly to the German authorities and executed. I don't know whether the driver of that other droshky just wanted to scare our driver or truly meant to catch him.

Many people thought it was madness to leave Warsaw. Everybody believed it was safer to be in the capital because of the huge concentration of Jews, including those who came from the small towns. Some reasoned that it was best to remain in Warsaw, rather than to be in a small town, because the Germans could easily murder a few people in a small town, but not the thousands in Warsaw. I agreed with this assessment: my intention was to return to Warsaw with my child and husband. I received a telegram while waiting that my brothers and stepfather were well. I looked for opportunities to return in every way I could, but there weren't any. It was no longer possible to return to Warsaw. The *aktion*, or liquidation, in Warsaw came like a bolt from the blue. It was so sudden, so unexpected! It had not occurred to anybody that they were preparing ovens in which to burn us. The only thought we'd had was that they would throw us into the Vistula River. Even the wisest people did not foresee anything direr. The deportation of Warsaw began on July 22, 1942, and went on until the Jewish uprising.

My stepfather and my brothers, Avrumce and Binim, remained in Warsaw with the rest of the family. I heard later that my stepfather had worked in one of the workshops the Germans had organized to support the German war effort. These workshops were run by Jews of the ghetto; because one such workshop, which manufactured shoes, bags, or brushes, was run by an Orthodox Jew, Abraham Hendel, he employed many of the rebbes, and probably also my brothers.

I was informed by survivors of the Warsaw ghetto that my brothers and stepfather were among the last to be eliminated because they worked in this factory. My stepfather passed away in an extraordinary way in the fall of 1942, as has also been described in various books dealing with the liquidation of the Warsaw ghetto, and as witnessed by one survivor. On the day the Germans entered the courtyard of his building, and the Germans were heard advancing into individual homes, my stepfather sat down in his chair in his prayer shawl (*tallit*) and phylacteries (*tefillin*), and said, "The enemy will not dominate my body." As the Germans entered the apartment, he closed his eyes and died. Nobody knows what happened to his body, whether it was possible to bury him or whether his body was simply discarded, like all the other Jewish bodies.

I was told different stories about how my two brothers, Avrumce and Binim, perished. One was that they were transported to Treblinka at the very end of the liquidation, sometime after my stepfather died. I was also told by a Hasid's daughter I met in the labor camp that my brother Avrumce and my stepfather's son from his first marriage were in the attic of the building, standing guard, and both were shot as they were looking out the window. **(My mother's voice here grows very anguished.)**

Following the Jewish uprising of April 1943, in which I was told my brothers may have participated, all was lost and the Warsaw ghetto was totally annihilated. The uprising was a futile effort. They just wanted to die with honor, even though they knew very well, from uprisings in other ghettos, that they would not accomplish anything. They knew that they would not save anybody; they just saved those who could not, or didn't wish, to join in; by sacrificing themselves they redeemed the rest.

From the time I started speaking about the Warsaw ghetto—what seems like ages ago in another world—until now, I can only wonder where are those people I loved, what happened to them? Where did they vanish, carted away to die? I cannot pretend that they each went somewhere and had an accident and died. They were healthy young people. They didn't do any harm to anybody; they were just pulled out and removed. I still cannot believe that they are gone. **(Neither can I.)**

Life in the Piotrków Ghetto

Piotrków, where Jews lived since the middle ages, had a thriving Jewish community before the war. My husband's family had lived there since the mid-nineteenth century. In more recent history, the Germans had established the first Jewish ghetto in Poland there, in October 1939. People came to it from other towns because it was considered safer, with a somewhat better chance of survival. The ghetto was never closed off by walls, for example. The Poles had to cross through the ghetto to get from one side of town to the other, and it was easier to trade with them, to smuggle things through and earn some money. Jews were also transferred by the Germans from surrounding towns to the small ghetto area of Piotrków. The conditions were appalling, but still better than in other towns, including Warsaw.

When I arrived in my mother-in-law's house in Piotrków in May 1942, I was barely able to recognize my child. She was not well taken care of by her grandmother or her father, who knew little about caring for children, or by other members of the household. Her hair was tangled up in knots; she was thinner, and a bit sad. She was not the same child I had sent to them months earlier.

My mother-in-law's apartment was already divided. She had once owned a large apartment, which after the German occupation became subdivided; she was left with two of four large rooms, which had a balcony and three windows. This was her salon, where she also slept. The dining room, a large room with two windows, was divided into two rooms by commodes. Half of the room had a separate entrance from the kitchen, and that became the besmedresh, the prayer room. She was left without a kitchen. The other half of my mother-in-law's dining room was a dark area with a bed, where my husband had slept. When I arrived in May, we all stayed in that room.

The other two large rooms were each divided into two to accommodate my husband's brother, his son, his daughter with her new husband, and his unmarried daughter. My mother-in-law could not accept the new conditions, and the fact that her possessions were being removed from her.

About five months after I arrived, on October 12-13, 1942, the liquidation of the Piotrków ghetto began. One of my husband's Hasidim and friends, who had a two- or three-year-old child, told my husband that he had a Polish friend who would take children into his home; naturally he would be paid very well. I did not want to let go of my child; I said I would go also, as did the mother of our friend's child. But it was impossible for the Pole to take the mothers. The question then arose of whether we ought to let only the children be handed to these people. My husband didn't want to give our child away; he believed that after the war she would not know where she belonged. He said he didn't want to leave a non-Jewish generation after him. He believed that whatever happened to everybody else would also happen to our child. We decided not to give her away; the friend arrived at the same decision. Actually, as far as I knew, no one left a child with Poles in Piotrków. Everybody seems to have held the same opinion as my husband. There was little trust that the Poles would raise the children as Jews, that they would return the children after the war, or that there would be relatives left to whom to return them. They would grow up not knowing they had been Jews.

The decision was not as easy as it seems from my telling it here—to give away a child or not to give him or her away, which could mean death. We talked, we doubted, we consulted one another; maybe our child would be saved. At the end, we all decided to keep our children with us. Some may have thought that my husband was committing a terrible crime because he didn't wish to save his child. It seemed to some that he wished to sacrifice her to maintain her Jewishness. I felt very badly when somebody thought that my husband made a disastrous decision. There were, of course, many other people in other towns who had relinquished their children to Poles. These people are not alive, and we don't know what happened to them or to their children after they were given away. But we learned later that many of the people who gave their children away couldn't find them after the war; they were not returned to the parents. Even though the Poles who took babies and small children were well paid, it is known that some took the money and killed the children, or they raised them in their own religion, placing them in cloisters and refusing to return them; most frightfully in some cases, as I mentioned earlier, the children refused to be returned to their "alien" parents, or they turned them over to the Germans.

I think my husband acted with great wisdom, like a tzaddik, a holy man. He devoutly believed that God would help our daughter survive and be Jewish. Extraordinary things happened. People remained alive, and one doesn't know why. A lot of people put in enormous effort to remain alive, but the overwhelming majority of them were murdered. My husband did not wish to sacrifice his child; he wished only to leave a Jewish generation. We had no way of knowing whether, if the child were raised by Poles, she would become an anti-Semite, part of the Hitler generation.

I had not known about this quandary before hearing my mother's narrative. As I learned about this compelling episode, I was astonished by my parents' determination to retain their religion, even at the risk of life itself. When I heard my mother speak on this topic I gained an even greater appreciation of what it means to have faith; to be religious, or perhaps, above and beyond the religion itself, to possess the powerful desire to remain who one has been for generations to come, under any circumstances. My mother was, however, greatly preoccupied with the way people interpret the actions of Jews during this period, and she was especially concerned with how she and my father would be judged for deciding not to hand me over to Poles.

Miraculously, many of the children of Piotrków did survive. They were taken chiefly to Ravensbrück and Bergen Belsen, as my child was, and they remained alive, except for those who had died of hunger, including the daughter of our friend. She died as she lay next to my daughter a day after the liberation of Bergen Belsen, I eventually learned.

During the few months when we were all together, after my arrival in Piotrków and before the ghetto liquidation, when we went into hiding, we looked for ways to save ourselves, to leave Poland, to hide in the ghetto, or to try to hide with some Poles. We were even told that there might be a possibility to go to Switzerland; we prepared the pictures needed for identification papers. It was one of the rare times my husband had his photograph taken. Nothing came of that ruse, though. Throughout this time I sought ways to earn some zlotys, and my brothers in Warsaw sent me packages with items **(these may have been rags)** that I could sell in Piotrków to earn a few pennies. Both my brothers in Warsaw remained active in petty commerce in the ghetto there, as much as it was possible.

We lived in constant fear, hearing about deportations in other towns and not knowing what was going to happen from one day to the next. I know that all of life is uncertain under the most favorable conditions, but our existence during the entire time of the war years was fraught with uncertainty from one minute to the next. It was totally dependent on the unpredictable whims of evil. During the war years we did not know which actions might protect us from death. And living with this type of uncertainty was another form of torture devised by the Germans.

We stayed indoors. It was dangerous for adults to leave the house. Because children were less noticeable, it was generally speaking less dangerous for them to go out. Thus we would send our little girl to the house of one of my husband's followers, a Hasid, to bring some potatoes and whatever else he was able to share with us. It was heartbreaking to see the child carry these heavy bags, knowing it was almost all we would have to eat.

My husband would send her, even before I arrived from Warsaw, to the old city to buy two deca (milligrams) of raisins, from which he made wine for the Sabbath blessing. We would laugh about this because by the time she returned with the raisins, she would have eaten half of them.

I. In My Mother's Voice

(My mother continued to laugh about that, expressing her amusement by this situation).

One time, in the summer of 1942, during my child's return from one of these little errands she was in grave danger from an SS man. William was a well-known SS officer in Piotrków who walked around the city with his huge dog that terrified people; he was known as "William with the dog", or as "the devil." When he showed up in the streets everything closed and everybody—children and adults—went running inside; the streets were empty. He would incite the dog and let him off the leash: the dog was known to tear pieces of flesh from people—especially children.

One day, as my little girl was returning from an errand, she saw William with the dog coming from the old city toward our house on Pilsutzkik Street, while she was crossing the very large beautiful grass field across from our apartment. We could see her walking from our window on that lovely summer day. We observed from afar how she walked, and suddenly stopped. She sat down on the grass. She wore a flowered dress and she looked like a flower growing out of the field. It was a miracle that William didn't notice her as he crossed the street. We stood at the window in agony **(My mother here uses the Yiddish phrase raysn fun zikh shtiker, "tearing pieces off from oneself")**; was she already lost? I ran around the field through the side streets that circled around the field to get to her from the back. When I reached her, William and the dog were not there anymore; she was just sitting down. I grabbed her and she said to me, "Mother I saw the dog, he did not see me, and I bent down so he would not see me." I started crying spasmodically and the people who saw the scene also cried with me because nobody could have saved her. I grabbed her and ran to Judin Street until we heard that William left the ghetto. Imagine how I felt as we calmed down and walked home. The joy! The intelligence the child showed, knowing that she needed to hide, to shrink. God helped me; she was saved because of the merits of her saintly father, her ancestors. Many miracles like that happened with my child. **(As my mother recounts this event, which I recall vividly too, she cried, and it brings tears to my eyes as well. It is not uncommon in traditional or Hasidic beliefs to hold that one's meritorious ancestors will intercede on behalf of the living to protect them, a belief my mother held on to throughout the war years, as we see later also).**

In Hiding

The way we survived the liquidation of the Piotrków ghetto was by going into hiding. There were nine people in the family: my husband, my child, my husband's older brother, his three adult children and son-in-law, my mother-in-law and me. In addition, two couples, neighbors and friends who helped organize the hiding place, joined us there. I didn't participate in any of the preparations; I did not even know until the last minute that my brother-in-law was planning on taking the family into hiding. It was all very guarded and secretive. I am not even sure that my husband knew. I did not wish to go into hiding, but my husband said that if I did not go, he would remain with me. Then his mother announced that she would go with us. And my husband's brother refused to go into hiding without his mother. The chain of refusals was broken when my brother-in-law's unmarried daughter, verbally pouncing on me, said that I would be responsible if the family would not go into the ready hiding place; she said, "We will all be destroyed." She was right. I should not have rejected going into hiding, and now I don't even know why I was opposed to it. I think it was because after July, when Warsaw was liquidated, we did not hear from anybody there. We lost contact with my brothers in Warsaw, and with my stepfather. I was greatly anguished, and I just wanted to go with all the other Jews on the trains. But since no person would go into hiding without the others, I agreed to join the rest of the family and not lead it to extermination.

The hiding place was well organized; it was located in the attic of the house where we had lived. The attic was the size of our entire apartment on the first floor. One corner, where we were to stay, was sealed off by bricks. A few bricks were left open to create a crawl space so that we could enter the big attic where the provisions were stored. The attic had no wooden or cement floors, only sand on which were placed my mother-in-law's carpets. My mother-in-law had many treasures like these carpets, although she was not pleased that they were used for such purposes. In the same way as we could not believe when people came to us in Warsaw reporting that Jews were being killed everywhere, my mother-in-law could still not accept as true, even at this time, that everything was finished and gone, that we were in great danger, that our lives might be over, and that it was no longer worth taking care of any possessions. She seemed unable to grasp the gravity of the situa-

I. In My Mother's Voice

tion, or to conceive of our destruction. It was a shock for her to learn, without any warning, that she had to hide in an attic. She was not a young person, and though she was wise, she was not always very kind. My brother-in-law had to make her understand that everything, including her carpets, were all inconsequential, and she finally agreed to have the carpets spread on the sand floors of the attic.

Once a person got through the crawl space from the little room to the big attic, he could go down to the kitchen on the first floor to get water. An opening was made from the kitchen ceiling to the roof, which also enabled us to draw water through a pipe. My brother-in-law's son, who was about 16 or 17 years old, also installed electricity. He pulled electric wires from outside of the ghetto, which were available to the Poles but not, theoretically, to the Jews, and he attached them so as to enable us to have an electric stove to cook on. He was an extraordinarily able handyman; he organized everything.

In one small corner there was a bucket that served as our toilet; it was emptied by my nephew every night, when he took the waste down to the courtyard. We remained in one place all day and night. There was no room for taking a step, or even to move. We could not stand up because of the very low ceiling. We had to lie down on the bedding we laid on top of the carpets for the entire three weeks we were hidden.

Only my brother-in-law remained in the large part of the attic. He had a little table with a chair and he sat there studying the Talmud at night. He may have stayed there all night. He would permit my child to crawl out from the little corner and stay within the big room of the attic for a brief moment. She had to be very quiet, and no one could be allowed to hear that there was a child there.

Everyone conducted himself and herself well, except for occasional rifts between one of my nieces and my mother-in-law (her grandmother), which her sister tried to smooth over; otherwise we all had harmonious relations.

We always spoke in whispers. Any sound could have given us away. But consider this one incident: my daughter suddenly started crying. Until that time she had not cried, and I cannot even recall the reason she was crying now. Naturally everybody tried to quiet her down, without much success. My niece's new husband, a big man, went over to her and put a pillow to her face and began suffocating her. He began yelling that she could destroy us all with this crying. He said, "Because of the child, everybody will die!" He wasn't a very nice person, although I couldn't blame him for his act—he believed she was endangering everyone else.

Picture it. The child is crying, and thirteen people's lives are at risk. What should the father and mother do? It was horrifying for my husband and me to live through. To fight with my niece's husband would have meant that we were willing to sacrifice everyone in that attic for our child. What could we do? We stood frozen, motionless, witnessing this terrible tragedy. My husband's brother and mother, thank God, would not permit it. My brother-in-law and my mother-in-law began pulling my niece's husband away from my daughter, to stop him from killing her. The two couples said nothing. My brother-in-law's daughters and son said nothing. They just lay there. My daughter was so frightened that she stopped crying. Like a true adult, she then apologized to everybody and asked that nobody be angry with her. Aside from this one episode, my little girl conducted herself like one of the adults. She helped with everything that needed to be done in that room when we prepared food, and always tried to make herself useful.

After three weeks, the Germans found us—but not because of my daughter's crying, which occurred about eight days after we moved into the hiding place. We were in hiding another two weeks after that, living in complete silence. We were very careful. At one point we heard people walking on the roof, before we were betrayed, but they could not find us because we could not be detected from above.

Only once did I deliberately close my eyes throughout the entire war: when we were in hiding, and we could hear the Germans walking over our heads, and we knew that any minute they could come to take us out. At the moment when they came, I closed my eyes so that I could not see how they would take my child away. But I opened them immediately after they got into the attic. They took us all out.

The Germans discovered us because somebody disclosed our whereabouts. There were other people hiding in the cellar of the same house where we were. We did not know them, and I don't know how they found out that we were hiding in the attic. But they seem to have noticed that we were storing a lot of provisions, and one person came to my brother-in-law and demanded that we give him some of them. My brother-in-law gave him a large portion of our supplies. When these people were discovered, we were later told, one of the women in the cellar said, "Why don't you go and look for the rabbi who is hiding in the attic."

The Germans then began to look for us even more systematically than before. They knew that the rabbi's family was not on their list of deportees; therefore the family must be hiding, but they didn't know where. They searched everywhere, and finally had luck. They didn't find us because they could hear noise from the attic: they found us because somebody betrayed us; regrettably another Jewish person. When the Germans saw how well organized the hiding place was, and how well concealed we were in our attic, they said that they admired the genius who thought up the hiding place, and that we could have remained there for years had we not been exposed by those people. Even once they got up on the roof it took them a while to find us.

In the Synagogue

When we were discovered we believed that our fates were sealed. We were removed from our hiding place and transferred to the Great Synagogue of Piotrków, considered one of the most beautiful synagogues in Western Europe, built between 1791-1793. **(The Germans deliberately violated the synagogue without totally destroying it, by having horses trample on its beautiful interior.)** About 2000 people in all were found hiding in Piotrków after the liquidation, and those people were transferred and concentrated in this synagogue.

There was no food in the synagogue, and we were starving. There were a few of my husband's friends, Hasidim, who gave us a few bread crusts they brought with them. My husband and I argued over who should eat them, and he would not have them. The conversation ended when we divided them: a bite for each of us, and the rest to our daughter. She was behaving in the synagogue quietly and like an adult, as she had for so long.

After we spent three days in the synagogue there was a selection. Some were to be sent off on the trains to be murdered **(in Treblinka)** and some to the small remaining ghetto to work as slave laborers in a glass and wood factory in Piotrków. They took us out to a large field where the selection took place. Of the nine persons in the family, the two most in danger were my mother-in-law and my child. Children and elderly people were usually selected to be transported to the death camps. Miraculously, our entire family was selected to go to the small ghetto. Except my mother-in-law and my child, we were all able to work.

My mother-in-law was 72 years old at the time, but because she looked twenty years younger, we could save her. We said she was 52. We said my daughter, who was 7, was 16.

When they called out our family, we all stood together and surrounded my mother-in-law and my child so that they could not be readily seen; this is how they survived this particular selection. Then they transferred us to the small ghetto work camp.

It is possible that our family was not selected for destruction because of the intervention of the president of the Judenrat at the time, who was a Hasid and friend of the family. It could have been that he was also given money to save us, but I don't know this as a fact.

I recall a dreadful scene during this selection when a mother held her child and it was taken out of her arms. They wanted to send the mother to work in the ghetto but not her child. She ran to grab the child and dragged it back. The German grabbed the child from her hands and sent it away. The mother again ran to grab the child. She ran back and forth several times. The mother fought for the child, but since she could not save it she went with it to an oven in Treblinka. There were many cases when they ripped the children away from their mothers; in this case I witnessed with my own eyes the unbearable scene.

In the Little Ghetto

When we came out of hiding, the ghetto had already been liquidated and those people who were not hidden were hauled away, we knew not where **(mostly to Treblinka.)** Of the 4,000 Jews left to work in the labor camps, about 2,000 had been in hiding. Those who were transferred to the synagogue, like our family, were taken from there to the little ghetto in the old city, the Jewish quarter. The area was much neglected, and they put us in decrepit apartments. We were nine people, and we were put into one room with a tiny kitchen. We divided the small kitchen, and my husband, my child, and I stayed there, and my brother-in-law, his children, and my mother-in-law had the other room and half of the tiny kitchen.

It is so difficult to speak about those times. But in those tragic conditions we were happy, the three of us. **(One can hear the irony in her voice as she says this.)** My husband, my child, and I were all together in this space with two little broken beds. My daughter slept on a wooden

I. In My Mother's Voice

slab on the floor; we were hungry and cold, and yet we were very happy that we were still together. It is difficult to grasp how our lives had changed, and it's so painful to think about. Had we all survived, we could have had a nice life.

The small ghetto was not simply a ghetto but a place where people were taken to work as slave laborers. The Germans had taken over two Polish factories **(the Huta Kara, a glassworks, and the Bugaj, a plywood factory)**. The people who did not work in the factories remained in the little ghetto and were assigned to work in the communal kitchen, peeling potatoes. My mother-in-law, my child, and my husband remained in our room with the permission of the president of the Judentrat and the Jewish head of the work camp. There were other people, some of the president's relatives, who also did not have to work in the labor camp. All others in our family, as well as the rest of the people in this ghetto, worked each day beginning at 6 a.m., returning at night.

While I was at work my child cleaned up the room. She kept it spotless. She also went out to collect broken chairs and broken pots and pans that she found in a huge garbage heap of junk the Germans threw out. The good things the Germans always sent to Germany. She went to the head of the Judenrat, who gave her a little wood, which we used to make a fire for cooking. My husband wouldn't eat the soup that was distributed from the ghetto kitchen, but she brought that soup for the rest of us, and she found potatoes, which she cooked for him. My daughter was very intelligent and mature for her age. Most admirable was how she knew what to do, how to clean the house and when to hide in a corner or under the bed when she heard something and sensed danger. It was very cold, and she would stand at the window in her coat waiting for me to return from the labor camp, and she would start singing, "Mother is coming, mother is coming,"

There were people who had money and could buy things. We only existed on what the Judenrat president gave us. Since my husband wouldn't eat the soup they distributed, we needed to get him some other food. He was weak; he needed extra milk and a roll. To get money for this food, I also worked extra hours for a wealthy family. This family had a girl a little older than my daughter. One time when my child was with me in their house, and my daughter saw that this girl did not behave respectfully to me, she wanted to beat her up.

In his capacity as the head administrator of these ghettos, the head of the Judenrat had police and other people who had worked for him managing the work camps. People wanted to kill him because he turned over inmates from the work camps to the Germans for deportation. He tried to save his relatives and friends.

We lived in this little ghetto until about February 1943, when the Germans ordered the president of the Judenrat to deliver 300 women. He told us that the Germans assured him they just needed 300 women to work in a camp. Who believed them? The Germans were constantly known to use deception, telling people that nothing would happen to them and then they were shipped to gas chambers. We didn't know whether this roundup was to send the women to slave labor camps or to annihilate them.

The Judenrat president furnished a list of people to deliver to the Germans. Once people learned they were on the list, they hid. Obviously, nobody wanted to go. In truth, none of our family members, the Radoszyce rebbe's family, was on his list. The Judenrat president wanted to save us.

The Jewish police walked around with the prepared list of names of people to be sent to Skarżysko-Kamienna; we were told later that it was an ammunition factory. They started combing the ghetto to find the people on their list. One of the women on the list stayed with my nieces in the other room where we lived. The Jewish police came to look for her, knowing she was with us, but when the police arrived in our living quarters, she was gone. She hid elsewhere. One of the Jewish policemen, a 16-year-old boy who acted as the middleman between the Germans and the Jewish community, and who was regarded as a traitor, insisted on being told where this woman was. It was 10 p.m., and we were all in bed. Both my husband and I told the boy that we didn't know where she was. He told us that if we didn't disclose the woman's whereabouts, he would take me. Wanting to save me, my little girl blurted out, "I know." When I heard her say this, I covered her little mouth and told her not to say anything, and I told the policeman that the child only thought she knew, but she didn't know anything. (We did know where she was, but refused to reveal the location.) The policeman left and started looking for her elsewhere. He couldn't find her, and he returned the next day and said to me, "If you don't say where she is, I will take you." We didn't, and he did. But they needed more women—300 in total—so they took my brother-in-law's two daughters and my mother-in-law. Since they still did not have enough women to meet their quota, they grabbed people

I. In My Mother's Voice

off the street, including my brother-in-law. My brother-in-law's son was at work in the factory and not in the ghetto, and he was not captured.

After an intensive search, they finally found the woman they were initially looking for. But I had already been taken in her place. Had they found her right away, I, and perhaps even my mother-in-law and my nieces, might have been spared the transfer to the slave labor camp. My brother-in-law, his two daughters (Malka and Sara), my mother-in-law, Sara's husband, and I were all taken to Skarżysko-Kamienna, the ammunition works. At the roundup, all of us were put into one room; then the women and men were put on separate trucks.

The moment of our seizure to go to Skarżysko-Kamienna was yet another moment of excruciating anguish. My husband ran around everywhere to try to find me. He went to the Judenrat president and other people in the hope that he could get me released because I was not on the list, but to no avail. They had by then already taken my two nieces and mother-in-law.

During the time my husband ran around trying to help me, he was terribly beaten by a German. He went from one wooden gate to another with my child, attempting to get me off the truck. When they chased him away from one gate, he ran to another. I saw him from the truck, standing at the various gates. Then there was a small riot. One man, who had a lot of money in diamonds and wished to save his wife from being sent to Skarżysko-Kamienna, walked over to the Germans standing guard, wanting to give them the diamonds to release his wife. The guard opened the gate and the man's wife came out, but as soon as she did, other people followed and the guards began beating everybody. One woman was beaten to a pulp. Her face was totally swollen, and later was blackened from her bruises. My husband was terribly beaten in the area around his heart, as he stood there with the other people. I could see what was happening.

But just before he was beaten, he was able to get to me, and he and my daughter stood next to me. The question was with whom my child should go. My husband and I were both undecided, conflicted. We stood there. The Jewish policeman in charge of this aktion, deportation mission, pushed me to go. I held my child by one of her hands, my husband by the other. We stood there, each asking the other what we should do. I believed it would be better if I took her, and my husband thought it would be better for her to remain with him. Neither of us could decide what was best. We asked her, "With whom do you want to remain?" She began crying terribly. "I don't know. Tell me, with whom should I go. I want to be with father, I want to be with mother. Should I go with you, or remain here?"

This episode was a watershed in my life that I have never forgotten; as I write this, it makes me shiver and I am still in anguish. My mother was crying while she narrated the incident.

All the time my child cried and repeated the question, "With whom should I go?" She stood there the entire time, cried and turned her head to me, and then to her father, like an adult standing at the crossroads trying but unable to make a decision. The moment didn't last very long, for the policeman came and tore me away. I didn't even manage to give her a kiss. He tore me away and pushed me into the truck. He made the decision for us. My child remained with her father and then he got beaten up by one of the Germans standing there.

It was fortunate that she stayed with her father. The women who took their children with them—I knew one such woman—could not keep them. The children were immediately sent back to the ghetto, since children were not permitted in the ammunition factories. The anguished moments of indecision were for naught. In fact, there was only one child in the entire camp, an 8-year-old boy, and I still don't know how he managed to be there.

After I was taken from Piotrków, my daughter took care of her father. The only one of the family left in Piotrków was my brother-in-law's young unmarried son, who was in another area. My husband passed away in June of 1943, and from then on my child was left by herself. All of the children who were left were distributed among families that were still intact. My daughter was handed over to a family by, I believe, the Judenrat president, so that somebody would watch over her. The man was a dentist, a family friend, and he and his wife had two boys around the same age as my daughter. This family was supposed to care for her but, regrettably, after the war I heard from various people how badly they had treated and exploited her.

Who can know what would have happened later had the Germans found the woman they were seeking in time and not taken me in her stead to Skarżysko-Kamienna? It might be that they would have taken me later anyway; it might be that if I had remained in the ghetto, my husband would have lived and been taken to a concentration camp. My brother-in-law's son remained in the ghetto, but then he was murdered in another place. Many who remained in the ghetto were taken to Częstochowa or other terrible places. What can we know after the fact? I do know that I was terribly wronged by this woman who failed to present herself to the policeman. I was unable to forgive her for a very long time. Years later, she once telephoned me in New York for some reason, and she admitted that she was wrong to let me be taken instead of her. She asked for my forgiveness. Since we cannot undo what happened, I told her that I forgot the incident, and that I forgave her with all my heart. But when it happened, it was a very tragic moment.

One consolation I have is that even though my husband was beaten and kicked in his heart, he passed away in his bed and was buried in the cemetery in Piotrków; I saw the headstone after the war. There were ten men at the funeral. A man who survived the war in Russia, whom I met in Poland after the war, showed me the burial plot. This man was a tombstone maker and the caretaker of the cemetery in Piotrków before the war; he was there when my husband was buried.

Skarżysko-Kamienna

I was taken to Skarżysko-Kamienna in February of 1943, and an even harsher chapter in my life began. As I recall how life was in the slave labor camps and in the barracks, and how we managed with the tiny portions of soup and the small pieces of bread, the ways we washed ourselves or our laundry, my grief returns. Of course, when I speak of this today it seems strange—to wash oneself without soap, to wash oneself with sand. It seems unreal, as if it happened in another world, but that is how those years seem. It couldn't have been on this earth, because even in a nightmare no one could imagine what happened during the war. Even the most frightening fantasies couldn't capture how people lived, how they survived. In both the Warsaw and Piotrków ghettos I was still surrounded by my loved ones, by my child, by my husband in Piotrków, by my beloved brothers and stepfather in Warsaw. Once I arrived in Skarżysko-Kamienna I gradually lost everyone, even those in my husband's family who were also transferred to Skarżysko-Kamienna.

CHAPTER 3
Working in a Slave Labor Ammunition Factory

As I listened to my mother's narrative of her experiences in the camp in Skarżysko-Kamienna, it was astonishing to me that she spoke about the events that follow without anger, without rancor, and in a matter-of-fact, inspiring voice. When I initially transcribed this section relating to her existence in the slave labor camp, I could only cry due to the unimaginable cruelty and humiliation I was documenting on the computer screen.

Arrival in the Camp

My memories of the years that followed my arrival in Skarżysko-Kamienna are even sharper. I recall a conversation with a woman in the camp. We talked about whether we would remember all our experiences should we survive. The woman said that if she were to survive the war she would fear all these unimaginable experiences remaining with her. She would wish to obliterate all her memories. I said I thought just the opposite. I was afraid that, if I survived the war, I might forget everything, and I didn't want to forget anything. One must talk about what happened to us in order to honor the saintly people (*kedoshim*) who were murdered and also to save one's own honor. With my memories, these events will never be forgotten. I want to remember them always. I believe that it is a betrayal of all the people who ceased to exist if we eradicate them even from our memories. I want to keep these memories as my diary, a living diary, in honor of those who were murdered. My memories will be their tombstones, for there are no tombstones or traces of the murdered now.

My husband has been in my diary all these years. A few years ago I felt him come to me to tell me, "Forget everything; begin a new chapter." These words in his voice made me feel a bit liberated, but not for long. The remembrances remain, and I don't wish to eradicate them. Now is the time to immortalize my loved ones and the camp years. I wish to put on record my experiences in the two camps I was in, Skarżysko-

I. In My Mother's Voice

Kamienna and Hasag-Leipzig / Buchenwald. Some of them I shared with others, but many were unique to me personally. I will begin with when I first came to Skarżysko-Kamienna.

We were put on open trucks between 4 and 6 a.m. and transported from Piotrków to Skarżysko-Kamienna on February 26, 1943, before Purim. We travelled all day in these packed vehicles. It was a beautiful, sunny day and we reached Skarżysko-Kamienna around 9 p.m. When we arrived we were wearing the same clothes we had in Piotrków. They registered us and gave us each a card with a number. There was an office that was administered by Jews, most of them from the Skarżysk region. They were brought to the camp after the town of Skarżysk was liquidated.

From the very first moment I arrived in Skarżysko-Kamienna I began to cry. I constantly wept. I walked around for the first week, the second week, the third week, with swollen red eyes. I cried unceasingly until the overseer (*meister*), a Pole, who was also a mean person, asked somebody, "Why is she crying all the time, why is she crying more than all the others?" I don't know what he was told, but he said to the woman that I must cease sobbing because he didn't like to see people crying. He wanted to hear people sing and see happy faces. He said that if I continued to walk around weeping, it would come to no good; I must stop. Germans wanted to see cheerful, satisfied people in accordance with the notice posted at the entrance of the camp, which read, "Work makes life sweet." This overseer, named Panchick, persecuted me a great deal, more than the others, because I cried all the time. Thankfully, he was not there very long. He was removed shortly after we arrived—but the others were not any better.

Naturally, I didn't listen to what was said and I don't know what happened to resolve the overseer's problem with me, but it took me several months to stop crying. At first I thought I would run away from the camp; that is why I cried so much. I was constantly thinking about how to run away. There was a Jewish man who said he was going to flee, and if I wanted I could escape with him. I would just have to find bread, because we wouldn't have anything to eat at the beginning of the journey. Once I found some bread, we could run away.

I don't know whether I told my plan to my brother-in-law, or somebody told him that I intended to escape from the camp, but one day he came to me and told me that I definitely must not try to flee. Three women I knew very well from Piotrków tried to escape in the first weeks after we arrived, and as soon as they got out of the camp confines they were caught. All three were shot. My brother-in-law asked me, "What will you accomplish? They will catch you anyway." That was how he tried to dissuade me from attempting to escape.

Then I walked over to the electrified barbed wires surrounding the camp. I had heard that if one crossed the wires and touched them one would be electrocuted. When I came close to the wires, I found that the first row of wires was not electric, but the second row was. Somebody saw me and stopped me. My brother-in-law heard about my attempt to cross over these wires and again stopped me from doing so because, he said, "It's sure death." I don't recall now all the arguments he used to deter me, but the fact is that he would not let me run away. I gave up. The man with whom I was going to run was told by my brother-in-law not to take me with him. Then this man decided he wasn't going anyway, and all my plans for escaping fell apart. That's when I calmed down and stopped crying. I recognized that I had to give up the thought of running away. It is interesting that as long as I had the hope that I could run away, I cried. The moment I saw that I couldn't accomplish anything I stopped crying. I had nothing to cry about. Nothing would help me. I would have the same fate as everybody else.

As a way of reminding us to be "happy" on our arrival in Skarżysko-Kamienna, after they brought us to the Economia building and assigned us bunk beds they "welcomed" us with music. The contrast between where we were and the music played by the prisoners already in the camp was shocking. In all probability some of these prisoners brought instruments, violins or what have you, with them. I remember the violins. The German overseer ordered the prisoners to begin playing when we entered the building. We understood, of course, that this was a joke played on us by the authorities, which only added to the anguish we were experiencing. At this moment we still did not know whether they were taking us to our deaths or to a factory to work.

Then, about two weeks later, during our 15-minute free period at night, this same overseer gathered the people under his charge, and the musicians who had "welcomed" us, and ordered everybody to sing. It is difficult for me to put in words what I felt at that time, but I knew it was a joke. He wanted to amuse himself so he traumatized people by making them sing and play music. I stood on the side, crying, watching this degradation and insult to us. The spiritual (geystlekhe) bitterness and pain this episode created is indescribable; the humiliation was as difficult to take as was the physical pain and hunger. I am, of course, speaking about myself; others may have just laughed it all off. But for me this, like so many other similar experiences, caused me unspeakable agony. If the overseer had put a knife in my heart it would have been more desirable than to hear the order that we should all sing and play.

I find it difficult to write about this scene. The cruelty had no bounds. My mother is right: a knife in the heart would have been less cruel. This little episode is more painful than most.

We did not go to work on the first day we arrived in this camp; they registered us and gave us numbers: mine was 224 or 226. The Germans were very meticulous and everybody had a number. On the second day after we arrived, we had to stand at a roll call before dawn; since my mother-in-law and I shared the same bed, we went together to the roll call. Roll calls usually began at 4 a.m. and we stood at attention till about 5:30 a.m. The work in the factory began at 6 a.m. Nobody could hide from the roll calls. Two Jewish commandants ran around in the halls and in the washroom with their clubs to see if anyone was hiding. When they saw me walking slowly with my mother-in-law, they gave us a few beatings to make us walk faster. They chased us out of the barracks, but my mother-in-law couldn't run fast like the others. There were a few steps down to get out of the barrack and I had to guard her from falling. The policemen began rushing people to come exactly on time. Once I came with my mother-in-law, and the policeman beat us because we were not there exactly to the minute. It was a terrible time for me. The roll calls also served to select those who would be sent away and those who would remain to work in the camp.

The Economia was a large stone building, once an empty factory that was situated some distance from the ammunition factory where we were to work. We entered on the ground floor into a long room where there were three- and four-tiered bunk beds lined up on both sides of the walls, separated by very narrow passages to enable a person to get in and out of them.

Yes, Jewish policemen were our guards; they escorted us to and from work and were in charge of allocating these very narrow bunk beds constructed of two or three planks, mostly covered with straw. Two women shared a bed. My mother-in-law and I were assigned to one of them. Two of her granddaughters were there also, but it was I who ended up with her in one bed. A doctor's wife and her daughter were in the bunk bed next to us.

We remained in the Economia building from February until shortly before Passover, at which time the construction of the barracks was completed and we were transferred there. These barracks were designed to accommodate 50 people each, rather than the 400 in the Economia building. The barracks were like a sukkah with a roof: they were small, wooden, feeble structures but, thankfully, the rain did not pour in because there were no cracks in the walls. Each barrack had two small windows at each end. In the summer there was light, and it wasn't as terribly dark and cold as in the winter.

There were about 10 barracks in the camp, which was very large and surrounded by pine trees. The Skarżysko-Kamienna camp was mainly comprised of women, although there were also some men, several of whom may have come "voluntarily" like my niece's husband, who wanted to be together with his wife. One of the men who came with us was a policeman in Piotrków, but gave up this good job to be with his wife.

The camp grounds were very sandy and muddy; all the barracks were separated from one another by some distance. The men's barracks were on one side and the women's on another; the two sides were not separated, and we could walk back and forth between them. In some cases men were brought together with their wives and they were able to be together.

In the center, between the rows of barracks, there was a flimsy structure made of patched-up boards with a door, and this was our toilet. There were also four water faucets on two sides with cold running water and a sink for washing oneself and one's laundry, located in another building like a poorly-constructed sukkah. Both of these structures were almost outdoors.

Two-tiered bunk beds were lined up on both sides inside the barrack. Two women occupied each tier; that is, four people slept in one such wooden bunk bed. Since there were two shifts, people rotated sleeping; when one person returned from the day shift and went to bed, the person on the night shift left. When the morning shift left at 6 a.m, the night shift returned, and only half the people who lived in the barrack were there at one time. Only on Sundays from 3 or 4 o'clock till Monday morning the people in both shifts were off together. The factories were idle then, and so we all slept together in the same bed. I should note that there were very few occasions when we could talk. When we woke up after returning from the factory everybody was busy washing. When we returned from work we just fell on the bunk bed and slept a few hours. When we got up we washed ourselves, and some women would visit different barracks to see friends or relatives. But communication amongst us was otherwise limited, except for those Sundays.

The bunk beds were set out lengthwise on each side of the barrack. In the middle of the barrack there were two long benches and an old-fashioned wood-burning round iron stove, with an exhaust chimney that conducted the smoke out through the roof. We picked up firewood not far from the barrack and also cut wood, which kept us warm during the terribly cold winters. Every day two different people cleaned, washed the floor, and spread it with wood shavings. We also found driftwood to fuel the oven in the winter.

Where did we cook? There was a tin sheet on top of the stove, and when the oven was burning we could cook, or warm up things, and water could be heated. The stove was a bit of a problem because everyone wanted to heat water to wash up, or to cook something, and there was not a lot of room on top of it. Some Poles who worked the machines with us did a bit of business on the side by bringing in products to sell to the Jewish inmates. The Poles were not checked when they entered the factory, and they could bring flour, kasha, potatoes, rice, or some *gritz* (type of kasha). It was not very much.

All business was conducted in the barracks. From time to time they distributed bundles of very old clothing. These rags and boots once belonged to people who were sent to the gas chambers. The Germans sorted these things, including clothing, into three categories: very good things, which they sent to Germany; goods not in tip-top condition, which those living in the area kept for themselves and rag-like items that were still wearable were distributed to us. The commandant sorted these out to catch things that may have contained valuables sewn into them; for example, people would sew pieces of gold or coins into corsets. I don't know who exactly did the sorting of this last category of things—the rags—but I do know it was not left for Jews to do. The Germans carefully scrutinized the people categorizing these items, seeing to it that nothing of value would be inadvertently left in any garment. After all the items were sorted out, they made packages of the rag-like pieces, and each person got one package.

Occasionally German vigilance failed. One woman from Piotrków found a gold piece and a gold coin concealed in the corset in the bundle she received. She sold the coins. Others sold what they received in the bundles, such as corsets, which were useless to us. I learned about the gold coins the woman found because she called me to her bunk bed. She was sick and she gave me 20 zlotys so I should buy something for myself and somebody else could benefit from her luck. Twenty zlotys would buy one saccharin tablet. In any event, I refused her generous offer and said, "Now you have it, but you don't know what will be tomorrow." I did not want to take the money from her. There were very decent people in Piotrków. This woman also may have known that I was a member of the rabbinical family. There were many people from Piotrków who knew the family and were even disciples of the family court. She may have distributed parts of her find to other friends as well. Also, there were people who wanted to help one another, even though one could not help anybody if one didn't have anything.

Another woman found a bathrobe in her bundle in decent condition; she proposed to me that I sell it in the factory and keep half of the amount. I did not take her up on this offer because I certainly did not have a talent for business of any kind, including selling things, and besides I could be observed by the Jewish police. There were people who were very adept at this kind of business, but not everyone is equally talented. As I suggested, she found another person to sell this precious bathrobe for her.

When these bundles were made available, we were told to pick them up to find some rags, shoes, boots, and other items. For a long time I did not wish to take any of these packages. I arrived in a cotton dress, with a skirt and blouse. But the dress got eaten up, destroyed by the machine oil that spilled on me while I was working. I don't remember what happened to my skirt and blouse; maybe they were taken away. The cotton dress was in shreds; it was so torn that strips were just hanging from it; it was falling apart like spaghetti. All my acquaintances in the barrack insisted that I get something to wear. I said I did not want to take anything from the Germans. After a few weeks, the Jewish head of the barrack insisted. She told me that it was awful how I walked around and who was I going to punish by not taking these clothes, the Germans would not know whether I did or did not take their handouts. She convinced me to take one of the packages. I got a skirt and a towel. I tore the towel in two and shared it with one of my bunk mates. I also went to get boots and then quickly ran back because, when I arrived at the barrack, I realized that both boots were for the same foot. I brought them back and asked them to change one of the boots. He told me to keep the boots and he gave me another one. Some people would find gold pieces hidden in the heels of boots. I gave him the one extra boot to look for something, but he found nothing.

Once I received a bundle that contained a blouse I began to wear and a good woolen skirt which I sold for 100 zlotys. I sent this money to my child in Piotrków. My husband was no longer alive at the time, and she was left by herself; she was with strangers and I wanted her to be able to buy something, which was still possible then. I don't know whether the 100 zlotys ever reached her. **(I don't remember, either.)** People were surprised that I sent money to Piotrków, because mostly people sent money from Piotrków to the camp, as my husband did once when he was still alive.

From the minute we were put on the truck in Piotrków and sent to Skarżysko-Kamienna, I was with my mother-in-law the entire time. She had two granddaughters, young women, and a son-in-law and her son; the men were separated from the women and could not go with her, and her granddaughters avoided her, I imagine not out of animosity but to sidestep difficulties for themselves. I was left to watch over her and also to share a bunk bed with her, which created various problems for me.

We were all confronted by the terrible shock of living in the Skarżysko-Kamienna camp, but my mother-in-law could not adjust to the events that overtook her and there were infinite day-to-day difficulties involved in having to care for her, especially to keep her clean. If we weren't clean, our hair would be cut off. There were faucets with cold water, as I described earlier, outside the building in the dilapidated wooden structure in the center of the camp. It wasn't so bad to wash oneself with cold water in the summer; the problem was in the winter, and especially when you were washing another person. Only a few people washed themselves no matter how cold or unpleasant the weather was, and I was one of them. We stood under these faucets and washed ourselves from head to toe. When someone had a pan, we could heat water in it on top of a stove and could wash our whole bodies in warm water. It was not very pleasant to wash with all the women around, but there were only women and we had to keep ourselves clean for our own self-respect. In Skarżysko-Kamienna we wore our own clothing, the rags we had from Piotrków, and we washed them under these faucets and dried them outside. I knew that if the body was clean then the undergarments remained clean as well. Not having any soap, we used sand to wash ourselves, rubbing our bodies with it and then rinsing it off with water. The head could not be washed with sand.

In all the camps the greatest fear was of lice because lice led to disease, mainly typhoid fever, which was transmitted from one person to another. When I arrived in the Economia, I was very clean and free of lice. Young people would manage to wash with cold water, but for older people, like my mother-in-law, that was hard. She couldn't keep herself clean enough and there were lice all around her. Our neighbor, the doctor's wife and daughter, realized the problem after the first night and, with some pull, managed to be transferred to another bunk bed. But I remained with my mother-in-law and it was not a pleasant feeling to be near lice. Those who couldn't keep themselves clean had various other problems I won't go into.

During the daily roll calls, older people were selected to be sent away, while younger people remained. Even though she looked young for her age, being an elderly woman, she could not walk in lock step and was unable to keep up. For example, after the first roll call we were marched to the factory. There were about 300 women marching in rows; my mother-in-law and I ended up in one of the middle rows. A Jewish policeman came over to us with a bat and began beating my mother-in-law to walk faster, and he also hit me with the bat, insisting I walk faster too. He wouldn't listen to any explanations. We hurried, of course. About these beatings, overseeing the Jewish police were the Jewish commandants, Krzepicki and Teperman, who were notorious for their brutality to the prisoners in their charge; they were both, as we say in Yiddish, "dogs", meaning cruel, sadistic people. Teperman was even worse than Krzepicki. I was beaten by Teperman, who was in charge of conducting us to and from the factory. He created a lot of trouble for me, especially when I had to walk slowly to the factory to keep pace with my mother-in-law. When he saw us walking slower than the rest, he beat me because we were holding people back. When I asked him to place us in the last rows, he beat me again with his rubber club. Another time he beat me because my mother-in-law could not walk down some stairs fast enough.

Finally, I went over to the head of the police before we lined up for the roll call and told one of them that I could walk fast but my mother-in-law couldn't. I asked him to place us in the last row, explaining that with about a hundred people behind us, in the middle rows, they also suffered because they couldn't push us forward and they, too, ended up behind. The head of the police heard me and placed us at the very end. In this manner we could walk slower but also keep up with the rest.

After we arrived, we met a few people who had arrived shortly before us. They were young people from Stopnica. I was interested in meeting them because they came from the same town as my father's second wife. I went to find out if there were any relatives amongst them. It turned out there was one and I wanted to know if one of my sisters, my father's second wife's daughter, had come to Stopnica from Warsaw after I had left. She hadn't and she didn't know what had happened to her. She told me that they had volunteered to come to Skarżysko-Kamienna to work because at the time they needed workers especially in one division (Werk B). They were assured that if they volunteered nothing would happen to them and they were promised better conditions than those in the Stopnica ghetto. She told me that 1,000 young people had volunteered, men and women. She herself came with six siblings. By the time they arrived in Skarżysko-Kamienna, however, all of the others were already murdered. She was the only one of her siblings who remained alive. Those who were not selected to be murdered received nothing more than we had, even though they had volunteered to come, not like us, who were brought to Skarżysko-Kamienna by force.

The Hasag Factory

The Hasag factory was the third largest privately owned ammunition factory, a subcontractor of the *Wehrmacht* **(the German unified defense establishment)**, which employed prisoners for slave labor. Before the war, the Skarżysko-Kamienna factory was a very large Polish ammunition concern, and it was confiscated by the Germans after their invasion of Poland in 1939. The factory was located on unpaved grounds, and when it rained enormous mud puddles were formed. The mud would slide right into the barracks. If it wasn't cleared out of the barrack, or wasn't cleared out on time, the Jewish policeman in charge punished not only the person responsible for the cleaning but the entire group living in the barrack. One time he took us outside and ordered us down on our knees to drain the rainwater on the ground with buckets. We had to sit a long time on our knees. And these were Jewish policemen who had such ideas. One such policeman wanted to show the Germans he was stricter than they were themselves.

In the factory, every group was assigned to a division where we worked. Here too I had special difficulties because of my mother-in-law. The younger people, like the granddaughters, were assigned to sections of the factory where the work was easier. The older people were placed in the most difficult sections of the factory, and I was assigned with my mother-in-law to one of these difficult units. I was in a division that made casings for grenades and shells for the German war effort. Among our various tasks was to place powder into the casings. We made two kinds of shells, some that were as large as a coffee pot and some that were smaller.

Organization of the Camp and Factory

The Skarżysko-Kamienna camp was divided into three *Werks*, or divisions: *Werks* A, B, and C. All those who were brought from Piotrków were assigned to *Werk* A, where we manufactured the casings—that is, the outer cylinder in which the powder was placed. Shells, grenades, small ammunition, and automatic weapons were also manufactured in *Werk* A. In *Werk* B larger ammunition, such as antiaircraft guns, were produced. From time to time they transferred people from *Werk* B to *Werk* A. *Werk* C was the most lethal; there they manufactured high explosive ammunition. I think the powder used there (in the TNT/ Picric Acid Department) burned the workers' hair, skin, and lungs, and damaged the heart. Men and women from Plaszow worked in *Werk* C, as did the better-educated population from Krakow. When they began liquidating Skarżysko-Kamienna, they brought the people from *Werk* C to *Werk* A, where everything was concentrated.

We were assigned to *Werk*, A and we were also exposed to two kinds of powders (one was called *tikrina*, the other I never learned the name of), which were terribly yellow, and we weren't given anything to protect us from the powder dust, which caused our bodies to turn yellow all over, clothing and faces, as if we were wearing a yellow uniform from head to toe.

The head of the camp was a German who was rarely seen, but when he came in, he ran around with a rubber stick as if he were searching for something. If he saw a person doing something he didn't like, he hit her with his stick. But he came very infrequently. In contrast, the internal administration of the factories consisted of the overseers (*meisters*), and they were also German. Every section had two overseers, one for a day shift and one for a night shift, but there may also have been a third shift. Below the Germans were the Poles, usually Volksdeutsche, or ethnic Germans.

The Poles were also workers in the armament factory; those who had worked in the factory before the war continued to do the same work as before the Germans took over. They considered having to work for the Germans a terrible ordeal, but they, unlike us, were paid for their labor. The overseers were also more lenient with them than they were with us; if they left the machines standing for a bit, it was overlooked.

The Germans manned the factories. I believe they were all from the Wehrmacht, not from the SS. (Generally speaking, the Wehrmacht people were considered less brutal than the SS.) There were two German overseers supervising us, and sometimes a third came. They stood and watched us all day and all night, depending on the shift, watching how we worked. For example, if the German was not around, we would hum to ourselves, or speak to somebody working at a nearby machine. One time I hummed a melody and was overheard by the overseer who may have been more decent than most. He came over to me and asked what I was humming. I said, "The Marseilles." He walked away. Another one came over and slapped me twice for the same offense. Below them, and present most of the time, was a Polish overseer. He was even worse than the Germans. He was a terrible "dog." He walked around the factory all the time, watching how our work was going.

The camp itself (which was separate from the factory) was administered by Jews, with only one German overseer. The camp director, or commandant of the camp, was a Jew from Skarżysk; he had two main assistants, the Krzepicki and Teperman I spoke of earlier, two especially infamous men whose official titles I don't know. They had an office and carried out all kinds of accounting, but I don't know what they counted.

They directed the roll calls. Below these administrators were the Jewish police that guarded us, the camp prisoners, and oversaw our daily life in the camp.

We watched out for the Jewish police. On the whole, they were not as murderous as the Germans or the Poles, but unfortunately, the one assigned to our barrack was an exception—quite as brutal as they were, and he gave us much trouble. Although there were many types of Germans, the majority were nasty. Occasionally there was one who had some feelings, who had some sympathy for people. But all the Germans were responsible for the selections that were made often, sending people away to be shot. We never knew then what had happened to people who were selected; we could only imagine their fate.

A Jewish policeman conducted us to and from the factory, which was about a 15-minute walk from the barracks. He brought our food, bread that he turned over to the barrack leader, a female commandant who made sure that the barracks were kept clean, with the floors washed; she was also in charge of the bread allotments. We were fifty women in a barrack, and every ten women had a leader who was in charge of the distribution of the bread ration.

One person who came in the morning was not a policeman; his task was to inspect the barracks for cleanliness. He may have been responsible for more than one barrack, I don't know. We kept everything clean. Every day a different couple of women had the chores of washing the table, chairs, and floors, and then throwing sawdust on the floor. The commandant, a woman, selected the people to carry out these tasks. The people on the night shift always went to sleep for a few hours upon their return; when they got up, they cleaned the barrack. Since it had to be cleaned only once a day, the people of the night shift ended up being responsible for this task. The people in the day shift returned to find everything clean.

Once I returned from the night shift to the barrack with a very high fever, and slept for two hours. I couldn't hold my head up and I could not get down from the bunk bed. The commandant told me, "Listen, you must do what you can. You have to clean up, otherwise the overseer will come in and he will scream." But it was impossible for me to move even one foot. The woman who was supposed to work with me was waiting. A short time passed, and a male commandant came in to ask what was going on. He was told that I was sick and I could not do the work. So he came over to me with his rubber bat and hit me and told me to get up; I somewhere found the strength and did the cleaning. Some people asked the female commandant why she did not assign somebody else in my place. But I did not hold it against her, because probably she would have been beaten herself if she, the commandant, did not complete the orders exactly.

Even the lowly hierarchy in this camp imposed its power by physical force, instilling perpetual fear in the prisoners. Getting slapped and kicked was thus a common occurrence and I don't even remember all the occasions I was slapped by the Jewish police or those above them. When I stood in front of the machine with the Pole, during the time I could not stop crying, an overseer came over and slapped my face twice. The Pole, or a Jewish policeman, had told him that I was not paying attention to the work. It may have been another Pole who wanted to malign me; probably he was the one who reported me. Or, it may have been that I had asked one of the overseers not to transfer me to another division as they had planned because he did not have any work for me; he said he would speak to my overseer. Once he did, the overseer kicked me so powerfully that I screamed, and I had to go back to where I had originally worked. When I arrived in the division and walked over to the machine where I had been before, the overseer gave me two slaps in the face, and a good beating. Actually, whether I cried or not did not matter. I cried because my child was taken away from me.

Work and Ammunition Production

Chiefly my division manufactured antiaircraft munitions. But actually, I also worked on several types of munitions. It was an enormous division, Werk A, with huge machines standing in an immense hall, creating an earth-splitting noise

Normally, I worked in the section of the factory where they produced the casings for grenades. Casings varied in size depending on their function; working on the casings was very difficult because we worked with huge ovens and chimneys. The Jews did the unpleasant and difficult job of standing in front of the very hot ovens, taking the pieces out, and placing them within the grenades. The Jews prepared the grenades, including the smelting of the irons in preparation for making the casings.

Working in a Slave Labor Ammunition Factory

We cut the casings for bullets that looked like thumbnails and were called *zunder*, detonators. One of the machines that I worked on cut the casings and I needed to shave off the edges from the "head of the thumbnail," the bullet itself.

There were two kinds of casings, those that were cylindrical, as large as a big coffee pot (about 20 centimeters long), which were used against antiaircraft; the smaller ones were used against tanks. Initially, my mother-in-law and I were assigned to the same section, where we both worked on the casing that held the explosive powder. It was easier and cleaner to work on these smaller casings. I also worked on the longer and heavier ones, which were manufactured on the very large machines.

To produce the casings, or shells, two people had to coordinate their activities. On one side of the huge machine a Pole sat raising and lowering the lever, while I, standing up, placed the iron pieces into the machine. These flat, round iron pieces had to be placed into one side of a big machine, and pulled out with pliers on the other side. They came out looking like little cups or rounded little plates. The machine went up and down in rhythmic fashion, and as the little plates came out I had to quickly remove them and put another piece of iron in. From there the pieces went to another machine, where they were made longer and thinner still, until they reached the desired size; then they were sent to another hall where each piece was dipped in a chemical and cleaned with water. After I removed the pieces and put them into a crate I had to be sure they had no defects. But we often damaged them, and many were ruined. When we placed the casings into a crate we put the bad ones on the bottom and the good ones on top. When the German overseer passed by to inspect it, he saw the good saucers; he saw that they were flawless.

There were two halls, one of which contained huge machines—I worked there. In the other hall we worked cleaning the rims—the flat, round, rusty pieces that were at the bottom of the casing, which held the explosive powder and looked like *matzlech* (little round matzas). **(Mother retained her sense of humor, even when telling these stories: she laughed when she used the word matzlech for this object).** People had to clean these rims to remove the rust. A Piotrków policeman saw to it that my mother-in-law was assigned to the division where the irons were scraped clean of rust. There were two other elderly women there, and each of those two was given paper to clean these iron rims.

My mother-in-law remained by herself to polish the rims of the shells, and I was very uneasy. I ran to help her with her job whenever I had a few minutes, whenever the foreman wasn't near. I would race over to her, grab two of the rims and clean them and put them in front of her to help her meet her production quota. Every time I had the opportunity, when my opposite—my partner at the machine—went out to smoke a cigarette, I dashed to help her keep up with her quotas so she would not be beaten up or selected for deportation from the camp. What mattered was the quota, not her age. The foreman and German overseers were everywhere, watching us work.

One day I had a very high fever and was very sick; I could not see what I was doing, and the Pole let the machine's lever down before I managed to get my hand out. But he realized immediately that I hadn't gotten my hand out, and he stopped the lever from coming down before I was seriously injured: I only had slight damage to my forefinger. The Pole called the German overseer and the Jewish policemen who supervised the laborers to make sure people worked and didn't sabotage the work. The German overseer took me to the infirmary where the Jewish doctor, whose name was Sacks, bandaged my finger and released me for one day from work; the German overseer allowed me to return to the barrack. But I used the opportunity to ask the doctor to say I needed an extra few days off from work for the finger to recover. The doctor was from Piotrków, or its surroundings, and he knew my brother-in-law, so with this influence I did get a few extra days off from the torturous labor. During those days I had a chance to care for my brother-in-law's daughter and her husband, who were in the infirmary. At that time there was a typhus epidemic in the camp. I felt protected from contacting the disease because I'd already had it in the Warsaw ghetto.

My brother-in-law's daughter, Sara, recovered, but her husband died in the infirmary. Before his death I managed to get a little milk, and I picked up his head and fed him a little bit of it. He could no longer swallow, and the overseer came over to say, "Why are you pouring it into his mouth? He is already dead." Then I removed my hand from behind his head, and his head lolled back. He died in my hands.

Everyone who knew me was surprised that I was put to work at these machines. When I came from Piotrków I was still dressed relatively better than most; I thought I still looked a bit like a dignified person. People could not understand why I was given this work, because in this division they usually placed "material" [people] who were designated to remain in the camp for a few weeks only and then be sent off on the trains—to the ovens. **(She used the word "material" referring to people and to describe herself. It seems to me that her usage of the word "material" is a form of ultimate dehumanization, to regard oneself as "material" rather than as a human being.)**

There was a section where they sent the young, those who looked most physically able and those who had some pull or influence, usually by bribery, but I seemed not to fit any of these categories.

Occasionally, but especially at night, when the Germans weren't walking around the factory floors, there were moments when we were left without guards. So we ran over to a person at another machine to ask about something. What did you used to read? Do you remember this and that book? We spoke about such things. There was one woman who could sing, and she knew all the arias of all the operas. So we asked, "Do you remember the aria of this opera, or that opera?" And we hummed it and we slowly recalled it. This was in Skarżysko-Kamienna. It was not like in Hasag-Leipzig, the camp I was sent to after Skarżysko-Kamienna was liquidated, where we stood very close to one another, one machine next to another. There, we did not need to walk away. We could stand at the machine and work and speak to one another. It was easier to exchange ideas and memories. We did everything possible to avoid thinking about food, or even that there was such a thing as food.

People sabotaged the work, even though doing so was incredibly dangerous. Because the administrators feared just such sabotage, our work was constantly counted. They calculated that in the general course of our work there ought to be about ten percent loss of production. But if more than that was flawed, they attributed it to sabotage. They got consistently less output than expected, and by the end they got fifty, rather than ninety, percent of the expected output.

Initially, when they discovered discrepancies in my unit's output, they investigated the matter. The German went to the Pole, and the Pole accused me of sabotage, and I was very badly beaten. I was lucky he didn't shoot me. I almost couldn't return to work, I was beaten so badly. It was said that in other divisions about 40 percent of the output was sabotaged. This was our way of fighting without guns and bullets.

In my own manner, I stood up to the Germans as best I could under the conditions of potential extermination. For example, we were not allowed to sit down in Skarżysko-Kamienna. There were chairs within our sight, but we were not allowed to sit down on them. Every now and again I walked through the factory and sat down for a second. One time the director of the factory passed by as I sat. One of the Poles saw me there and warned me with his finger. I did not get up, and he walked away. This was a daring act under the circumstances, but I acted with *chutzpah*.

I generally refused to accept anything from the administrators. One "bonus" I did accept, however, was when I stood in front of the machines by myself and needed some rags to polish them. A temporary foreman, a decent Pole, not the regular one who was very nasty, told me that his child was sick, and asked whether I knew of any remedies. He described the child's symptoms, and I told him what I knew, based on his description, from my experience. He was very grateful for that. He went with me to a storage room and selected a few rags that I could take with me to the camp and maybe find a use for. I got a few rags for the machines, and a piece of a serviette, and some black silk cloth. Later these few rags were useful. I had a serviette to put on the table, to pretend that I had a table with a cloth. I managed to piece together something like a skirt from the black silk. The one skirt I had was falling apart, so it was a relief to have a "fresh" skirt.

Sometimes my luck caused me more torment than pleasure. I seem to have been destined to be tormented not only by the Germans but also by my own scruples. One time I walked on camp grounds and saw something sticking out of the ground, a piece of paper. It looked like paper money. I bent down and picked it up. It was a 20 zloty bill. This piece of "luck" created a problem for me. I could not take this 20 zlotys; I needed to find out to whom it belonged. When I returned to the barrack, I immediately asked if anyone had lost something. I did not say, "I found 20 zlotys," because then everyone would wish to be its owner. Everybody said they had not lost anything. I asked the same thing when the next shift returned to the barrack. Again, nobody reported having lost anything. I was now faced with the dilemma of what to do with the 20 zlotys. I began thinking about who could have lost this money. Could it have belonged to an office worker, to the commander, the policeman—all Jews, who had various tasks in the camp? One policeman took us to work; another inspected our barracks for cleanliness. Or perhaps it belonged to one of the two policemen who were in charge of the daily roll calls, who counted us to make sure no one was missing. Could one of these two brutal people have lost the money? If I asked them I would have to give it to them, and I did not believe that it was a good deed (*mitzvah*) to return it to these people. I asked not only people from our barrack but any other inmates I ran into if they had lost something. Nobody had. I waited a long time. I didn't want to use the money until I knew if anybody from the camp had lost it. But this was a test for me (*nisoyen*). I held on to the 20 zlotys for about a month; then, since nobody came to claim it, I decided to spend it. Not much could be bought with 20 zlotys; whole bread cost 100 zlotys. I could buy two or three saccharin tablets to sweeten the water they gave us. As I recall this episode now, it seems that I was more bothered by the fact that I could not return the 20 zlotys than happy that I had this money. I didn't want to use it. I wouldn't tell this story to anyone then, because people would laugh at me.

We lived with constant fears of selection, especially when they transferred people from one factory division to another. One time they sent me to a section called *Drzendzufke*; they produced incendiary bombs (*tzindes*) there. They would select 8 to 10 people in one section and move them to another until the overseer came and selected a few people from this group to be sent away. I recall how one woman came to warn me to do something to avoid being selected. I could do nothing. I left it to fate.

Another time, luckily, I was transferred to a different section where the work was not heavy and for a few weeks I had peace. As it turned out, we learned later, they lacked the raw materials to make the casings. Since they didn't wish to close that section, they sent us elsewhere until they obtained the materials. But we didn't know this, so before the supplies arrived, we lived in great fear that we would be selected for the ovens. Most often, people whom the overseer did not like, or who looked weak, were selected for extinction. Rumor had it that the Germans wouldn't send people away because they wanted to keep the factory running, and in this way all those supervising the slave workers would not be sent into the battlefields. But such speculations failed to allay our fears. **(Karay[1996] makes the same point: that there was talk of eliminating Skarżysko-Kamienna, but the German staff did everything in its power to avoid it.)**

Before the war the Polish workers in this factory had rooms where they could rest and closets where they could change their clothes. Now they lacked such conveniences, but they had a separate room for hanging their clothes, which was watched over by a Polish woman. She had a Jewish assistant who cleaned and organized the overseers' rooms and washed the floors. This took about an hour, and after that the entire group could go back to the camp. And it was when I worked here that I got two containers of soup because the Poles would not eat the camp soups since, as I remarked earlier, they lived in their own homes, off the camp grounds, and cooked for themselves. One of the Polish women told me to bring a vessel for what would have been discarded soups. I felt enriched by all this extra soup, which I could share with others. This was a very good job. The other great advantage of being in this section was that there was not much work to do; we sat around, and got the soup. When they called us back to our regular section, the Polish woman told me to ask the overseer if I could remain in her section. I did not intend to ask, or beg, but the overseer himself asked my section overseer if I could remain in this section. He said "No," shouted at me, and sent me back to the regular section.

Major selections were done, as I noted before, during roll calls. Two Jewish commandants counted us when we stood at the daily roll calls. The counts in Skarżysko-Kamienna were not as precise as they were later in Germany. During the roll calls the head overseer looked the people over; when he saw somebody who looked weak, and he judged that the person could not work, she was removed immediately. One such selection in Skarżysko-Kamienna stands out especially in my mind. **(Amazingly, my mother's voice was usually matter of fact when narrating these horrors and degradations; but when describing this incident, her voice was punctuated by deep sighs.)** We were taken outside; one woman quickly gave me a red pencil that she used during her work hours, to record the work done, and then she gave it to one woman after another to paint their lips and cheeks to give the appearance of health. She told me, "With this you will look healthy." I refused. I said I would not do this; let them do what they wished. The woman said, "You are risking your life." I would still not do it. The other women did, and they needed it, because many were so pale and gaunt that they looked like ghosts, like death itself; despite their efforts they were quickly removed and sent away. As long as we looked like we could work we would remain alive; otherwise we would be sent to our deaths. People who were selected were put onto trucks that took them away, and they were never seen again.

Selections in the infirmary were much more frequent than in the barracks. Only those who could thrive remained there. It was said that not far from Skarżysko-Kamienna there was a forest where the sick were taken and shot. I recall one selection where they killed those selected in this manner.

Sickness and Disease

There was only one doctor in Skarżysko-Kamienna for the Jews—also a prisoner—and one for the Poles, but Poles could go to doctors in their communities outside the factory. The Red Cross did not exist in Skarżysko-Kamienna, and the doctor attended to people who seemed able to recover, either from illness or from accidents at the machines.

A typhoid epidemic raged in Skarżysko-Kamienna in1943. The infirmary, divided into male and female sections, with sawdust spread on the floor, had a few bunk beds, but many sick people were just lying directly on the sawdust. Those who were not afflicted by typhus, who may have had colds or other mild conditions, but couldn't work temporarily, were brought to the infirmary; once they recovered they were sent back to work. Those who were very ill, or half dead, were simply removed.

Our entire existence in the camp was tragic and traumatic, but there were some moments that were beyond the daily painful experiences; such was the moment when my mother-in-law was removed forever. She did not remain long working in the factory; she lasted only a few weeks before she was taken to the infirmary after a selection because she was simply unable to keep up with the regimen. It was difficult for me to witness her fate. From the time we were brought to Skarżysko-Kamienna, I do not remember hearing her utter a word. I don't know whether she did not speak because she was almost like a vegetable, or because she was too bitter to speak. I brought her in and sat her down wherever she was supposed to sit to do the assigned job, but she did not work for long. She was in a state of shock. She didn't sigh, she didn't cry. When she was asked something in the factory or in the camp she did not respond. She had the same experiences as everybody else, but since she was older she just could not comprehend what was happening to her. Perhaps she spoke to her son, my brother-in-law, but she did not say anything to me when I did the work for her, or when I came to see her at the infirmary.

I took care of my mother-in-law the entire time and ran to her in the infirmary as often as possible; I brought her soup and bread. The last time I came, she held on to the bedcover she'd brought with her from the barracks and pulled on it with both hands, and her eyes were lowered. I asked her if she wanted anything, but she did not answer. Lying there, she seemed as if she had lost her faculties. My brother-in-law's daughters and I had separate shifts; I don't know whether they were present when they took her away. I only know that one day when I returned from the night shift at 6 a.m. I ran to the infirmary to help her, but she was no longer there.

There were people there, including men among the police, who knew her and could have made it easier for her, but they did nothing. I don't know whether my brother-in-law may have attempted to help her. I was convinced she was still alive when she was removed, that she knew she was being taken to her death. Had she not been alive when they removed her from the infirmary, well, that's another matter, but if she was still alive and knew that she was being taken out, and where they were taking her, if she still had a little consciousness, then it was a terrible thing for her. It was difficult to live through seeing my mother-in-law's end. I struggled, but it was very difficult to experience.

As I said, I was convinced my mother-in-law was still alive when she was selected. One of the Jewish commandants, who assisted the Jewish director in Skarżysko-Kamienna, was from Piotrków; he was a disciple of the Radoczyce court whose name was Wilek. I gave a loud scream in the infirmary when he told me that my mother-in-law was removed, and I went back to the barrack. Wilek then came to my barrack to say, "You think she was alive, I can tell you she was not." He claimed that they took her away because she was already dead. I was scandalized and blamed Wilek for her having been removed and murdered. He claimed he was not responsible. I did not spare him and I did not think about the consequences to me for doing so. But he did not do anything after I strongly scolded him and told him he lied. "You took a living person and put her into a grave. She did not speak but she knew what was going on" He defended himself, repeating that she was already dead when she was hauled away. When I saw her a day earlier she was still breathing, even though she did not speak. She was not treated, but I don't know if she was brought anything to eat in those very last days. My brother-in-law may have smuggled in a little bit of milk. There were various followers of the Radoszyce family who may have brought her a small piece of roll or a sip of milk. Parenthetically, I may not be entitled to bear a good name, but I feel my conscience is clear in the way I took care of my mother-in-law.

They took all the people from the infirmary, including my mother-in-law, and put them on trucks, usually between shifts when nobody was around to witness the removal of the sick. The Germans seem to have feared to enter the infirmary, and they depended on the Jews to do this dirty work for them, including in this case the selection itself. These lackeys justified their actions by saying that they distinguished between people with a mild condition who would recover, and those that would not. That was Wilek's justification. He repeatedly insisted that my mother-in-law was dead, but there were people who were still breathing who were taken to the forest and simply shot. Wilek's excuse was perhaps logical, in that it was better to send a person who was almost dead than to take one who could potentially recover. Such a moral argument might apply to strangers, but when we are confronted with our own, such as me facing this happening to my mother-in-law, that kind of logic loses its potency. As long as my mother-in-law was breathing, and she knew she was being taken to her death, he should not have permitted her removal.

The death of my grandmother must have been especially heartbreaking for my mother, because she spoke about it repeatedly and extensively, even though my grandmother was not especially kind to her throughout her married life.

Food and Living Conditions

How did we survive the hunger? What food did we get, and how was it distributed? When the bread was brought to the barrack, it was turned over to each leader of ten women to distribute. Everybody stood around her, watching to make sure that she did not cut one piece bigger and another smaller. People in the barracks formed into groups of ten—usually those who felt close formed such a group. Each of the leaders of ten women would take the allotted "kilo" of bread for the group from the commandant and cut ten portions out of it. The bread was never a full kilo; it usually weighed about 800 grams (about 1 lb., 12 oz.). If it had been a kilo, everybody would have had 100 grams, or 3.5 ounces, for the day; but since the allotted portion was short of a kilo, every person received about 80 grams or 2.8 ounces of bread a day. I don't know what the bread was made out of. It tasted like paste. It was not hard; it was not really baked well. It was terrible. It stuck to the hand. People said it was made out of some dark rye flour and dried potato peels. We had to eat it, there was no choice. We even looked forward to that piece of bread. We stood watching that all ten pieces of bread were cut evenly.

A ceremony was enacted during the bread distribution. Every group had its own place in the barracks during the bread-cutting ritual. The person assigned to cut the bread would bring it to the bench and begin. She placed the bread on one side of the bench. First, she marked out the pieces so that each piece, when it was cut, would not be one millimeter larger than another. All the portions had to be exactly alike. There was only one exception—the person who cut it. Because this was a very important task, it was decided that her portion should be slightly larger. But the nine remaining portions had to be precisely the same size. To carry out this mission with such precision one had to be an artist, because we had no measuring tools to determine the exact size of each piece. The nine women stood watching, even though one could trust the woman or she would not have been chosen to be the distributor of the bread. Nevertheless, all nine of us watched her cut the bread. We usually received only bread and some soup. Occasionally, they also added some sugar with the bread. We did not receive any coffee.

I don't know if it was wise, what I did with my portion of bread. I would eat it at once so that later, until the next day's distribution, I would not think about it. I did not want to cut it up into smaller pieces when I got my portion. There was a woman who told me that when she received her bread she sliced it into four or six pieces and took it with her to the factory. When she returned she washed herself and went to sleep. Every two or three hours she ate a piece of the bread to assuage her hunger—to revive her—and the entire time she was busy watching the clock. She was thinking about this piece of bread all the time. I had another approach. I ate it all up and knew I would not have any more until the next day, so I didn't think about it and I could think about other things. I told the woman, "You are standing all day and you are thinking about those two hours until you eat each piece of your bread; then for another two hours you are again thinking about the bread. Your thoughts are on the bread the entire day; I do it differently. I eat it up and I forget that there was any bread at all." I was sated for a half hour, but later I was not bothered because my thoughts were occupied with completely different things. I thought about a book I had read, I thought about many other things, just so as not to think about bread.

I organized the women who stood closest to me working the machines. In the section where I was, four machines were lined up in rows, with four Jewish women at each machine. I suggested to the young intelligent women among them, those who had gone to school, who had higher degrees, had matriculated, that we should think about the books or articles we had read, or remind ourselves of interesting experiences and exchange our thoughts amongst ourselves. We could not engage in a discussion, but occasionally we could tell one another what we had read and our ideas about these readings. Such were our exchanges about books, articles, theater performances. We occupied our thoughts with such matters and we had no time to think about food. And so the time passed. My daughter, by the way, did not follow my method of calming her hunger. She told me after the war that she made about ten transparent slices of bread from her ration, and every few hours ate a slice.

When we went to and from work, we walked five in a row, and people began talking about food, what they would eat and cook should they survive the war. But to talk about food reminded us about our hunger. Better to talk about the dresses one wore. Better to describe the dresses one would make after the war, and how we would look in them. One woman said to me, "Look at the way we masquerade in the rags we are wearing." People walked around with rags around their necks. Others had paper, or straw around their feet, anything they could find. One wore whatever one could to keep warm and not injure one's feet. One woman said, "Let's forget we are in a camp and pretend we are at a masquerade ball, considering how everyone appears." My idea was to speak about everything except food. Some people were helped by this, but others were not.

In addition to the bread, we received soup. It was apportioned by the Jewish policemen who escorted us to and from the factory and guarded us so that everything functioned exactly the way the Germans wanted. It was distributed when we returned from our shifts—at either six in the morning or six in the evening. We got a large ladle of soup, which consisted of... well, I don't really know what was in it, because one could not see what it contained. It seemed to us that it was made of potato peels mixed with something else. He placed the barrel in front of the barracks and people lined up to get their portions. We were hungry 24 hours a day and everyone wanted to get a little bit of the watery concoction. People pushed. The Jewish policeman who dished it out was a young, mean-spirited person. He made a business out of the soup distribution, and wanted more for himself. Instead of mixing it with the ladle so that everyone could have the same thickness, he left it unmixed. Thus, the thickest part remained at the bottom of the barrel for him; the soup was very watery for the first people who were served. At first we didn't realize what he was doing. We each had a tin can for the soup. We actually got the cans illegally from a pile lying around, but people got them anyway. Somebody brought me one such can. People finished their portion of soup as soon as it was distributed, before even getting into the barrack. Those who were last in line had got the thicker soup from the bottom. The policeman kept for himself the thickest portion of the soup.

I had a few particularly unpleasant experiences when the soup was apportioned. At the beginning I stood in line with everybody else, but I didn't push, as the others did, which meant I was left at the end of the line. I would often end up getting half a ladle of soup, rather than a full one, but since it was from the bottom of the barrel, what little I got was thick. People complained and asked why I was getting thicker soup than the others.

There were people who stood behind me claiming that I was also pushing for soup. When I heard this, I decided not to get in line until everybody else got her portion; I wouldn't miss anything if I were the last one. But by being at the very end of the line I ended up, again, with thicker soup. I did not know why I got the better soup until later, when we realized that the policeman did not stir it. Once people realized that their place in the line determined how thick the soup was, there were three or four people who lined up right away, and the rest stood by the side waiting till the policeman reached closer to the bottom of the barrel. When the policeman saw that no one came for the soup, and he realized what was going on, he took his club and began rushing people to line up for the soup. Nothing helped; people did not rush to get it, which meant that he had to be around longer. He then started hitting people over the head, and they had to line up and get what they could.

The winter in Skarżysko-Kamienna was not too difficult. I don't recall any snow. But there was a terrible frost, and when the Jewish policeman handed out the soup outdoors, not in the factory, he had to be careful not to lose a drop since he had to distribute 50 to 60 portions. **(A portion consisted of 0.75 liters twice daily or 25.4 ounces)**. A little bit may have spilled over occasionally, and on a freezing day one or two men would stand near the barrel, and they would bend down and catch the frozen drops of soup with their tongues, or fingers, from the rim of the barrel, which had sand around it. There were people who could not control themselves and conquer their hunger. Some people were swollen because of starvation.

Religious Life

The practice of my religion, or as much of it as I could observe, kept my own and others' humanity alive; it showed the Germans that our dignity could not be torn away from us even under these unimaginable circumstances. Our religious values and beliefs nourished our defiance, but at our peril. Ironically, after the war, when I came to the United States and worked in factories, I needed to conceal my religious sentiments from my fellow Jewish workers, who disvalued religion and its practitioners.

I lit candles every Friday night in the barrack, as did a few other women. I believe that our barrack was the only one where candles were lit. There were many religious women there. We lit small pieces of candles that burned out quickly in a corner of the barrack, to conceal them as much as possible. Germans rarely, if ever, came into the barracks. There was one German, the camp commandant, part of the SS administration, who, as I mentioned earlier, would occasionally run around with a club to see whom he could beat up. We guarded against him and anyone else seeing the candles, but chiefly we had to guard against the Jewish police, who did not permit us to light them. Most of them did more than was necessary; they wanted to be more like the Pope than the Pope himself, as the expression goes in Yiddish. They did not need to carry out many of the acts they did; their behavior was just out of meanness. There were a few decent Jewish police. There was one, an elderly Jew, who would close the faucets in the shed that served as communal washroom if we left them running. He feared that another policeman would come, or a German, and immediately punish everybody. Nobody had asked him to turn off the faucets in the shed; he did it out of decency.

But there were also some not-so-decent people. One woman from

Piotrków, who shared a bunk bed with me after my mother-in-law passed on, was not a decent person. We had no difficulties sharing the bunk bed; she was all right in that regard, but she was annoyed with me because I was an observant Jew. She did not like that I lit candles on Friday. If there was a way to obey the Sabbath, I did, but she could not bear it. One time, in February, I bought eight matzos with a few found coins; some people had smuggled in flour to make them. There were a number of observant people among us who managed to bake matzos that one could buy from them. I bought eight *matzolech* **(using the diminutive suggests they were pretty small)**. I wrapped the tiny matzos in a rag and hung them inside the bunk bed so nobody could touch them, since I could not take them with me to the factory. This woman could not understand why I bought the matzos. When I returned from the factory, I saw that the matzos were crushed. I asked her why she crumbled them, and I made a bit of a speech to everybody about how we were all in the same situation and yet we didn't treat each other well. I said that what this woman had done demonstrated her character—something to that effect. She was ashamed. From then on she behaved well.

How did we get candles to light anyway? Since the Poles who worked in the factory lived outside the camp, it was possible to trade with them and buy rags, potatoes, bread or candles. There were two sisters from Piotrków who were businesswomen, and ran a business in the camp, so to speak. They were friendly with some Poles. They may even have traded jewelry for money. One of the sisters who lit the candles exchanged bread for candles. Those who had money could buy most everything in the camp. In this one respect, Skarżysko-Kamienna was not terrible. I didn't have any money except when I had 20 zlotys I received from the 100 my husband sent me, with which I bought a piece of bread. I bought the candles with a piece of my bread and some of my soup because otherwise I had no money except what I found the one time I mentioned.

We also decided to light candles on Yom Kippur eve in 1943. It was a very dangerous act. On Yom Kippur I was working the night shift. We left at around 5 or 5:30 p.m. for the factory. We decided that we would light candles no matter what happened; we lit them and were extraordinarily happy; it gave us remarkable satisfaction to have done so. First, because we could celebrate Yom Kippur; second, because we were doing something against the Germans; third, and this was the most important reason, because it made us feel that we were not being dehumanized.

There was a small room with a door and we decided to light the candles there. Everybody wanted to light candles; even the single women wished to light candles, although traditionally they were not required to do so. Everyone brought one candle, and three or four women entered the room at a time to light theirs. We placed one woman to guard the door. In the event that somebody came, we would extinguish the candles and quickly hide them. The Polish overseer, Pinchuk, noticed that there was some unusual activity going on. Generally speaking, we knew him to be a terrible anti-Semite and also a nasty person, a criminal. Nonetheless, we told him that there was a Jewish holiday and explained what we were doing, and it seemed as if he was moved. Maybe he began thinking about sacred candles in his own religious practices. The Pole pretended he did not see anything, and we were able to walk in and light the candles. When we decided to light candles on Yom Kippur eve, we did not think about all the possible consequences this action might have. Undoubtedly, if the German saw us lighting candles, we would have been shot on the spot. We wanted to show, if only to ourselves, that we are Jews and that we follow and celebrate our holidays.

It is Purim today as I am recording this memoir, and I remember that shortly after we were transported to Skarżysko-Kamienna in February (1943), and before our family—me, my brother-in-law, his daughters, and my mother-in-law—was separated, my brother-in-law read the *megila* in his barrack. His barrack included a lot of observant Jews, but I don't know how my brother-in-law obtained the megila. I must also explain how it was possible to hear the reading of the megila on Purim. Those of us who worked the night shift left at 6 p.m. and returned at 6 a.m. We read the megila at dawn rather than at night, and the overseers did not notice what we were doing. I went to the men's barrack, and I was the only woman at the reading because not all could come, if they had the day shift and had to work. Even my brother-in-law's daughters were not there, as they were on that shift.

My brother-in-law also blew the *shofar* on Rosh Hashanah, although I could not be there to hear it; one of the Orthodox men in the camp got hold of a ram's horn and paid one of the Pole machinists to carve it out to the required specifications, using the machines there.

This shofar is currently displayed in Yad Vashem. After hearing about this from my mother, I was able to find an account of a man

I. In My Mother's Voice

in Skarżysko-Kamienna who managed to smuggle in a large sum of money and ordered a ram's horn from a Pole, which another Pole, working the machines at the factory, carved according to his instructions.

I was at great risk the day I sat *shiva* **(if one cannot remain sitting in the home for the seven days, one day is observed)**, after my husband passed away two days after Shavuot **(June 14)**. I did not go to work that day. We succeeded in getting permission from one of the Jewish policeman in charge. I don't know what he said, but the German head overseer ran around and kept asking, "Where is the rabbi's daughter? Where is the Rabbi's daughter?" He confused me with my brother-in-law's daughters. It was best, of course, not to call attention to oneself.

It was very painful and miraculous that I sat in the barrack by myself; the night shift came at dawn and went to sleep when the day shift had left. It was very quiet. People had left things in the barracks and were not afraid that someone would take them. We were all on an equal footing. Well, maybe some had a bit more, maybe they had money and could buy something extra to eat. But they even left bread in the barracks. There was a rule: nobody touched anybody else's things or food. There wasn't any occasion for anyone to touch anything, because nobody had ever remained in the barracks by herself. Each shift came and went together. If after the roll call a person was missing, the policeman ran looking to find her. He had to bring back to the factory the same number of people he came back with to the barracks the day before. There was never any opportunity for anyone to take another's things. To sit there by myself and know that in some corner there was a piece of bread that could be taken to revive me was a test. Well, people did try to save themselves as best they could. Thank God I was not punished by the temptation to take somebody else's things. This was the only time I remained by myself in the barracks with the nightshift asleep.

Our spirituality could not be taken away from us. In Skarżysko-Kamienna, where there were both men and women, there were, of course, many different types of people. There were many religious people who, like me, attempted to hold on to our practices. In fact, there were several men who were my father's followers, Hasidim, one of whom said *kaddish* on my husband's *yartzeit* **(anniversary of death)**, a year after his passing, while I was still in this camp. He even brought a prayer book

(a siddur), and managed to obtain a little gas lamp to light on this day. **(Culturally, it is important to have a light burning for the full 24 hours of the anniversary of a family member's death.)** The men also prayed together to commemorate his life. I did not attend the service that time. I very rarely went into the men's barracks. One time, of course, was when my brother-in-law read the megila on Purim. The other time was a very different situation. My father's Hasid had proposed conducting a se'udah shelishit on Saturday whenever possible. These Orthodox men managed to organize this event, and at their se'udah shelishit ate their ration of bread. There were several Modzitze Hasidim who knew my father's compositions, and sang melodies he had composed that were well known in the Hasidic community throughout Poland. The Hasid invited me to come to hear them sing the songs. He was one of my father's followers and he also knew my brother; he said it would give me satisfaction to hear a few of my father's songs. I was persuaded, and one Saturday I was able to go. These men avoided walking around the camp, where they could be seen and harassed. I had never met them before, and I didn't even know where they worked. In the division where I worked I don't recall any religious people. One of the men I met among this group was from Otwock.

These types of religious activities show that Jews could not be destroyed spiritually. During such an event one did not think about food, and we took strength in the fact that the Germans could not break us.

This is not to say that there were no kowtowing, compliant, or damaged people who lost their decency, honesty, and honor. There were people who abandoned their spiritual upbringing and behaved dishonorably. I have heard about people writing how terribly people behaved in the camps. They may have seen individuals behaving improperly, and generalized about everybody. As I described earlier, men lay on the floor licking the soup that spilled over from the pot after it was distributed. I witnessed one person licking whatever drop of soup spilled on the floor itself. But this incident can be seen from different perspectives. The person can be judged as despicable; he grabbed whatever came his way to satisfy his hunger. But it could also be regarded the way I regarded it, and my heart burst with pain when I saw it happen, for I saw it show that the man was unspeakably hungry; he could not control his hunger or even stand on his feet. So he latched on to the one drop of food he saw on the floor. It didn't matter whether he ate sand or not, he tried to quell his hunger. These people were a cut above some: rather than stealing soup from somebody, better to lick it from the floor.

Thank God that I came out of the camps morally unscathed. I did not need to lower my eyes or head—I had no reason to be ashamed of my actions during my years in the camps. I could walk proudly; I didn't fear to meet people after the war. I was saved from doing terrible things and I came out of the camps the same way I came in.

I am reminded of a woman from Piotrków, whose family had great respect for my husband and was close to the family. The woman and her two daughters, in their early twenties, had worked with me in Skarżysko-Kamienna. We met occasionally, depending on our shifts. I mentioned to her, "We don't know what will happen to any of us, who will come out alive from here, but if God helps us and you come out of here and meet our people, give them my regards and tell them that I have not shamed anybody in my family. I conducted myself the same way here as at home. I came in the same way as I left it, without any blemishes." Yes, she promised me, but then she asked, "Why do you want to protect yourself like this?" I answered that I wished people to know that I had not morally wronged anyone.

It is a testament to my mother's ethical breadth that she saw unethical acts against another inmate to be as terrible as any of the experiences in the camp.

People Helping One Another and General Conduct

By and large, people didn't help one another, especially with food. How could they, if everybody received exactly the same quantity of soup, and the same portion of bread? It was simply not possible to give away one's own allotments when one was starving. But there were times when people managed, when they had something extra.

The first weeks after I arrived in Skarżysko-Kamienna, my husband sent me some zlotys from Piotrków, transferred at a high cost by Poles, who were free to travel and enter and leave the camp. A person could give a Pole money to deliver to a friend or relative who worked in the camp. In this manner, people who remained in the smaller ghetto in Piotrków, like my husband and child, could help family in Skarżysko-Kamienna. These were very small sums, and 80 percent of what was sent was siphoned off by the Pole. Naturally, I bought bread, and with this bread I could help somebody. For those few weeks I had extra bread and could share it with somebody else. I gave a piece to one woman, a relative of one of my father's wives. Well, it may have seemed silly and unbelievable to others to give away one last piece of bread. I describe the food sharing as "silly" because it had an unexpectedly unpleasant consequence for me.

I did not have much opportunity to see the woman I shared my bread with, because we worked different shifts. I could only see her when the shift changed and there was a little overlap time. During these few minutes when we stood at the roll call we could speak a few words. At such a moment I was able to give her a piece of my bread. She was in a very difficult situation, as was everyone else. But, unlike many others, who may have had some money or things sent from their home towns, including Piotrków, she had no one whatsoever to aid her with an extra bit of soup, or a piece of bread. One time a strange thing happened when I gave her a piece of my bread. I hid the piece of bread under my blouse; when we stood at the roll call and I saw her, I took the piece of bread out and gave it to her. Later this woman told me that it was claimed that I had stolen the piece of bread and for that reason I hid it. It had not occurred to anyone spreading this rumor that I was sharing my own piece of bread with someone. In fact, I would give her a piece of bread from time to time when all I had was the miniscule portion they gave us.

There were people who had brought money into Skarżysko-Kamienna, hidden; they, of course, could buy more food—they were rich people. But these people did not share with others what they had, and one could not blame them. In most cases if somebody was fortunate enough to have someone in Piotrków who would send them money to purchase food, they could still not afford to share it with another; in all likelihood the person would not even take it.

Yes, there were still decent people. For example, I discovered one woman, who had married a member of the Eiger family, my uncle's son. We became very close and she had a lot of respect for me. She miraculously managed to bring her eight-year-old boy with her, and he stayed in the men's barracks; nobody really saw him. From time to time she would cook something for him. Once she cooked a potato soup when I was sick, and she brought me some. I did not want to take it from her. She insisted. I wouldn't take it. I explained that she must not sacrifice the child's needs for mine. After that she never brought anything. I don't know what happened to her later.

On another occasion I shared my own soup. I worked in one division for a few weeks, where, as I mentioned, one of the Polish women gave me her soup and I handed it out to people close to me. They could not understand why I was giving it away. And when I had some extra bread and shared it, as I said before, it was believed that I must have stolen it.

My mother cited the incident of having been accused of stealing the bread several different times, which suggests to me how hurtful this experience must have been to her.

Liquidation of the Skarżysko-Kamienna Camp

The Russians were closing in on the Germans in Poland, and in the summer of 1944 they crossed the Polish border into the area of Skarżysko-Kamienna. The Skarżysko-Kamienna camp was closed in August 1944, and all those who survived the last selections, and were not shot, were sent to Germany.

In Skarżysko-Kamienna, they mostly let people live because they needed the "material" to work in 1943 and 1944. By the end of that time, the Germans had already "cleaned out," killed out, almost all their prisoners elsewhere. They had to leave a certain number of people to labor for them. The last week before evacuation, nobody went to work. All were in the camp, and we just walked around. The evacuation created a panic because nobody knew whether we would be taken to gas chambers, be transported to another camp, or be shot in the forest. We were never told throughout those frightful years what would be done with us. We were always kept in the dark about what the next minute would bring; consequently we lived with ongoing terror all those years.

They began removing people from the camp on a Monday, the first day of the evacuation. It was announced that we must report in the open field and place ourselves in rows of five. There were people who were very anxious. One of my acquaintances, who had survived the Jewish uprising in Warsaw and was later taken to Majdanek, and from there brought to Skarżysko-Kamienna, stood in the rags she had with her; she was asked why she was taking her belongings, as she would not need them. She answered, "What harm does it do me? I can always throw them out. Let me take them." She was a practical person. When I walked out, she called out to me and said, "Line up also, we will walk together." My thoughts were that I didn't do what I wanted, but I left myself to fate. What will be will be. I decided to sit in the barrack, and if they called me or chased me, then I would go. I would not go of my own will. What did I know about where it was better and where it was worse? I refused to present myself to anyone. I didn't know where they were sending the people lining up. I didn't wish to reprimand myself later, so, I told the woman, "No; I will not go on my own."

When I went later, I saw how people were taken into train cars. The trains were not far from the camp; they were freight trains and there was one little window. Only one face could fit in this window to allow a person to see what was outside. We saw how the people went in. I went back to the barrack; most of the people I knew did not go.

On Tuesday another group was sent out, both men and women. I remained in the barrack. On Wednesday they chased out all those who still remained and ordered us to go into the trains. Now there was no choice. Everybody had to go. I went together with the people I knew. There were a lot of people I did not see again. The people from Piotrków did not leave of their own accord; they went only when they were forced. The reason for our refusal to go right away was, as I said, that we did not know where they would take us, and whether they would take us to be shot.

Each car was completely full and there was no space to even sit down on the floor. People had to curl up sitting, or stand. But they switched with one another. Those who were sitting got up, and those standing sat down. It was chaotic. I was one who went last on the train, as were my brother-in-law's daughters. One of the daughters was known to have a weak heart, and she was sufficiently respected that the others let her sit down at the entrance to the car. Because of her heart condition, she needed a little extra air to breathe. We all sat together at the entrance where there was a little air coming through the cracks of the door. One could suffocate in these cars. In addition, when we needed a toilet, there was something set up in a corner, although I did not go there for the entire trip.

On the first days of evacuation—Monday and Tuesday—they took people to Częstochowa; on Wednesday, people were sent to Germany. Those who went first into the cars, we learned later, and were sent to

Częstochowa were liberated three months sooner than we were. They also travelled only one and a half days, because Częstochowa is in Poland and thus closer to Skarżysko-Kamienna. We travelled for three days. But I did not know that at the time, of course. We all believed we were being taken to our deaths. Again, we lived in a constant state of unknowing. For this reason, many people did not present themselves; like me, they waited to be taken on the last day of evacuation. I don't know what was done with the people in the infirmary, whether they were taken in the trains, or brought somewhere else to be exterminated. I often wondered about the woman with her young son, but I have never learned what happened to them.

On the last few days before we were removed from the camp, I learned that some underground Jewish organizations had sent money for us there, to be distributed to the people in the camp. This was completely new to me. I was in Skarżysko-Kamienna over two years, from February 1942 to August 1944, and I did not have any idea about any money. One acquaintance told me that there were people who had received such funds.

The National Jewish Committee records indicate that in 1944 it sent 50,000 zlotys to 13 camps, including Skarżysko-Kamienna, to be distributed to members of certain organizations present within the camps.

The entire camp was evacuated. No one remained but the liquidation commandants, all men, who were overseeing the process. They remained to the very end, and it was thought later that they were actually murdered after everybody was shipped off, but I don't know whether that was true or not. Twelve hundred women were brought from Skarżysko-Kamienna to what we later learned was Hasag-Leipzig—in Germany. We went to the cars early in the morning, and were in them three days and three nights. There were some who looked out of the tiny window as we were moving; they could see when we passed a station but could not tell where we were going; the Germans, of course, didn't tell us.

After we had been on the train one night, it stopped at a station during the day. We were guarded by an SS man who watched the cars so we wouldn't jump out and run away once a car door was opened. If there was an opening, or a large crack, in the door, one could jump. Indeed, when the train stopped, somebody from another car did jump out to get some water from a water pump, but as soon as the person was seen he was immediately chased back into the car. We did not have any food or water in our car; we weren't given anything to take with us. Some people may have had a piece of bread they bought from a Pole in Skarżysko-Kamienna, but I did not have anything.

When we arrived at night after the third day, we did not know where we were. They ordered us to leave the cars and at that moment a terrible panic swept over us. They conducted us into a room and told us to get undressed. I wore boots, and I kept a letter that my daughter had sent me from Piotrków in these boots, the only place I had to hide it. They did not tell us to remove the boots, otherwise we remained standing fully naked. Here we remained, and we did not even think about whether it would be a gas oven or a shower. We were simply frozen motionless. My entire body and my head were dead. We could not even think at all: my head stopped functioning, and we could not even begin to consider what they were going to do with us, where they would take us.

CHAPTER 4
Working in a Slave Labor Factory in Germany: Liberation and Return to Chaos

Hasag-Leipzig

It was midnight. 1244 women were led into huge, well-constructed buildings. A Polish woman conducted us to a room where there were showers, and we washed. Then they steered us to another room where they gave us slips to wear. We finally learned where we were: a place called Hasag-Leipzig, an ammunition factory. The SS administrated the entire Hasag-Leipzig camp, holding 12,000 or 13,000 women from many countries, including Russia, Belgium, and France.

From the showers they took us to a huge room containing bunk beds, where there were two workmen repairing the floors. The building was not yet ready for people to move in; they walked us around for two or three days in those rooms without sleep, dressed in the slips they gave us, which, it turns out, were striped inmate uniforms.

There were regular toilets around the registration area. We had controlled ourselves for a very long time in the trains; when we first arrived in Hasag-Leipzig we were relieved to see a normal toilet bowl, even though it was terrible to see how people were running to these very filthy toilets.

People standing near the windows saw other prisoners dressed in similar prison-type slips, striped with dark lines. They saw the prisoners outside signaling to us, using a writing motion with their hands, and shaking their head in a "no" movement to indicate that we should not sign anything. These were Belgium, Polish, Dutch, or maybe Russian or even French women.

At the registration, we were given numbers. My number was 1242, out of the 1244 women transported from Skarżysko-Kamienna to Hasag-Leipzig. After we were assigned numbers, a German SS man, sitting at a table, gave us the papers to sign that the women below had warned us not to sign, stating that we admitted we were prostitutes, thieves, and other types of criminals, and for this reason we were brought to the camp. We had to confess to all these things. One woman from Piotrków, who knew German very well, took a look at the papers and confirmed what was written there.

The civil administrators of the camp were Polish women, brought to Hasag-Leipzig after the Polish uprising in Warsaw on August 1, 1944. One woman looked like an aristocrat, and the rumor was that she was of the Polish nobility (*chrabina*), and had also been involved in the uprising. All kinds of rumors went around about these Polish women, including one that said one of them was the daughter of a Warsaw opera conductor, part of the Polish intelligentsia.

After registering us, they took us to the blocks. The Polish woman conducted our whole group through a large corridor; she asked us to be quiet—not to wake the women of the night shift. She brought us into a huge hall that was converted to dormitories, or "blocks," with two windows, filled with bunk beds where 450 women were to stay. These spaces were once factories and were now converted into sleeping facilities with three- or four-tiered bunk beds. As in Skarżysko-Kamienna, the bunk beds were separated by a narrow passageway with a little ladder for getting up to the fourth tier.

When one block was full, people were taken to the next, and each block had a number. My number was 20; the others in our group were in block 19 and 21. As we entered the block, people began pushing terribly, because everyone wanted to get a bunk bed close to the window. We already knew that having a bunk bed near a window gave one some fresh air, although I don't know where the air came from, because the window was never opened. But there was also light near the window, whereas near the door it was very dark. So there was a lot of shoving and running to grab the best-situated bunk bed. I was a schlimazel. I did not run, I did not push, and therefore I got a bunk bed in a dark corner close to the door.

My bed had one advantage. Normally, there were two women assigned to each bunk. (Actually, it was as though there were four women, because each bunk bed was very close to the next.) The tremendous benefit of getting the bunk bed I got next to the door was that fewer people could be squeezed into that area, and I had a bunk to myself.

While in Skarżysko-Kamienna there was a flimsy shed with mostly outdoor cold water faucets for washing, in Hasag-Leipzig the conditions were slightly better; there were cold water faucets in the basement of the dormitory building where we could wash ourselves and our things.

The two workman who were there when we arrived left pieces of wood and glass on the floor when they left; we took these pieces of wood and glass lying around and made spoons out of them to eat with. The food was brought in barrels and distributed in cans.

Like the Skarżysko-Kamienna ammunition factory, the Hasag-Leipzig factory was owned by the Hasag Company; its directors were in Hasag-Leipzig. **(The Hasag-Leipzig factory in Germany was converted into an ammunition factory in the 1930's, specializing in the production of bullets for infantry rifles and rocket shells for combat planes.)** Unlike in Skarżysko-Kamienna, where we were involved in producing several different parts of casings, in Hasag-Leipzig the factory was much more automated and we produced only one component related to shells of different sizes and shoulder missiles that fired a projectile.

The factory was located outside of Hasag-Leipzig in a place called Schoenfeld, about two kilometers from the camp. When one looked out of the block window, one could see open fields and further still the Hasag-Leipzig houses. Outside the camp, as well as inside, there were only German administrators. SS women escorted us to and from the factory, and inside the factory there were other Germans administering the labor force.

While the name of our camp was Hasag-Leipzig, it was under the authority of Buchenwald by the time we arrived there. I am not familiar with the exact organization, but as far as I know Buchenwald was comprised of a central camp with many divisions dispersed in various places around the vicinity. The camp known as Buchenwald was the head camp and there were many branches, also called Buchenwald. There was Buchenwald 1, 2, 3; our camp in Hasag-Leipzig was Buchenwald 10. The last transport of men that had left from Skarżysko-Kamienna on Wednesday, we learned later, was taken to Shlieben-Buchenwald.

Unlike in Skarżysko-Kamienna, Hasag-Leipzig was a camp for women only, with 10,000 women from many countries and among them 1,500 Jewish women. There were no Jewish policemen, only SS women who conducted us to and from the factory; we were really afraid of them. If somebody bent down to pick up something, the SS woman would not ask any questions; she would immediately shoot the person in the head. However, as I said earlier, there were Polish women administrators in Hasag-Leipzig also. When we were brought to Skarżysko-Kamienna, the first Jews transported there were made the administrators of the camp. In Hasag-Leipzig, the Russian women had been there for awhile; because they had been captured on the battlefield, they refused to work in the factories, claiming they were prisoners of war. They went on strike, asserting that the Geneva Convention applied to them. One of the Russian women who spoke a little Polish told me that they were sent to work in the kitchen, cooking. But they refused to be enslaved factory workers. They and the Polish women managed the internal affairs of the camp, and the SS women were their bosses.

The directors of the camps were Germans, but their immediate subordinates were drawn from ethnic Germans, or Ukrainians. Uniformly, the immediate prisoner guards were other prisoners in all camps; however, the ethnicity of those guards varied by the location of the camps. Within camps situated in Poland the inmates were guarded by Jewish police appointed by the Jewish Councils (Judenrat) usually men of the upper echelon of the Jewish secular community. In some camps in Poland, where I was, in the Bugaj, for example, the guards were Ukrainians and Jewish. In camps located in Germany, where prisoners originated from other countries, like in Ravensbrück, or Leipzig, the guards consisted of hierarchically organized ethnic groups, often based on who was brought into the camps first. In Hasag-Leipzig the guards were Polish women, managed by SS women, whereas in Ravensbrück, the guards were SS women with some French women prisoners as their subordinates, as we see later.*

Many women spoke French; they gave us courage to go on. They told us to hang on, the war was coming to an end and we would not suffer much longer.

In Hasag-Leipzig there existed a Red Cross, but it had no authority. The German Red Cross attended the Germans. The Red Cross used to send some things for us from time to time; once they sent herring. However, the German authorities did not distribute the herring outright, as the Red Cross intended; it was used as "bonuses" for people who exceeded the quota of 1000 pieces of ammunition a day. The bonuses

---

*   Much of this information comes from Christopher Browning, personal communication; see also Browning 2003, 2004.

I. In My Mother's Voice

were apportioned in the form of coupons denominated in 5 or 10 marks. This paper "money" was handed out to those who produced the norm. The more points one had over the quota, the bigger the bonus. This was yet another type of German theft; exploitation to get us to increase our production. With this bonus one could get a piece of herring, or some toothpaste, once even shoes. I don't imagine anybody took the toothpaste; the bonuses were kept for something more important. The Red Cross, it seems, sent wooden clogs, which one could get for a large number of bonuses.

The German Red Cross assisted only the German war effort; however, the International Red Cross was allowed into the camps in Germany because of the international population there, but as we see even their meager assistance was used to exploit the Jewish prisoners. The International Red Cross was not admitted into camps located in Poland.*

The formal Red Cross employed two nurses in Hasag-Leipzig. One time I was taken to the Red Cross office. I began feeling sick one night, not terribly sick, and I did not say anything. In the morning when we needed to present ourselves at 4 a.m. at the roll call, I began feeling very feverish. I felt burning hot. I told the head of the block that I could not go to work, that I had a very high fever. She told me that if I had told her this the night before she could have reported it to the administration, but now it was too late; there was nothing that could be done for me. I had to go to the factory. I went to the factory and stood in front of the machine but my head kept falling down. It fell in all directions: I just could not hold it up. The German overseer, who was considered the worst of the SS men of the day shift, saw the jolting head and asked what was wrong with me. I don't recall now what I answered, but he conducted me to the office. This was not out of consideration for me, but for the Germans' benefit; they were very afraid of people who might have a contagious disease. At the office, the nurse took my temperature and asked the overseer, and also the SS woman, why they had brought me to work when I had a temperature the equivalent of 107 F. The SS woman

---

* Gerhard Weinberg, personal communication; see also Weinberg 2005.

said that she did not know I was sick; I had walked with everybody to the factory.

The nurse had a small bag of cookies; she opened the bag and offered me two cookies. I thanked her and I said that I wouldn't take anything from Germans. She looked at me. Here I had this great opportunity to get something without even begging, and I refused. The overseer, the SS woman, and the nurse all looked at me as if I were a very strange, crazy, woman to decline an offer like this. The nurse finally understood that I was a person who could not be crushed. She took the cookies back.

The SS woman walked me back to the camp and took me to the infirmary, which was in a better condition than the one in Skarżysko-Kamienna. There were two doctors there, unconnected to the Red Cross, one Russian and the other Ukrainian. The bunk beds there were clean and covered with white sheets. There was also food and soup. I did not have to go anywhere to get it; they brought it to the bed. The doctor examined me and told me I had influenza, or something similar, and that it was very serious. She told me there was no medicine for it, but she would see how long I could remain there.

The doctor was pretty decent; she wanted to help everybody. Even when I no longer had fever and felt pretty well, she came every morning to examine me and told me that I still had fever and could not go to work. She would not even allow me to get off the bed because, she said, I was still sick. She let me stay in the clinic for eight days, until it was announced that there was going to be a selection of the sick. Those no longer able to work would be dispatched. The doctors were afraid that the Germans would see they were holding a healthy person, so they discharged me along with some other people who had recovered, and we returned to work. Everybody was surprised that I came back; they were convinced I would be sent away. They didn't know why I was gone for eight days; they knew I was sick but not that the doctors were holding people to avoid having them go to work. When people in the block saw me they thought it was a miracle I had returned. I have not told this story to share how I was sick but because of the cookies the nurse wanted to give me, which I refused. There were others who also refused, if a German wished to do them a favor. That was one of the many ways we could fight back.

The factory was located a fifteen- or twenty-minute walk from our block. It was a pretty walk, with apple and pear trees on both sides. As we walked, debilitated by hunger, we saw the fruits on these trees. Those who were at the ends of the rows saw the fruit lying on the ground. One person wanted to pick some up, but people began screaming and stopped her because, if she bent down, she would be beaten and her entire row of five women would suffer for this transgression. It was terrible. A Polish policewoman conducted us to and from the factories, and she was as brutal as any SS man. We thus walked and stared at the pears. We talked amongst ourselves how to pick up some of these forbidden fruits, but it was impossible to do so without being detected. We just walked on and dreamed about the pears that remained lying under the trees. We saw the trees, we looked at the trees, but we walked on to the factories. The Germans picked the fruits up. Maybe if a fruit had fallen on our heads we could have eaten it, but unfortunately nothing fell on us.

People did everything they thought would help them gain even a slight advantage in survival. There were two young women, one 16 and another 17 years old, one a very gifted painter and the other a poet. They originated from Krakow and Plashow, towns in Poland known to have had a highly educated Jewish population. I did not know these girls in Skarżysko-Kamienna because they had worked in *Werk* C, the worst of the three divisions of the Skarżysko-Kamienna factory. The young woman painter painted on a piece of paper she had found—the same type of paper that came in a notebook I had found and used to write my prayers and calendar, which I will come to presently—a lovely picture of a girl standing at one of the machines. She gave the picture to the overseer for Christmas. He liked it and said nothing. Another woman obtained a cake with some money she had, which may have come out of her bonuses, and gave the cake to an overseer for Christmas as well. This overseer may not have been happy with this gift. He said to her, "I don't know why you are giving me this cake, this gift; we torture you." It might be that they respected people who stood up to them more than those who tried to please. I wonder. This overseer seems to have regarded such ingratiating gestures as inappropriate, as I did.

As I had in Skarżysko-Kamienna, I acted in Hasag-Leipzig with *chutzpah*. When they handed out the bonuses, I told the German overseer in a sarcastic tone to keep his "money" so that they could make more ammunition. I turned around and walked away and returned to the machines. I was scolded by the people around me. People said, "What are you doing? You said something to him. It smells like sabotage." I said it made no difference to me. I believed we had already been condemned; the question simply was when the execution would take place. Therefore, let me have the satisfaction of saying a few words to the German. This particular German was, by chance, from the Wehrmacht, not from the SS. He was an elderly man with a limp that he may have gotten by being wounded at the front. He was a somewhat milder man than most of the guards—in fact, he was the same man who refused to take a cake from the other woman. The German did not respond to me, but he may have called someone from the office, for when someone came he pointed to me. I thought that now I was finished, but I was not punished due to this incident; I just remained without bonuses. In a similar incident when they distributed herring as bonuses, I also refused.

The goal of the Germans was, in addition to wanting to destroy us physically by starvation and hard labor, to break us morally. They wanted to drive people to the point where they would become like wild animals, lose their humanity. That was the Germans' goal. But they did not succeed in crushing us morally or spiritually. **(As can be seen, this is a recurrent theme throughout my mother's account; I retain the repetition because it was so central to her narrative and existence in the camps.)** Maybe there were a few who allowed themselves to be destroyed in such a way, but on the whole people maintained themselves with great dignity. Whenever we could, we would stand up against the Germans, not follow their rules, although we could not have the satisfaction of spitting in their faces, so to speak, because we could be immediately murdered. When we sabotaged the work, we felt great satisfaction. They did not kill us because Hasag-Leipzig, like Skarżysko-Kamienna, wasn't only a concentration camp. We produced their ammunition, and they needed us.

Religious Life in Hasag-Leipzig

There were other ways we maintained our dignity. Many of us did so by attempting to observe our traditions, here as we had done in Skarżysko-Kamienna. For example, unlike in Skarżysko-Kamienna, in Hasag-Leipzig we would be given "coffee" at 2 a.m. on the night shift. They brought kettles with black warm water that they called coffee. All Jewish laborers sat down for a few minutes to drink it. On Yom Kippur eve, 1944, we did not take the coffee. The same SS woman who guarded us and also conducted us to and from the factory could not understand what was happening, why we did not come. Luckily, she did not do anything. It was our great delight to openly demonstrate that we were Jewish people and that we followed our traditions; they could not make us inhuman. I still don't understand why they did not do anything to those of us who refused the "coffee" on that evening.

We kept our dignity and humanity in other ways. For example, we did not get paper for hygienic needs. There were huge garbage cans outside containing everything the Germans threw out, and in one of these cans I found a newspaper that could be used for such purposes. I also found a pair of slippers, cards showing the name of the factory, and a notebook that I still have to this day. The notebook showed the work we had done. In Hasag-Leipzig, we worked on what were called fire bombs. We worked on one part of these *tzindes*, incendiaries. The tzindes were attached to the bombs and with them the bombs were lit and fired. About 20 or 30 machines cut a little piece of metal for each tzinde that looked like an open thimble, a thimble with its head cut off. This piece needed to be straightened and cut around. These thimble-like pieces were handed from one machine to another. I don't know how the incendiary was put together, since I only worked on the thimble-like pieces. A foreman recorded in these little notebooks what needed to be done.

Earlier I referred to a notebook I found, an especially big find for me because I could write in it. I reconstructed a religious calendar based on the dates I remembered. I knew when Shabbat was but not when the holidays, like Rosh Hashanah and Passover, were. They did not tell us when Saturday or Sunday was, but those days were easily calculated because of the work schedule. However, I had no similar clues about the Jewish holidays. I guessed the dates as best I could. There were a few women who knew when the month of January occurred in the Jewish calendar, and based on that I created a calendar of all the Jewish holidays, recording them in the notebook. I wrote out the days, Sunday, Monday, and on to Friday, following the dates. After liberation, when I returned to Lodz, Poland, I checked the accuracy of the dates I constructed from memory. I showed people my calendar and they found that it was very accurate, and there were no mistakes about any of the dates of the holidays.

While I was still in Hasag-Leipzig, I recorded in the calendar yartzeit days, including my mother's. I also was able to know when Hanukah was, and I lit candles for Hanukah along with one or two other women who knew the laws of the holiday. I tried whenever possible to keep up with the Jewish holidays **(see Appendix 4)**. This calendar also served everybody well later on when we were on the death march.

Along with the notebook I also used cards we were given to keep a record of how many pieces we made in a day. I took a few of these cards with me and on the blank sides of them wrote down passages from *Tehillim* (Psalms) which I remembered, especially *Al Naharot Bavel*. **(On the Banks of Babylon, Psalm 137; she also wrote down excerpts from the morning prayers, especially Birkot HaShahar (see Appendix 4))**. There were two other young women present, who had been teachers in a religious school, and they helped me remember some other ones. I still recall when I wrote them. It was on Sundays when we returned from work early; every Sunday afternoon I wrote a little. I kept these like a treasure. I watched and cared for these pieces of paper, keeping them safe so that if, or when, I was liberated, they could show that no matter what, we guarded some of our Jewishness. These are among the only "souvenirs" from the camp I have kept, along with a little comb and hair net they handed out so that our hair would not disrupt their machines.

The calendar and prayers are displayed currently in The Museum of Jewish Heritage in New York City, and have travelled to various other museums; they were also shown in a special exhibit in Yad Vashem in Israel and reproduced in their book titled, *Spots of Light: To Be a Woman in the Holocaust* **(Imbar 2007).**

The recording of the psalm brought out my mother's "feminist" side before this notion entered the collective conscience. As is pointed out in the book from Yad Vashem, she reworked the prayers, beginning with writing, "Hear, my daughter (rather than son), the instruction of your father and do not forsake the teaching of your mother." By making the change to "daughter," significantly, she also altered the grammar of the entire prayer to conform to the feminine Hebrew grammatical structure, which normally women do not do when they say this prayer.

While I was in the camps I had various dreams. It may sound fanatical or superstitious, but the entire time I was in the camps I was sustained by dreams I had about my child. I dreamed especially that my mother had saved her, and also that my husband had saved her because of his holiness and because of his merit.

I grasped at straws to console myself that my child was alive, that nothing had or would happen to her. I had a few dreams in connection with her survival. In one dream, and I don't know where it took place, there were stairs going down, in much the same way as they do in the subway in New York. I walked down two steps and turned my head, looking backwards, and I saw my mother. She wore the same outfit I saw her wear the last day of her life, a brown skirt and a gold sweater. She held my child by the hand and brought her over to me. I remained standing, and she placed her hand into mine, and said, "Here is your child." She turned around and walked away. When I woke up from this dream I was sure my daughter was alive. There was a woman from Piotrków, Dincha, whose sister was my daughter's age. The children worked together in the camp in Piotrków. Dincha always lamented that they were lost and dead. One time after I had this dream, when she came over to repeat her sad thought, I said to her "Dincha, I can now assure you with 100 percent certainty that our children are alive." I told her about this dream, reassuring her, "My child is alive, and so is your sister." **(Her sister and I were very close during the war, and she did survive. She went to Israel after liberation.)**

This was one dream. I had another dream that I was in Piotrków. Half of my mother-in-law's apartment was taken away from her, and there my child and I slept in one bed, and my husband slept in another large room where there was a sofa. In the dream, my husband was in the middle of his prayers; he had on his prayer shawl and tefillin (phylacteries). "Where is your head cover?" he asked (my head cover always fell off when I was sleeping). "I want to bless you." Then I woke up. This was the second dream that convinced me that my child was definitely alive. I calmed down. This certainty gave me the determination to survive the extraordinary misery we were suffering. We couldn't do anything, only run away, which was certain death. But it gave me faith that it was worthwhile to remain alive so that my child would have a mother.

I had heard a rumor that my daughter was transported to Ravensbrück, but I knew nothing else about her. This knowledge and my dreams reassured and comforted me; it made me feel less despondent. There was some hope that, God willing, I would live through this hell and see her again.

I also had many fantasies during the years in the camps. It may sound silly to say and write this, but when a person is drowning she catches at any straw to save herself. For example, as I described earlier, women who were brought from Piotrków to Hasag-Leipzig were assigned numbers. They brought over 1200 women from Skarżysko-Kamienna and other camps to Hasag-Leipzig. The Jewish women were registered separately and given special numbers on arrival. I and another woman were the last to be registered. We were in no hurry to register, so my number was 1242. Why do I remember this number so well? I was brought up in a Hasidic home with Hasidic ideas, and so I interpreted the 1242 to equal to exactly 18. I calculated as follows: one is ten, two plus 4 is six, and another 2 is eight, which totals 18. Eighteen is the numerical value of the word *chai*, or life, and I took this as an indication that I would remain alive. This was of course a stupid, idiotic idea, but just as I said: when one is drowning, one grasps at anything.

This refers to gematria, a system of applying numerical value to a word in the belief that the two are thus connected. The number 18 is the sum of the Hebrew word chai, or life; it is ironic that my mother used a number the Germans assigned to her to create "life."

I had another childish fantasy. I imagined and considered myself dead. It was true that we all had a death sentence on us. All those who were in the camps had been sentenced to death; it was just a matter of when the decree would be carried out. I wanted to make the pain easier for myself by picturing myself already dead. I am condemned to death and every minute I am in danger. Well, I am already dead. When I looked at all that was happening in the camp, I saw myself as someone who was buried in a grave, sticking out her head and looking at what was taking place. It was not happening to me; it was happening to others. I saw others but nothing was occurring to me, for I was already in the grave.

Until now, I believed that it was better to be silent about those years when I worked for the Germans. But now, here, I record it all. I should have forgotten the disgrace of working at the ammunition factories, and that I worked there at all. Those were the years of shame. It is difficult to explain the everlasting harm it did to my dignity. From time to time I resisted, but my resistance was the voice of one crying in the wilderness. It wasn't easy to live and it wasn't easy to die with the thoughts

I. In My Mother's Voice

I constantly had, about whether my brothers and my child were alive. What kept me from committing suicide? Was it my cowardice? Was my strange fantasy a kind of insanity before committing suicide, or just healthy thinking? It's difficult for me to judge impartially. I would like to be the most rigorous judge of myself, but I don't know if my approach to these circumstances is rational. It is hard to be objective, no matter how hard I try.

The Death March and Liberation

I am writing separately about the liberation because I think about it a lot. I will never forget it. Around February or early March, when bombing began **(The bombing of Dresden, about 70 miles from Hasag-Leipzig, began on February 15, 1945),** airplanes started flying over the factory and camp where we were. We then heard sirens, and they took us down to shelters, when we were in the camp, where we remained by this time. The shelters were well prepared, but they were not prepared for us. They must have been well-equipped before the war. We sat in the basement on benches, and there were tall narrow windows facing the street level. The camp was, of course, surrounded by a double line of electrified barbed wire. At every corner there was a watchtower with SS guards, or military men, sitting on top of it.

The bombing came on; we saw it was very bad. But we did not know whether they would also bomb us. They could throw bombs at the factory when we were there. As it turned out, the planes were flying low, and they threw down leaflets. One woman stuck her hand out of the shelter and managed to pick up one of the announcements that fell close to the window. I don't recall whether it was in English or German, but we managed to read that we shouldn't be afraid, they wouldn't bomb us. The words were "Time is close to liberation." They gave us hope. The notes also instructed us to run away, if we could. But the area was being bombed. The wires were cut and many did run, not the Jewish women but probably the Russian and the French, who had more contacts with the outside. The Polish women prisoners, like us, wore striped uniforms, so they could not run either. We heard bombing from afar, and we stood and watched. We saw one woman hit by a piece of shrapnel that also tore up a clump of earth. We then went upstairs. I stood at the window and we saw people running, but they did not escape. Some were brought back, many fell as they ran, and others were shot. The electrified barbed wires were quickly repaired and the camp was again tightly closed off.

But we saw that this was the beginning of some end, either for us or for the war. While we did not know what was happening, we understood that if bombing had reached Hasag-Leipzig, it meant that the war was going badly for the Germans.

By mid-April the Western Allies were closing in on the area, and things began to be stirred up in the camp. The factory was closed, and all the supplies were removed. We were left starving. Evacuation from the camps began at this time. But no one seems to have known where to take us. The front was now very close, and the Germans could no longer use empty trains to send people to any camps.

They began marching us out in rows of five. We didn't know where we were going; the marching around was a mystery to us. It looked like there was no one directing the march. The Polish administration and the women in charge of each barrack were gone. Only the SS women remained to give us orders about what to do and where to march. They did not seem to know what to do with us. They all seemed to be waiting for a command from Germany, from Hitler, from camp directors, or from Eichmann. We speculated on how they could get instructions from Berlin; the people in charge of us, it seemed, were not permitted to decide. They were not allowed to kill several thousand people without instructions from a higher authority. Those were our speculations about what was happening.

There were about 400 Jewish women in block numbers 18, 19, and 20; when we were told to gather on the ground floor, we thought there would be a selection. They instructed us to bring our blankets, which were the only possessions we had. Nothing else. We had nothing to take, anyway. Perhaps somebody had a piece of bread. They gave us a double ration of bread at this time. It was Friday, very late at night; after they lined us up, we were told to start walking. Every group had an SS woman leading it. The rows were separated just enough so that we wouldn't walk on top of one another. At the start of the march, I was not yet very tired or sleepy. We all walked normally. But later, we all got exhausted and very sleepy. It is still hard for me to believe how I walked with my eyes closed, catching a nap while walking. The nap must have lasted a minute or two. One cannot walk for very long sleeping. I saw in front of my eyes huge buildings. Later, when I arrived in America and I saw the skyscrapers, I said to myself, "I saw these already. I saw this at that time." As I walked, putting one step after another, I fell on top of the "buildings." Actually, I didn't fall on the building; I fell on the woman walking in front of me. She began screaming, "Why are you pushing me?" I told her I didn't intend to push her; I just fell. This happened to me several times. I fought with sleep. Others probably had the same struggle, but I only know my own experience. During this march I kept walking and falling asleep, falling on the person in front of me, all the time thinking I was falling on buildings. This was a terrible march, and it was just the first night. It was especially terrible by the time we approached our first stop, where we saw a sign for Wirtzburg (maybe Weurtzburg). Then it was already light. At least the weather was nice; in Hasag-Leipzig the winters were mild. When we started the march, the days were beautiful.

The name of the first town they reached was difficult for me to hear on the audio tape; it sounds like Wirtzburg or Weurtzburg but I could not find such towns on any maps. The closest sounding town name is Wittenberg, which is located on the Elbe River about 70 km, or 42 miles from Leipzig.

We were in the last row, near to the German commandants; we asked them where we were going and they themselves told us that they didn't know, they were waiting for an order. To our surprise, those commandants left in the camp seem to have acknowledged that they didn't know what to do with us.

They at least knew to take them on the march rather than to leave them there; it is gratifying that my mother could still enjoy a beautiful day, under these circumstances.

We kept walking. When we reached Witzburg **(perhaps Wittenberg)**, the town looked dead, deserted. They told us to walk close to the walls of the houses. The planes flew over our heads and flew away; they did not throw any bombs. We still did not know whether these airplanes belonged to the Germans or the Western Allies.

Whichever town we walked through, this town or others, it was small and very nice. We walked in the middle of the road and did not see people in most of the towns, but in one of them we saw Poles; they may have lived there. These Poles yelled to us in Polish, "Hold on, we are close to the end of the war." They, too, gave us courage. We occasionally saw a person behind a window curtain, opening and closing it quickly. They seemed to be curious.

We walked all day in one town. On the second or third day, at night, after passing fields and gardens, we arrived at a sunken area. We walked on top of this spot and below we saw a lot of people. We immediately recognized that they were prisoners, like us, by their striped uniforms. I could not tell whether they were Jews, or non-Jews, but I imagine that they were probably Jews.

As we marched, we heard airplanes flying, but again we could not see whether they were German or the Western Allies. We were not frightened. It would not have helped if we were afraid of the airplanes. We marched on until they brought us to a field and told us to sit down. The field was surrounded by barbed, but not electrified, wire; it may have been a field of pasture land. On the other side were men wearing the same striped uniforms as we did; they were brought from other camps. The men came closer and they told us to hang on, to keep strong, help was near. Maybe they knew something we didn't, or perhaps they just guessed.

We all lay down and covered ourselves with our blankets so they wouldn't take us for members of the military. Now the airplanes flew very low, but they didn't drop any bombs or pamphlets either. Somebody yelled, but I never knew from where the scream came. We had no white scarves to wave for the airplane pilots to see that we were not Germans but their prisoners. Some people thought these were Allied planes. After we rested for about two or three hours, we were forced to go on further. They wanted us only to walk at night to avoid bombings; but sometimes we walked at night and sometimes during the day. Later I found the town of Wirtzburg **(Wittenberg)** on a map; it was not far west from Hasag-Leipzig, away from the Russian front, which was swiftly coming closer to us. The SS wanted to get away from the Russians. It is interesting that there were specific expressions invented relating to the camps which we now have forgotten. For example, the word "kertin" came into use, referring to the people who were on their last legs. They were extremely weak; they were "kertin." We were "kertin."

We marched like this for eight days. They led us around, day and night. We read various names of villages but no longer Wirtzburg **(Wittenberg)**.

We were much further away from Hasag-Leipzig. The last day we arrived at the water—the Elbe River. But they walked us away from the river, for the Russians were close to there, and they were terrified of the Russians. **(The Elbe River is about 30 km or 18 miles from Hasag-Leipzig.)** Here we kept walking within the same small area. We remained standing a bit and walked on. When it got dark we walked into a forest.

The first two days of the march were calm, and there were no battles, but at dawn after the third night we arrived at a place we had passed the day before. One day we were in one place, and overnight we walked, and the next day we walked and came back to the same village where we had been. We surmised that they had nowhere to take us. One walk took us east, another west. The Allies were coming from the west, and the Russians were coming from the east. They took us back to the sunken area where we had seen that large group of people. The second time we went through there, all the people had been murdered. There were several hundred people in that depression. We were not far away, and we were on the high part of the valley while they were below. We could see that they were dead. We saw people stacked one on top of another. We no longer knew what to think. Each person had a different opinion when she saw the dead people below. When we saw all those people dead, we concluded that they were looking for a place to murder us as well. Then they told us to walk, and we walked.

As we passed one field, we saw a young boy of about six or seven years old coming out of one of the village houses with a jug of water. He came over to us, but when the SS woman saw him, she chased him away. He ran behind a fence.

At this point they gave us raw potatoes. The Polish woman, the "aristocrat" who had been our manager in Hasag-Leipzig, remained with us and still had some human feelings. She told us to sit down and brought us these raw potatoes that they must have brought with them. When we stopped, we gathered some driftwood and made a fire. In the end, though, many of us ate the potatoes raw, as not everybody could get to the fire to cook them. I myself ate mine unwashed and uncooked. We were still five in our row. We put down our blankets when it became dark, and we lay down after our potato "meal." The days got longer; by now it was the beginning of April.

At this time I had a terrible problem with my stools. As soon as we left the Hasag-Leipzig camp, I did not have any stools for days. Then

I started needing to go, and had such terrible pains that it was worse than delivering a baby. I needed to evacuate and couldn't. I cannot even describe how painful it was. Once I at last passed it, I lay down and could not move from forcing myself so much. I became very weak.

We continued to walk, but I am not sure in what direction we were walking. We passed one village where we saw a dead woman wrapped around a fence. She must have been a German killed by a bomb.

They walked us around in circles; we kept coming back to the same places. We could not understand why they were walking us around? **(She utters this sentence with a question mark. She is still puzzled, even years later.)** We walked around a half day and saw again the same sign for the town we'd seen a day earlier. I don't know how many kilometers we walked, but I do know that we walked around the same place for several days. We did not see any Germans except a few SS women. We understood that these women had not received any instructions about what to do with us. It looked to us as though they had the same fears we had. They could kill us, but then they would be punished for murdering us. Yet, how long would they be going in circles with us? So they just led us around and around and around, and they would continue to walk us around until they brought us someplace. **(The repetition of the theme of going in circles reveals the disorientation and trauma felt at this march beyond the physical hardships.)**

At one point, we walked all night until we came to another forest surrounding the road. We crossed the road. A short distance away from us we saw different parts of the forest burning. It may sound as if I was dreaming that we walked into a burning forest, but no, the forest where we were was not burning; it was burning further away. We were able to walk through the short forest passage. It did not take us long to cross it, but we saw the fire from both sides. The scene of the burning forest became engraved on my mind.

We continued to walk in rows; mine was in the middle, closer to the end of the group. It was hard to know what row exactly, because we were several thousand people marching. We ate very little and had nothing to drink during the march. Some people had a little bread they brought with them. And we had the potatoes they gave us. I still cannot understand how we had the strength to march. I look back on it and wonder, how could we have walked? We rested one night, sleeping on the blankets we took with us, but another night we just walked and walked. The most dramatic moments of the march are especially imprinted on my mind. According to the calendar I constructed, we reached one of the fields on a Friday and lay down with our blankets under us and wrapped around us. It rained terribly at night, and here something strange happened. When we stuck our noses out of the blankets we saw that a very heavy amount of rain had fallen, but the blankets remained dry. When day came and they got us up to move on, the blankets were still dry. Perhaps it did not rain that long, and the blankets dried during the night. This may sound impossible, but it did happen.

We saw people alive one day, and dead the next. We lost hope. Most of all, we could not understand why they were leading us around. The Germans marched people from many camps, not only from Hasag-Leipzig. We saw them killing people: why did they not kill us? Why were they schlepping us around and where were we going? Why were they dragging us around and around? Even though many ran away, there were still some Poles, Russians, and French women in our group. After a few days we did not see many SS women; there were very few of them and they were 30 rows separated from us. We were totally baffled.

The horrors of the Holocaust culminated in the infamous death marches. Beginning in 1944, as the Allies were closing in and the Russian fronts were coming closer to the locations of the camps, the Germans had three conflicting policies concerning the remaining Jewish bodies: sell Jews for money, and thereby use them as" bargaining chips" with the Allies; eliminate them completely so that no survivor could tell his or her story; or thirdly, no policy, which led to the death march. In the end, the death marches were ordered by Himmler in order not to allow prisoners to fall into the hands of the enemy alive. He did not want survivors to give testimony, and wanted to hide all the German atrocities. According to Daniel Blatman,* the first death marches took place in January 1945 and continued until April 1945. There were no general instructions and this led to great confusion. The chain of command broke down. The orders from above were unrealistic, and untenable in light of what was happening on the ground. Because the roads were blocked, the prisoners could not be taken very far; this is why my mother's group

---

* Personal communication; see also Blatman 2011.

was going in circles. As we can see from my mother's account, the death marches reflected the total breakdown of the German hierarchy by this time; but their guards' confusion was also disorienting and threatening to the prisoners.

We saw the same areas again and again. Later we realized that the Russians were approaching the Elbe River, but still far away. The Western Allies were on the west side of the river and the Russians on the east side, and it looked as though the Russians were coming closer and closer. The SS women had to walk us around in such a way as to avoid the Russians. I don't know exactly how far away the Russians were, probably between 20 and 50 kilometers **(12-30 miles)**.

One late afternoon during our march, when we reached a village, one of the SS women told a group of us—about 100 women—to enter a granary there and go to sleep. The Germans were good householders, and these granaries were filled with hay. Of course, we did not sleep very well, and many who were awake saw several of the SS women take off the uniforms they wore under their military coats. They removed all of their military wear to look like civilians, and left the granary, in civilian clothing with capes. They disappeared eventually; we never knew what had happened to them. But then, nobody was really interested.

One person ran out in the middle of the night, when it was very quiet, and discovered carrots in a hole in the ground. It looked like a peasant had hidden and buried carrots in the winter in preparation for summer. I was not among the first group to take advantage of this, but people from this group came running back inside bringing carrots with them and telling everyone to go and get more from the large supply; many went. Nobody was watching us. I was just resting there, inactive the whole time. I couldn't move. People urged me to go to get the carrots, but I was immobile.

In the Warsaw ghetto, during the bombing, and even later in Piotrków, I was very active and energetic. As I recounted before, when the bombs started falling the first days, many people gathered in our house, and we packed them all in. I took care of and fed everybody. I was very enterprising in the ghetto. But here, from the time they took us from the Hasag-Leipzig camp, I was totally brutalized and numb, like a stone, totally ineffectual. I wouldn't even say weak, just immobilized, like a hand that has fallen asleep, numb, and cannot be moved. So was

I. In My Mother's Voice

I: my head and my entire body were like that.

People slept everywhere: in the granary, in the mill, or in a barn, everybody was hidden. In the morning we got up and the remaining SS women appeared; they gathered us in one place and we marched to the shores of the Elbe. I don't know how the Elbe is usually, but at that point and season the river was narrow and low; there were beaches and houses on both banks; we did not see any people.

We talked about running away, but how could we? If we walked away by ourselves, if we fled, we were sure the Germans would come out from somewhere and shoot us. We feared that if we ran away and were seen in our prison uniforms, the striped navy and gray *pasakis*, and there were Germans around, they would shoot us, murder us. They would not know why we were there alone.

We asked one of the SS women where to go, and I can still hear her saying distinctly, "Sit down and wait—they will come for you." So we sat there till late afternoon. We sat spread out on the grass and on the riverbank. A lot of Germans in uniform started coming; we didn't know where they came from. They threw things at us out of their pockets—crackers, chocolates. This was the military, the Wehrmacht, not the SS. They were still fighting, but we did not know where they were running. A little further we saw some kind of barges; the German military was being transported on them to the other side, away from the Russians and toward the Western Allies. They loaded several groups, and the last group left after dark. From the direction of a village, we heard a child crying "Mother, Mother"; it must have been lost. Everybody, including the townspeople, ran quickly out of the houses, wanting to get on the barges also, but they were full. All the civilians wanted to get to the other side, where the Western Allies were. There were terrible screams. Terrible screams; people were also falling into the water. After the last barge of military personnel left, civilians from the village got on the barges themselves, to get to the other side. We heard people speaking German, saying they were terrified of the Russians; they wanted to be captured only by the Western Allies, and not by the Russians.

We ran away from the SS women while we were at the banks of the Elbe River; we ran and ran and ran kilometers, until we arrived at a camp where there were Polish officers. Later we heard that some of the prisoners even caught an SS woman, cut her hair, and beat her up.

As I was recording this part of my mother's narrative, I wondered why the prisoners had not run away immediately. But actually it was not possible to do so. The local population felt threatened by them and could have attacked or shot them even if the guards hadn't, as my mother notes. But additionally, these women were so starved that they could not run away fast enough anywhere. Then, as we hear from my mother's refrain, they did not know where they were, and they did not know where to run. Moreover, it is very clear from my mother's narrative that the local population was hostile to them and not very helpful. According to Blatman, and as we also learn from my mother's account, the German civilian population made no efforts to assist the camp prisoner, and even feared them.[*]

In truth, when we marched with the Germans we did not have to think, we could not think, we could not do anything. I don't know how we survived this march; all I know is that we could not consider anything anymore—what would become of us tomorrow, or what was yesterday. We were as if asleep. The only thing we knew was that we were walking with a death sentence upon us.

But fortunately, our destiny was not what we expected: most of us remained alive. When we were liberated, when we walked by ourselves with the SS gone and the Russians occupied the area, we felt good. But unanticipated tragedies continued to happen. There was a 21- or 22-year-old woman from Piotrków, Irka, whom I remember also from Skarżysko-Kamienna, where we talked about how we did not know whose fate it was to remain alive. We spoke about not dishonoring our family names, and said that we would be known by our conduct. She would see me praying, after our day shift. I recalled all this about her because, ironically, after we were liberated from the Germans, she thought she was already safe; but as she was walking back to Poland a Russian soldier began molesting her. She ran away from him and he shot her; she died on the spot. After all the horrors she survived, she ended up being sacrificed. The Russians bothered several women I knew of: one miraculously saved herself, and another ran away, but Irka was shot dead.

Now we no longer saw German commandants from the camp, and there were no SS women. When we began walking by ourselves we could

---

[*] Daniel Blatman, personal communication.

walk more slowly and calmly; we did not need to rush. With the Germans gone, we were free, we breathed freely, and we were freed from hell. The first few days we did not think about anything; all we knew was that we were free like birds; we could fly anywhere we wished. We could stand where we wanted, we were totally emancipated people. We no longer belonged to anybody, not to a person, not to a place. The prevailing feeling was as though we were in a vacuum. But a few days later, when we were coming to accept this feeling of being alive, we began to reflect on who else remained alive of our children, our relatives.

It took us a while to become accustomed to our freedom. We had not believed we would be liberated—we had not believed we would live that long. Until the moment of liberation, we thought that it did not matter what happened to us, since we were condemned to death. All we thought about, as they were taking us round and round from one place to another, was how they would kill us. We would be in a pit and all those in it would be murdered, one way or another. We knew that nothing better than death was awaiting us.

But now we saw peasant houses, and deep trenches in the ground that looked like hiding places, or perhaps pits for the animals that were part of the village economy. The houses extended from the banks of the river to the village, and the entire area was surrounded by trenches. We heard shots and screams, and we did not know what to do. We hid in the pits and lay there. We heard more and more shots, but we did not hear any Germans.

The shooting we were hearing was begun by the Russians. This was the battle to gain control of the Elbe River. On one side, where we were, were the Russians, and across the river was the German military; the German soldiers were shooting at the Russians. We were stretched out in the pits and heard the bullets flying from one side of the Elbe River to the other. The shooting went on for a long time, and we in the pits were literally in the middle. I am only speaking about our group; what others heard I don't know. We did not know whether we would end up with the Russians or the Germans again. We did not know who would get to the pits first, who would prevail. All we heard was shooting.

After a while we heard the sounds of heavy wagons that were being brought from the other side of the river. We could not see them because it was dark. We imagined an armada—military vehicles, tanks. They stopped not far from us, and we heard people speaking Russian.

We realized that the Russians, coming from the east, had reached our side of the Elbe River, but we did not know whether it was just an isolated group shooting, or whether they had captured the entire territory around the river. We were hearing them arrive with very heavy armaments. We were afraid they'd think we were Germans hiding. We were in a terribly tight spot, fearing that they would start shooting at us. One or two women began shouting in Polish, "We are prisoners." When the Russians heard them, they responded and came over, and we all yelled that we were prisoners, and one woman called out, "Give us a piece of bread, give us something to eat!" The Russians responded, "Be calm," and indicated that there was a terrible battle going on and we should lie low and wait. They advised us that when the battle ended and it was quiet, we should go down to the river bank where there were a lot of wagons filled with food, clothing, and everything that the Germans were planning to transport across to the other side of the river. After the battle started, they left everything standing. The battle began at the banks and moved in inland.

Of the first Russian soldiers we met, one of them recognized us as Jews. He told us we should not say we were Jews; we had to guard ourselves. We asked him for a note saying that we were Poles coming from the camps.

We were already calmer when we realized that they knew we were prisoners and would not shoot us. Gradually, we stopped hearing shooting; the Russians ceased firing, and it was quiet on the other side. We remained in the trenches until dawn. Then people began running down towards the river, and my friend Guta along with one other woman were the first to run down. They brought back bottles of wine, juice, and bread, and cans of sardines, but we had no opener to open the cans. Whatever they brought they distributed, and each person ate a piece of bread.

We had no food or water until we began coming out of the trenches in that pre-dawn darkness and exploring. When we started entering the empty houses, we discovered plentiful provisions stored in their basements: jams, juices and numerous other items. The peasants had prepared for war, and their basements were stuffed with food, very good things. The most daring of the former prisoners went the farthest afield. People grabbed things with great joy after having gone for so long without any food or water. As I think about it today, again and again, it is incomprehensible to me how we survived without any food or water—on an empty stomach—all those days until we found this food.

I. In My Mother's Voice

From the day before we left the camp until we reached the Elbe River, we hadn't eaten anything except raw potatoes. I still cannot picture it. It seems that human strength cannot be measured or judged. Under such conditions we realize a person's capacities. Even weak people managed to stay alive without food or water, and later with just a few onions and sardines. But a lot of woman fell ill, developed stomach problems, and died just at the war's end.

Finally, we were beyond doubt liberated by the Russians on April 21, 1945. When they found us in the trenches, they told us that not far from where we were there was a camp with Russian and Polish officers where we would get food and drink. The Germans had held that camp, but the Russians had already liberated it.

We got out of the trenches and started running. There were many, many people. We did not hear shooting, but we ran very fast to the officers' camp. We must have run for two miles. Polish officers met us and told us that they, too, had been prisoners in German camps. With the Russians there, there were no Germans anymore. The officers told us to go into the barracks to get water to wash ourselves and they would bring us food.

I was in the first group of ten or fifteen women to arrive in this camp. We entered the barracks and sat on bunk beds; it wasn't long before they brought us a tub with buckets of water. In the meantime, more and more people arrived, and there was a bit of a commotion with one officer turning over responsibilities to another. Then, I don't know why I caught the attention of these officers, but one of them chose me to take charge of the others. I actually told him that I was not good at such things. He asked me to see to it that everybody got some food.

We lay down on the bunk beds and rested. We took off our prison uniforms, the striped slips, washed them, and hung them on a rope line to dry. People went to some storage place and found us dresses. I did not want to go, but somebody brought me a cotton dress and I put it on. Other women came up from the shore and showed us what they had gotten from the wagons. Many people went down during the day to get more things. All the women were from our camp. We thought we would remain there, but we were in this camp for a very short time.

All told, we were a large group. Suddenly a Polish soldier came in to the barrack where we were to tell us that we must leave right away, fast. There was a terrible battle going on. We ran down quickly, and I was so sorry I did not grab my prison uniform; I wanted to keep it as a souvenir. Whatever a woman had hanging she had to leave and we had to start running east. We ran very fast because we were in danger once again. There were now many people from other camps running as well. As we ran, we heard yelling: "Avanti, Avanti." We assumed that these were Italian officers. They yelled to us to run faster. Once again there was a lot of shooting; it was said later that of the last group that ran and was spread out all over, a few people were hit. I don't know how long we ran. It was late in the day, and we continued running. We ran and ran, following those in front of us. Those ahead seemed to know where they were going, but actually there was nothing to know; they were running in the fields, there were no roads. We ran and ran until we came to a village; it was dark. There was still a battle going on. The Russians who stood guard told us to rest there until dawn and then keep running. We walked into a house. It was dark, and people were stretched out on the floor and on the table. It was extremely chaotic. We didn't know whether we were alive; we didn't know if we needed to run right away. Then the Russians told us to run. We did not know where to run, but we ran.

We arrived in another house and came into rooms where there were people stretched out everywhere; we had to walk over them. Somebody mentioned that there were pots with sour milk standing on the windowsill. We were constantly impressed by how much food the Germans had prepared for themselves. We drank the milk from the pots; we shared it by passing the pots around from one to the other. Then we sat down to rest. It was terribly dark, and we couldn't see anything. We left at dawn because we heard yelling that there would be more shooting. And there was. But there were no more Germans here. We were already several miles away from the Elbe River. There were no more Germans, or so we thought. Actually, there were some in hiding, shooting from their hiding places when they saw people who wore different uniforms, like Russians or Italians from the Army of Badoglio. When these Germans started shooting, the Russians shot back, and therefore there was still a small battle going on; thus we ran away.

General Badoglio fought the Germans; the men from their division were arrested and placed in a concentration camp.[*]

---

[*] Gerhard Weinberg, personal communication.

I. In My Mother's Voice

We walked east for several days. Russians arrived on trucks, and some of the women asked to be taken on one of the trucks. A few of us just sat down. A car came with a Russian in it. He asked if we wanted a ride. He said he could only take us a short way. Several of us got into the car; he took us several miles. We left the car, sat down to rest, and hoped to meet up with the women who went on the truck. There were many other people there too.

The Russians left us at some point, because they were going in a different direction. They told us to go east. It seems we were three kilometers **(1.8 miles)** north of Dresden, and there was a terrible battle there. So we started going farther northeast. But we didn't know whether we were still in German territory, or whether we had reached a Polish area. We were totally disoriented. It was an extraordinary time; one cannot imagine it, nor can one picture the total pandemonium.

When we came into a village and saw how well-furnished the German homes were, how opulently their basements were stocked with many different foods, we remembered, and wondered later why they complained how bad it was for them. How could they say they were hungry when they had so much wealth? This we saw in the villages, but even earlier we had seen their wagons loaded with food, and stacked high with other goods. The fact was that when people saw all these riches, many ran to get them. We gave it the name *szabrawen* (*szabrowac´* or *r*ummaging), meaning selective looting. I am not sure what the word means exactly, but that is what we called this activity. It meant that when people went into a village they took whatever they saw and needed.

We walked from west to east, so what was left in these villages were remnants, because the Russians, coming from east to west, did their own *szabrowac´* and not much by way of riches was left. The Russians took everything they could. They especially wanted clocks, alarm clocks, and hand watches. We knew that they looked for clocks because one time when we came into a village and went into a German house to ask for something to eat, they told us they had no food to give us, but we could go upstairs where there were beds with bedding and we could lie down to rest. They had some potatoes and some greens, but no bread. Shortly after we lay down, the German woman came upstairs and told us that the Russians would come here very soon. They were walking around the houses looking for clocks and watches. The German woman begged us, if the Russians came, to tell them that there was nobody there. She and her husband hid in the basement. A Russian military woman came upstairs and asked us whether there was anyone there and we told her we did not speak Russian and we did not know where there were any watches; we came from the camps. She went downstairs and did not bother us. We remained there overnight.

In the morning we left the house of the German couple and continued walking. We saw an empty house, and walked in thinking maybe there would be some food there. In the basement we found a lot of food: jams and various marinated foodstuffs. We now had eaten a lot of bread, and anything else we found. We walked on. We had to clear our bowels. I got diarrhea, probably from the food I ate, and one time became so weak I could not continue. I told the girl who walked with me to go ahead, because I could not go on. I would just remain until I felt a little better, and then I would catch up with her. But she would not leave me by myself. She stayed with me, and I felt terrible. I lay a bit on the grass, very weak. I had to relieve myself constantly, and there was no place to go. This was a big problem. I rested; at last we went on. We arrived on a hill, and there we stopped running; we started walking. We passed a house where we saw a bottle of blueberry juice standing in a window. I walked in and took the bottle and drank its entire contents. I think this bottle of blueberry juice stopped the diarrhea and saved my life. I shouldn't say this, but I will: it was a remedy sent from heaven. The blueberries brought me back to life. Before that I said I could not continue, I was feeling so terrible.

Thousands of people walked and walked. Most people seemed to walk in the same direction. We continued to walk east. By now there were not many in our group. The others had run sooner. Everyone did what she thought she should, and nobody knew what to do. Now we no longer ran; now we walked slowly. We went further and arrived at a place where there were Russian soldiers. They told us to keep going, because there were still battles going on and they didn't know what would happen.

There were still sporadic skirmishes, especially with the Germans who came out of their hiding places and shot at the Russians on guard. We went away from the shooting—going east—and one night arrived in a German village. There was a man and woman in one house and we asked for food. They said they had none, for many of the Germans weren't willing to give us any food. But in the meantime two French officers came down from upstairs. They asked us where we were coming from and in which camps we had been. We weren't wearing our prison uniforms anymore, so it wasn't obvious to them from looking at us. They asked us if the Germans were giving us any food, and we answered that we were given only potatoes. The French officer spoke German and told us to go upstairs, where they had many kinds of foodstuffs. We went upstairs and found all types of delicious foods to eat—wine, potatoes, herring. Guta, my friend, peeled the potatoes, we boiled them, and she distributed them to the others there. As we were walking upstairs, somebody opened a window downstairs and three German soldiers jumped out to run away. They ran across the fields, and we heard shooting coming from there. It looked like they were afraid to remain in the house. We had nothing to fear: we would not be harmed by the French. But the Germans were afraid that they would meet certain death.

Suddenly, as we were eating, we heard people coming, and the French officers told us to go into another room and close the doors. They were very decent people; they calmed us down. They told us not to be afraid. If the people coming were Germans, the French officers said, "We will say that you are our family. If they are Russians, we will tell them that you are our wives, and they will not bother you." These French officers showed great understanding and empathy. A Russian woman soldier came upstairs and said she wanted to see what was there. She saw and she left. She told us to be calm, not to be afraid, but that it would be better if we left because there would be a battle shortly. In the meantime we could remain there. We heard shooting again. We ate and the French officers suggested we go to sleep in the bedrooms. It seems that the German peasants had two-story houses, and upstairs they had the bedrooms and downstairs the dining rooms. They had huge kitchens. The French officers also took what they could find; they too looted. At dawn someone came in to say that we had to go further east; we left the house and started running once more.

We left in the morning, when it was light; the officers announced that they were going in a different direction from us and we could not go with them. We were going east toward Poland, and they were going south in the direction of France. There were large numbers of people wherever we went, as I mentioned earlier; who they were, whether Jews or Christians or whatever, I don't remember exactly, but Italians were also walking. We left the house and followed them. We arrived in a village and walked into a house where there were women on the beds, covered with blankets. We heard that the Russians were coming, so we asked the Italians to say, as the French had, that we were their wives. They said that they couldn't do that. They were from the Army of Badoglio. They said, "We are in danger also because we are from the Badoglio army, and if a German comes he will shoot us. We are not as afraid of the Russians. They (the Germans) may or may not have arms, but we cannot help you in any way. Don't depend on us."

The Italians told us to rest and cover ourselves with blankets, and we would not be seen. They said, "When they come in we will say we don't know who's here." It was a terrible feeling after the French treated us so well that here the Italian officers didn't wish to do anything to protect us. There were several rooms downstairs on the main floor, and they were in another room; they closed the doors and didn't want to know what would happen. In fact, some soldiers, speaking Russian, entered the house and walked around with flashlights, but since they didn't see anyone, they left. We were saved without the help of the Italians. In the morning we came out, and the Italians said we could walk with them.

Walking Back and Being Back in Poland

Once we were liberated from the Germans and the shooting ceased, only Russians were everywhere. My friend and I walked back to Poland; there were just two of us by this time. Our immediate thoughts turned to where we could find a piece of bread, but there were also the wonderful feelings of being free after all our suffering. Nobody reigned over us anymore; we could go in all directions. However, we did not know where we were, only that we were walking in the direction of Poland. If we managed to get to Poland, what awaited us there? I couldn't imagine what we would find. My thoughts were constantly with my child: would I find her? Would I find anybody else? Was there anybody left? Later, I found out that my daughter and I were the only ones who remained of my close family.

We reached Rausch on foot. **(While my mother seems to have said Rausch, I was not able to locate such a town on any map within this region; in all likelihood the town was Rawicz, situated approximately 300-310 km or 180 miles from Leipzig. I have, however, retained my mother's pronunciation in this book.)**

I. In My Mother's Voice

We heard that there were already trains leaving from there for Poland. This town was once at the boundary between Poland and Germany. Later I saw it on a map; I believe it was in the Posen area. When we were coming closer to Rausch, all I could think about was whom we would find in Poland. Yes, we knew that Warsaw was evacuated before the Piotrków ghetto. I hoped that my younger brothers Avrumce and Binim, and my stepbrother Menachem remained alive. Why should I have remained alive and they not? I couldn't believe that these young people would not survive; they had a better chance of remaining alive than I did. It hadn't occurred to me that I would arrive in Warsaw and not encounter anybody, that I would find such *tohu wa-bohu* **(emptiness and chaos, a description in Genesis 1:2 of how the universe looked before God created the world).**

We reached Rausch, a small town. When we walked into the town's station, there were already people there, young women. We asked a conductor about the train to Poland and were told that there were open freight trains leaving for Poland from there, and they allowed people to get on them, but we needed to wait at the station for a long time; the train would come today, tomorrow, or whenever. The people managing the trains were Poles; they told us to just sit and wait next to the rails.

The girl who had walked with me decided not to return to Poland after all, because there was a hospital in Rausch where she was promised a place to stay and employment. She would have food there; she would no longer need to search for food everywhere. I told her I would go on to Poland; there were other people who were going back there also. I believed that anyone who remained alive would return there to see if anybody was left. I would also learn when and where people disappeared. Even though I had by then already learned that my beloved brothers, Avrumce and Binim, had been murdered, I still fantasized that, whether together or separately, they would still return to Poland to look for family and friends. I believed it would be easier to discover more about my family there than if I remained in Germany.

I also wanted, of course, to look for my daughter. I had a sacred belief that she was alive somewhere. I wouldn't find out in Germany where she was; whom would I ask? Perhaps my life would have been easier in Germany. There were displaced persons camps there, and those who got to them were in a good situation. People who remained in Germany did well for themselves; they did business. But I didn't think about this. I only considered one thing: my child. After I found her, I would look into what happened to the rest of my family. These were my only thoughts.

When we left the camp, we only knew what was happening to us personally. We didn't know what had happened elsewhere. As I mentioned before, I had heard rumors that my daughter had been taken to Ravensbrück from Piotrków. I also knew that my youngest sister, Basia, went to Russia in 1941 to join the war effort there. She got married there and lived in a place called Ludme; she once sent us a card from there. Since at that time the Russians were not involved in the war, Ludme was secure. But then when Russia had entered the war, we no longer knew what happened to people there. Did she go deeper into Russia, or did they stay in an area which was later taken over by the Germans? We did not know any of this, about where she, her husband, and their child disappeared to.

I got on an open freight train that transported coal and scrap iron from Schlesien (Silesia) in Germany to Poland. I, along with others—Jews and non-Jews, climbed up on top of the train and sat on iron and coal. At that time, one could not tell who was a Jew and who was not, since everybody wanted to pose as a non-Jew. One man riding the train went back and forth from Germany to Poland to loot small villages in Germany, bringing back various things which he then sold in Poland. This was his third trip.

Many people collected things from houses as they were walking past the villages. I have to admit that I am a schlimazel, and except once, I did not take anything from a house only food. But, when I found a useful thing on the road, I picked it up. I picked up two or three towels, a slip, a blouse, whatever I found while walking. We did go into one house, but there was little there. Everything had already been looted. It was a mansion, the palace of a rich German. There were torn hand-painted pictures thrown around and a lot of broken things. The Russians would go through these houses, and what they didn't want they broke. I did find a hand-knitted woolen cape among a lot of rags in this mansion, and took that with me.

The train made stops on the way to Warsaw-Lodz. At one stop, I believe in Demblin, the train remained for a long time. Poles came up and asked if we had things to sell. They wanted to buy everything, and I sold a towel for a few zlotys. We travelled on the train for three days. One of those days was May 8, the day Germany unconditionally surrendered to the Allies. On the morning of that day, we passed a village, and I opened my eyes to see many Poles yelling in Polish, "There is peace, a peace was concluded. We can now be calm." On that day I also sold my other things to get some more money. We passed Auschwitz, not far from Posen; from Posen the train travelled to Warsaw. It was not far, but this was a freight and mail train and not all tracks were open, so it took a long time. Since most tracks were destroyed and had to be repaired, there must have been only one track in each direction.

We reached Warsaw on May 10, at the Zachodnia station, several miles from the capital, where freight trains arrived. We looked around and there were not many people. Now the problem was how to get to Warsaw. There was a Pole standing there with a horse and carriage, a type of wagon that had wooden planks on which one could sit down, who took people to Praga, a two-hour trip from the station.

Praga is a district of Warsaw situated at the east bank of the Vistula River, and has always been considered part of the city of Warsaw. For this reason, my mother uses Praga and Warsaw interchangeably. Unlike most of Warsaw, Praga was not destroyed during the bombardment.

People saw immediately by the way I looked that I had come from the camps. I wore torn clothing and an old coat made for a man. The Pole said he was going to Warsaw and I jumped up on his wagon, along with several other people. A man sat down next to me. I didn't know whether he was a Jew or not, but he was well dressed. I don't know why he was there; he didn't come off the train. Possibly he came to await somebody, since people were conducting all kinds of business. He asked me *amkhu*, meaning "our people." When I agreed, he understood I was Jewish, but we spoke Polish nevertheless. Everybody spoke Polish; no one wanted to show they were Jewish.

I asked the Polish wagon driver how much the trip to Praga would cost, and told him I only had a few zlotys to pay him. The man told me to tell the driver that I just came from the camps and he wouldn't want any money. If he did, I shouldn't worry, for he would pay. But the Polish driver didn't mind taking only my few zlotys. He didn't seem to notice that I was Jewish. He didn't know what amkhu was. The man and I spoke Polish and included a few French words, and the driver did not harass me. He thought I was a Pole.

The man who had offered to pay for me asked me to tell him about myself. I recounted that I was just liberated from a camp in Germany and asked him where I should go in Warsaw. He informed me that we were going to Praga rather than Warsaw proper because Warsaw was totally destroyed and there was nothing left there. Everything now was concentrated in Praga. There was an organization there called the Joint **(the Jewish Joint Distribution Committee)** which was assisting people returning from the camps. He told me that I must go to Lodz where there was a Committee (*Comitet*) where people registered to let others know they were alive. They helped people find a place to sleep and also issued announcements on the radio that these people were alive and where to find them.

While we were travelling in the wagon this man and I talked about how Warsaw appeared now. We passed the Kierbedź bridge, linking the right and left banks of the Vistula River. It was terrifying to see the remains: not even a kitten or a bird could be seen. It was just one ruin after another. The city was totally desolate. I must say in all honesty that I did not pity the Poles, given the way they treated the Jewish people throughout the history of Poland. Unfortunately, Jewish property was destroyed too, and the entire Jewish section of the city was demolished, including Nalefki Street and Marszałkowska Street, which was one of the main thoroughfares in Warsaw.

Only a few places in Praga were destroyed. The Russians had occupied Praga from the beginning of the war. They had reached the Vistula River and Praga, and then they stopped and occupied Praga. Later, of course, once the Germans were gone, the Russians took over all of Poland. In Praga, we could even see houses where people lived and little stores, but there was nothing for sale.

We arrived in Warsaw on a Thursday and went to the office of the Joint Distribution Committee right away. I asked about close and distant family and about friends. There was nobody. People were just beginning to return from the camps, and the Joint didn't have any names that interested me. I requested to have them announce on the radio the people I was looking for at a cost of five zlotys; I paid for this out of the few zlotys I had gotten by selling the items I'd picked up along the way.

This office gave me a few zlotys and also a ration card for bread and sugar. Actually, everything else was rationed too. The office gave me a train ticket to Lodz, and they sent me to a place I could stay temporarily. There were trains to Lodz every second day. The next train I could take was on Sunday, and it was Friday. I wanted to go to Lodz right away since there was nothing in Warsaw, but I had to stay there for two days.

I went to the address the Joint gave me. The building was once a three-story house, but now only a single large room remained. It was on the ground floor, and there was a table, desk, and sofa, and many, many people. They were stretched out wherever there was space near a wall. On one side of the room were women and on the other men. A man who was one of the first to arrive in these quarters was sitting on the table, looking comfortable, acting like the boss, ordering people around, telling them where they should lie down, and charging them money for a better place on the floor. Because this was a very large room and a lot of people could sleep on the floor, some spaces were better than others. Whoever gave him some money, or any other item, like a towel, could buy a better spot, and he saved the best locations for such people. For example, the worst sleeping space was next to the door, because it was exposed to a lot of wind. If someone paid him, he found the person a place to sleep on top of the very large table. When he saw somebody like me, who had nothing, he assigned me an undesirable place. The few things I possessed I made into a package that served as my pillow. I used the coat to cover myself. I slept two nights there. I don't want to accuse this man of anything. Perhaps if he had not taken money, people would have started fighting about a place next to the window and not next to the door. Because money was involved, it seemed like a smooth process. People immediately began doing business.

I remained in this sleeping quarter on Shabbat **(Jewish Sabbath)** and until Sunday. It was still day when I arrived there, so I just sat until night. During that day, a man came to ask me if I had anything to sell. I became a bit confused. When he heard I had just come from the camps, he also asked me how many Germans I had killed. I asked him what he meant. He said, "I killed 100 Germans after liberation." I looked at the man as if he were crazy. "You had the opportunity to kill Germans?" I asked. In all likelihood, where he was liberated, people took revenge. The administrators were no longer there, and he sought vengeance for the wife and children he had lost. I asked him if we were like the Germans, to just kill people. I couldn't understand it. How could he do that? There is no merit in retribution. They deserved it, but we couldn't slaughter people. He said he could not forgive them.

I said that I hadn't killed anybody; I hadn't hurt anyone. Actually, I told him, I'd tried to avoid the Germans as much as I could. He asked me what I was going to do now. I told him I wanted to go to Lodz as quickly as I could, since there was nothing to be done here; I came without money and must do something. He said, "You know, I have an idea. I have a room and I am a tailor by profession. There are people who need clothing to be altered, repaired. I can hire another person to earn a few zlotys." I agreed to come with him since I could sew; my mother had taught me how. His room was in Praga, and so I could remain there even though everything seemed to be concentrated in Lodz.

I went with this man to where he lived and he gave me some buttons to sew. I didn't like it. He said, "I am here by myself, and you will be with me." I realized then that he was interested in some things more serious than sewing. I told him I was not really up to this job. I declined his offer, suggesting that maybe he could find somebody else, and thanked him for wanting to help me.

Right there in Praga there were people who engaged in business. Those who had found things in Germany brought them back to Poland and started a business in Praga, like the man on the train who went back and forth between Poland and Germany picking up goods and rags. The man who invited me to work for him was not a businessman, he was a tailor. He found work sewing immediately upon arriving at the office of the Joint. Everybody who arrived there came in torn clothing, wearing rags, and could use a tailor.

On Friday night, I lit candles. I used my ration card to buy them. I endured a couple of days in Warsaw. I left the sleeping quarters on Sunday and went to the railroad station in Praga. We had arrived at the Zachodnia Towarowa station in Warsaw, but I was now leaving on a windowless train for Lodz from a different station in Praga. Still, it was a train. I left with only a small package in my hand, unlike other people who had brought many things back from Germany.

I arrived at the Lodz station in May. The city was not destroyed; it had remained completely intact. The Germans captured Lodz without bombarding it. From the station I went directly to the Comitet of the Jewish Council, where there were many people who had returned from the camps. The office was on Tczelinski 45, and they gave me ration cards so I could buy bread. Everybody gathered there. When I got to this office, first I needed to register in case somebody wanted to find me. They also issued identity documents. Since we had no formal identification, we each needed to provide a name and birth-place to reconstitute our identity. And I made a mistake here. Here I said that my name was Golda Finkler, and that my father's name was Saul Taub. By giving my father's name as my maiden name, I felt I was being dishonest. This deception tormented me for a very long time, even though it was silly of me to have guilt feelings about it. When I was asked what my maiden name was, I thought for a moment about what I should say, even after all this chaos. I said Taub, thinking that here was an opportunity to correct a mistake so that from now on it would no longer be a problem. Later I regretted it, because if the name was not changed, even during my adult years, I should have retained the name Eiger. Usually I accede to other people, and here I should not have made an exception.

When my documents had been submitted for my visa to the United States, they bore the name Golda Taub. My father had never commented on it, but now I was bothered by making the change permanent, even though there were better things to worry about. I may even have disadvantaged myself by making this change at the time because people knew me by the name Finkler/Eiger; I could have been discovered sooner than I was had announcements gone out in the name I was known by. Few people knew that my family's name was actually Taub. I went to the Comitet office every day to see if anybody had heard anything about my family. It was by a chance meeting in Lodz, while I was standing in the Comitet office, that I made the first contact with a family member, as I shall recount shortly. Before that, I was put into contact with a friend.

While I was in the Comitet, a man who had been in Skarżysko-Kamienna and then taken to Częstochowa approached me and asked where I was staying. I did not know. This man had already been in Lodz for a little while, and he wondered whether I knew a woman by the name of Handelsman, who had been in the camp with us. She was a manager here, and he suggested I speak to her; she would find me a place to stay. When I walked into her office, she recognized me immediately. She too came from Częstochowa, where she was liberated in the winter months. The Comitet began functioning from the time the first people returned to Poland. She was very happy to see me and wanted to know where I was staying. I told her I had just arrived and didn't know where to go. She told me not to worry. She remembered that I had shared soup with her and another woman, Regina, in Skarżysko-Kamienna. Regina was also here and had an empty apartment with a kitchen; I could stay there. I was very pleased, because we were good friends. This woman gave me the address and told me that Regina might not be there during the day because she sold cans of shoe polish in the market. I went to the apartment and sat on the threshold, waiting for Regina until she returned. When she finally came back, she was very happy to see me alive and there. She lived in this empty apartment and slept on the floor. It had been her apartment before the war, but the ethnic Germans who remained in Lodz had grabbed it from her during the war. These Germans remained in Poland, hiding from the Russians when they came. Now the Poles and the ethnic Germans wanted the apartment back. She had to be careful not to let anybody in, because they would take the apartment away from her. She said I could sleep there with my package under my head and the coat I found in Germany as my cover. I had my ration card for food, and I could stay there until I oriented myself and found a place. I remained in her apartment for four weeks.

When I arrived in Lodz in May, there was still no mail. The mail began functioning in June or July in Praga, but I did not wait that long. The first letter I sent was via the man who had been meant to care for my child in Piotrków, who I chanced to meet in Lodz. He was on his way back to Germany. I gave him a letter to mail to my father in America. I did not have an exact address. I remembered something like South 5th Street, but did not recall the number of the house. The letter reached him anyway because there weren't any other Rabbi Taubs in Brooklyn.

I hesitated to write to my father to let him know I was alive. I had my reasons for not writing. Then I thought that one must forget all lesser wrongs after the disaster that had happened. I once read a short novella—I don't remember its author—about a young man who was going to travel somewhere. He waited for the train in the station, and either he missed it or he fell asleep when the train came; in any case, he did not get on it as he was supposed to. He went on another train. And after this accidental change, his whole life turned upside down. The story has many more details, but the author concluded that sometimes a person takes one small step and that one step alters his life. I felt that when I contacted my father the course of my life would take a momentous shift in direction.

I sent a postcard to my brother Leibl in Palestine, whose address I remembered exactly. I also sent a card to my brother Shmuel Eliahu (Smilele) who had left for Palestine in 1936. I knew only that he had lived in Tel Aviv. I knew they did not receive the cards because they did not respond. They found out that I was alive some other way.

Every day I went to the Comitet to look for my child. Also, I walked the streets to see whom I would meet; just walking in the street one would meet people who were in Skarżysko-Kamienna, or people from Piotrków. I hoped someone could tell me something about my child. I knew that she had been in Ravensbrück. I met a woman from Lublin on the streets of Lodz who had just returned from Germany, and she told me that she knew my child was alive but not where she was. She was with her in Bergen Belsen. She told me that my child was stretched out on the bunk bed and could hardly breathe. Many children had died of hunger and weakness just lying there. Many remained faint; they could barely breathe anymore, and my daughter was among them, scarcely alive. As I learned later, it was a miracle that the English came quickly and that the children were taken to Sweden. The Swedish king had sent a boat to bring them from the camp to stay in sanatoriums there until they recuperated.

Now for the first time I had some positive information. Later, in Lodz, when I ran into the man to whom I gave the letter to my father, he told me that his wife and both children were in Germany, and he had just returned to find some things he had buried in Lodz. He too said that my child was alive; he knew the children were taken from Ravensbrück somewhere, but he had heard that she was alive. He suggested I go back with him to Germany, where I could more easily learn about her whereabouts.

But I did not accept this offer. I remained in Lodz. Regina left in the morning and returned in the late afternoon. We cooked potatoes, for there was nothing else to cook. One could buy a piece of bread in the market, and some tea to drink. On Fridays I bought two candles to light. She had no objections to this, although she was totally nonreligious. She was a communist. I prepared the stove for Shabbat so we could have hot tea. She said, "I will make the tea in my way and you in yours," And would put on a separate pot of water for her tea. We heated the stove with pieces of wood and coal and had hot tea all day. Daily I went to the Comitet asking about all the people with our family names: Eiger, Kalish, and Somberg. I thought that Basia Somberg, a cousin, would be alive, because when I was in Warsaw, before I left for Piotrków, she and her family procured papers attesting that they were Poles. I did not know to look for the name Shymanski, which was their official Polish surname. I looked for Somberg. Nobody responded. I received one letter from a Kalish (my stepfather's surname), but it was not from anyone in our family, and another from a distant cousin, Abraham Finkler. I also tried to find out what had happened to my sister Basia, who had gone to Russia. I wrote letters to various people, but I didn't receive a response from anyone. Most of the people who had gone to Russia were sent to Siberia. Basia, like others in our family, perished in Russia. I heard previously in Skarżysko-Kamienna that my brother Avrumce might have been shot when he was found in an attic on the lookout for Germans. My brother Binim fell ill and was taken to the u*mshlagplats* in Warsaw, and was transported to Treblinka together with all those who were still in Warsaw during the Jewish uprising. But I still hoped they were somewhere. It is so difficult to talk or write about this. **(Her sorrow can be heard in her voice as she retells this sequence.)**

After my searches in Warsaw and Lodz, I finally gave up hope that my brother Binim may have survived. I did not need to try and find my beloved stepfather: I already knew what had happened to him. The way he died is now well known. It stands out in my mind and I have spoken of it often, how he said that the Germans will not take him, and remained sitting at the table with his last breath gone. They couldn't take him because he had closed his eyes and died.

Now, after the war, I was overtaken by depression. This was not the same as when I struggled with death in the camps. I had foreseen in the camps that the real tragedy would begin when, with God's help, we would be free. The nerves had been strung out for so long; now that we had arrived on the shore, they broke, and there were no arms with which to raise myself from the spiritual (geystlekhe) depression. But I should not digress.

I received a telegram, not a card, from New York—the first communication I had from my father since the war. It took a long time for the telegram to reach me; by the time it did, it was already the middle of the summer. The telegram said that my child was alive. He believed that she had been transported to Bergen Belsen by the Germans and liberated there. Then another telegram came, stating that she was already in Sweden.

I. In My Mother's Voice

At last I heard from my child herself. The first letter I received from her was from Sweden. She did not know where I was, so she sent it to the Comitet. The letter remained there for a long while. I don't know who received the mail in the Comitet, but I know that one person told them there was an Abraham Finkler who was working for the organization, and when they spoke to him he realized that a letter from Kaja Finkler might be for me. Abraham Finkler did not know that I was in Lodz, but the man who had made the connection did, and he told him about me. Abraham did not really know me because we were very distant relatives. He found out where I was and obtained Regina's address. The letter, thankfully, arrived while I was still there.

Regina instructed me from the day I moved in not to open the door to anyone, because, as I mentioned earlier the Poles, or ethnic Germans, wanted the apartment back, and there was the possibility that somebody from a Polish office would come to reclaim the apartment. I followed her instructions. Usually nobody ever came anyway when I returned from the Comitet. The apartment was on the ground floor, and the windows faced the courtyard. One day, as I returned to the house, I saw a man in the courtyard without a hat, with a briefcase, who looked like an office employee. I came through the gate and waited to see where this man was going, thinking that once he left I would enter the apartment. I was afraid that if I came into the courtyard he would start questioning me about who was living there. I waited a long time, and then I lost patience and walked into the courtyard where the man was standing.

Next to the apartment there were stairs. I started walking up the stairs and the man addressed me in Polish. He asked if I knew who lived here. I said I didn't. He asked if Regina Finger lived there. I said I didn't know and started walking upstairs. It seems that the camp was still written on my face. He looked at me and asked me if I knew a Finkler who lived there. I said yes. I did not wish to say immediately who I was. He told me he was looking for Golda Finkler. After I acknowledged that this was me, he gave me his name. Abraham Finkler, my husband's cousin. I explained to him why I could not allow anyone to come in, and since that time, every time we meet he has told the story of how I would not let him in.

Abraham let me know how we were related, and that he used to visit my mother-in-law. He seemed to know a lot about my husband's family. He told me that he and his brother, the only ones to survive, were residing in a large apartment with a kitchen. He suggested that I move to their apartment, where I could have a home. I considered him a stranger and did not wish to live with strangers, so I declined his invitation. He invited me to visit him and meet his younger brother, see how his apartment was, and decide later. A day or two later I went to the address he gave me and met his brother. I looked around and I left.

Before I had time to decide about moving in with the two brothers, something else happened—I bumped into a relative, as I mentioned earlier. On one of my daily visits to the Comitet, a very elegantly dressed woman showed up there also. She wore a beautiful and rich looking outfit, and she didn't look as if she had come from the camps. I looked at her and then went on in the long corridor. She did not turn around. All she saw was a woman dressed in one cotton rag on top of another. I was still dressed the way I had arrived from the camp, in rags. At least I wasn't still in my striped camp uniform.

I saw the woman again on another day. I looked at her and she seemed very familiar. By the third and fourth time, she also looked at me, but she walked on. It was pure chance that we were in the Comitet at the same time. One time we arrived and I looked at her and suddenly recognized her. I gave a scream, "Basia!" **(As I write this I get the shivers and tears come to my eyes.)** At just that moment she, looking at me, cried out, "Golda!" We finally recognized one another. Calling out her name was a dramatic moment for both of us. For about five different days we had seen each other and we had turned our heads away from one another, but after the fifth time we finally turned around and exactly at the very same instant, we both yelled out each other's names.

Basia's grandfather (Shlomo Eiger) and my mother were siblings, and I knew her from my childhood in Lublin. Now that we were reunited, I went to live with her and her husband and son. When it was suggested to me that I go to Germany, they dissuaded me, arguing that there I would have to be in a displaced person's camp waiting for handouts. Moreover, if somebody were looking for me they wouldn't look for me in Germany. They would look for me in Poland. I allowed myself to be persuaded and remained in their home.

By then I knew that my daughter was alive, since, as I said, I had already received a letter from her from Sweden. I also was aware that my two adored brothers, Avrumce and Binim, were murdered, nevertheless, I still kept asking everyone if they had information about them. I had already paid for an announcement on the radio that was supposed to be transmitted all over the world when I first arrived in Warsaw, but I had received no response. Somebody told me later that it was not heard by anyone. The announcement may never have been aired. Besides, few people even had radios. I wasted the money I spent on the announcement, yet I had to spend it: I believed in miracles.

My child had been found by an English chaplain and journalist named Hershel Klepfish, who knew our family. He came to England with the Anders Army **(The Anders Army was a Polish division under British command)**, and to Bergen Belsen with the English army when they liberated the camp. My daughter remembers the details of this extraordinary event. All I can say here is that after some miscommunications, Klepfish wrote to my father that my child was alive, and my father wrote to me the glorious news that she was alive in Bergen Belsen. **(I will recount this episode in greater detail in my own story in Chapter 6.)** My father then learned that she was in Sweden, and he sent me her address. From then on she and I corresponded until we met in Sweden.

I spent nine months in Poland after the war. I left for Sweden in January 1946, after I was issued a Swedish visa in Warsaw. Thanks to my father's efforts, I was able to see my child after an almost four-year separation; and every day had felt more like a century. Once I was reunited with my child in Sweden, we went to the United States. I will leave it to my daughter to tell about our joyful reunion in Sweden later on.

To conclude this chapter of my life, I will repeat a point I have stressed all along because it is important to me to convey that more than taking our lives, the Germans aimed to purge us of our humanity. But at this they failed. They could not take away the spiritual (*geystlekhe*) core of the person even under these horrific circumstances. They hoped that the Jews would destroy themselves by destroying one another under the conditions they had created for us. It was known that when it was pointed out to Hans Frank, the governor general of Poland, also known as the Nazi butcher of Poland, that Jews were not committing suicide as expected, he said, "Be calm. We will put them into such a situation, we will create such conditions, that they will kill each other. They will eat each other up. The Jews will destroy themselves, we don't have to do anything, they will do it themselves, and they will kill one another." The Germans were disappointed. The Jews did not "eat each other up." Not only did they not "eat each other up," but whenever possible people helped one another in the ghettos and in the camps. We did not harm one another. Of course, there were malevolent people, including the Jewish police I talked about, who tried to advance themselves at our expense, but such people were not the rule. And above all we did not commit mass suicide, as the Germans seem to have calculated.

PART II

IN MY MOTHER'S VOICE

CHAPTER 5
On Being a Refugee in the Land of Gold

My life and my mother's intersected with our meeting in Sweden, followed by our transition to the United States. Coming to the USA was one of the most difficult periods in my mother's life. One would have thought that reaching a new land would usher in a new and happier beginning after the misery of the previous years. Alas, the war had not left her, or me, and the life that awaited her was harsh in ways she had never anticipated. This part of my mother's life, particularly her work history, causes me tremendous distress now, as it did at the time, watching her experiencing new kinds of humiliation. In her eyes, she fell from a very high social position in her milieu before the war to a very low one in America. Of all the difficulties facing refugees, the change in social position may be the most intractable, especially because it is so elusive.

I left Lodz on January 31, 1946, after having stayed with my cousins for over six months. I had learned from my father that my daughter was already in Sweden and that all my other loved ones were gone, annihilated. I arrived in Stockholm on February 10, 1946, after having waited in the Polish port city of Gdynia for a boat for four days.

My reunion with my daughter, after almost four years of separation, was overwhelming. It is difficult to describe the joy I felt seeing her after all that time; we became inseparable. I met her in the home of a rabbi **(Rabbi Jacobson)**, who had lived in Sweden for many years and who assisted refugees after the war. My daughter had stayed with the Jacobson family for about a month awaiting my arrival. We remained in Sweden until March 26. There were great difficulties at that time in obtaining an American visa, but my father managed to get one for both of us, with the help of some of my younger brother's machinations. My daughter's visa had arrived during her stay in Sweden before I arrived, but mine was not settled until I reached Sweden.

To get one of the very scarce tickets for a boat trip to the United States at that time was also almost impossible, and the ticket could not be purchased until my visa had arrived. The visa arrived two days before the first passenger boat after the war ended, the S.S. Drotningholm, was scheduled to cross the Atlantic. With Rabbi Jacobson's special efforts, we managed to get two tickets on this boat, and we left Stockholm on one day's notice.

Arrival in the United States

We reached New York on April 8, 1946; I believe there were several hundred Jewish refugees arriving at this time. We were received with some fanfare and a kingly reception. My father, a portly, imposing figure, awaited us at the boat with an entourage of people, including my whole family at his side, my siblings from his second and third marriages who had been here since 1941. Numerous reporters came also. Naturally, there was great interest, and the press wanted to learn how things were in Europe. The reporters ran after me and my daughter for interviews, but I was not disposed—not in the mood—to give interviews. I was elated that I had finally arrived on American shores and could see my family members with their very young children. I was not concerned with what reporters would write; it didn't matter to me. I wanted to rejoice with my family. I had no interest in speaking to all of these strange people, and since I am a very impractical person I did not wish to exploit the situation.

We were photographed, questioned, and subsequently written about in all the newspapers, clippings of which I still have. There were various errors in the articles, albeit insignificant ones and I soon realized how inaccurate newspaper reports could be. Shortly after our arrival, both my daughter and I realized that it was best not to speak about our experiences, because at that time people could not comprehend them. For example, some people asked whether we had toilet paper, as if that was the major problem we faced. Both my daughter and I have kept silent all these years.

Immediately after our arrival I was approached by various people asking me to give talks, for pay, around the country about my life during the war. I was shocked by the suggestion. I could not capitalize on our extraordinary suffering. I wrote only one article, the first summer after we arrived in the States, at the request of some people from Piotrków. I wrote about the Piotrków ghetto, and how the Germans prepared the synagogue, not far from my husband's house, to temporarily house people that were found hiding. After this one article, I did not write or speak about my experiences until I began recording this account.

Unlike many refugees who came later from Germany, bringing with them numerous possessions, I arrived with a small suitcase and one dress. I was a bit ashamed that I brought nothing. After the wonderful reception, I imagined that we would be brought into a pleasant home of our own, where we could rest our heads and have some relief. We were instead brought into a little room in my father's house that contained a chair and a narrow bed on which we both slept. I did not care much, for I was with my family, but when visitors came they expressed surprise at my quarters.

After my initial joy of being together with my siblings, it became increasingly clear to me that it would be difficult to remain in my father's house, particularly because of difficulties presented by my father's fourth wife. It was suggested that I seek assistance from the Joint Distribution Committee, which was also active in helping Jewish refugees in the United States. I refused to seek their aid, thinking that it might embarrass my father, who was a public figure, that I needed financial or other assistance. It is distasteful to me to speak about this period of my life, but I did not live in a vacuum; I did not come into a forest where there were no people; I was and I am dependent on and connected to others. Thus the difficulties presented themselves from the start, and for this reason I had to leave that small room.

My aim was to have my own apartment, no matter what size, not a little room with a narrow bed. I was told that there were no apartments. I was "green," as newcomers were referred to: I could not speak the language, nor did I know where to go by myself. Nevertheless, I decided to go it alone, to seek work and to find a place to stay, which at that time was indeed exceedingly difficult because of the scarcity of housing in New York after the war. I did find a very little room with a small bed, table, and chairs through the Yiddish newspapers. The rent was four dollars a week, which at first I paid with some money my father gave me. I could not cook or eat there, only sleep; they also did not permit children. Since it was now summer, I sent my daughter to a summer camp (through *Beit Yaakov*), and when she returned, since she could not stay in that room, she went to stay with my sister and her family, where we also ate our meals. I looked for another place to stay. My sister had moved to a large house in another neighborhood, and she suggested that we both come to live with them for the time being. We relocated there after the holidays, and remained there for several months. My family had counted on my remarrying so I would have an apartment and could reestablish a new life. However, having come out of the hell I had survived, remarriage was not in my plans.

I desired to retain my independence. I decided to move out of my sister's house and find a place for myself not far away. I found a small apartment on a nice street with a large room, and a large window with a view of a few trees. The room had two beds, one of which was a bit broken. The iron spring jumped out of it one time, tearing my daughter's calf and leaving her with a very visible permanent scar. But the room also had a little kitchen area with a stove where I could cook; in the hall there was also a bathroom. The owners of the room were decent people, and I could pay to use their telephone. We lived there until the summer of 1949, when we went to Israel.

My father did not assist me in finding a job or a place to live, but he did give me a thousand dollars, which I wished to use to buy a sewing machine and leave for Israel, where I had initially wished to settle directly after the war. But until Israel became an independent state, it was impossible to get an entry visa. Once there was an Israeli state, I packed up my possessions, which I could count on my fingers, and we left in August of 1949.

I stayed in Israel for eleven months, and my daughter stayed there for an additional month in the summer. I returned to the United States mainly because, according to the immigration laws of that time, had I remained in Israel for longer than a year I would have lost the possibility of becoming an American citizen. I decided to seek American citizenship because that period was one of the most difficult in Israel's history. It was the year after the War of Independence, and people were starving. Everything was rationed. I did not wish to lose the opportunity of citizenship in the United States because I wanted my daughter to have as many options as possible, especially since conditions were so bleak in Israel.

When I returned to America in July I had nothing, not even a glass or a pot. I came just as I was born, with only a few personal things. I did not have a place to stay, and I returned literally without a penny because at the time one could not leave Israel with more than five dollars. I was on a boat for fifteen days, where I spent my only five dollars. I didn't know who would await me at the boat, and I needed a few dollars for a taxi to take me to one of my relatives. Fortunately, my siblings waited for me and I did not need to borrow money from a fellow passenger. My brother's family was in the mountains and I was able to stay in his apartment for the rest of the summer.

Once again I needed to find a place to live. I found an apartment in the Borough Park section of Brooklyn, where I rented a room from a very nice elderly woman who lived on the second floor of a two-family house in a rented eight-room apartment. She was left by herself after her children had married. She remained in the apartment because of the low rent. The landlord lived downstairs, and this woman feared that if the landlord could hear her walking or talking, he would evict her. One could not speak on the telephone loudly; one could not do this or that. She herself walked on the tips of her toes. As long as I was by myself, it did not bother me. I could watch myself; I didn't jump and dance. I lived there for the rest of the summer, but when my daughter came back in September to return to school, it was too difficult to live there. She wanted to jump and dance and the woman did not permit her to take even one step.

From there I moved to a railroad flat in the Crown Heights section of Brooklyn, where I lived till about 1956, when there was a terrible fire and I had to move out quickly. We moved in with one of my brothers, who lived in the same neighborhood, until I found an apartment with three rooms, still in the same area of Brooklyn, and my life stabilized a bit. I remained living there until everybody I knew moved to Borough Park, which became increasingly heavily inhabited by Orthodox Jews.

Work in America

Shortly after I got off the boat, I had to find work, since I had no financial resources whatsoever and had to support my daughter and myself. I didn't wish to seek assistance from any charitable organization. This brings me to the most sorrowful chapter of my life after I arrived in the United States: my work history.

I didn't know the language, and I lacked an occupation. My studies in law at the university in Poland were worthless here. I began looking and asking: a naïve thought occurred to me. I had worked for the

Germans in an ammunition factory; I could do the same work here. I had a lot of experience in this type of work, so I could work in this field. But where does one go to look for an ammunition factory in Brooklyn, or even Manhattan? That was my naïveté. Initially, I thought it would be very simple. It turned out to be a ridiculous idea because such work was available at the time, as I was told, only in a government-related factory. I dropped this comical thought and forgot about it. I tried to look for something different, some more realistic employment. I started thinking about Yiddish; I speak, read, and write the language very well. I could do some kind of work with Yiddish, office work in an organization, wherever the language could be used. This was a realistic idea, but I did not know where to look for that kind of work. When I mentioned it, people laughed at me; where is there such work, who hires people with Yiddish? I didn't think it was a dream, especially since when I arrived in New York in 1946 there were several Yiddish newspapers and various Jewish organizations. This was not such a wild idea, but I did not have the right contacts, and I had to forget all this as well.

I needed to search for other ways of finding a paying job. I began looking for work six weeks after I arrived in April; I began working for a livelihood for the first time in my life when I arrived in the United States. I started by learning to cut diamonds. At the time, two of my brothers had a small diamond-cutting factory and it was suggested that I learn this craft. The diamond-polishing machines were strange; I needed to learn how to work them. I did, even though it was not that easy, but the fact was that at first, when I learned the work, I only managed to polish one stone or two stones a day. With time I produced more. I was paid two dollars for polishing one stone. Later, I succeeded in polishing eight stones in a day. During the last days I was earning $16 a day, but God helped, as we say, and there was no work for me. By the time I learned the craft of polishing diamonds, the factory closed. With this ended my hopes of learning a trade.

It was not easy for me until I was able to find work in a shop that produced veils for women's hats. At that time, hats with veils were very fashionable. These veils were sewn on the hats on a Singer electric sewing machine, and one needed to know how to work the machine. I knew how to work on a sewing machine, but not an electric one. I had a hand machine at home in Poland, and I knew how to use it. Perhaps there were electric sewing machines in Poland before the war also, but I did not see one there. I did know that it was not difficult to learn how to work on an electric sewing machine. I also did not know people who had worked in factories. I knew that there were workers, but I was unaware of the existence of unions, or that workers had a union. The factory working world was remote from my background.

This factory was owned by a religious Jewish man who had various kinds of people working for him, but since I couldn't speak English I couldn't communicate with anybody. Nevertheless I could start working for pay. I learned quickly how to work the electric machine. We worked on piece work. Then something happened; the thread got tangled up and the machine stopped working because of the tangle. A whole mishmash ensued and this episode made a very strong impression on me. The foreman in the factory was a German Jew and his wife was a non-Jewish German. They both came to the United States before the war. While the foreman's wife was a very nice woman, he behaved like a real German. He started screaming at me terribly about what I had done. People stood there, astonished at his unimaginable outburst. His wife calmed him down; I remained in shock; I felt as though I'd received a slap in my face. I did not expect this kind of explosion because of a tangle in a machine. Someone came over right away and fixed it; I continued to work. A few weeks later, God helped, and again I was told that there was no more work, and I needed to look for a job again.

Then I set out to look for work myself by searching in the Yiddish newspapers, the *Forward,* the *Day,* and the *Morning Journal*. I read the *Morning Journal*, even though I tried to read the *Forward*, the most important Yiddish paper in those days; but it was very difficult to read because, even though it was a Yiddish newspaper, their articles contained more English than Yiddish words. Since there were so many English words in their articles I could not understand them at the time; I had no interest in reading it. The *Morning Journal* had very good writers, and they wrote in pure Yiddish.

I found in the *Morning Journal* an ad for a job in a women's leather belt factory. Since by now I had already learned how to work an electric sewing machine, I went there, this time accompanied by somebody; but it didn't take long until I started travelling by myself. I sewed belts there for several weeks, but then this factory also closed. During that summer period I worked at several places for a few weeks, and at each place the work just ended.

When my work finished in the belt factory, I said that I was afraid I would be sent away from America because I was ruining the American economy. The government would require me to leave because wherever I went the work disappeared or ended, or the factory closed. More seriously, I never knew whether I lost the job because there really was no work, or because I didn't know the work. I knew that various factories where I had worked did close, but while I was there they still had some work left. And that was how my first efforts at finding work ended.

I had to continue looking. I looked in the *Morning Journal* to see what kind of work was available. I noted that garment factories were searching for finishers of ladies' coats and suits. I didn't know the meaning of a "finisher," nor what "coats" or "suits" meant; I had to ask for the definition of the terms "finisher of coats and suits" ; I was told that a finisher is one who makes the holes and sews buttons on a garment. I sewed my own dresses at home, as well as clothes for my daughter. I knew not only how to sew but also how to cut dresses very well. I could learn how "finishing" was done here.

So I began my "career" in the garment center on 7th Avenue in Manhattan, as a finisher. When I came to one shop and met with the owner, I told him right away that I had not been in the United States very long. He wanted to know what I could do, and I indicated that I knew how to sew very well but I understood that here they sewed a bit differently from the way I had learned in Poland; if I were shown how it was done here I could learn quickly. I may have told a little lie, suggesting that I was a seamstress, but it was true that I sewed at home.

The owner agreed. He walked me over to a table where people were sitting on all sides. Those working on machines sat on one side, and the finishers sat on the other. There was an empty chair next to a woman finisher, and across from me sat a man. I had brought a thimble with me, which was not a tailor-type thimble. My thimble was closed and here the finishers sewed using an open tailor-type one. They gave me one, along with needles.

When the owner brought me to the table, he told the man sitting across from me that I had just recently gotten off the boat, that I knew how to sew but that he would like him to show me how to sew here. The man responded, "I am not a teacher." I didn't know what the word "teacher" meant. The man said, "I don't know and I don't show." After the owner, who spoke Yiddish, told me what the man had said, I thought

I would have to leave. Once again, I felt I had received a slap in the face when I learned what the man said to the owner. I felt crestfallen. **(As I transcribed this, it made me cry for the pain she must have felt during that moment.)** But the owner told me, "Don't let this bother you. Sit down, I will send you a person who will show you."

I sat down and the foreman came over and brought me a jacket to work on. He showed me what I needed to do, how I needed to baste it and I, naturally, understood his instructions. A Jewish American woman who could not speak Yiddish sat next to me. She was very nice; she explained to me how I should hold the garment; she showed me how to baste it; later, when the foreman came over he told me that it was fine. He instructed me to cut the ticket from the jacket, to write down a number, and to bring the jacket to the people who line it. I began sewing and kept the ticket. The tickets were handed in at 4:30, when we stopped working.

Later, I realized that the man across from me and a woman who spoke Italian were working as a team. I saw that he sewed a jacket and threw it to her, then she sewed it a bit and threw it on the floor; they worked like that unceasingly. Every ten minutes, he sewed and then she sewed, and I observed that they sewed about 50 jackets together. Afterward, I found out that they divided the work according to what each did best, enabling them to work very quickly.

I worked on one jacket for about one hour. By the end of the day, they had sewn a whole mountain of jackets. I went over to the owner and told him that it looked like here one had to work faster than I could. He said, "Don't worry; don't be bothered, you will make more later. How many did you do today?" I said about six pieces; he said, "Tomorrow you will make 12. Don't worry. Sit and work." I said that I was sitting there occupying a place, while somebody else could sit in this place who knew the work. He said, "Don't let any of this bother you. You come tomorrow morning at 8:30 and you will sit and work." I agreed and decided to come and see what would happen. If he was not bothered that I was sitting there working at my own pace, I had nothing to lose. I would produce as many pieces as I could. I left with a heavy heart. It is not just that the work was different, it was also that I was just not used to this kind of work. I didn't know what "baste" meant, and other such things. I was lucky to have met the woman I mentioned before, an extremely nice middle-aged person, who was always willing to show me what I did not know how to do.

Afterward, I found out that we were working by piecework, not by the hour. Originally, I did not know the difference between piecework, hourly, or weekly wages. My new friend explained all that to me. I oriented myself very well and quickly, but the occupation was not that simple. When I had first arrived at this factory, the owner only wanted to know whether I was a member of the union. This being my first experience in a very large factory, it was the first place where I was asked about union membership. Indeed, one advantage of this job was that the foreman told me he would see to it that I became a union member. Without a union card, one could not work anywhere. In fact, a few days later the union's business agent came over to tell me that I would receive a book, and he would register me with the union. He told me that it cost money to join the union, and I agreed to pay it.

I came the next day; I sat down and quickly oriented myself, and I already knew what the job consisted of. The foreman complimented me on my work, as did the woman who sat next to me. As he had promised, I actually made not six, but twelve, coats that day. The owner was also reassuring, telling me that I would make more with time, calming me down. I was very glad.

I soon learned what a "paradise" working in this industry was. There were women there who had begun to work there when they were children. Years later, people told me they had started at the age of nine. One middle-aged woman remembered that she could not even reach the table when she had begun; they had given her a little box to stand on so she could see what rested on the table. She told me that she had been very happy during the war, for she made a lot of money. Later, I saw what it meant to work in the garment center. I worked in this shop until we left for Israel, and when we returned I was employed at various other ones. At none of them did I have pleasant experiences.

When I decided to go to Israel in 1949, I left the factory in mid-season and the boss was very annoyed with me. July and August were the high seasons in "coat and suit" factories. Normally there was a slack period during the winter, until July Fourth, and then a new work season began. Since I realized I could not find a livelihood in Israel, and wished to become a naturalized citizen, I returned to the United States on July 11, 1950. I was not a citizen as yet, but I needed to find work again. I immediately began looking for a job and returned to the same place where I had worked before leaving for Israel. They did not want to believe that

I had left the country, and thought I was lying, but since they needed people, the bosses agreed to let me work there. Now that I had a job I knew I would have a few dollars.

I worked in finishing women's coats until I retired. The work was not stable; I could have four weeks of work and then be unemployed for two weeks. I constantly had to look for work. I earned about $55 a week, working piecework but after tax and other deductions I had $30 net pay. I worked in different places; when a job ended in one factory I found one at another, until I retired at age 65 (in 1968).

I begin to shake throughout my body just recalling the two decades and more that I worked in the garment industry. It was not the work alone, but the various intrigues and deceptions that went on in these factories that had a terrible impact on me. My legs begin to quiver and I begin to shiver when I think of my experiences during those years.

When I worked in the garment center shops, people were constantly fighting to get more or better work than the others. There were always quarrels. I used to think about what would have happened if these people had been in the camps. They would have torn one another's eyes out. We were starving, we received a little soup once in 24 hours, and we worked unimaginably hard. What would these people have done if they had worked in the ammunition factories? I wanted to picture it. Perhaps had they been in the camps they would have behaved differently; they would have behaved better. We all got the same thing to eat; we suffered in the same way. I continuously thought about this as I sat in the shop: in the two years I was in Skarżysko-Kamienna, there was only one single incident of a serious quarrel, as I described before, around the stove at the barrack. Otherwise people deferred to one another. I behaved as I was accustomed to behaving; being in the camp did not change me. People have wondered how people who lived in closed quarters, who shared the same bunk bed, can live in peace. But I did.

Because I wanted to free myself from the garment center, I occasionally made various attempts to find other types of work. While I was in the Warsaw ghetto I had studied accounting, so I took two courses in accounting in Brooklyn College at night, thinking that perhaps I could get a job as an assistant to an accountant, since I didn't have the experience to become a professional accountant. I didn't receive a diploma, but according to the professors I did very well in the accounting courses. From March until July was usually a slack period in the garment center;

I looked for work in bookkeeping during that time, but it was very difficult to find work in this field. I interviewed at one place in a one-person office where I would have had to keep the books by myself. I declined that job because I lacked the experience. Actually, the man told me he would show me, and encouraged me to accept the job, but I was afraid to assume the responsibility. If I started working there I would not be able to return to the shop if the bookkeeping job didn't work out.

Then I took courses to become an X-ray technician, at a private institute for different types of medical assistants. I took the courses at night after work during the winter, running in the evenings from the garment district to 57th Street and 8th Avenue, the location of the Institute. The courses lasted four months, and again I did very well in them. I got one hundred percent in all of the subjects. Here I received a diploma. **(On August 31, 1955, my mother was awarded a diploma by the Manhattan Medical Assistants' School for having completed 150 hours of "advanced X-ray techniques," certifying her as an X-ray technician.)** When my work in the garment center ended for the season in April, I was advised to do a practicum at a hospital to get some experience in the field. At the time, St. Johns Hospital was one block away from my house. The hospital was a union hospital, and they accepted me. I was not paid. I was there for a few weeks, and liked the work very much. The head of the department was an Arab from Lebanon, and he was a very nice man. But when the season began in the garment center, I had to give it up. He was very unhappy: he told me that I was a very good technician and it was unfortunate that I could not continue working there, for after six months I could receive a license from the city and would then be able to get a job in any hospital anywhere in the country. He could not understand why I was leaving, and even scolded me for it. I could not tell him that I worked to live, that I had nothing to live on if I was not working, and that therefore I couldn't stop working for six months.

Then I changed my mind: I found out that there were jobs available immediately working for the city, if only I passed an examination. But if I had a Bachelors of Arts degree I would not even need to take the examination. I was advised to go to New York University, and if I had 120 credits I could get the degree. I wrote to the consulate in Poland, asking them to send me the documents showing that I had studied at the Wszechnica Polska. After a few weeks I received the documents in Polish; I obtained an official translation of them into English that showed that Golda Eiger **(my mother laughs ironically, when she says this—I assume it brings back all her memories about the issue of her name)** attended the University, and listed the courses I took there. **(The transcript from the Polish Free University [Wszechnica Polska] states that she began her studies in 1927/1928, and completed the Law exams in 1932.)** When I presented the transcript to the registration official at the University, he told me that I had enough credits for three college degrees here. I was what we called in Poland *absolwent*, meaning that I was a graduate of a university, having completed all the requirements for a degree. I was told that I could receive credit for the work I had done in Poland. I could be admitted right away, but there were two subjects I was required to take at the university here: English language and American history. Those were mandatory courses for everybody. I needed to attend for one year and take these two courses once or twice a week. I registered for the courses; it was not too expensive, and I started going to school again while I was working. **(As I write this I am amazed by how indomitable she was.)** I studied, but when I came from work I was very tired and had no energy to sit and listen in class; I did it anyway. After a while I realized that it was impossible for me to do this; it was simply too difficult to work and also study. I did not complete the two courses. I attended only for half a year, for four months after registering in the fall. In the shop I was compelled to work overtime and it was very hard. I have the papers from the Wszechnica Polska translated into English, and also the documents that I had registered for the two courses, although I may have thrown them out. With this failed endeavor I ended my adventures, my efforts to get out of the garment center. I studied one thing, then another thing, and I had to give it up. I had to remain in the garment industry. I did not earn a lot of money there, but I did have three months off a year, sometimes even four, and for me that was a great advantage. Thus, I continued to work in the garment center until, as I said, I retired. **(She also received a certificate from the New York City Board of Education, showing that she completed a course of study in English at an evening elementary school.)**

Even though my mother worked in the garment center for almost two decades, working there diminished her. It was an extraordinary fall from being a person of very high status in her Jewish com-

munity in Poland to perceiving herself as having a very low status because of having to work in a factory, and with people with a very different background. I witnessed in many instances over the years how demeaning she felt this work to be. One can see how degraded she felt from the following part of her narrative.

In the first years after I arrived in the United States, I wanted to get in touch with Professor Rafael Lemkin, who was in New York. As I mentioned previously, he was an assistant to one of my professors at the Wszechnica Polska. I had various conversations with him at the time. But then I thought I would make a fool of myself when I would tell him I was a "finisher" in a garment factory. There was a man I had met here by chance who was from Lublin, an art collector, and when we met at a Jewish lecture he would laughingly say to me, "You are still sewing buttons." I did not wish to tell Professor Lemkin that I was "sewing buttons," so I dropped the thought of contacting him

I feel in exile. I don't know why I came here. Mainly, we ran away from "there," a there that no longer exists. It would have been wiser to go to Israel rather than to America, but it was not possible for me to live in Israel. I tried in 1949 and returned because of my child and her future. She could ask me why we went to Israel, where there were wars all the time, if we had the possibility of living in America. It was a difficult decision to make, not because of my fate but because of my child's fate. Even before I had found her, once I knew she was alive, I believed that I should go to America, although I did not know what she wanted. Only afterwards did I learn that she wanted to go to Israel; she was not that excited about going to America. I made the decision without her; I thought it was important to have American citizenship when we were stateless. Our lives would have taken a completely different turn had we gone to Israel without having the option of becoming American citizens.

From the beginning I found that in America there exists a different philosophy of life; it is not really bad, but it is founded on a different premise from mine. People seem to think about themselves all the time rather than about others. For example, I observed in my first months here that a dominant approach is "Mind your own business." I took this to mean that one should not interest oneself in others, not get involved in or concerned with another person's life. If one saw somebody lying in the street, dead or in a faint, one need not stop to try and help the person. Here it seems to be understood in a positive way, but in my opinion this is a negative approach to life.

Living and working in America, there is no time to think; nevertheless I subscribe to many papers. In the morning I get the *Morning Journal*, and now that I read English well, I get the *New York Post* in the afternoon. I read *Life* and *Look* magazines every two weeks, and a literary journal every week both in Yiddish and English. From time to time I also get a monthly magazine. Because of the years I lacked any newspapers, it is my revenge on Hitler that I read much more than one would expect.

When I was working, there was not even a minute to stop to reflect; during the actual working day in the shop, one could try to think, but there was always some disturbance. Now that I am not working, I think about all the people I have lost, especially as I am preparing this memoir. The people I lost stand in front of my eyes, and I keep asking myself: where are they; where did they disappear? I think of this person, of another person **(as she speaks these words her voice is painfully soulful)**. I constantly think of my brothers Avrumce and Binim and all the others. I always picture how Avrumce died. I know he was shot when he was in the attic of the house in Warsaw. How did he feel the moment he was being shot and when he fell? These thoughts can break an iron heart. And what happened to Binim? I know nothing about how his life ended. Maybe he too was among those who were shot, but I don't have the same information about him as I do about Avrumce. I think all the time about all these people. I keep asking myself where they disappeared to. I ask myself who was burned, and who was gassed. Unfortunately, we do know where they went, but this thought cannot be comprehended. We don't know where they vanished, but this we do know: they are no more. They were slaughtered—somebody living may even have seen them being murdered—but in the end we don't know the place where they are. This is a tragic thought. People said, "Don't think about this, and forget it." People said that thinking about this would make me sick. But that is not a way to calm down a person; the best way to calm down a person is to speak about it again and again. Forgetting makes a person sick. It is more consoling to speak about these painful events than to keep silent and try to forget. As I mentioned before, some people wished to forget, they feared they would remember; I wished to remember, and feared that I might forget. But I cannot, and never will forget. There were seconds when I did forget, but I made an effort to remember so I could continue with my life.

Only seldom did mother cry when she recounted her life in the camps, but I could hear her weep when recounting her response to listening to the news about Reagan's visit to Bitburg; she cried for her people, as we can see from what follows.

I am recording a new chapter in connection with the 40th anniversary of the war's end. The world celebrates the end of the war; there is nothing for Jews to celebrate. For Jews a fresh storm was awakened when the American president (Ronald Reagan) was invited by the German Chancellor to visit the cemetery where 49 SS men were buried. The president agreed to do so and placed a bouquet of flowers on their graves. This created a terrible storm in the American Jewish community, among World War II veterans, and in the media. Everybody seems to have agreed that the president had made a mistake. It suggested that the Germans should forget all that had happened. The president didn't apologize for his actions, but in his speeches he attempted to justify himself. The more he did so, the more he entangled himself. He gave various rationalizations: he wished to console the Germans for their suffering during the war; the Germans were now lamenting what happened. This made people in the Jewish community even more embittered. He did not seem to plan on visiting a concentration camp, but after intense pressure he finally did. The suggestion was that we needed to forget what had happened and start anew. **(Mother sighs.)** All these words infuriated me, Jews in general, and even non-Jews.

The political problem this created for the president made no difference to me. But when he gave the speeches, my heart was broken. How could a representative of 240,000,000 people wish to console the Germans? I felt worst when I heard him give a speech justifying the Germans, when he said that we need not remind the Germans of their acts during the war; they had already faced God and He had judged what was right and what was wrong. An American patriot once said in English, "It is my country right or wrong." This the President said about the SS, about the Germans. He said **(and my mother quotes this verbatim in English)**, "They long ago stood before their maker and he judged them right or wrong." With these words he put a knife in my heart. Since that time I became a little weak. My heart began beating terribly for an hour. I could not calm myself down. His words hit me as if he had plunged a hammer into my heart.

What was right about what the Germans did? We were not war victims. We were victims of murderers and bandits. We were not soldiers. Soldiers are a different matter. Normally, when there is a war there are victims; if one cuts wood there is driftwood. But we were not military people, but innocent unarmed civilians. The entire episode destroyed me; I lay down for about an hour until I calmed down. From then on I had palpitations. People asked me why I was taking this whole matter so much to heart. This question pained me even more. True, 40 years have passed, but the people are not here; should we forget them? Such questions are insensitive. The only positive outcome of this controversy was that people were shown what actually happened. It may have opened the eyes of many. They showed when the English entered Bergen Belsen, where the president went after Bitburg, and where my daughter was liberated. They showed all the victims, their emaciated bones, their skulls, in pits. These were terrible pictures to see. One Englishman cried, when he saw it; the military could not believe it; it seemed like a nightmare. The English ordered the SS men to dig up the pits. The British were right in forcing the Germans to dispose of the bodies in these pits; a photographer recorded these scenes and now being televised. I sat at the television watching them. This photographer took pictures not only of the liberation of Bergen Belsen but also of other areas near the Elbe River where the Russians came from one side and the Allied armies from the other. Now I relived all my experiences. That was where I lived through that terrible April night when the SS left us and told us to stay there till the Russians would come for us. As I recounted before, this lasted a whole night; the bullets were flying over our heads and we lay in a pit; the Germans made these pits to hide themselves. Above us the Russians and Germans were fighting. This photographer took pictures of both armies standing at the Elbe River; he also photographed Dachau, Auschwitz, and the gas chambers. It was terrible to look at but I could not tear myself away from the television, even though it affected my health and I knew it would make me sick. Since that speech I have been feeling weak. The doctor put me on a 24-hour monitor to assess why I have these palpitations. I will be OK. I just feel weak.

II. In My Mother's Voice

I do not know if my mother had ever studied Freud's theories of dreams, but, irrespective, she attributed significance to them, as we saw during the war years. Before she passed away, she spoke of the following dream:

I had another dream a few weeks ago. I dreamed I stood in front of an open window, and there were a lot of animals outside. A camel stuck its head inside, and two of its feet. I wanted to stop him and I started pushing him back with my fists. I expended a lot of strength, as can be imagined, and pushed him back. I woke up. How does one interpret this dream? My first thought was that I fought with the angel of death (*malach hamavet*). I did not want to tell my daughter that. I added later that the dream showed my strength, that I was able to fight with this camel. That I can push away a camel—that is a sign that I am strong. That I am strong geystlekh (spiritually) is true; I am stronger spiritually than physically. What I have experienced was a miracle, OK....

(She stopped at that thought. Indeed, she had an inner strength that one can only stand in awe of. Then, as if by premonition, a year before she passed away in 1991 she summarized her life.)

It is now 1990; it is far away from 1910. At that time I had a childish thought (I was seven years old) that fits 1990. In my childish mind I thought that 1910 would last forever, probably because it was connected with a momentous happening in my life. My great-grandmother, Bubbe Basia, passed away that year. It was impossible for me to conceive that there would be a 1911, and my Bubbe Basia would not be there.

What does that have to do with 1990? I never believed that I would live to 1990. It seems to me like a similar thought. From 1910 to 1939 the time galloped by with one breath. I don't know where that time disappeared. Those were my very best years, and they passed very fast. From 1939 to 1946 the miserable months dragged on, but there was a glimmer of hope for better times. From 1946 to 1990 was a new chapter; the years moved slowly, and it was like a *cauchemar*, a nightmare. As a child I must have heard something about the world ending somewhere. I thought about it; where does the world end? In my mind the world would end at a tall mountain and a deep valley. These ideas occupied my mind when I was a child. And I could not understand how it could be that the world ended in 1910 and then 1911 came. Today I am beset by the question, how did I get to the year 1990? In 1946 I started life again; suddenly I found myself in a new and strange land. It was not physically strange. I knew about strange places from reading many books before the war. The strange place was spiritually foreign—strange in the sense of being exactly opposite to my whole being: odd concepts, unfamiliar customs, alien comprehensions. Everything seemed peculiar. I needed to begin from the beginning to change completely to a different way of life, to a new world.

PART III
IN MY VOICE

CHAPTER 6
A Child-Adult Remembers Home, War, Loss, and Liberation

Unlike my mother, who vividly recalled her life in great detail and with fine nuance, I have only an average memory, and my recollections of the war are those of a child. My experiences of that time are set in sequential scenes, lacking my mother's acute observations, but even so they are very vivid in my mind till this day. The experiences I describe have framed my existence, especially because of their clarity. They are engraved on my mind as if they happened only days ago, but I must emphasize that I don't recall dates. My body recorded time not by the calendar but by my experiences of climate—was it cold, or warm. Later, I was able to corroborate my bodily barometer with more official chronologies.

I recorded my reminiscences before listening to my mother's narrative, because, as I noted earlier, I did not wish my memories to be influenced by those of others, including hers. When we were not forcibly separated, my own and my mother's experiences have obviously intersected and our narratives may, to some degree, overlap; naturally, she recalled many more details for events than I do. At the risk of some repetition, I report in this chapter my own recollections of experiences when they over lap, although where our memories of a happening are exactly the same, I note that mother has already described it. Our shared experiences, and later separations, have probably contributed to the greater-than-usual attachment we had to one another, which was a source of both joy and difficulty in our lives, as such attachments generally are between mothers and daughters.

My mother often spoke about how she had grown up in a large and rich world, notwithstanding the painful divorce of her parents and the external environment infused with anti-Semitism. She was afforded a sure footing from birth to adulthood, supported as she was, by her loving maternal family, mother, grandparents, great-grandmother, stepfather, brothers, and by the larger extended family that respected and cherished her. At the risk of sounding maudlin, I must say that, regrettably, I lacked a similar advantage.

My maternal grandmother had passed away before I was born, and therefore, as is customary, I was named after her. I have only brief recollections of my maternal grandfather, from whom my mother was estranged for much of her life. I had only very brief contact with him before the war and then briefly after we came to the United States. He left for Israel a year after we arrived, and soon died there. Ironically, the night before he passed away, my mother had a dream that foretold his death.

My paternal grandfather had passed away years before my birth, and my paternal grandmother, whom I do recall, was aloof. My father died in my arms when I was eight years old. I have only loving memories of my father before his death, and of my mother's stepfather and her brothers, whom I adored. To my great sorrow, I was separated from them during the war, and later they were annihilated. I always believed that my mother rested on a firm foundation, which may also explain her extraordinary resiliency—a resiliency I, to some degree, lack. I consider myself to stand on "mushy soil." Yet I do recall boasting a bit when I was a child that, unlike anyone else, I had three grandfathers: my paternal grandfather, whom I did not know; my step-grandfather, whom my mother considered her real father, and whom I venerated; and my mother's birth father, whom I recalled from occasional visits to our house, when we lived in the same town and he brought me, once, an electric train and chocolate.

The war deprived me of what otherwise would have been a glorious childhood; in actuality, it robbed me of any childhood at all. I began functioning as an adult at the chronological age of five. The first ten years of life were gone, even though my first four years were the happiest of my life. When I hear people recollect certain children's stories, and the experiences of a normal childhood, I listen with a blank gaze. My happy childhood memories, and the stories my mother read to me, all happened in those first years of my life. When I write this tears come to my eyes; I mourn those lost years that can never be replaced, and the people I loved who can never be revived. This is a sorrow I shared with my mother. I also do not have the happy memories of the holidays that my mother recounts. The first Passover I remember is the one immediately after our arrival to the United States, when my grandfather officiated at the Seder. Subsequent Passovers and other holidays are always dimmed by memories of those gone.

As I mentioned before, I returned to Poland, with great hesitation, to visit the places that I remembered and where my family resided. Warsaw was badly bombed initially, but the entire city, including Pavia Street, was totally demolished by the Germans in 1944 in reprisal for the Polish uprising. Consequently, there was no evidence of the existence of Pavia Street or any of the other streets I remembered. I did stroll through the beautiful, but reconstructed, Krasinki garden, and it was as I remembered it from before and even during the war. Lublin, the city where my mother grew up, still exists, but the Jewish section was destroyed by the Germans. Only present-day Piotrków, my father's city, remains as I remember it to have been, and it was the highlight of my trip.

Childhood Before World War II

My life began with difficulties for my mother. I was born in a birthing center, as was customary in Warsaw at the time, but my mother was in labor for more than a day, with her life in danger. There came a point, as my mother noted, when the obstetrician asked her family, especially her stepfather, who was always consulted by the family and his followers about crucial matters, whether to save the mother or the child. He, apparently without any hesitation, ordered that foremost the doctor must save my mother. My mother attributed this difficult labor to the trauma of her own mother's passing away a few months earlier.

Aside from the difficulties of my arrival, I had an exceptionally happy childhood from birth to about age four or five; I was surrounded by people I adored: my parents, my step-grandfather, and my mother's two younger brothers, Avrumce and Binim, the children of my grandmother with my step-grandfather. We met these people in my mother's narrative, but I mention them again now because I continue to long especially for them.

I was brought up bilingual from my earliest days. When I learned to speak, it was in Polish to my mother and Yiddish to my father. It was not uncommon for men in Hasidic families to speak only Yiddish and Hebrew, and for the women to speak both Polish and Yiddish. My mother was equally versed in both these languages and in Hebrew as well.

We had a large apartment with big windows and a veranda in Otwock, a town where various Hasidic rabbis lived and held court before the war. Otwock was a suburb of Warsaw in the Warsaw District; it was connected to Warsaw by a 25-minute ride on an electric train. The town, surrounded by beautiful pine forests, was known for its hotels and health resorts, including sanatoriums for "lung disease" or tuberculosis, from at least the beginning of the twentieth century until World War II. Jews ran the hotels and most of the stores in the town. The area was rural, with many goats all around; we used to drink their delicious milk. The Hasidic and Polish communities lived separately and had minimal contact; they only intersected in commerce, or when Poles would make snide anti-Semitic comments, or occasionally physically assault a Hasidic Jew in the streets. Some behaviors of the Poles were regarded negatively by Hasidic Jews. When I tried to whistle at a very young age, my father said to me, "Only Poles whistle; Jews do not whistle."

My father was a talmudic scholar, and also a rabbi with a modest following. His older brother was the head of the rabbinic court known as Radoszyce; he inherited by the rule of primogeniture most of their father's followers. My father, who had beautiful teeth, a warm smile, and delicate hands, was a very gentle person; his entire life was dedicated to religious study and teaching. I remember sitting on his knee, watching him study Talmud as he sat on the veranda; it was incomprehensible to me when he would turn back to pages he had already read. Only after I became a scholar did I understand, as I too found myself returning to pages I had read before.

Other scenes from this same period that stand before my eyes: my father bathing me in a tub, walking away for a moment as I call to him in Yiddish, "Look how I am swimming like a fish." My father also liked to carry me on his shoulders and cry out, "I have a lamb (*shepsele*) for sale, I have a lamb for sale" and I would laugh my head off. I also recall how my father would say with me nightly the prayer central to the Jewish religious cannon, " Hear O Israel, the Lord our God, the Lord Is One," before I went to sleep, and how he would teach me to ask the four questions recited by the youngest children at a Seder.

Once thieves attempted to enter our apartment, and my father stood up on a chair, beating at the ceiling with a cane and calling for help from the neighbor above us. The robbers left before they even got inside.

My mother did not speak much about my father in her narrative, except for discussing the time they had to decide whether to give me away to Poles during the war. She would always say that he was a holy man. Since he died when I was barely seven years old, I often wonder whether, if he were to walk down the street today, I would recognize him. My mother's brother Leibl did say more about him, even though he didn't know him well because he moved to Israel three years after my parents married in 1932. My uncle described him as a good-looking man, well built, with a sensitive face and an aristocratic bearing, much the same as I remember him. He described his elegant and well groomed beard, with every hair in its place, and spoke of his "worldly demeanor." It had surprised my uncle to discover that my father was very conservative in his thinking, like his Radoszyce ancestors, who unlike my mother were backward-looking rather than forward-looking. This came up in reference to what my father deemed to be her inappropriate (*es past nisht*) mode of dress for a rebbe's wife. The phrase *es past nisht,* "it is not befitting," was used as a common form of decrying behaviors that were regarded as improper for a person's position in society, as I also learned later, beginning in my adolescence. As my uncle remembered him, my father didn't believe my mother dressed with sufficient modestly for the wife of a rebbe; he objected, for example, to an eyelet dress she had made, because of the fabric's transparency. My uncle heard my father complain to my step-grandfather about this issue. But rather than agreeing with my father, as one might have expected, my step-grandfather supported my mother, especially since she had never transgressed any religious laws.

My mother didn't work before or after her marriage, and didn't take advantage of her education after she married. It would have been inconceivable for a rabbinical daughter to work outside the home, or be employed by strangers, although women would run small businesses in their homes while their husbands dedicated themselves to religious scholarship. My mother, however, had no talent for business, nor would my father have permitted such efforts on her part had she possessed such talents. After she gave birth she dedicated herself completely to raising me, her child, as she describes.

She proudly recounted to me on numerous occasions how she had followed the most advanced theories of child rearing. I recall how she prepared grated carrots daily for my afternoon meal, and how my lunch consisted of spinach and other vegetables. I recall her bathing me in a tub in the sun every day at noon, weather permitting, because according to my pediatrician it promoted healthy bone development.

All her efforts paid off greatly during the war. During my first four years of my life I was exceptionally well developed, so much so that a few years later, when I was brought to the Ravensbrück labor camp and asked my age, I immediately said I was 16 years old, though I was actually about eight, and the woman who signed me in accepted it. Since the war, I have often attributed my survival in the camps to the healthy diet and loving care my mother gave me during those early years.

Mother subscribed to a Polish children's journal from which she read me stories, and she read to me also from various books. I still recall one such book by Julian Tuwim, a Polish poet, who also wrote stories for children. While I no longer speak Polish, I recall the first sentences of this book about the life of a locomotive, in Polish titled *Lokomotywa* (Locomotive), which read (I translate, naturally), "A locomotive is standing in the station, beautiful and huge, and sweat comes down from her brow..."

I also recall occasional visits by my mother's birth father and brothers, when they brought me presents; my memories of these first years of my life are sporadic, but very joyful. My memories become much more vivid from the day the war began when I was four and a half years old.

Beginning of World War II in Warsaw

The scenes from that first day, when World War II officially began, are still engraved in my mind.

The family, as my mother recounts, lived in a large apartment on Pavia 16, which consisted of several immense apartment buildings with an inner round courtyard. At the entrance to these buildings there was an iron gate that was always locked at night. The street name meant "prison," and indeed there was a prison not far away.

The apartment was located on the first floor; at the entrance there was a long corridor leading into a large kitchen with a massive coal stove. From the kitchen one entered another long corridor that led to various rooms, one of which was a big room where my step-grandfather spent much of his time. When the war began, my father was in Piotrków. As Mother recounted, a few days earlier his sister had died, and he had travelled to Piotrków to sit in mourning for her (to sit shiva). His niece had also married a day before the war. Once the war began he could no longer travel to Warsaw to join us because he was dressed in his Hasidic garb; he would not disguise himself as a Pole as other people had done in order to travel.

When the war began, my mother and I lived with my mother's stepfather, whom my grandmother had married in 1910 or 1911, and with whom she had four children, three of whom lived with us when the war began: Avrumce, Binim, and the youngest daughter, Basia. Also living with us was one of my stepfather's sons from a previous marriage, and these were the people at the very center of my life. My step-grandfather was not very tall; he had a long beard, wore a very large round hat, and very much enjoyed when I, sitting on the table, would pull his hat down on his face. He would pull it up again and again, and he would laugh and laugh. This little game could go on for a long time, until I got tired, even though many people were waiting to meet with him. My step-grandfather was a holy man and numerous people would seek his advice, especially when they were ill, and also his blessings; even Poles came to ask for his blessing.

My step-grandfather ate very little; actually, he ate no food for much of the day, but smoked a pipe and drank coffee all day. From the time the war began coffee was not available, but a coffee-like beverage was made out of chicory. He only ate a regular meal on the Sabbath, because on that day there is a commandment to eat. On Fridays, at sundown before the Sabbath began, he would run about the house announcing that the Sabbath was coming and that it was time to light candles; his voice still echoes in my ears now. My uncle Avrumce was an exceptionally handsome man who stood tall as he looked out the window smoking cigarettes. When I began smoking as an adult, I always recalled my uncle Avrumce with his cigarette.

The day the bombing began, my mother, my uncles Avrumce and Binim, a neighbor, and I went up on the roof. We saw Warsaw burning. I can still see the fires and smoke coming out of the buildings not far away. I was fascinated by hearing the sounds of the air alerts, and seeing the fires; the city burned until the end of the siege of Warsaw on September 27, when Poland officially surrendered to Germany. Once the bombing stopped, we could go out onto the street and, as my mother described, life began returning to some routine.

After the bombardment stopped, I was even sent to a kindergarten where the children spoke Polish. The school was located in the teacher's one-room upstairs apartment, furnished with what would be described today as antique furniture. My mother brought cookies and a bottle of sweet wine for all the children to celebrate what was probably my fifth birthday. Although my family did not usually celebrate birthdays, the school did, and I joined such festivities. I was the *solenizantka*, or celebrant, for that day. During this time in the Warsaw ghetto I recall still being happy; I was surrounded by all the people who meant the most to me in my life, and still do. I even remember wishing that I could live forever, and being angry at Eve because, as I understood it at the time, had she not eaten the apple we would all live eternally.

During these early months, my mother would take me to the theater and to the beautiful Warsaw gardens. I recall a puppet theater, and also a place with kaleidoscopes, at the ends of which there were pictures of Japanese people, and Japanese women twirling their colorful umbrellas. These images stayed with me, especially when I visited Japan as an adult.

Until the ghetto was sealed off, people were still able to travel. My uncle Avrumce's wife came from her native city in Galicia, where she was trapped when the war broke out, although later she had to return. While she was with us she would still bake braided challahs in the big black oven for the Sabbath, and I loved watching her braid the dough. Just as the war began, my step-grandfather's brother was brought to Warsaw to have a leg removed; the operation was conducted in the house, and I witnessed the procedure. I believe the man survived the operation but not the war.

When my step-grandfather held the traditional third Sabbath meal, se'udah shelishit in the late afternoons on Saturdays, he always insisted that I sit near him as he was expounding to his followers, his Hasidim, about some points of the Torah. He was very solicitous toward me, the only child in the household. I still can hear his voice calling out, "Where is the child, where is the child?" when he did not see or hear me. Since food was very scarce during those times, he always insisted that I must be fed first, even before him.

During the time of the Warsaw ghetto I still looked like a healthy child. Both my uncles conducted "business"—illegally, of course—in the ghetto. Binim sold lottery tickets, and Avrumce engaged in various small enterprises. Our family, unlike most, was not in want of basic food. I would even get a cup of cocoa with milk at times, in a special child's cup with a smiling face carved on it. While our family still managed to have some food, the images of the beggars and emaciated bodies lying in the street have never left me. Starvation in the Warsaw ghetto was rampant. My mother remembered that I still looked healthy and well, and that one time when we were walking down the street a German stopped us to say, "What a beautiful little girl." Rather than arrest us, as she had feared, he let us go on our way.

My mother, her two brothers, and I moved out of the apartment on Pavia Street to another apartment (Mila 37), so that my uncle Avrumce could conduct his business from there and not endanger my step-grandfather. Also, he wished to protect his father from the terrible typhus epidemics rampant in the Warsaw ghetto, beginning in 1940-1941, during which between 4,000 and 5,000 people died in the streets daily.

One day a policeman came to the apartment building, grabbing people to send them off to work as slave laborers. He caught my uncle Binim, wanting to take him away. I screamed, yelled, and was dragged along with him because I would not relinquish his hand. By some miracle, the policeman let him go because of my ranting and crying. Everybody said later that I saved Binim's life at the time. In her narrative, mother remembered what I do not: that without any prompting I had told the policeman that Binim was my father.

People gathered in the Mila Street apartment and incessantly spoke about the political situation. I listened to all the talk. Mother recalled that somebody remarked that I looked like Mussolini, having retained my chubbiness still. In response to this characterization of me, I immediately responded, "No, I look like Churchill." I have retained my interest in international politics throughout my life, having been made aware so early that our lives are always affected by global affairs.

My first separation from my mother and the rest of my beloved family occurred during one of the typhus epidemics I mentioned above. Both of my uncles fell ill, one after the other. When Binim became sick, I was sent to a relative's house, and then when Avrumce contracted the disease, I was transferred to another relative's house. My mother was the last one in the family to fall ill. She has told me that I, too, had an extremely high fever. I recovered after 24 hours, so it may not have been typhus, but nonetheless the family decided to send me to my father, who was in Piotrków.

My appearance was stereotypically Aryan, contrary to German images of Jews. They were amazed when they saw me on the street, shocked that a Jewish child could look so Aryan, with blond hair and a round face. My uncles hired a Polish woman to take me to Piotrków and I travelled as her child, even though she was short and looked less Aryan than I did. I don't know how they found her, or how much she was paid: such arrangements with Poles always involved a payment and were done in great secrecy.

People in Warsaw were paralyzed, not knowing what to do: would it be better to remain there, or to seek ways to leave for a smaller town? As my mother observed, it was believed to be madness to send me to the smaller city of Piotrków, because surely the Germans would kill people in small towns before exterminating them in a large city such as Warsaw. Nevertheless, I was sent out of the city because of the fear that I too would become sick.

Despite all the warnings, I left the apartment at night with my uncle Binim, who took me in a *droshka* (a horse-drawn carriage) to the ghetto wall. My uncle propelled me up the 10-foot-high wall that surrounded the entire ghetto, and pushed me over it to the other side. I did not cry at this time. The woman waited for me on the other side. She took me by the hand, and together we went to the station to take the train to Piotrków. There I was reunited with my father, who would visit his mother quite often in Piotrków before the war, but I did not remember, nor did I see, my grandmother before I arrived. When as an adult I returned to see Warsaw, I revisited the spot where a small segment of the ghetto wall still remains, bringing me back to the day I scaled it.

After my mother recuperated from typhus, she was longing to see me and insisted that she must go to Piotrków. The rest of the family remained in Warsaw until the liquidation of the ghetto. I learned later that everybody had urged my uncles to try to leave Warsaw when the liquidation began in 1942, but they would not leave their father, despite his urging them to go. As my mother recounted, until the liquidation my step-grandfather and uncles worked in a factory administered by a Hasidic man. Since they were working in a factory, we were told, they were among the last people to be liquidated, and my step-grandfather simply closed his eyes and died as the Germans came into his apartment to take him, which to this day I find an extraordinary feat.

I have been mourning the deaths of my step-grandfather, Avrumce and Binim, and that of my father, all my life. My only solace from having endured these irreplaceable losses is that throughout my life since then, when something unpleasant happens, something that distresses me greatly, I can console myself that the worst thing had already happened to me: nothing could be as bad as having lost these people. My first painful separation and loss occurred when I scaled the wall to escape from the ghetto, and there were many further separations during the war; consequently, separation and loss have been undercurrents in my personal life; they surreptitiously lay down a template for my actions thereafter. As much as I wish to discount or refute the influence of the war on me, it has had its consequences on my life to this day.

In Piotrków Ghetto

When I was brought to Piotrków, my father lived on the second floor of an apartment house located in the heart of the ghetto, on Pilsudski Street. By that time, the large apartment had already been divided into several dwellings. The main large room (which was meant to function as both dining and living room) was furnished with traditional furniture. What have always stood out in my mind are the beautiful demitasse cups and golden spoons that were among the numerous knick-knacks my grandmother had in her credenza.

My father and I lived with my grandmother, who at the time was 72 years old. She was a rotund, short woman with a round face and lovely skin; and she was not a particularly loving grandmother. My father's older brother and his family—two daughters, one of whom, as I mentioned, married a few days before the war began, the other of whom was unmarried, and an unmarried son in his late teens—resided in the same building, in one of the dwellings split off from my grandmother's apartment. During this time I was not fussed over as I was by the family in Warsaw. The Finkler family, including my grandmother, was actually inattentive to me, perhaps because my father and his older brother were estranged. This kind of friction regarding who was the true successor to a father's court and followers was not uncommon in rabbinical families, as we also saw in my mother's account of the disputes among her maternal uncles after the death of her maternal grandfather. There were those, I learned later, who had wished my father to become the official Radoszyce Rebbe, and those who anointed his older brother.

Also, I understood later, a tension existed between my mother and grandmother. As can be deduced, I don't have warm and fuzzy memories of my paternal grandmother. To this day, I think of her as a self-centered and selfish woman who probably dominated my father, her youngest child, if less so than she did her older son. My one surviving cousin, who at the time was one of the young women in the house, remarked years later that our grandmother was not very welcoming to her daughters-in-law either. She seemed to be interested only in herself.

I spent much of the time by myself, since my father's family did not pay any attention to me. Perhaps the two young women in the house did not know how to care for a little girl. Certainly my father, who had played with me as a baby, did attend to me, but he did not know very much himself about caring for a child. To amuse myself, I would go down from the apartment and stand in front of the building, watching people. I wore the little coat with fur inside that my uncle Avrumce had made for me in Warsaw, as my mother has described, as well as a hat and muff trimmed with the same fur. The

Germans required Jews to hand over all their valuable possessions, including jewelry and furs, and we surrendered the fur inside my coat. But my father did not trim the fur off the hat and muff, which I wore when I went out. I still recall the fear I felt of being seen by a German, because of the trim on the hat and muff. When one would pass I would turn around so he couldn't see me. I don't know at what age children develop a sense of fear based on "not obeying orders," so to speak, but I certainly experienced such dread at the age of six.

The joy I felt being with my family, even under the dire conditions of the Warsaw ghetto, was not present in my grandmother's house. There was a gloom hanging over the apartment in Piotrków, and my existence during those days, until my mother arrived, was dismal.

I was reunited with my mother when she arrived in Piotrków in May 1942; she was smuggled out of Warsaw in the same manner as I was. My mother left her beloved brothers, whom she had raised since their childhood, determined to be with me. Ironically, the typhus epidemic in Warsaw saved our lives because, otherwise, we would have remained in that city to be liquidated with the rest of the family.

My mother's arrival in Piotrków was totally unexpected, and that day still remains clear in my memory. Curiously, she did not dwell on this momentous event in our lives in her narrative, perhaps because immediately after she entered the room and saw me, she cried, "What have you done to my child! What have you done to my child?" These words still ring in my ears.

The cry was an expression of absolute shock when she saw my long blond hair unwashed, tangled up in knots, and dotted with lice; it must not have been washed or combed for many weeks. I had the appearance of a waif. When I was sent to Piotrków I was still a bit on the chubby side, a little girl with beautiful long blond hair.

The same day she arrived, she washed me and shaved off my hair to get rid of the lice. She was very angry at my father's two nieces and my grandmother for their neglect. My head was once again shaved later when I reached Ravensbrück, but I am getting ahead of my story.

Piotrków Trybunalski, situated 90 miles from Warsaw and 16 miles from Lodz, is one of the oldest towns in Poland, established around the twelfth century; Jews were present there since 1487. The town had its first formal rabbi in the eighteenth century. Approximately one third of its 20,000 inhabitants were Jewish by September 5, 1939, when the town was occupied by the Germans four days after the outbreak of the war. The Germans established their very first ghetto in Poland there on October 8, 1939. It was at that time that the Judenrat was established, and all Jews had to put on the infamous yellow badge; and also surrender all their possessions, including furs, in the middle of the 1941-1942 winter. The town was policed by the Germans, especially, as my mother noted, by the notorious German SS man known as William with the Dog. Since my father feared leaving the house because it was especially dangerous for Jewish men in Hasidic garb to be seen in the streets, he would send me, even before my mother arrived, to one of his followers living in the Old City to get the two deca (milligrams) of raisins from which he made the wine for the Sabbath Kiddush blessing. My mother remembered, as I do, and my parents laughed about it even then, that by the time I returned to the house I would have eaten half the raisins.

I do not recall how many trips I made to get these raisins, but I do remember the incident Mother mentions. One time, on my way back, I saw William appear with his dog as I crossed a large field. As I write this, I still feel the fear that I felt then, when I saw William with his huge black wolf dog, which we called the devil. I immediately hid in a courtyard until they were out of sight. It was often said that the dog had bitten many Jewish children in Piotrków. My mother described better than I can this frightening episode in our lives—although she considered it miraculous, since she recalled many more details. Indeed, my mother regarded this as one of several miracles we experienced, attributing my being saved from being eaten alive by the dog to the intervention of our ancestors. When we arrived in the United States and I saw a person walking with a dog, I would run to the other side of the street. It took me many, many years to get over my fears of dogs, but gradually, as I grew older, I became a lover of them and all animals.

People began to search for ways to save themselves, including ways of getting to Switzerland. With the illusory hope that a visa for Switzerland would materialize, my father allowed himself to be photographed for the first time in his life. According to the tradition of that time (which has subsequently changed), Hasidic men avoided having their picture taken. This custom was based on the premise that, since humans are made in the image of God, they should not be photographing Him or His facsimile. This was the only picture I had of him, but it was subsequently taken from me.

Obtaining visas to Switzerland was actually quite a remote possibility, probably just a fantasy, but the family found another option: to go into hiding. We did so in October 1942.

I remember our hiding place clearly, especially the crawl spaces. There were two crawl spaces, one set off from the other: a small space where we all lay without moving, and a larger, higher and more open space in which it was nonetheless safer to crawl on our bellies. From the larger crawl space one could descend to a balcony that wrapped around the entire first floor and also looked out into a courtyard and the large field across from the apartment. We had water and electricity, which were hooked up by my father's brother's young son, and he also built a provisional facility for waste. We had a food supply to last twelve weeks—by which time, people thought, the occupation would end. We mostly ate kasha, or something called gritz. There was also a huge barrel of water standing in the large space. There were thirteen people in this hiding place: our family, my father's brother's family, my grandmother, and two unrelated couples. We could only get out of this crawl space at night, as I did on occasion. Our days were spent lying on the floor in absolute silence, living as we did in continual fear of being discovered.

I had all my belongings in a little blue cloth backpack that I brought with me to the hiding place. One day I couldn't see it, and I began crying or wailing and wouldn't stop. My cousin's husband Shia, an enormous man—unlike my father, who was slight—took a pillow, put it over my face and began smothering me. The man remains in my memory as a big brute with a long red beard, towering over me. As my mother recalled, my parents could not, and did not, say anything. I finally stopped crying, although I don't know whether this was because I was being choked and couldn't breathe or for another reason. The image of this person trying to kill me still stands before my eyes.

I can also still hear my mother's words when we were found in our hiding place by the Germans. She said, "I am either imagining, or I feel as if somebody was walking on my back." She sensed, before everybody else did, that the Germans had found us; they walked on the roof and with some effort discovered us. They marched us out of our hiding place and corralled us into the Great Synagogue of Piotrków, where hundreds of other people, who had also been found hiding, were already warehoused.

We were brought to the huge synagogue, where we were kept three days without any food before being transferred to the smaller Piotrków ghetto. I can still see the enormous room, originally the sanctuary, painted in blue, where they had put us all. The elderly and the children were earmarked for extermination, but because my grandmother looked younger than her years, she was passed off as an able-bodied worker. I was still tall for my age and could pretend to be older than I was. Nonetheless, our appearances could not be trusted. The president of the Jewish Council or Judenrat, Szyman Warszawski, who I recall as being a short man in his 50s, was in some measure a follower of the Radoszyce court. He paid the Germans to overlook my grandmother and me; we were also concealed by the bodies of the rest of the family. I learned later that once we were transferred to the small ghetto, there were people who were resentful that the president of the Jewish Council used his influence to save my grandmother and me. Indeed, he was a controversial figure. Some thought he had saved many lives, as he did mine and my grandmother's, but because he complied with the Germans' demands to present them with lists of names of Jews to deport to labor camps, he was regarded as a collaborator. I was very fortunate that I was concealed, because we could all see babies being shot in front of us, and the majority of the Jews in the synagogue were murdered. I witnessed some of the killings as they took people out of the synagogue. I heard later that many Jews were taken to the nearby forest and told to dig their own graves beforehand.

Between October 13 and 21, 1942, five months after my mother's arrival in Piotrków, the entire ghetto was liquidated: 5,000 people were transported for extermination in Treblinka each day. At this time we also went into hiding. This aktion, as it was called, was carried out by the SS, and by Ukrainians, with the aid of Polish police. In total, 20,000 men, women, and children were deported, including those who were subsequently brought from nearby towns.

By the time we were transferred to the small ghetto from the synagogue in 1942, there were about 4,000 Jews left in the town, including those who were discovered hiding, and two thousand who may have had work cards. By 1943 Piotrków was, as the Germans liked to say, *Judenrein*, meaning "cleansed of Jews." This was the status Hitler intended for the entire world.

Once we were brought to the small ghetto, my mother, father, and I were deposited in one small cold room with one bed; the rest of the family was placed in an adjacent room. I do not remember where we prepared any food; there may have been a small stove.

I was extremely enterprising at this time. We arrived into a small empty room, and I roamed around the ghetto in search of things we could use in it. There were heaps of things discarded by the Germans, piled up as high as a small mountain, and I managed to find in these piles broken chairs, a table, pots, plates, buckets, pans, and other such items which we used in the little room. I would also search for wood to make a fire for cooking, although I do not, as I said, remember where exactly we cooked. Searching for such things was known in Polish as szabrować, or shabreven in Yiddish. These words are the only ones I know that describe accurately what I did during that time; my mother's narrative of the death march, and when she trekked back to Poland, similarly speaks of such activity, when the women entered German villages and tried to find things in the debris the Germans had left. In the small ghetto I was referred to as a "super child" because of such activities.

One day, police came to the house in search of a woman, a close friend of one of my cousins, who stayed in the adjoining room. Since she was not there when they came, they grabbed my mother instead. There was an aktion, when people were seized, mostly at random, if they could not find the person the police was looking for, and dragged off to a work camp. An order had been issued to capture 300 people; nobody actually knew whether the purpose was to kill them or to take them as slave laborers.

My father and I ran from one place to another to find my mother until we reached a fence, from which we could watch her being put on a truck. This was one of the most defining moments of my life, and the ensuing scene has never left my memory.

III. In My Voice

Just before she was shoved on to the truck, we were separated by a fence, and my mother and father kept saying to me, "Come with me!" They did not know what would be a better course of action: my father believed it would be preferable for me to remain with him, and my mother thought it would be best for me to go with her. Since neither one could decide, they asked me with whom I wished to go. I cried terribly saying that I did not know with whom to go. I wished to be with my mother, and I wished to be with my father. I can still hear myself weeping, "What should I do?" I cried until my lungs ached, repeating and repeating, "What should I do?" My mother kept saying, "Come with me," my father, "Stay here with me." Neither my father nor my mother knew what was best; I could not make the decision myself; finally, the choice was made for me when my mother was hauled off before I could decide, even had I known what to decide. My father and I stood watching as the truck my mother was on moved away. Later I was told that they didn't take children anyway; they either sent them back to the ghetto, as was the case of the child of one of my mother's friends, or killed them. My mother describes this as another episode especially tragic for us all. I suppose no decision, in this case, was a good decision. Prior to that time, my mother recounts that I knew exactly what to do, where to go, when to hide. At that moment I was lost.

While I do not consider myself an indecisive person, there have been various times in my adult life when I wavered about which choice to make. On such occasions, I keep reverting to that moment when I stood sobbing, asking what I should do. This instant was decisive in saving my life, but I also wonder how influential it was in later life when I had difficulty making choices.

Immediately after my mother was seized, in February 1943, the rest of the Finkler family members were also caught, although they were not on any list. Except for my father, my uncle's son, and me, all were taken together with my mother to the Skarżysko-Kamienna munitions factory, a slave labor camp, which she so carefully describes, where relatively small ammunition were produced for the Werhmacht. At this time my experiences and my mother's diverged, until we met almost four years later in Sweden.

My father fell ill around the time we were brought to the small ghetto; subsequently, he was stopped and badly beaten when we were trying to find my mother during the aktion that took her from us. He began spitting blood and became emaciated. I stayed with him and took care of him. He would not eat the soup provided by the Germans in the ghetto kitchen because it was not kosher; I sought ways to prepare him a little food, and I still succeeded in having theological conversations with him. I asked him what the meaning of God was. He told me, "God is like a ball of fire." To this day that is my image of God. Also during this period, as I was lying on the bed, I kept thinking about how I could stop thinking. I wished to empty my head of all thoughts. I couldn't.

One day, four months after my mother was captured, as I was walking around the big piles looking for items we could use, a man came over and tapped me on my shoulder. I remember it being a very warm and sunny day. He told me to come with him. He took me by the hand, and I ran with him to the room where my father, still alive, was lying with blood coming out of his mouth. I picked his head up, held it, and screamed. He died in my arms very soon afterward. He was 43 years old. With the help of the president of the Judenrat, my father's followers were able to bury him in the cemetery. When my mother returned to Poland after the war and learned where he was buried, she placed a headstone on it. More recently, I arranged for the grave to be refurbished and the headstone replaced with one that shows his name clearly and visibly, an important Jewish tradition to commemorate a person.

Being in the small ghetto of Piotrków was more traumatic than surviving the ghetto of Warsaw, despite the fact that, generally speaking, conditions for adults in the Piotrków ghetto were considered, in relative terms, more tolerable. There was less hunger there; there wasn't a wall cutting it off from the city, and there was the possibility for commerce with the Poles. Jews would exchange their possessions for food with the Poles. But for me, while in Warsaw I was surrounded by my loving family, who cushioned all the distresses of ghetto life; in Piotrków ghetto I lacked such shields once my father passed away in 1943. At the moment my father was gone, I was left all alone to fend for myself. The head of the Judenrat, Mr. Warshawski, believing, I suppose, he was doing my parents a favor, asked a Jewish family in the Piotrków ghetto to take care of me. They made me into their servant. I was greatly traumatized by their treatment. They forced me to work for their family; clean their room, wash the floor, and do other such chores, as their maid. Years after my stay with them in the ghetto, when we arrived in the United States after all that had happened, I would continue to recount how miserably I was dealt with by this couple. Recently, I met a woman years older than I, who was also in this ghetto, and the first thing she asked me when we spoke was whether I still remembered how I was treated by that couple, how I was exploited by them. Their abysmal treatment of me was what stood out in the mind of the woman I spoke with, even after all those years. I cannot forgive this Jewish family for their deliberate cruelty. There was only one bright instant during the time I spent with them, when I may even have acted like a giggly child for a second: the couple had two boys, perhaps a bit older than me, who introduced me to smoking. They got cigarettes clandestinely and gave me a puff to try.

My father passed away on June 14, 1943; in July 1943, the last Jews, 1,720 working-age people, were transferred from the small ghetto to labor in three glass and one woodworks factories located in Piotrków. I was one of 1000 persons, as was the president of the Judenrat, who were moved to the woodworks factory, the *holzenwerke* owned by Dietrich and Fischer, known as the Bugaj that was cordoned off by wires. They built wooden barracks for us and set us up in bunk beds. There, I was forced to work by forming part of a chain of people relaying plywood planks from one person to another. The plywood I transported served to make tables and benches for the military. It is said that Dietrich and Fischer maintained the factory to avoid going to the front; they claimed they needed the people to produce these products.

Once on the Bugaj, I was no longer under the "wings" of the nasty couple; we were moved to barracks, where I was together with my cousin, my father's elder brother's son. The factory provided a minimal ration of bread and sometimes sugar on which I survived. People were, however, able to cook in this barrack and some even prepared potato dumplings of sorts (*kopitka*). I would see my cousin from time to time, even though he worked in the glass factory, but, actually, I was on my own.

When we were brought to the Bugaj, my little rucksack that I had wept over in the hiding place, which contained my possessions and my father's one and only picture, was taken away from me. All possessions removed from people were piled up in a large empty lot. I frantically ran looking for my rucksack, hoping to find the picture of my father. I also had several baby pictures in this backpack, and pictures of my mother on which she had written on the reverse side my grandfather's name and "Brooklyn, N.Y." I managed to find the rucksack with some of the pictures but, to my great sorrow, my father's picture was lost. Fortunately, the name and address my mother wrote on the back of these pictures enabled me at the time of my liberation in Bergen Belsen to tell a chaplain that I had a grandfather in America.

Whereas the little ghetto was guarded by Jewish police, the Bugaj was guarded by Jewish and Ukrainian police. It was not uncommon for Germans to use Ukrainians as their assistants. When we arrived the first day at the Bugaj we were lined up to get soup. I was close to the end of the line, probably the smallest and youngest person. To my amazement, one of the Ukrainian soldiers came over to me, pulled me out of the line and placed me in the front of it. Later, ironically, the Ukrainian guards, who were normally known for their cruelty, became my "protectors"; they had me sit with them in the evenings when they sang songs in Russian, a few of which I still recall.

I worked in the Bugaj between July 1943 and the end of November 1944, when the glass and woodwork factories were closed down. The Russians were advancing on Poland and the Germans began moving out. Indeed, six weeks later, in January of 1945, the Russians entered Piotrków. But the Germans, needing slave labor, transported us to Germany, and we were deported to various slave labor camps there. The men were sent to Buchenwald; the women, including me, to Ravensbrück. But our transfer from the Bugaj to Ravensbrück may also have been simply sheer luck; it is said that our transports were initially designated to go to Auschwitz, but by this time Auschwitz was refusing to accept new prisoners because it was overflowing with victims and in the process of shutting down. Sending prisoners to slave labor camps was still an opportune option.

Before I leave Piotrków and turn to life in Ravensbrück, I must note here again that my return visit to Piotrków in 2008 was especially moving. I relived the war years I spent there; I felt excited, overwhelmed, and also removed from that painful past. I was able to see the synagogue, which has been converted into a library, with only one hidden vestige of a painting of a Torah scroll riddled with bullets; and visit my father's now beautifully refurbished gravestone. Seeing my father's gravestone reaffirmed that I actually had a father.

Because the city of Piotrków was not destroyed during the war, I was able to find and recognize the three-story house where we lived in the center of town, albeit now in a decrepit condition; I saw the field across from it where I barely escaped from William and his dog, and where I would nibble at my father's raisins meant for Sabbath wine; most remarkably, I was able to revisit the attic where we hid. It was as dark as it was then, but now empty; the crawl space and the large room were exactly as I remembered them. The balcony wrapping around the second floor is still there.

I also returned to the Bugaj, where the woodworks factory continues to exist. With some reluctance the current owners allowed me to enter the premises, and I saw myself relaying wooden planks in the courtyard, as I had done as an eight-year-old.

In Ravensbrück, Germany

Ravensbrück, located 55 miles north of Berlin, was initially opened in the spring of 1939, before the war began, to house chiefly non Jewish dissident women, including communists, Jehovah's Witnesses, foreign female political prisoners from the occupied territories, including Poland and France, and only a small percentage of Jewish women. It was uniquely a camp for women. Not until 1942 were Jewish woman brought to Ravensbrück en masse, at which time the camp became a true warehouse of misery, housing 1000 women in a barrack designed for 200. At the beginning of 1944, there were 17,300 women in the camp; by the beginning of 1945, the prison population had risen to 45,637, and it is said that the influx was so sudden that not all prisoners were recorded. In the last days of its six years of existence, Ravensbrück was turned into an extermination camp, with crematoriums built after the closing of Auschwitz. There were also slave labor camp sections, especially the Raven Siemes factory, which produced ammunition, including bombs and airplanes, as well as uniforms for the fighting SS.

In 1944, certain medical experiments were performed on Jewish woman, and other types were performed on Polish women. Mercifully, I was saved from this evil. When the gas chambers were established in Ravensbrück in January of 1945, 6,000 women were gassed in them. Those sent to the gas chambers were the sick, the old, and those too debilitated to stand up.

It was the German policy to save German labor for the front, so the day-to-day operations in Ravensbrück, including the notorious roll calls, were managed by the prisoners themselves, overseen by SS commandants, often very young women for whom such jobs represented upward mobility. In her book *Jewish Women Prisoners of Ravensbrück* (2007) Judith Buber Agassi printed the identification number each prisoner was assigned by the Germans. I was stunned and overwhelmed when I saw my name on this list with the number I was given on arrival. My identification number in Ravensbrück was # 90184. The list verified the reality of my existence at that time, although I will hasten to add that I never doubted the reality of my memory.

We were transported to Ravensbrück after being herded into a freight car that was totally bare, with only a single small window. I was fascinated by the movement of the train. I could still see out of the little window, and I wondered how it was that the trees were all moving behind me. The trip was interminable; the train made one stop in Częstochowa in the middle of the night when we were able to go down to relieve ourselves. Otherwise, there was a bedpan-type container in the car. We were not given any food on the train. The train left Piotrków on a Tuesday and we arrived in Ravensbrück on Friday, December 1, 1944, in the middle of the night.

From the train we were steered into a big room where there were French women in charge. We were lined up and the woman who inspected me was tall; the first thing she asked me was "How old are you?" I immediately responded by saying that I was 16 years old, when I was not yet nine. After the war I was frequently asked how I knew to say I was 16 years old. Nobody had instructed me to do so, since I was on my own; it just popped into my head to give that age. I still do not understand what prompted me to come up with it, although I may have heard that age 14 or 16 was the cut-off separating children from adults. Even now I can see clearly the look

III. In My Voice

on the woman's face—presenting both a faint smile, and doubt—when I told her I was 16 years old. Undoubtedly, she did not believe me, but nevertheless she let me through. I may have been a bit tall for my age, which I attribute to my mother's nurturing before the war; regrettably, from that time on I stopped growing. My reply to the woman, along with her willingness to act as if she believed me, saved my life at that moment; upon arrival to Ravensbrück, children were usually promptly murdered.

Once I passed the initial inquiries, we were directed to an inspection, which began with the shaving off of our hair. I ended up with a totally bare scalp, unlike the very short cut my mother gave me to rid me of my long, tangled, lice-ridden hair when she arrived in Piotrków. Here the hair was cut to the scalp; from that time until I reached the age of 40, I never cut my hair.

We were taken into barracks, furnished with an endless number of three-tiered bunk beds. I was assigned the top one. On the next day, after we were brought to the barrack, we were stripped naked and ordered to go into the showers. I refused to go. I screamed and yelled, and the barrack guards dragged me naked on the floor, but I would not go. When I remember myself being hauled now, I still fail to understand why I was not simply shot. As I am writing about this incident, I am reminded of the various occasions my mother openly, or clandestinely, refused to conform whenever possible.

Each morning, except Sunday, at around 4 a.m., when it was still dark, we were assembled for the brutal roll calls. Since I was there during the winter months, and it was freezing cold, I still shiver when I think of those bitter hours when I stood there barely dressed. The roll calls were unrelenting and endless; to this day when I am exposed to great cold, I am brought back to the days I stood at the roll call, and I crumble. Some days during the roll calls there were selections; I recall a big fat SS man standing, with his thumb constantly moving to the left and to the right, as we were marched in front of him. When his thumb moved in one direction, one lived, and when it moved in the other direction, one was sent to the crematorium.

While I was in Ravensbrück I was put to work, and my task was peeling potatoes. I became an expert potato peeler; after the war I boasted about my potato-peeling proficiency. According to Judith Buber Agassi,* the people who were brought from Piotrków received somewhat better treatment because it had been arranged with the Piotrków industrialists (Dietrich and Fischer) who had factories in the ghetto to take these workers and use them in Germany; this may have been another reason we were sent to Ravensbrück rather than to a crematorium. Perhaps this explains the puzzling fact that I was one of a small number of Jewish people to work in the kitchen, whereas the norm was to assign the worst kind of work to the Jewish women, such as cleaning sewage, or loading wagons, or performing other heavy manual labor.

We were given a ration of bread every three days, and soup made out of rutabaga. A ration consisted of about 200 grams, or about 7.05 ounces of bread. To this day I will not touch a rutabaga, which we were given daily; I don't know who received the potatoes I peeled. Unlike almost everybody else, including my mother, as I learned from her narrative, I did not eat the entire ration in one full swoop. Most commonly, people finished the meager bread ration immediately after they received it; my mother explained that she did not save pieces of her ration to avoid the need of thinking about the bread. From her perspective, once it was gone it was gone; she didn't think about it anymore. I was the only one, I believe, in that particular barrack who cut her ration of bread into translucent pieces and ate one translucent piece every day until the next ration. I did not observe anyone else cutting their rations into thin pieces. I guarded my bread in my bunk bed.

One time I developed a fierce diarrhea for several days; I couldn't eat the bread or the rutabaga soup. I saved the bread. During the time of year I was in Ravensbrück it was extremely slushy; I had a torn coat and very torn shoes. I accumulated several rations of bread when I had diarrhea, and I went to a place where I was told I could exchange the bread I had saved for shoes. Rarely did I venture out of the vicinity of my barrack as I did this time, and I walked through an area full of mud. I exchanged my bread for little boots, but for some reason did not put my "new" boots on when I got them. Instead I put the boots under my very torn coat and walked back to my barrack. As I was walking, an SS woman stopped me,

---

*   Personal communication.

and as I write this, I still experience the fear I felt then. I was convinced that when she found the boots under my torn coat, it would be my end. When she stopped me, she asked me what I had under my coat, and I had to show her. To my shock, she walked me back to her very nicely furnished room, sat me down, and put the shoes on my feet. This was the only act of kindness I experienced during the entire war years after my mother was taken away and my father died. Although, perhaps I should include the Ukrainians who placed me in front of the food line in Piotrków and the French woman who accepted the fiction that I was 16 years old.

As I sat on the bunk bed, which I always shared with at least one other woman if not more, I would dream of one food: hot chicken soup with rice. I thought of this dish all the time. I would also pick lice from my head and crack them between my nails; a cracking noise I can still hear now. Sitting on the bunk bed, I saw repeatedly a particular image. I heard people speak about how the Allies and the Germans were trying to get a special bomb, and whoever got the bomb first would win the war. I pictured a huge field containing an immense ball in the middle and the two adversaries on each side rushing to get this humongous ball. I imagined that this race to get the ball first would determine the outcome of the war.

Alas, the ball did not come soon enough. In mid-March 1945, there was a selection by the fat SS man and I was selected to be shipped off to Bergen Belsen. We were transported to this concentration camp for reasons that are still baffling to me; I constantly keep thinking: why did they ship us to Bergen Belsen rather than kill us? I recall hearing at the time that the Germans had run out of bullets so they could not shoot us, or that bullets were so scarce that they did not wish to waste them on us. Instead they decided to starve us until we expired, and they almost succeeded with me; some even said they poisoned the little water we got. Scholars of the Holocaust (especially Christopher Browning, with whom I have discussed the issue) who have analyzed German strategies suggest that since Ravensbrück had become exceptionally crowded by then, and the Germans wished to maintain living Jewish bodies as "bargaining chips" with the Allies, they shipped people from Ravensbrück to Bergen Belsen and elsewhere, even if they kept them only barely alive.

In Bergen Belsen, Germany

Bergen Belsen, situated in Northern Germany, is so well known that even to a person entirely unfamiliar with the evils of the German regime, it needs very little introduction; it came into prominence to the American mind particularly during President Reagan's visit, as described by my mother. We were transferred there, to a concentration camp where people were brought to die, a place which brought into bold relief the depth of Germany's depravity.

Whereas I recall suffering from bitter cold in Ravensbrück, especially when we stood for an hour at roll calls, in Bergen Belsen I recall being warm, occasionally even hot. When we arrived there, we were deposited on the sandy floor of a barrack. There were not even bunk beds. We were very closely guarded by an SS woman who had a room in the barrack, separated by a flimsy wall. In this room she cooked, and I could even smell the food. Keeping this very close watch was as irrational as anything else the Germans did. Did they think anyone was capable of running away?

In actual fact, people died like flies, to use a proverbial if mundane metaphor, from one minute to the next. We were not given any food at all; later I learned that there was a virulent typhus epidemic during the time I was there, from which I was miraculously spared. We were intended to just expire. I was lying on the floor next to Renatka Milioner, who was one year younger than me, also from Piotrków. On my other side there was woman who died as I turned towards her to say a few words.

I somehow came across a piece of cheese, although I do not recall how it got to me. I have been told that there was a woman in Bergen Belsen who worked in a kitchen, and she managed to smuggle out some little bits of food to distribute to the children. When I received this precious miniscule piece of cheese and a tiny piece of bread, I searched for my closest friend at the time, Henia Mlynarska, who was in another barrack, before I was totally immobilized by hunger. Henia was one year older than I, and was also from Piotrków; I shared my unexpected good luck with her. I do not know how she came to Bergen Belsen—I do not remember her from Ravensbrück—but in Piotrków, and later in Bergen Belsen and Sweden, we were inseparable. I say this only because it is sometimes said that people in camps were totally selfish, but I do not believe that people failed to share with others if there was something to share, as is also attested by my mother's narrative.

On the way to Henia's barrack, when I could still walk, I passed a heap of beets lying nearby and I vividly recall that as hungry as I was, I thought that I must not take any because it would be stealing and it was wrong. I did not take even one. When I recall that moment, I often wonder at what age children develop a moral conscience. By that point I was already ten years old, and I suppose notions of right and wrong had already been instilled in me.

There is little that I can say about my interminable stay in Bergen Belsen. As the days passed I became weaker and weaker. Having had no food for days on end, I could no longer walk and could barely breathe. People were dying around me. The Germans almost succeeded in achieving their aim of killing us all. But then we were liberated!

Bergen Belsen was liberated by the British army on April 15, 1945. That day is indelibly engraved in my being. Vehicles full of soldiers arrived, wearing strange-looking berets and announcing over loud speakers, "We are here to liberate you. We are your friends." As I write this now shivers still make my body tremble. They must have spoken in Polish, or else in German, which I had picked up a bit during the war. On the day the army arrived the soldiers brought with them bread, sardines, barrels of hot soup, chocolate, and Lifebuoy soap that had a terrible smell. They distributed these foods and the soap as their trucks were entering the camp. When I received the food I did not immediately eat it, as so many did; at first I only ate a little piece of the bread, and then only gradually I ate a little bit more. I did not eat the soup or the sardines straight away either. Ironically, Renatka ate the food at once when it arrived; she died the next day, as she lay next to me. Numerous people passed away after liberation from eating the food because it was difficult to digest so much of it—especially a rich soup—at one time after months of starvation. But I especially recall Renatka because we were close in age. Mother recalled her in her narrative as well, because she and Renatka's mother were together in Skarżysko-Kamienna and they, along with Henia's sister, speculated incessantly over whether we would survive; like my parents, the Milioners had considered for a moment turning their children over to a Polish family, until they, like my father, rejected this possibility.

I weighed less than fifty pounds at the time of liberation. I could no longer walk or speak. With Renatka's passing I may have been one of the youngest people from the Piotrków group, or perhaps even in the whole camp, who managed to survive until liberation and after. Judging by a short list of prisoners and their birth dates that I saw published after the war, Renatka and I may have been the youngest people in the camp. I still cannot understand what constrained me from eating the food immediately after receiving it. Perhaps I was just too weak even to eat. The British meant well, of course, but the consequences were dire.

Mountains of emaciated dead bodies were piled up everywhere in Bergen Belsen by now; it presented an iconic picture of the German atrocities seen everywhere. The British rightly required the Germans to dig giant pits to bury them. We stood watching as the Germans were throwing the bodies with shovels into the giant pits they had to dig. I stood cheering with the little energy I still had; we all cheered. Watching the Germans' miserable faces was the first sweet moment for us all in many years.

It may perhaps not be fitting to reveal the revenge fantasies I harbored during the war and for many months after it ended. My mother in her narrative rejected notions of revenge. I did not. I visualized taking each German I saw and cutting off parts of his or her body, and saying, "This is for my step-grandfather, this is for my 28-year-old uncle Avrumce, this is for my 27-year-old uncle Binim, and this is for my 43-year-old father." I don't know if others had similar images in their minds, but I say unashamedly that they were vivid and I relished them. I speak of it here because this fantasy was very much a part of my childhood experience. I don't know if I would have acted on it even if I'd had the opportunity at the time. I may not have the capacity for this kind of cruelty, but I certainly imagined it then.

Immediately after the liberation there was a lot of activity in Bergen Belsen and people acted with great urgency. I began to take food slowly, but was still very weak. There were all sorts of people there shortly after the liberation; people of various nationalities came into the camp from everywhere. Those first days, after I gradually regained the ability to move slowly around, I began searching and searching for my mother, speaking to anybody I saw, inquiring whether they had seen her anywhere. All survivors searched for somebody from whom they were separated. I went over to one person, then another, asking the same question. While my mother was convinced I was alive because of the dreams she had after we were separated, I had no such dreams but, for some unexplained reason, believed my mother must be alive. I simply felt it: she must be alive.

As Mother also recounts this fortuitous event, a man by the name of Hershel Klepfish, a British citizen, entered Bergen Belsen together with the British Army at the time of the liberation. He spoke to all the children and asked them what they knew about their families. When he questioned me, I told him that I had a grandfather in America. My mother had told me to remember that my grandfather was in the United States; she also wrote his name on the back of a few baby pictures I'd managed to save.

When I told Mr. Klepfish that I had a grandfather in America, he believed that I was confusing the countries because he knew a man in London with exactly the same name as my grandfather, Saul Taub, and he insisted, to my chagrin, that I had simply made a mistake; my grandfather actually lived in London. He immediately notified the man in London that I was alive. As it turned out, the Saul Taub in London was my mother's cousin, who even knew my father and instantly recognized who I was; he telegraphed my grandfather at once that I was alive.

My grandfather, after receiving the card my mother sent to him in Brooklyn, knew her whereabouts, and wrote to me that my mother was alive and living in Poland, having walked back there hoping she would find somebody from her family there. He wrote to my mother that I was alive. She and I were reunited in Sweden a year later, when she was finally able to get a Swedish transit visa, after our four-year separation.

Among the numerous people who came to Bergen Belsen to assist us after the war was a Norwegian woman who wished to adopt me, probably because I was very young and very weak. The Jewish authorities who took charge of the children would not permit any child to be taken from the children's group they formed; those children who remained without any family were to go to

Palestine, but were taken as a group to Sweden first.

I left Bergen Belsen three months and nine days after liberation, in a group of forty-six other children. We were taken to Sweden on a boat provided by Count Folke Bernadotte, a Swedish diplomat, active in the rescue of Jews during the war. The trip to Sweden took us from Bergen Belsen to Bergen and to Lübeck by train, and from there by boat to Malmo. After one day and one night at sea, we arrived in Malmo on July 24, 1945. I had never been on a boat before, and for the entire day crossing the Baltic Sea I was deathly seasick, in addition to being extremely weak.

As I noted before, I believe I was the youngest of the remaining children comprising the group that left Bergen Belsen. Upon our arrival in Sweden, the children, who were mostly in their teens, were divided into two groups, depending on their health; those who were very sick and required rehabilitation were separated from those who were just weak. Together with a handful of others, I was placed in the very sick group; I was separated from the larger group once we reached Sweden, and also from my close girlfriend Henia Mlynarska. I was sent for treatment to a sanatorium in Fiskeboda, in the vicinity of Katzinehom, Sweden, where I spent a month. Once I recovered, I was reunited with the rest of the group, including Henia, which had been sent directly to Bergsjö, Halsingland, in Northern Sweden.

If there were any happy times in my life after my first four years, they were the year I spent in Sweden from July 1945 to April 1946, when we arrived in the United States. Actually, I wished at that time to return to Sweden. My memories of Sweden are of an idyllic life, from the moment I got off the boat.

We were treated royally during the month we were in Fiskeboda; we were given all kinds of therapy to bring us up to normal weight and make us healthy. I was literally brought back to life. My grandfather sent me money; I was able to buy a watch and a bicycle, and to my delight learned how to ride the bicycle. The sanatorium was situated in a beautiful area of the country, near a lake; there was an abundance of food and one particular dish we were fed seemed very strange: fish cooked in milk. I began to regain my weight, but not my height for my age. The starvation may well have stunted my growth, and I have remained about the same height ever since. I recently returned to Fiskeboda, but the sanatorium was turned into a school and I could not recognize anything there now.

When we recovered, we were transferred by train to Borgsjö. Our stay there was a very happy one for all of us. There I learned from my grandfather that my mother was alive; I was also reunited with my friend Henia. I learned how to speak Swedish, and how to write Polish fluently; I wrote letters to my mother and grandfather, some of which I have in my possession but, ironically, can barely read now.

From the moment my grandfather learned about my survival until I left Sweden, I engaged in a vigorous correspondence with him. These brief letters—in Polish—remind me of both our momentous and our immediate concerns. When he reported to me that my mother was alive, I wrote to him about my longing to see her, and how I thanked God that I still had a mother, but I then added, "I lost my dear father. It is difficult but maybe that was the way it had to be." As I read this sentence now I'm taken aback by my fatalistic sentiment. In another letter I complained to him that after I met my mother in Sweden she would not buy herself anything new to wear.

Most of my grandfather's correspondence to me, which he wrote on a typewriter in Yiddish, concerned the logistics of getting visas for us to enter the United States. First, my mother needed one to enter Sweden. To accomplish this feat, he entrusted me with sending the necessary papers to my mother, because at the time there was registered mail between the United States and Sweden but not between the United States and Poland. I was still the child bearing adult responsibilities.

Since I may have been the only one in the group who had family in America, I suppose I was a bit better off than the rest of the children. My grandfather sent me money twice—50 dollars, a fortune at the time—and I shared whatever I bought with Henia. We alternated wearing the watch I bought in Fiskeboda; she wore it one day and I the next. I have retained some of the memorabilia from that time to this day, including a little white furry reindeer that I keep with me.

We lived a heavenly life in the small provincial town of Borgsjö. The winter was long, the town was covered with beautiful white snow; we became children again, playing in the snow, designing figures on it, stretching out on our backs. We learned Hebrew songs, although I don't know where and when I initially learned to read the language. At the time of the Christmas holiday, about which

I had no knowledge, people from the town came to serenade us with traditional candles and songs; I especially recall enjoying the beautiful Swedish Christmas carol, "Santa Lucia."

When I returned years later to Sweden, I found a list of children brought to Borgsjö in the Swedish archives in Stockholm, which included my name. Again, when I saw my name I cried out in surprise. I also visited Borgsjö at that time, and introduced myself to the local mayor. I received a very warm welcome.

I arrived in Borgsjö around September 1945, and remained there till January 1946, when I was moved to the home of a Rabbi Jacobson in Stockholm to await my mother's arrival. From there we were to leave for the United States. Stockholm, too, was wonderful in the winter. My grandfather obtained a visa for me, but it was more difficult to get one for my mother, and we had to wait in Stockholm for its arrival. It was delightful to stay with the Jacobsons, who were exceedingly kind and generous to me. They lived in a spacious, warmly furnished apartment, and they made me feel very welcome there. They bought me skis, in the Pub department store; both the skis and the department store were marvels for me. I learned how to ski and move around in the city that way in the winter. There was also a Rabbi Wolber, who may have been a convert to Judaism, who was very attentive to me. Everyone with whom I came into contact was affectionate and caring; a very welcome change from the years in the camps. Every time I return to this city, even in recent years, I delight in it.

One day in February 1946, February 17 to be exact, I came into the Jacobson house from the outside; when I walked in, Mrs. Jacobson pointed to a little suitcase standing in the entrance hall. I can still picture the suitcase and I was puzzled as to why she was showing me a suitcase. I looked and gradually my mother entered the hallway from the other room. I nearly burst with joy on seeing my mother. The reunion with her after all those years of separation was overwhelming. As I write about it now, I can relive the joy, shock, and excitement of seeing her again. By then, of course, I had known she was alive for quite some time, but to see her in person was astonishing.

After my mother's arrival, Rabbi Jacobson moved us to yet another exquisite place, the Grand Hotel Saltjebäden, about half an hour away from Stockholm by train, where we waited for my mother's visa to arrive. Being in Saltjebäden was sheer happiness. The Grand Hotel, a luxury hotel of great elegance, is situated on a lake; at the time we were there, the lake was completely frozen and we were able to walk on it. I had never seen such luxury, and we wallowed in it. We had a stunningly furnished large room, and the staff brought us breakfast served on a silver tray and in silver dishes. Tea was brought into the room in silver tea sets. I return to the hotel every time I visit Sweden. While I may find it less impressive today because I am more accustomed to such amenities, it remains an elegantly appointed hotel, and even now has the same magic for me. Here we exchanged information about our war experiences, about which later we spoke little.

When we met in Sweden after the long separation and sat watching the frozen lake across from the beautiful hotel, I told her what had happened to me from the time of our separation. My mother may have heard some of it from people she had met after the war, especially people from the ghetto in Piotrków. They told her about how badly I was treated by the Jewish family to whom I was entrusted by the President of the Judenrat when my father passed away; this was probably the first fact about my life during the war that I told her. Being harshly treated by "one's own" was as unbearable, or even more so, than the German's treatment, precisely because the Jewish family's behavior toward me was personal, whereas the Germans handled everybody the same. I learned about my mother's experiences during the war in general terms. I knew she had worked in ammunition factories, but not the details she narrates here. Much later I learned about the calendar and prayer book she wrote, but she never spoke to me about having been on the death march.

We remained in the enchanted environment of the Grand Hotel of Saltjebäden about three weeks, until my mother's visa arrived in April. We returned to Stockholm right away to prepare for the trip to the United States. My mother describes the difficulties involved in obtaining a ticket for a boat, for which my grandfather paid, but which we could not purchase until she had her visa in hand. Rabbi Jacobson miraculously managed to get passage for us a day after the visa arrived. We left Stockholm running for the airplane to get to Goteborg Port. I was saddened to leave Sweden but both my mother and I were grateful to Rabbi Jacobson for his magnificent assistance. I was sorry too that, because we left so suddenly, I left my skis behind; we arrived in the United States with only one small suitcase. I was terribly airsick on the airplane to Goteborg, to such an extent that there was some talk about the airplane making a special stop to leave me off. The flight was not long, but it seemed fatal.

We traveled on the S. S. Drottningholm, which carried 840 passengers, for 14 days. The boat went around Scotland to avoid the English Channel, which was still mined at the time. Our cabin was located on the bottom of the ship. I don't know whether this was due to cost or to lack of availability of a better-situated cabin, but I was seasick and in misery for the entire trip. I was actually lifeless most of the days on the boat, until we reached shore. When we arrived in New York, I instantly recovered; that is the nature of seasickness. Because most food on the boat was not kosher, the only food available to us was canned salmon; when I was awake I was given the fish with some bread, but I could not hold it down. I would not touch canned salmon for many years afterwards.

As I write this, and it is the first time I have spoken about my war experiences since the war ended, except to my mother in Saltjebäden; I continue to be amazed that I remained living. I still do not understand how I managed to fall through the cracks, so to speak. I celebrate being alive, but while I do not recall having cried during the war years except when I was separated from my mother and when the police wanted to take my uncle Binim away in Warsaw, I cry now over those years and all that I lost, including the kind of protected childhood that I discovered in Sweden was possible.

My mother spoke mostly dispassionately when recounting her war years. I still feel rage seething; and I have not stopped meditating on how it was that I, a child left by herself from about the age of seven, stayed alive and endured. How I managed to hide from William and his dog; how I avoided being smothered by a relative; how I was not selected by a German's flip of the thumb for a crematorium when we left the synagogue in Piotrków, or in Ravensbrück when such selections took place; how I knew to declare myself to be 16 when we arrived in Ravensbrück; how I knew to eat only tiny portions of food upon liberation. My mother believed that our ancestors saved me. I would like to think this is so, but perhaps it was simply luck, with some assistance of wits. I often look at children of that age now and wonder whether they would have managed to survive in those circumstances.

Unfortunately, I am an only child. When I asked my mother why she had not had any more children, she immediately said that given the talk of war soon after my birth, she believed it was best not to bring any more children into the world, even though, as she recounted herself, they never imagined atrocities of the magnitude that came to pass. She was prescient, but I have been, naturally, greatly dismayed all my life by not having a sibling. Perhaps she would have pushed her luck in having more than one child, but that lack of a sibling is yet another effect of the war on my life.

CHAPTER 7
The Child Becomes an Adult

An account of my life when I reached full adulthood, with all the twists and turns my professional and personal lives took—all the turmoil, tribulations and satisfactions—properly belongs in a separate book. Here I briefly sketch the beginnings of my adulthood after we arrived in the United States until I graduated from college; during this period my own and my mother's lives overlapped, albeit with different experiences. After I graduated from college our lives diverged more than before, although we remained inexorably tied; we never lived completely separate lives until her passing.

When we arrived in the United States on April 16, 1946, we were received not only by my mother's family but also by many reporters. A picture showing me standing next to my grandfather's commanding figure was published in numerous newspapers. The reunion was overwhelming. All my mother's many-years-younger siblings received us: five brothers (the youngest one was one year younger than I), two of whom were married, and two sisters, both married. We were immediately taken to my grandfather's house in Brooklyn and given a little room with a small window and a single bed. In Sweden I was taught to curtsy to older people and I did so at first. By then I still spoke Polish, Swedish, and even some German. Yiddish was our language of communication with the family.

Looking later at the various newspaper clippings, including one from the New York Times, I realized as my mother had that newspaper accounts were often misleading. Some of the articles gave my age incorrectly; others reported mistakenly that we came from Belgium. My mother and I also became aware that telling people about our experiences frustrated rather than relieved us, because such events were incomprehensible to almost everyone, especially immediately after the war, when little was reported about the murders, crimes, and camps. As my mother observed, we both concluded that it was best to be silent, as I have done till now.

Shortly after we arrived I received countless "fan letters"—from children (pen-pals) my age from different parts of the country. I could not read them myself, or, regrettably, respond to them then, not knowing English, but these letters were heartwarming. The writers, mainly young girls, were desirous of my friendship, as I learned from my mother's younger sisters' translations. As I reread them now, I marvel at their warmth but also at their different concerns from mine at the time: these letters speak of their ages, pets, schools they attend: all such interests were alien to me then.

During those first weeks I found many things strange, such as the bridges, and the empty trolley cars moving through the Brooklyn streets. I was unable to understand why no one travelled in them and felt sorry for the drivers that they had no "customers." But most of all I was puzzled, at first, by seeing people coming out of the subways into the street. I had learned early in life that when the Messiah comes, the dead would rise and come out of the earth. When I saw people coming out of what I learned later was the subway, I thought the dead had arisen and that my own father, step-grandfather and uncles would come up. I was disabused of these thoughts quickly, but I still recall them now.

My mother describes how difficult it was for her from the very beginning to find a suitable place to live, and to provide a livelihood for us both. While I was conscious of how pained she was by our new situation, I was unable to help her. I felt helpless watching her anguish. All I did was cling to her—at the beginning I would not leave her even for a moment.

My mother's father expected my mother to remarry immediately after we arrived. He had an appropriate suitor in mind, but she was so shattered after the war that she could not contemplate marriage. I cannot say I gave her any encouragement in that regard, fearing that she would be taken away from me once again. Later, when she might have considered remarrying, it seems that no suitable suitors were available. At first, whatever tension my mother had felt relating to her father dissolved, despite her discomfort in living in the tiny room in his house with his very unpleasant fourth wife. Perhaps the reason he did not prepare comfortable living arrangements for us was because he thought my mother would want to remarry shortly after we arrived and create a home of her own. He failed to understand that her selfhood was destroyed by the war;

she wouldn't recoup her vitality until much later. Actually, he knew little about his firstborn child and the independent person that she was. He held to the traditional view that a woman must not be without a husband and must marry, as indeed most people surviving the war did, establishing new families.

We arrived a few weeks before Passover, and I recall the first Seder we celebrated with my mother's father and the family. It was a joyous occasion. As is customary, the house was made especially spotless in preparation for the holiday; a long table was set out in the basement room, the largest room of the house. My mother's father composed a special melody, known as "Golda's nigun," to celebrate our survival. My mother's next-to-youngest brother, regrettably now deceased, sang especially enthusiastically my grandfather's many compositions for the Seder. The entire evening was filled with song and dance around the table. I asked the four questions in the Haggada that I vaguely remembered from the time my own father taught me to ask them in Otwock. Curiously, I did not recall a Seder in our own house from before or during the war, including in the Warsaw ghetto; this was the first Seder of which I was aware. My mother's father had a sonorous voice indeed, and I also loved to hear him movingly pray. Yet, despite his love of music and his religious fervor, my memories of him are of a tall man with a huge belly that seemed even more prominent when I saw him lying on the sofa. In contrast to his letters to me, he was aloof, unlike my mother's stepfather (whom, like my mother, I had also called Fete, or uncle), who never ceased attending to me. True, at this time I was no longer a cute little child. I was an unhappy, anxious eleven-year-old at the threshold of becoming a young woman.

Shortly after our arrival in the United States, my mother began to search for ways to support us, as she so poignantly recounts. My mother's work history in the United States was an exceedingly painful chapter in her life, and as I return to considering those years the hurt I felt for her then also returns. It is difficult to convey how demeaning it was for her to have become a "finisher." A woman who was raised in the hub of a Hasidic court, serving as an example for numerous others in her surroundings, now lost her social standing in her own eyes. As dehumanizing as it was being in the camps, everybody was similarly doomed; but here people lived normally, even prospered, yet her attempts to escape that "lowly" position met with failure, leaving her even more impotent than during the years in the camps, arguably, unless she had quickly remarried.

I was placed in school, and needed to dedicate myself to study, while feeling helpless, unable to aid her in her searches or by working since I was still too young to seek any kind of employment. Besides, she did not even consider my getting any job that would detract from my education. She placed my education at the forefront of our lives. Until we came to America, I'd had an unsystematic and rudimentary schooling. I had a lot of catching up to do academically.

My mother placed me in a religious school when we arrived. After about one term, she felt the school was not providing sufficient classes in secular subjects and decided to transfer me to a public school. When we arrived in the United States I spoke various languages. It was extremely difficult at first to learn to speak and write English; English spelling was especially torturous. My mother would sit with me before every spelling test and drill me on each word. Whatever Polish words I had learned, I could spell as they were pronounced. English was a great mystery, since there are so many words consisting of silent sounds that cannot be spelled phonetically. I labored on words such as "enough," and many others that I could not memorize by pronouncing each letter. Perhaps because it was so tough for me to learn the language, in later life I became sensitive to errors in spoken or written English. I find it grating to my ears when I hear English mangled. But I must hasten to add that until the age of "spell checks" I could not say I felt secure in the spelling of English words.

I attended primary school for about two and a half years. My memories of this school are associated mainly with its requirement to pledge allegiance to the flag, which made me uncomfortable for reasons I cannot explain even now. The school authorities encouraged me to take the entrance examination for Hunter High School, one of several special high schools for bright pupils in New York. Unfortunately, I was informed that I had failed the English part of the examination. It is worth noting at this juncture how difficult it is to be a refugee in a new country, not only for adults but also for children. The drawbacks include not only having to learn new ways, customs, and language, which children learn quicker than their elders, but also ignorance of the opportunities available to them. Nevertheless, I was fortunate that the elementary school authorities directed me to this opportunity. I recognized later, after graduating from high school and beginning to search for jobs, how little a new immigrant can know about educational and work opportunities, especially before the internet and other such technological tools were invented to make such information more easily accessible now.

To compensate for my lack of Jewish education, my mother sent me to an afternoon Hebrew school. I cannot say that it was a profound educational experience. I was happier when she also sent me to ballet lessons despite her meager earnings, but as much as I loved dancing, my talents lay elsewhere, although at the time I did not know where. To her and my regret I could not learn to play the piano because we had no possibility of buying one, nor would we even have had a place to put it, since we lived in one room.

My mother had always yearned to go to Israel. The British left Palestine on May 14, 1948, and Israel was declared a State that year, at which time all Jews could enter it. In 1949, my mother decided that we would move to Israel, greatly encouraged by her brother Leibl, who was a pioneer there. She had the same feelings for this brother as she had for the two brothers, Avrumce and Binum, that she had lost during the war; they were almost like her sons, since she nurtured them as children during their mother's illness.

We went to Israel in the summer of 1949, when I graduated from elementary school. Once we arrived, I was placed in a high school in Jerusalem, where my uncle lived, that offered both a religious and a secular education. Now defunct, at the time it was considered one of the best high schools in that city. I began learning Hebrew formally, and all other subjects were taught in Hebrew. To my mother's satisfaction, I received an excellent secular education that year. Included among the various subjects was Arabic, which I found fascinating because it seemed so similar to Hebrew, but also challenging, with a teacher who had a terrible temper. He was of the old German school, believing that if a student failed to learn correct Arabic verb conjugations it was appropriate to pull the student by the ear out of the classroom and into the courtyard and beat him. He would strike a girl more gently with a ruler on the hand for the same failure. Fortunately, I escaped his ire, but I was deathly afraid of him. The other teachers in the school were actually pleasant, and much of what I learned that year I have still retained; alas, Arabic not so much. I also improved my English writing skills, taught by an Englishman, which at the time were still not well honed.

My uncle, who was an autodidact and had a special love for the Hebrew language and for me, decided to enlist one of his friends, a specialist in the Hebrew language, to privately teach me Hebrew grammar. I always think of this very gentle woman and her instructions with great affection; and while my Hebrew may be at times a bit rusty due to lack of practice, I have retained a good knowledge of Hebrew grammar and have no difficulty communicating in the language. I found great joy in learning Hebrew grammar, which I found especially logical. I discovered that by knowing the syntax I could construct new words that I had not heard before but which were part of the Hebrew language. I loved learning new languages and subsequently learned others. Some I have also forgotten.

We lived with my uncle and his family, including his wife, who was my mother and uncle's first cousin, and their three children. My mother recounted earlier how difficult it was in Israel at the time; aside from the food rationing and shortages, my uncle had few economic resources, and it was tough for the entire household to make ends meet. In preparation for our arrival, my uncle moved his family from a one room to a three-room apartment in the same house, despite his meager income. The apartment was on the second floor of a nineteenth-century stone house with stone floors that was cool in the summer but freezing during a Jerusalem winter; the 1949-1950 winter was one of the rare ones when it actually snowed there. The shower was on the other side of the balcony, heated by a gas burner. Taking a shower there was actually an adventure, especially in the winter, requiring much preparation for heating the water with a propane tank. We had a large sunny room, furnished with comfortable beds and a chest of drawers. One day, I went over to the chest of drawers and there were five tiny kittens lying inside. I have no idea how they got into the room or the chest of drawers, but when I saw them I yelled in terror, since at that time I still had a great fear of any living animal.

Aside from unemployment, poverty and the difficulties resulting from the national food shortages at this time in Israel's history—my aunt made "chopped liver" out of eggplant, and prepared fish to taste like meat—we were happy to be with my uncle's family. They had a lot of friends, and people would visit daily but especially on the Sabbath. Or we would visit my uncle's very devoted friends about an hour's walk from our house on the Sabbath, when it is common in Orthodox households for people to visit one another. The holidays were especially happy and the one Seder we spent with my uncle, his family, and their friends was jubilant, even though food was scarce.

During the week my mother, too, studied Hebrew, and I was in school most of the day. I made friends, even though I was still learning the language and it was difficult to communicate with the other children at first. I made friends especially with one girl who had lost her mother and whose father had a terrible temper and spent his life locked in the house reading mystery stories. I suspect our friendship was founded on a shared sadness. When I was not in school and wished to be by myself, I would read novels in English, but I do not remember the titles. I definitely recall that these books were about young girls like me, but they lived in beautiful houses.

As my mother relates, we returned to the United States after a year for various reasons, mostly because economic scarcity and unemployment were so great in Israel that she could not see any future in remaining there. But once we were back in New York, it was again a terrible struggle for my mother to find lodgings and work.

I wished to attend what then was considered one of the best high schools in Brooklyn, Erasmus High School, but we lived out of the district. To get around this problem, I gave my aunt's address as my residence. This was partially correct, since I spent many days in my aunt's house when my mother was at work. The high school gave me full credit for my year of study in Israel, including language credit for Hebrew. I thus completed high school in two years and two summers when I was 17 and a half years old; miraculously I had been able to catch up despite the lost years of the war.

In my first English class in high school, we were required to write a composition about the book *Wuthering Heights* by Emily Bronte. I was in agony. I was sure I did not know how to write a long essay. I consulted with a classmate, but she knew even less than I. I finally managed to compose something and with great trepidation handed it to the teacher, thinking that this would be a disaster. The day the teacher returned our compositions, she asked for Finkler to stand up; hearing my name being called out, I was certain she would use my essay to instruct the students how not to write one. To my astonishment, she did read my composition to the class, and then announced that it was the best composition she had received in many a year from any student.

But high school was not all that easy for me. Not only did I feel estranged, but I did not do well in classes with unkind teachers. I especially recall my algebra teacher, who did not like me. I thought she was a sadist; she frightened me, as she may have other students. Needless to say, I did poorly in algebra, although I managed to squeak by. I had a wonderful teacher for geometry, flourished in that class, and excelled in the subject. Because I wished to finish high school as soon as possible, in my last semester I enrolled in two required English classes concurrently rather than consecutively. In one class I did extremely well and in the other I didn't, because of the helpfulness of one teacher and the disdain of the other. Young people can flower only with caring teachers who encourage them; this was probably the most important lesson I learned from my high school experience, and I attempted to apply it when I became a university professor.

The high school assigned a special teacher to work with me on eliminating my accent. She was a kind, somewhat elderly woman, but unfortunately, she would fall asleep while attempting to teach me correct Standard English pronunciation. I don't know if her instructions would have helped even if she were wide awake when she taught me. At home my mother and I spoke Yiddish. As I mentioned, following the war my mother refused to speak Polish to anyone. After some years, when I became a fluent English speaker, albeit with a slight unidentifiable accent, my mother, who learned English as well, wished to speak English with me. I could not do so. I felt her frustration, but to the last days of her life I could only converse with her in Yiddish. I always tried to explain to her that to speak to her in any other language would be as if I spoke to a stranger.

Because my spoken English remained influenced by other languages, and a bit accented, when I became a professional anthropologist and interviewed for my first professional position outside

New York City, I wondered if I would get a job at all. I assured myself that I had a chance at getting a position with my slight accent because at the time Henry Kissinger was Secretary of State, and he had previously been an academic at a university, speaking with a much more highly pronounced German accent than I. Listening to Kissinger, I consoled myself that I too had a prospect of being hired in academia. Indeed, people outside of New York usually take my accent to be a variant of "New Yorkese."

In the last month before I was due to graduate from high school, I developed measles, which seemed like a tragedy to us because I was unable to take the Regents exams that were required in New York State in order to graduate. To my great relief, my history teacher Mrs. Andrews, whose name I still recall, intervened, and I was excused from having to take these examinations on the strength of my overall grades. I recovered in time to attend my high school graduation and have my picture entered in the 1952 yearbook. My mother gave me a beautiful gold necklace for my graduation present, which she was able to purchase at a much-discounted price. I still cherish it.

Whether by temperament or because of my past experiences, I felt alienated from my classmates both in elementary and high school. I believed that I knew what they never could know. I didn't feel I had anything in common with them, although I did enjoy playing handball after school with some of the children in elementary school. I disliked being in high school, and to this day I still find it strange when I hear people speaking with nostalgia about their high school years, or attending high school reunions. Because at first I lived outside the high school's district and far away from my classmates, I made very few friends. I didn't participate in any extracurricular activities in high school, nor did I attend the prom or pay attention to it. I didn't know anything about it. When classes were over, I immediately went home. My circle of reference was my family and my mother's friends. My mother loved the opera, theater, and movies, as I do now. We would purchase standing room tickets at the Metropolitan opera. We would go often to the movies, the most affordable entertainment for us, which for my mother was certainly a moment of escape. "Let's go to the movies" was a refrain we had when either of us was especially unhappy. I particularly recall our outings to the Paramount Theater in downtown Brooklyn; it was an impressive edifice with elegantly appointed seats. Sharing the same images with the crowds of movie-goers—movie houses were always full then—was comforting and even thrilling. But most of the time we went to neighborhood movie houses that were not as special as the Paramount, although also teeming with people. The trips to the theater or opera were more special, of course.

Since we had very little money, throughout the years we would amuse ourselves by reading the advertisements in English newspapers, and if we dreamt of traveling here or there, we always ended up saying jokingly, "Well, let's go to the Bronx." For us, Brooklynites, the Bronx seemed the outer extension of the universe. But we never did go there for leisure travel purposes. We played chess and monopoly. Various people, including my mother's siblings and several Yiddish writers, would come to visit us, and there were discussions about politics, foreign affairs, literature, and other such weighty matters. I essentially grew up among adults, very much enjoying being among them.

Throughout my years in elementary school, high school, and when I was a full-time student in college I cleaned the house and prepared supper for us so that my mother would not have these responsibilities. I would eagerly await her coming home, and I always knew she was near the apartment when I heard her distinctive, sure-footed steps in the hall. I found it sad to arrive home from high school to an empty apartment. I waited for her during this period in much the same way as when we were in the small ghetto in Piotrków and I stood at the window waiting for her to return from where she worked. Even during the years I attended college, I loved coming home if my mother was already there. But more often she was at work.

Knowing how unhappy my mother was at her various jobs, as soon as I graduated from high school I insisted that she stop working. I said I would work to support both of us, and I began working immediately after graduation. It was extraordinarily distressing to me to see her despondent; even her description of her efforts fails to convey her anguish during those years. Despite my insistence, it was disillusioning to me that she refused to cease working; in truth her earnings were greater than mine at the time. I still kept urging her to leave her employment, but she, being fiercely self-reliant, continued to work until she was eligible to retire and receive Social Security.

The summer immediately after my high school graduation, I worked as a camp counselor at a hotel in the Catskills. In the fall, I found my first job at the Metropolitan Life Insurance Company of New York at $37.50 a week, where, I believe, I may have been the first Jewish person hired at the company. I began by working at what seems today like a primitive copy machine, and was told that I would be groomed for various jobs in the company hierarchy. The work was terribly boring, but it held promise for advancement. Not long after I began working, the Jewish holidays came around; naively, I requested time off. The company refused to give me a few unpaid days and I was promptly fired.

After my experience with the Metropolitan Life Insurance Company, I taught myself to type properly on a typewriter and began to look for office employment, including bookkeeping, among Jewish people who would allow me to take off for Jewish holidays. I worked for one of my uncles in his office, and while I have forgotten, I may have had several other such jobs. In one of these work places, the owner, not a relative but known to my family, had designs on me that I didn't appreciate. I left immediately. I hated having to look for jobs, normally by answering want ads in the newspapers. I found it mortifying. Finally I landed a bookkeeping job in the garment district of New York, among secular Jews, who agreed that as long as I got my work done, I could take any time off I wished. This type of arrangement suited my temperament best; the job gave me responsibilities and the independence to decide how I used my time as long as the work was done. Since I had to prepare a weekly payroll for over 40 people, during the Jewish holidays I would take the work home and complete it when the holiday was over at night. I still recall fondly this workplace, since I functioned as my own boss, so to speak, and the owners appreciated my dedication.

While working in this office I began to attend Brooklyn College, taking courses in the evening. I worked and studied. It was a heady period in my life, despite having to get up at a very early hour, travel to my job on the subway for one hour, then travel for another hour to school, after finishing work at 5 p.m. When classes finished at around 10 p.m., some classmates and I met till about one in the morning, when I would travel on the subway for another hour to return home. During the period of work and study, I spent about three hours on the subway daily, and unknowingly must have honed my anthropological skills as an observer of people. Since I did much of my reading of newspapers and class assignments on the subway, I wished to have a seat when I got on the train in the morning and on my return from Manhattan to college in Brooklyn. I developed a strategy of guessing who would get off at certain stops, and I would stand in front of the person I assessed would get off well before my own stop. Once the person got off, I could sit down and do my reading quietly, oblivious to my surroundings. I was surprised how often I succeeded in getting a seat, using my improvised tactics.

Shortly after entering college I met two fellow students, Margot and Jerry, in my Comparative Literature course, and we began meeting at a bar after class to discuss literature and anything else that came to mind until late into the night. And when Jerry, the oldest and most erudite of the three of us, mentioned a book, I ran on Sunday to the splendid Grand Army Plaza library, which I had delighted in throughout my elementary and high school years, to get the book and read it on the subway. During that time, I read numerous books that I have not forgotten to this day. I especially recall reading Franz Kafka, and James Joyce's *Portrait of the Artist as a Young Man*, in which Joyce recounts a sermon given by a priest about hell that was so foreign to me I simply dropped the book on the subway floor in astonishment. Our group of three mushroomed to about twenty people, meeting regularly until we left the school. The three of us were poor. I lived with my mother; Margot lived in a third floor walk-up cold-water flat on 20th Street, and Jerry resided in Greenwich Village. It was during this period that my friends introduced me to Greenwich Village, the café Rienzi and other such haunts that I frequented on occasions. I think of this as one of my most exhilarating phases in my life, despite my exhaustion at times.

During this period of my college career a couple of my male college mates had sought me out, but I did not take them seriously enough to consider dating because they were not of my background. I lost contact with various people of that time in my life, particularly after I left for Europe. Correspondence by letters usually lost its intensity after a certain time. O, but for the advantages of email then, if one had chosen to continue a friendship! But I met two women who have remained my friends, who I visit when in New York. They were the only ones in college who knew my history, only because they, in different ways, were both of similar backgrounds. The three of us went on a memorable vacation together, my first as an adult, to Nantucket and Martha's Vineyard, an experience I still cherish. We composed songs about our travels by plane, boat, and bicycle. I even had a brief fling during the trip with a young man I was certain my ancestors would not have deemed appropriate for me. But then, early on I often wrestled with the thought of whether my beloved deceased family would approve of any persons I felt were appealing. It was also during this period that I began to move away from my religious upbringing and move into the secular world experientially but not physically.

I fantasized about meeting fascinating people with exciting ideas. I distinctly recall wistfully thinking then that by leaving Orthodoxy, I might lose the possibilities it offered and the rich ritual life. I still recall how overwhelmed I was during High Holiday prayers at the synagogue, which inspire me to this day. Perhaps I absorbed my ancestors' mysticism from one side of my family and the rationality from another. Yet I did leave, which took me on a totally different course from my ancestors, my peers in the Jewish community in New York, and to some extent from my mother. The world I came into on my own was stimulating but also disappointing because, as I have found, I entered a world where human relations tend to be arid, competitive, and much less gratifying than what I had anticipated when I left my natal community. But I did not know that at the time.

Even before I entered college, I aspired to travel, to see the world, to study, to engage in life in ways I could not living in an Orthodox community and following all the commandments. I eventually fulfilled my aspirations, at the cost of abandoning the prescribed rhythm of life into which I was born, a rhythm punctuated by observance of dietary commandments, the Sabbath, and the holidays. Time was marked by the sacred calendar: whether an event took place or was to take place before or after the Sabbath, before or after a specific holiday. You either looked forward to these days or looked back after they had passed.

When my mother was a young woman, she was exposed to French and Russian literature, and having one foot in the Polish intelligentsia at her university, she, like Polish intellectuals of that time, looked toward France for her intellectual nourishment. She instilled in me the appreciation of the French language, which she had studied privately. So I devised my own version of what is now common, but was at that time rare, a study-abroad program. Since my mother had not stopped working, I saved $200 dollars from my employment, and decided in 1955 to leave the secretarial-bookkeeping job in the garment district that I liked to spend a year in France at the Sorbonne and the Alliance Française. I did so from 1955-1956, also one of the most stimulating years of my life, studying the French language at the Alliance Française, and French civilization at the Sorbonne. Since at the time the French government subsidized all students living in France, I benefitted from numerous discounts in restaurants, theaters, and train travel. I resided in the American Pavilion of the Cité Internationale Universitaire de Paris, where I first met people from all over the world. I learned from my American southern roommate that, to my astonishment, Christians were not an undifferentiated category of people, that Protestants did not like Catholics. I heard Spanish spoken for the first time—a language I subsequently became fluent in but at the time found exasperating. I became fluent in French, however, with the help of a French boyfriend, Noel; I had one or two other romances, including a suitor from India (I had never before met a person from India), who brought me flowers for the Jewish New Year. Noel followed me to Israel, hoping that we would marry.

During my year in France I supported myself by giving private English lessons. I had several pupils, one of whom was the owner of a well known art gallery on Paris' left bank, where I met some renowned painters. This particular pupil felt she needed to learn English, despite the fact that, as she reminded me often, for 500 years her ancestors would not speak English. To her misfortune she had to learn it now because of the many Americans that came to the gallery. I struggled to keep her attention on English, but she was more interested in taking me to haute couture houses to look at their collections. She invited me to her Swiss chalet, situated in a lovely Swiss village, and taught me curling; to my frustration she continued to resist learning English. During school breaks, friends and I took brief trips to London and Italy, each trip marked by various adventures that would take up too much space to describe here.

After I completed my year in France and before leaving Europe, I returned to Israel to visit my family. This was in 1956, at the time of the Suez crisis. My mother sent frantic telegrams that I must return immediately to the United States. To allay her fears of my being in great danger, I did so. I returned on a boat, where I also met a wonderful fellow who was two years younger than me. At the time I felt the age discrepancy jarring; he was from California and dreamed of flying a plane, an exotic occupation in my view. He asked me to return with him to Los Angeles. He was my first true love, and I wished to go with him despite these reservations, but my mother mobilized her sister to dissuade me from leaving with him; besides, they said, he was not a fitting mate for me. Throughout my adult life, I have always said that I usually regretted that which I had not done, rather than that which I had done.

Once I returned to New York in 1956, after this stirring romance, I enrolled as a full time student at Brooklyn College, then regarded as one of the city colleges sometimes referred to as the "Harvard of the poor." I continued to live at home with my mother since, in my family, children left a household only when they married. Actually it had never even occurred to me that I could move away from my home and parent. In our Hasidic subculture, children do not become independent of their parents ever, and the norm is that they do not move out of their homes until they are ready to set up their own family and household. I lived with my mother in her home until I graduated from college, except for the year I lived abroad. I only moved away to the Bronx when I began working as an office administrator at a university there, because it seemed terribly far away to travel to work from Brooklyn, even for a New Yorker. Later, after I began graduate school, I moved to Manhattan, close to my school. But all that would take me too far afield to dwell upon here.

When I returned from France, Margot and Jerry were no longer attending Brooklyn College, nor were the other people in our group. When I had attended college in the evening I took disparate courses that led me in different intellectual directions, but when

I returned as a full time student I decided to major in philosophy because of my Israeli autodidact uncle, who always philosophized about everything, and in psychology because I believed courses in psychology would enlighten me about the inner turmoil I was experiencing. They did no such thing. I hasten to add that I had magnificent professors in psychology, one of whom was so persuasive that he turned me into a Freudian for a long time. I realized later that Freud's theories might even have been destructive to me, since I usually applied all the theories I learned in college to my personal life. I firmly believe that those who were guided by Freudian theorizing in and out of academia, especially those theories relating to women in general and to mother-daughter relations in particular, may have been more harmed than enlightened by them. Conversely, I have never forgotten Dr. Austin Wood, a psychology professor—who was not a Freudian—who after my graduation hired me as his assistant and whose seminar I attended in my last year of college. Professor Girden, in experimental psychology, along with Dr. Wood, encouraged me to pursue a graduate degree in psychology. They suggested that I apply to schools outside of New York, which seemed to me an outlandish proposal. To leave New York, and move elsewhere! To move west of the Hudson River had never entered my mind until I completed my graduate training in anthropology and was offered my first professional position, in Michigan.

My undergraduate college years were exciting, except when I had to pass a swimming test to graduate. I had to dive into the pool to get my swimming certificate. After many days of standing at the pool fearful of jumping in I finally asked the instructor to gently push me in. Once she did, I found jumping in the pool invigorating. I learned from this very minor episode that sometimes we need a light shove to go on with our existence.

After two years at Brooklyn College and a summer term at New York University, I completed the Bachelor of Arts degree. I had wonderful professors and fellow students, with whom I have regrettably lost contact, with a couple of exceptions. Some years later, when I began graduate work in anthropology, the environment was tension-provoking and competitive, the competition not infrequently generated by professors, unlike in Brooklyn College.

During my very last semester in college I stumbled into a course in anthropology and discovered that the anthropological view of cultural differences explained my confusion, discomfort, and estrangement in ways my study of psychology had not. Nevertheless, after graduation in 1958, I entered a graduate psychology program in City College at the urging of my two psychology professors. I didn't think that a graduate degree would eventually become a source of livelihood, but I hoped my studies would somehow illuminate my feelings of not fitting in. The discipline of psychology explained little, if anything, to me because it tended to ignore cultural differences. I also recognized that I stood on a weak foundation, despite having, as some would say "the resilience of youth," because of the years of separation from my mother and father and my experiences in the camps, in addition to my very different cultural background. I thus concluded that it was not my faulty psyche that was the problem, but the disparate, conflicting and multiple cultural environments in which I lived and which molded me, each in separate ways.

I abandoned my study of psychology after a year in graduate school, partly because my mother had a gallstone operation and I needed to tend to her, and partly because of my realization that the discipline did not suit me: it didn't explain why I felt so much like an outsider. My past experiences, along with my limited exposure to anthropology at the time, led me to grasp that I was living in two worlds: the world of experiences not shared by those in the world of work and college, and the Hasidic world of my ancestors, which was highly esoteric even to most Jewish people in the United States, let alone to the rest of the society. It is, after all, as I said at the outset, a subculture of a subculture of the Jewish minority. Having come from a very high-status family in the Hasidic world, one in which we had yikhes (pedigree), my mother would always ask me, referring to the secular world, "Do people you interact with know who you are?" I had to explain to her that such people had never heard of or had contact with Hasidic life and Hasidic dynasties; they knew nothing about rebbes and rabbinical courts. In the Hasidic world a person was simply given recognition because he or she originated from a pedigreed family, while in America's presumably egalitarian society family origins have little meaning, unless, arguably, you live in a small southern town or among the highest echelons of the American elite.

Actually, I took it for granted that everyone spoke two languages, even three, and it always surprised me when other people knew only their native tongue. Thus growing up bilingual was not an exceptional experience for me, as I sometimes hear others say. But I should add that my personality changes a bit depending on the language I speak. It is usually fun to speak Yiddish because of its many amusing idiomatic expressions that provoke a smile in me even when I just think about them. I usually feel a bit more formal when speaking English, even though it is my principal language.

But growing up in dual cultures with different values, norms, and rules of social interaction was disconcerting and often disorienting. I was taught humility and modesty, a core value in our circle, but especially practiced by my step-grandfather, who was a vast influence in my very early childhood. We did not speak about ourselves unless asked; we did not put ourselves forward or seek the spotlight, which I observed American people doing and which I was unable to do. I am still amazed how self-referential people often are in social and professional situations. To be assertive was to be vulgar, and I shied away from competitive situations. Once I entered the academy, my particular cultural background was frequently disadvantageous professionally. When we first arrived in the United States I clearly recall how my mother was appalled when she heard one of her young nephews born and bred in the United States say, "This is a free country and I can do what I want." She never forgot this little boy's assertion. She taught me that we could not always do what we wished, and that we must defer to others. As I was growing up she would always remind me that I had to think about the good of others and I must consider how others would judge my actions. In Hasidic society people are always surrounded by family, followers, and friends, to whom they have obligations that may conflict with their wishes and needs. I learned that I could not do only that which was convenient for me alone, despite living in a "free country." It was not difficult to relinquish religious traditional practices, but the values and norms I inherited were highly ingrained in me and I was unable to shake them off. I never believed what is held almost axiomatic in contemporary society—that to be human is to be ruled by self-interest, which springs fundamentally from our "human nature." When I relinquished religious practices, my mother regarded the rejection as an abandonment of my responsibility to others in our community and a violation not of God's laws but of community norms, which became a major source of friction between us, as was my desire to be autonomous. She did not always recognize that I had actually internalized the values, if not the practices, and that they ruled my actions throughout my life.

Many have asked how people could continue to believe in a God who seemingly had abandoned them during a period of such horror, who allowed such atrocities to be perpetrated against "His" people. Without a doubt many have forsaken Him after the war, turning away from any religious practices. Paradoxically, for some, including my mother, their religious feeling intensified during the war. Such people believed that to have survived World War II was miraculous. As we see, my mother sought heavenly signs, as when she even "grasped as straws," resorting to gematria to foresee a shiny future for herself and for me. Granted, her Hasidic belief that one's illustrious and righteous ancestors will intervene with God to achieve positive results for their descendants and will protect them from all evil was particularly comforting to her as well. She was certain that our ancestors, and especially her own mother, would at least save me. As it was wisely pointed out to me, the belief in ancestral intervention may calm one's fears and answer the very basic questions of "why me and not someone else" that human beings everywhere may pose at times of adversity.

Since I was a child, I was oblivious to such theological musings, although I did ask my father about the nature of God before he passed away. But even as an adult, and until I entered college, I did not question God's existence or his intentions. Thereafter, and particularly when I studied the religions of others, it became difficult to accept my own religion as the only one, although its rituals remained important to me. Actually, I appreciate the rituals of all religions, but feel most comfortable with my own because I know them best.

Indeed, my desire to enter a cultural milieu in the secular world created in me conflicts that also reverberated with the tensions between my mother and me when I became a full adult. To be sure, my mother's concern about my having moved into the secular world caused friction between us for other reasons as well: my rejection of religious practices, if not of the religion and its traditions, was very disturbing to her, as was her worry about what people would say about my "leaving the fold." She was highly sensitive to the opinions of people in her community, adhering to the notion of "es past nisht"; it was not befitting to have an unorthodox daughter who failed in her obligations to the community. It was also difficult for my mother to accept my aspirations, especially when her existence in the United States was very painful, when life for her here seemed hopeless. But I could not accept with equanimity her frequent reference to the judgments of others, which often guided her actions. Paradoxically, she took great pride in my subsequent accomplishments as a professional, and she was usually enthusiastic even about my minor unconventional deeds, as when I returned from a trip in Bolivia and brought back, as part of my collection of cultural amulets, a mummified llama fetus, which is sold in the local markets there and believed to bring good fortune. My mother delighted in its exotic nature, whereas everyone else I showed it to in my family circle was repelled. Until the last days of her life, she would send me clippings of articles in large print (she was declared legally blind in 1977) about any topic she deemed would be of anthropological interest to me.

Nevertheless, unlike American parents, she had difficulty in acknowledging my desire for independence as an adult, and my secular stance; before the war she was able to be a maverick, to be immersed in the secular world yet remain within the bounds of her family and community as I was not able to, given contemporary circumstances. I wasn't enveloped by a close extended family, as she was in her youth. So, my relations with my mother in my early adulthood were more conflicting than hers were with her mother when she wished to act atypically by attending the university. While I have until the present great admiration for my mother's exceptionalism and great love for her, the generational divide between us was much greater than that between my mother and my grandmother. In the past, in my mother's milieu, parents were the final arbiters of all that their children did and even desired; but within the American environment, along with my aspirations that could only be fulfilled outside the community, my push to disengage myself from her at certain points in my life was problematic for both of us. Despite tensions along these lines, we were together much of the time because

I could only gradually and partially detach myself from her. Besides, I did not really wish for full separation.

Undeniably my wish for independence aggravated my relationship with my mother. Mother-daughter interactions are possibly the most complex of all human ties. Our attachment was greater than normal because of our separation during the war, as I reflected earlier. I recalled how when we were reunited I clung to her, but as I grew older I sought a provisional independence from her, uncharacteristic of my background, leading me to feel guilt not only for abandoning the religious life but also for attempting to detach myself from her. The detachment was an illusion. We were connected by both an invisible cord and a very visible telephone cord that kept us united.

Yet, despite the frictions, we enjoyed one another's company; she loved going to Macy's and I would accompany her. She loved to sew the newest fashions for both of us, because she was an excellent seamstress. I always had a beautiful and original wardrobe at a cost we could afford, and she remained the elegant woman she was before the war despite our meager resources. She always wished me to dress similarly elegantly. We took vacations together. Until the penultimate day of her life, we spoke on the telephone daily, unless I was abroad; but even then we would maintain weekly, if not daily, telephone contact. She would tell me with great enthusiasm how much she enjoyed the various organized trips she took on her own and the people she had met. Once I moved away from her house, I loved to return especially on the holidays and always on Passover, our favorite holiday, when her house felt especially fresh and she would have my favorite foods prepared. In later years, unless I was out of the country doing research, we would always spend Passovers together either in her house in Brooklyn or in mine, whether it was in Michigan or North Carolina, where I subsequently resided.

The basic anthropology course I took in college that focused on cultural differences began to unravel the enigma of why I felt so much of an outsider. For this personal reason I was drawn to the discipline. But while anthropological concepts further helped explain my confusions, after I became a professional anthropologist and moved to a southern university, I encountered to my surprise that, even though I found, and still find, anthropological ideas highly stimulating, challenging, and applicable to my daily life, the discipline's practitioners, many of the anthropologists I interacted with who professed to understand people of all cultures, barely understood their own, other people or themselves. They are as conformist-intolerant, competitive, narrow, and petty as any non-anthropologist; one or two even reminded me of some of the "clicking their heels" Germans. Here I will just add that mitigating these unpleasant circumstances were, fortunately, the relish I took in my teaching, the interactions with my students, and the satisfaction I got from my research and writing activities. The many years I spent in the field in Mexico and in the United Sates were some of the most gratifying days of my professional life. In my role as an anthropologist and as a participant observer in Mexico, I lived with various families, participated in their daily lives, trained as a spiritualist healer, and maintained ongoing personal contacts with numerous people from many levels of Mexican society. Regardless of great physical discomforts while living among rural peasant and urban poor populations, I cherished the many, many hours I spent in extensive interactions with the hundreds of people I met and interviewed in their temples and their homes. However, I was saddened by their lives and the harsh economic conditions of their existence. I deeply empathized with them. I continue to retain my contacts with various families; on my return visits we delight in one another's company. I observed and wrote about their difficulties in eking out a livelihood, about family interactions, and most of all about their experiences, and especially women's, of sickness and healing as practiced by spiritualists and by physicians. I observed the people's harsh living conditions and listened to them talk about their difficult personal interactions. It gives me great satisfaction to see their children, some of whom are my godchildren, grow through the years, with, in some cases, their circumstances improving.

There were various reasons why I could not speak about my experiences, and now am doing so only on paper. Most important, when I say something about my early life history, I immediately begin to cry. Only on rare occasions, when speaking to people with the same background, particularly when I contacted those who were in the same camps to prepare to write this book, could I avoid tears welling up. Writing this narrative has made it easier for me to think about the war years with a little less pain, even though on various occasions tears came to my eyes when I wrote this narrative.

My crying on such occasions is yet another indication to me of the "mushy" foundation I stand on, which was nourished by separation, by unexpressed anger at my plight, and by the unceasing humiliation that I felt as deeply as I expect it was felt by adults. I often meditate to what degree our childhood experiences influence our actions as adults, specifically my childhood during the course of my life. I reject the common notions often advanced in psychology that one's childhood experiences rule or even determine a person's actions and feelings in his or her adult being. I like to think that we continually evaluate our thoughts and acts throughout our lifetime and respond according to the circumstances that present themselves to us in any given time. I believe that my own and my mother's actions in life have been taken inexorably in certain directions because of the external circumstances. But while I say I do not accept a kind of "our childhood is our destiny" viewpoint, I cannot deny that my war experiences have framed various spheres of my life. Unlike my mother, who was sustained throughout her life by the knowledge of having had a loving extended family, irrespective of her adverse relationship with her father, which she could not let go of, I lacked a similar pillar to mitigate the "mushy base" I wrote of before. Certain feelings and scenes from my childhood "bubble up" at crucial moments, and have probably affected my actions throughout my life. I have always feared separation and have avoided putting myself in a position where it could happen again. My mind always returns to the scene of my separation from my mother when she was being hauled off to the slave labor camp, or the separation from my uncle as he pushed me over the Warsaw ghetto wall.

I believe that I learned early in life a fierce desire for self-reliance. Unfortunately, the self-reliance, even defiance, I learned during the war did not prepare me to confront the wider world with the self-confidence I needed. I lost my sure footing navigating an unfamiliar world, attributing falsely to those in it a mastery I believed I lacked. The cultural baggage I carried with me into that world did not serve me well either, be it humility or avoidance of trumpeting one's own self worth. Indeed, I did not learn to live otherwise. It was only my stubbornness to persist that propelled me to achieve relative success in the wider world, in my profession, though at an emotional cost. I was also profusely influenced by my mother's standards, by her example of independence, perseverance, and determination, by her aspirations, if not by her religious practices. It was her influence that enabled me to achieve what I did in my life, even though she may not have realized it.

I will conclude at this juncture by saying that though my life took various distinct directions professionally and personally after I graduated from college, which I mention only fleetingly here, it also continuously interconnected with my mother until the end of her life: in effect, the mother-daughter bond was never severed. But how could it be? We were separated and we were reunited. Now that I have recorded her life, the bond is stronger than ever.

Epilogue

At the outset I commented that I began this endeavor with trepidation, afraid to hear my mother's voice after she passed away, afraid to relive the war years, and even afraid to revisit the early years in the United States. By the time I finished listening to and transcribing all the cassette tapes, I regretted that they came to an end. I wished to continue hearing my mother recreate her world before the war, hear her engrossing, if very painful, narrative of her life in the camps that I had only known about in general terms. While I knew about the religious calendar and prayer book she had constructed from memory in the camps, I had not realized until hearing her how religion had nurtured her, giving her strength and protection against the perfidious assaults on her physically, on her personhood, on her dignity, and on her humanness, giving her, too, the strength to resist the brutal onslaughts, even if only in small ways. As I translated and transcribed her words I became conscious once more of how much is "lost in translation," especially the beauty and expressiveness of her language and the richness of thought that is encapsulated in the expressions she uses.

My mother was not a celebrity in the contemporary sense of the word, famous in current society. She was known by those who originated from the same Orthodox society as she had, and was widely respected within Hasidic circles before World War II. To me, of course, she was a remarkable woman, a maverick ahead of her time who possessed great fortitude, admired by all who knew her. She was an inspiration to me all my life, despite our various conflicts, but she was even more of an inspiration after I heard her narration of her struggles: how she faced humiliation and adversity with valor, maintaining an upbeat demeanor under the worst circumstances. After the war, till the end of her days, she was able to enthuse about the smallest event and thing, be it a brief trip she took, a visit from a friend, a television program she saw—even with her poor vision—or a strange object I brought back from a foreign land.

When I completed writing this work I felt enriched by an even greater appreciation for my mother, and my ancestors' commitment to their religion. I gained insights into religious beliefs about which philosophers, anthropologists and religious scholars have written innumerable tracts. I, myself, contributed to that literature, in a small way, in my professional writings, having researched the efficacy of spiritualist healing and its religious foundation in Mexico. The insights I gained observing and participating in these religious rituals led me to recognize the power and pleasure religious beliefs give their adherents.

For much of humankind, for my ancestors, for my own father and for my mother, religious beliefs gave satisfaction, an anchor, stability, and community. Beyond that, they communicated people's humanity, as my mother repeatedly reminds us. Under persecution people often may "dig in" more, rather than less, to their religion and ethnicity. During the war, religious Jews were sustained by the knowledge that there is only one God; that theirs was a very special God who would protect them against German perfidy, when the Jews, and especially Orthodox Jews, were regarded as vermin. Whereas many people abandoned their religious beliefs because they held that their God deserted them, my mother, my father, and my ancestors, who suffered the indignities of anti-Semitism, never doubted for a moment that they would be protected from their persecutors by Him. He and only He would safeguard them at the end. This faith enabled them to maintain their decency, their morality, and their nobility under these unimaginable degrading circumstances. Alas, He did not protect all of them.

I cannot say that religion sustained me during the war, because at the time I lacked any real understanding of its precepts or even prayers. Actually, I do not know what sustained me during those years, except a desire to survive, my wits, the knowledge that I had the love of my mother, my father, my step-grandfather and the extended family; the confidence that my mother would find me—and yes, my desire for revenge. I abandoned this wish years later. I suppose, too, that paradoxically, under conditions of such horrific dangers, mortality is no longer a metaphysical matter. Clinging to life is.

Parenthetically, when, as a professional, I was invited to give a lecture on my work at a university in Germany, I deliberated over whether to accept the invitation. I had vowed never to return to Germany. After some persuasion, I agreed to accept the invitation but, when there, avoided speaking with anyone I judged to be born before the war. I was, however, delighted to see how the younger generation seemed deeply conscious of its country's past, more so than the American president Mother spoke about. Actually, whereas the first invitation came from the faculty, the second originated with the students, and this time I agreed to revisit them and give another talk without hesitation.

When I began college I removed myself from my forbearers' and parental religious rituals, prayers, and practices, knowing that I was also forsaking not only them but the community that had nourished them. I knew that I was leaving a relatively protected life. Although I had never lost contact with my surviving family after the war, I have longed for the people that were lost, the family I remembered from childhood and still remember. Other than my professional life, the connection to family was more important than anything else in my adult life, but that very professional life separated me from the remaining family members because it was secular and very different from theirs. I would visit them in Israel and the United States, and delighted in the warm reception I always received, but then I returned to my secular impersonal world, remaining "unknown" to them. In contemporary life, the idea of kinship alone is usually insufficient to hold people together; some commonality beyond blood ties is necessary to cement people's connections.

Many memoirs, biographies, and autobiographies are being written at present. Arguably, they seem to have become the literary genre of choice. But why write them other than for self-revelation, for the satisfaction of unburdening oneself, for bringing forth what seethes inside that is difficult to talk about, even as one gets older? Until recently my early experiences were hidden in me. Writing this work released what I have been carrying within me all my life. But there are, of course, other reasons: to memorialize that which must never be forgotten, to honor those near and far in the past. Additionally, and equally important, the memoir, biography, autobiography, such as this, cannot disconnect the personal experiences from the historical times in which they occurred. As this work brings into bold relief, the private life of the individual cannot be understood outside the context of the society, culture, and history of the times; it thus is also a unique record, an ethnography of the places and events that reshaped the modern-day world, for the young people of today and future generations, which they would otherwise never know about.

We must, however, guard ourselves against generalizing the events recorded here to other venues, other periods of human history, because by doing so the magnitude of each atrocity becomes diluted and reduced to meaninglessness, notwithstanding some commonalities all atrocities may share. Each crime against humankind has its own unique roots, history, actors, and intentions, and these must not be conflated. Too often the German crimes of the mid-twentieth century are becoming simplified and diminished to an "everyman" or generic evil, thereby impoverishing every evil, which has its unique configurations.*

Only a memoir can reveal the unique personal dramas and moral dilemmas each individual must confront separately at a time of historical calamity, conundrums like whether to "sacrifice" a child's life or to save it, even if it may eventually live a life alien to one's own being, as my parents had to decide; or whether to "sacrifice" a child's life to protect the larger group, as in the situation that presented itself in the hiding place; or the bewilderment I faced, as a young child, having to decide with which parent I should go, with each of them tugging me in a different direction.

Among the several leitmotifs of this work is memory, even unsettling memory, but that which must be told. In contemporary America we are urged to go on with our lives and to free ourselves from the past. As my mother recounted, even she debated this point with a fellow inmate in the camps who wished to forget, if she survived. On the contrary, as she makes clear, this trauma cannot be healed by forgetting but by remembering. Only individual narratives can bring back to life the violation perpetrated against an entire people. Time does not heal these wounds; to forget is to betray all those who were murdered, a desecration of all those who were slaughtered. As my mother states so wisely, her memory is their tombstone.

My mother's narration brings forth yet another overarching theme through her very repetition of certain experiences: the disbelieve by the people in Warsaw when they were hearing about the plans the Germans had for them. This disbelieve was at first perplexing to me, but became comprehensible when I recognized that in everyday life human beings are generally unable to believe in catastrophe, atrocity, sudden and utter change that they had not witnessed before. This is echoed in her repetition of how the Germans kept people in the dark, how they didn't know from one moment to another what would happen next, be it in the

---

* See also Rothstein 2011.

ghettos or in the factories and camps. They were kept in deliberate ignorance, as well as fear, which together barred them from exercising any possible will—yet another way of stripping them of their humanness. Most compelling, however, was the disorientation she, and others, felt when they were taken on the death march; when they totally lost their bearings because of not knowing where they were. It is heartrending to hear her repeatedly enunciate the terror brought about by disorientation and ignorance of their whereabouts. I retained, too, my mother's refrain throughout the narrative referring to the Germans' failure to strip them of their spirituality, of their ethics, of their integrity, of what distinguishes humans from animals that nourished her strength to resist and thus the Germans failed in their attempts to dehumanize them. Jewish prayers are repetitive, as are the liturgies of most religions; therein rests their power. My mother's repetition of such themes mitigated the panic she felt even when she narrates these nightmares many years later.

Yet another leitmotif woven through this work is the matter of assimilation that has beleaguered our ancestors and is still a frequent topic of discussion: is it possible for people who have followed a certain way of life for numerous generations to abandon it and assimilate into the larger society: to leave behind their "difference?" For my mother this was not even a meaningful question because she was able to navigate both worlds without necessarily meditating on the matter. I have not completely discarded the old life, especially since my mother's passing, but I have not felt fully integrated into my adult milieu, although this particular milieu, and profession, was one I chose in the main because it seeks to comprehend people from different cultures.

In this narrative, my mother has covered very personal and the most significant events and thoughts of her lifetime, including her relationship with her father, which weighed on her all her life. Many of these events were a revelation to me; they expose mysteries about the human heart and interactions in general as well, especially about parental relations. Only after hearing my mother's tapes did I realize how her parents' divorce and her subsequent estrangement from, and perceived rejection by, her father had affected her life and reverberated in my own. It led me to wonder when we need to let go of childhood traumas, such as those that had caused my mother everlasting pain. I profoundly regret that I did not know about her relationship with her father before she passed away, especially about the distressing episode concerning her surname, which had plagued her even after the war. I could have consoled her and eased her grief, but she tried to shield me from it.

I stopped my narrative at the point of my graduation from college. Once I became an academician, to some extent my professional life dominated my existence until my very recent retirement. It gave me great satisfaction that in my own way I defeated the Germans. I was able to overcome my early deprivation to build a satisfying career, albeit with some obstacles. But I do not believe that my professional and personal lives call for further telling here, as my mother's did. Her narrative reveals an extraordinary and courageous human being.

APPENDIX 1
*Mother's World and Our Family before World War II**

Jews in Eastern Europe

Our ancestors originated in Germany, and Hungary, but in the nineteenth century members of our branch of the family reached what is now recognized as Poland, where they lived until 1939, as did four-fifths of world Jewry, with a large majority residing in Warsaw. But the history of Jews in this part of the world may go back as far as the twelfth century.

By way of painting the background in broad strokes, while historians may have different takes on the social and economic position of Jews in Poland and their relation to the Polish people, there is a consensus regarding their overall situation there throughout the ages.

Jews may have arrived in Poland as early as the eleventh century, and established permanent settlements by the twelfth century. Following the Black Death in the fourteenth century, more communities of Jews were expelled from German-speaking lands and moved into the more tolerant Polish commonwealth. Polish monarchs were known to be hospitable to their country's Jewish population, welcoming them to facilitate commerce and even protecting them; they faced only sporadic, if horrific, persecutions. Actually, in the sixteenth century, nobles depended on Jews to administer their estates, and to be their craftsman, especially since Poland was an agrarian peasant society.

Jews in Poland were granted a good deal of autonomy in governing their communities, and Jewish religious and material life thrived, although the chief rabbis were appointed by the Polish king. Jews had the power to tax, although the revenues were unequally shared between the Jewish communities and the monarchy; they were also free to elect their mayors and other community officials. In the late sixteenth century, an umbrella institution, the Council of the Four Lands (*Vaad Arba Arzot*),

---

* The materials in Appendix 1 and 2 are based on numerous sources, including academic monographs on Jewish history of Poland, the history of Hasidism, interviews with relatives steeped in the history of Hasidism, and family history, as well as the internet, which was especially helpful for verification of dates and spelling of place names.

instituted a court that issued decisions based on Jewish laws. During the sixteenth century talmudic academies were established in towns like Lublin, where they flourished and became highly influential in the lives of the communities, corresponding to the general prosperity enjoyed by the people. In sum, the Council of Four Lands had extensive powers, and Jewish spiritual life achieved great heights.

Throughout the era of the Polish Commonwealth during the sixteenth and seventeenth centuries, about half of all its Jewish inhabitants lived in urban areas and in large communities, usually in the center of a town around the markets, like the communities my mother refers to. Curiously, demographically the Jewish populace grew faster than the Christian population. This was attributable to several factors, including their hygienic practices, diet, absence of alcohol use and venereal disease, and the custom of kest **(see Glossary)**, which my mother describes in various contexts; the custom of parental support of young couples is still practiced in Hasidic circles, allowing for a lower age of marriage, which contributes to larger size families.

Although generally speaking the Jews were affluent through the previous centuries, in the seventeenth century their life was marred by the infamous Chmielnick or Chmielnicki Revolt (1648), when 20 percent of the Jewish population, and about a third of the entire Polish population, was decimated by Ukrainian Cossacks. The Cossacks accused the Jews of selling them to the Poles and turning them into slaves. Even though this revolt may have been aimed at the Polish nobility, the Jews, who had worked for the aristocracy, largely by distilling liquor, were considered their associates. The Chmielnick Revolt unleashed in Poland wars that led to the destructions of numerous communities, including Piotrków and Lublin, where our families resided later. Once the hostilities subsided, the Jewish population grew again, and the Polish kings continued to remain supportive of it until the division of the Commonwealth beginning in 1772, when Poland ceded territory to the Russians, and lost its independence completely around 1793-1795. By then, Poland in effect disappeared from the map. The country was partitioned by the end of the eighteenth century among three competing powers: Russia, Austro-Hungary, and the Kingdom of Prussia (which later became Germany). With the partitioning, Poland declined economically, and the Catholic Church became increasingly influential and intolerant of the Jews; serious persecutions of the Jewish population greatly intensified and persisted from that time on.

Toward the end of the seventeenth and the beginning of the eighteenth century, Jews were restricted more than ever in trade and excluded from craft guilds and from moving into many towns. On reading about East European and Polish Jewish history, it is difficult to comprehend Jewish survival in Poland under the unrelenting persecutions that followed the "Golden Age" under the Polish commonwealth. Virulent anti-Semitism reared its ugly head, and legal edicts of exclusions and prohibitions were enacted, greatly incited by the Catholic Church.

During the chaos of the eighteenth century, when almost a million Jews lived in Poland, Russia acquired Central Poland, Prussia gained Warsaw and the surrounding areas, and Austria was left with what was known as Little Poland, around the Krakow region. Lublin was first acquired by the Austro-Hungarian Empire and its population was about fifty percent Jewish, as was the population of many other towns, but in the early part of the nineteenth century the Russians became its rulers. Then, in 1915, the city reverted to Austro-Hungary. As Mother observes, by that time the family needed passports to travel between Warsaw and Lublin, because these towns were situated in different countries.

The Jewish population's circumstances varied depending on the power that ruled the region where they resided. With the partitioning, Polish Jewry began to separate along the disposition of the different conquerors. For example, under Russian rule Jews encountered the most misery and isolation: young boys were captured and forced to serve in the army for 25 years. Kosher meat was taxed, as were candles; people without any visible occupation were to be exiled, and, most significantly, Jews were prohibited from owning land.

In the Prussian, or German, sector, the authorities aimed at suppressing Jewish minorities with policies such as allowing only one child to marry, or subjecting married couples to a special tax. In this region there may have also been the most assimilation, especially in the nineteenth century.

Assimilation of Jews into the larger society in which they lived was the single greatest concern of the Orthodox population, including our ancestors Akiva Eiger (1761-1837) and his son Shlomo (1785-1852), who resided in the Prussian region **(see Appendix 3)**. They fiercely desired to preserve Orthodox Judaism within the Jewish population. Actually, in the latter part of the nineteenth century, intense conflicts divided Jewish communities between those supporting the Jewish Enlightenment and traditionalists, as was the situation in Posen, located in the Prussian sector of what was once Poland. The dissension among the Jewish communities between traditionalists and modernists comes into bold relief in the history of my family when Rabbi Akiva Eger (Polish spelling Eiger) was nominated for Chief Rabbi of Posen. He encountered strong opposition from those who wished to advance a more modern, secular agenda, whereas Akiva's supporters advocated traditional Orthodoxy. In this instance, Akiva prevailed, and he was granted the position.

Integration of the Jewish population became a central concern of the Polish intelligentsia in the mid-nineteenth century as well, when an important intellectual movement arose, known as Polish Positivism, referred to by my mother in her narrative of her childhood and youth. Polish intellectuals attempted to find a solution for the "Jewish Question" by recognizing the legitimacy of the Jewish presence in Poland, providing that the Jews relinquish their Jewish practices and integrate into the dominant population. The movement called for modernization of Jewish society, strengthening the entrepreneurial and middle class, and Polonization of the Jewish masses. In short, Positivism advocated dissolution of a distinct Jewish life within Poland. While this movement was regarded as supportive of Jews, many interpreted it as having an undertone of anti-Semitism because it advocated the disappearance of Jewish culture. But the Polish revolt and its defeat, followed by riots in Warsaw against Jews in 1881, gave a blow to the Positivist program of Jewish assimilation. Poland became progressively nationalist, which further intensified the existing anti-Semitism in the twentieth century.

Although our family had reached Poland before there was a Polish state, they were the inheritors of the anti-Semitism that had reigned there by the time they resided in what became known as Congress Poland in the nineteenth century. Congress Poland was chiefly, though not exclusively, ruled by Russia, and would remain so until Polish Independence in 1918, despite revolts by the Polish population.

When Poland became an independent state following World War I, the Polish government granted Jews their rights, but its population continued to be virulently anti-Semitic. Between the two world wars, while the Polish government may have agreed to give Jews civil rights, there was an economic campaign against them. For instance, they may have had legal rights but little access to higher education, as my mother's narrative shows. She was not admitted at the national university in the 1920s, and therefore attended the Wszechnica Polska. In the late thirties, there was a campaign to expel the Jews from Poland altogether because of their presumed social, cultural, and economic influence. The anti-Semitism of the Polish population came into the fore especially during World War II, as we can also see from my mother's narrative.

Genealogical History
The Eiger Dynasty

The genealogy that appears in Appendix 3 will be useful to this section.

Our ancestors and their ideologies continuously pervaded our lives, and in large measure shaped our existence. The Eigers were my mother's maternal forbears, who from their known beginnings were distinguished rabbis and talmudic scholars residing in Germany, where they may have settled as early as the twelfth century. Our earliest identified maternal ancestor was Abraham Broda (1640-1717), rabbi of Raudnitz, Prague, and Frankfurt am Main, who established several talmudic academies in these cities as well as in Metz; he was also known by the name of *Eschel Abraham*, named after the title of one of his books.

The actual founder of the Eiger lineage was Rabbi Akiva Eger, whose maternal grandfather, Rabbi Akiva Eger the Elder (1720-1758), was recognized as a great scholar, an authority on the Talmud, Jewish Law, and *Halakhah*, or "the path that one walks." He was born in Halberstadt, Bohemia (Germany), a vital center of Jewish learning as early as the seventeenth century; he became rabbi of Zülz (Silesia) and later rabbi (in 1756) of Pressburg.

Of Akiva Eger the Elder's two sons and one daughter, Rabbi Yehuda Loeb Eger (1741-1814) and Rabbi Benjamin Wolf Eger (1744-1796) established well-known talmudic academies as well. Yehuda Loeb demonstrated his oratorical talent and the far-reaching esteem in which he was held, by his funeral oration on the death of Frederick the Great (1786). Rabbi Benjamin Wolf Eger continued the family line as rabbi of Halberstadt. Akiva Eger the Elder's daughter, Gitel (1740-1811), married her relative, Moishe Gins or Guens (1705-1790), and her son, Akiva Eger (Eiger), became the known founder of the Eiger line.

Akiva Eger (Eiger) was born in Eisenstadt, Burgenland, Hungary (currently in Austria), the town of his paternal family, which was an autonomous Jewish community and an important center of Jewish learning. He was slight and frail; nevertheless, when the family realized his brilliance, he was sent in 1774, at the age of 12, to study at a yeshiva in Breslau (the capital of Silesia that formed part of Prussia) that was headed by his mother's brother Benjamin Wolf Eger. Akiva, whose full name was Akiva ben Moishe Gins or Guens, changed his name from Gins (Guens) to Eger to honor his maternal grandfather and mother's brother. (The name Eger was derived from the Bohemian city by that name, where Jews are known to have lived in 1322; shortly after the outbreak of the Black Death [1348-1349], a mob incited by a monk's preaching attacked and nearly massacred them all. Their property was appropriated, including their books.) After the Jewish expulsion from Eger, some of those remaining alive moved to Halberstadt, including Akiva Eger's ancestors.

Of the six children of Moishe Gins, or Guens, and his wife Gitel, three sons and three daughters, Akiva became the most prominent. At age 16 he married the 16-year-old Glueckchen Margolies (b. 1763), the daughter of a wealthy merchant from Lissa (Leszno), part of Poland at the time; his father-in-law gave the young couple a house there and supported the new family, following the custom of kest, which allowed Akiva to pursue his talmudic studies. The couple had four children, two sons, Shlomo and Abraham, and two daughters, Sheindel and Sarel. After about 18 years of marriage, Glueckchen passed away, and in 1796 at the age of 35 Akiva Eger married his wife's niece, Brendel, who was 16 years old at the time. She bore him 14 children, and he has many living descendants.

Akiva Eiger's numerous works on Jewish law and ethics are studied by Talmud scholars to this day; his contemporaries turned to him for advice and decisions on points of law. Not only did members of the Jewish community seek him out to adjudicate disputes, but non-Jews wanted his counsel as well. To them he was known as the "Jewish pope" (*Judenpapst*).

Akiva Eiger was renowned for his great intelligence, sharpness of mind, and humility; there are many stories recounting his humble and selfless acts. He was opposed to receiving any titles of honor bestowed on rabbis of his stature. In 1831 a severe cholera epidemic swept through Eastern Europe, including Posen, when he was Chief Rabbi. He ignored the quarantines, entering into the stricken sections of the city to care for the sick despite his delicate constitution. He set up a commission that established, under his auspices, regulations to strengthen the community's resistance to the epidemic. The government commission for the prevention of cholera reported that owing to Akiva Eiger's activities on behalf of the sick, including the regulations he instituted, mortality caused by the epidemic was relatively low in Posen. He also created a fund to support a local nursing home for poor Jews. As a result of his communitarian activities during the epidemic, he received a special letter of acclamation signed by King Frederic William III of Prussia. I often heard about this letter, which was a source of pride to the family.

When Akiva Eiger passed away at the age of 76, on his tombstone in Posen was inscribed: "He was a servant of G-d's servants." The tombstone was destroyed by the Germans during World War II, and the stones from the cemetery were used to construct roads.

Of his four children with his first wife and fourteen children with his second wife, generally speaking the descendents of his first wife remained Orthodox, as he had wished in his will. Especially significant was his daughter Sorel, the youngest of his and Glueckchen's children, who married the renowned talmudic scholar known by the title of his most famous book, *Chatam Sofer* (Moses Schreiber, 1762-1839), who was most influential in his vigorous opposition to the reform movement in Austro-Hungary during his lifetime. The numerous descendents of his second wife, who at the time was regarded as a woman more disposed toward life in the modern world, may have followed their mother's proclivities.

We are the direct descendents of Akiva Eiger's second son, Shlomo, son of his first wife, Glueckchen. He was born in Lissa (1785-1852) and assumed his father's mantle. As custom dictated, marriages were contracted in the rabbinical world between families that either had yikhes (pedigree) or wealth, as mother recounts **(see also Appendix 2)**, no matter how far away the two families resided from each other. Shlomo married Golda Herschensohn, who lived in Warsaw; her father was a wealthy merchant and one of the most prominent members of the Warsaw Jewish community. Shlomo lived in Warsaw for 35 years, where he too became an affluent merchant; later he was appointed rabbi of Kalisz, and after his father passed away in 1837, he succeeded him as rabbi of Posen. Like his father, Shlomo was an important talmudic scholar who unrelentingly supported his father's traditional approach to Judaism, emphasizing strict adherence to Jewish law as prescribed by the Talmud, fervently believing that talmudic-rabbinical laws—and the oral law codified by the *Shulchan Aruch*—were sacred and indissoluble: to doubt them was to commit heresy. And, like his father, Shlomo was engaged in disputes with luminaries of the Reform movement, some of whom, including Abraham Geiger, believed that a progressive Judaism was more adaptable to the modern world, and thus opposed Shlomo's appointment as chief rabbi of Posen. Shlomo, nevertheless, served in this post for about 13 years, when he seemed to have lost the battle to Reform Judaism and returned to Kalisz.

During his tenure as rabbi of Posen, Shlomo advocated for the idea that Jews ought to engage in agricultural activities; he urged his constituents to become farmers, even suggesting to the King Frederick William IV of Prussia that he should help them establish agricultural villages in the province of Posen. Alas, the project fell through because of political upheavals at the time.

Shlomo left eleven children, six sons and five daughters. The oldest of the eleven was Yehudah Leib, my mother's great-grandfather. Yehudah Leib (Leibl) (1816-1888), to Shlomo's lament, became a Hasid. He established the Hasidic court of Lublin, which was, to my knowledge, the only Hasidic dynasty within the widely dispersed Eiger lineage. Our family knew little about Shlomo's siblings and their descendants, probably because they likely did not turn to Hasidism.

Leibl was born in Warsaw; at age 19, in 1835, he married the 17-year-old Batsheva Grodshtyn (1818-1911), later to become "Bubbe Basia"; she was born in Lublin, and was the daughter of a prominent rabbi who was also a forest and wood product merchant. I heard a great deal about Bubbe Basia, my mother's beloved great-grandmother, from my mother all her life. After their wedding, Batsheva and Leibl moved to Lublin and, following the custom of eating kest, were supported by Batsheva's parents so Leibl could study Torah and Talmud.

Lublin was a vibrant Jewish community throughout the centuries, and continued to be so until World War II. It was one of the important hubs of Jewish life in Poland from the beginning of the Jewish presence there. Jews are first mentioned in Lublin in the fifteenth century, despite a royal edict prohibiting them from living there. They established settlements on the periphery of the town, having to pay a special tax for the privilege. At the end of the fifteenth century, Lublin was a market center, and rabbis would assemble there as at other market centers to adjudicate disputes among Jews, arrange marriages, and collect taxes from the autonomous Jewish communities. Community internal affairs were regulated by Jewish law; the community was permitted to establish a slaughterhouse, butcher shops, and a cemetery where three of my Eiger ancestors are still buried.

Lublin was one of the earliest centers of Jewish learning; academies were established there as early as the sixteenth century, and before the partition of Poland the town was even described as the "Jerusalem of the Kingdom of Poland." Hebrew books were printed there as early as the sixteenth century. The last, and probably most famous, talmudic academy was Yeshiva Hokhmei Lublin, the "Wise of Lublin," built in the 1930s by Rabbi Meir Shapiro, its first rector. Its last rector was Shlomo Eiger, one of my grandmother's brothers, who was there until 1939. In 1940 Yeshiva Hokhmei Lublin's twenty-two thousand books and ten thousand volumes of journals were confiscated by the Germans. Most of its students and faculty were murdered, and the building was desecrated. After the war, the building was turned into a medical college, but recently it was being restored to its original design, as I saw on my visit to Poland in 2008.

Before World War II, Jews comprised one-third of the total population of the town. There were Jewish representatives in the government Town Council; they had their own schools, but there were also state elementary schools for Jewish children, cultural organizations, and Yiddish newspapers. The city had numerous synagogues and private prayer houses, three cemeteries, a Jewish hospital, an orphanage for children, and an old people's home.

According to the Polish historian Robert Kuwalek,[*] Lublin had a low level of assimilation in comparison to those of other large communities in Poland. Most of Lublin`s Jews were traditionally Orthodox, with a very strong Hasidic orientation.

Initially, Leibl followed his father and grandfather, dedicating himself exclusively to Torah scholarship. After arriving in Lublin, he studied in his father-in-law's yeshiva, but then, rather than follow in his father's footsteps, to the astonishment of all he became a devotee of the disciples of the Seer of Lublin, one of the earliest proponents of Hasidism

---

[*]   Personal communication.

in Poland **(see Appendix 2)**. This was particularly shocking to his father and father-in-law, both fervent opponents to the mystical movement. Leibl traveled first to the rabbi of Kotzk, then to the equally famous rabbi of Izbica, who had broken away, along with others, from the rabbi of Kotzk, becoming a rebbe himself. After the rebbe of Izbica died in 1854, Leibl became the head of the Hasidic community in Lublin, the city of birth of his wife, Bubbe Basia.

When Leibl became a Hasid, it created a great upheaval in the Eiger family, as my mother recounts. Akiva Eiger was regarded as tolerant and indifferent to Hasidism; he believed that all paths lead to the same destination, to God. But Akiva Eiger's son, Shlomo, and Leibl's father-in-law were ardently opposed to this movement; that is, they were fervent *misnagdim*. In fact, before the marriage of his daughter Bubbe Basia, Leibl's father-in-law insisted he sign a condition of marriage (tnoyim), that he must never even speak to a Hasid.

When Bube Basia refused to divorce her husband at her father's direction, he disinherited her and left them to fend for themselves, refusing to maintain them (give them kest). Bube Basia encouraged her husband to travel to the rabbinic courts, even though Hasidim would often leave their homes to spend months or years with their rebbes in their courts, leaving their wives to attend to the household and its needs. At first, Bube Basia sold her dowry possessions. Then she became a grain merchant and, accompanied by one of her sons, travelled to surrounding towns, negotiating with traders, thus enabling her to support her husband financially while he was away for long periods at a time, studying with his mentor, the Rebbe of Izbica.

At one point, Leibl's father arrived in the court of the Rebbe of Izbica to get his son, believing the Hasids to be drunkards, but he saw his son revered by very sober court followers and ceased his opposition to Leibl's newly acquired devotion to Hasidism. When the Rebbe of Izbica died, Leibl became a rebbe himself, famous for his writings. He returned to Lublin and remained there permanently until his passing in 1888.

Although Bubbe Basia gave birth to either seven or twelve children (the exact number is not known), only five of them lived to adulthood, three sons and two daughters. Abraham, the oldest of the three boys, succeeded his father and became the Lublin rebbe. The Hasidic rabbinic dynasty thus continued with Abraham Eiger, my mother' adored grandfather, whom she recalls with great love in her narrative. Of Bube Basia's other children, her second son, Shlomo Myer, was a businessman; he married a woman from Russia, where the couple went to reside. The remaining son died as a young adult. Of the two daughters, Hadasah Breine married a well-known talmudic scholar from Lublin, Rabbi Zytman, and Gitel married into a distinguished family, the Rokeachs; she moved with her husband to Romania. I often wondered how Bubbe Basia felt, "losing" two of her four surviving children, a son and a daughter, when they moved to foreign lands after their marriages, in an era when communication and travel were difficult. But among Hasidic families of a certain social standing within the Jewish community, it was not uncommon to contract marriages with families living at some distance, possibly even losing contact with the child, if it was for his or her benefit: if it was a good match.

The Eiger family became one of the most prominent Jewish Orthodox families within, and even outside of, the Hasidic community. Leibl became the leader of the Hasidic community in Lublin,[*] and by entering the Lublin rabbinate he also functioned officially as a rabbi, as well as a rebbe. In the role of rabbi and member of the rabbinate, he became eligible to receive an annual salary from the community.

Most members of the Eiger family were officially registered in the archives as merchants; they owned houses on Sheroka Street, known as the street of the wealthy. Leibl derived his wealth from his business activities in addition to his annual governmental salary; as a member of the rabbinate, he received a salary from the municipality for adjudicating numerous religious matters, such as what was or was not kosher; he also received 10 percent of the 10 percent of the Jewish community's taxes that they were permitted to retain.[**]

Abraham (1846-1914), Leibl's son, got married at age 13 to his 12-year-old bride, Hana Zylberberg (1847-1924), who gave birth to 17 children. Despite this astonishing birth rate, only five sons and one daughter, my grandmother, lived to adulthood. Abraham followed in his father's footsteps, becoming rebbe, albeit unwillingly. After the death of his father, he became the undisputed spiritual and social leader of the Hasidic community of Lublin. Subsequently, he was elected to the County Congress of Representatives, indicating not only his great

---

[*] Robert Kuwalek, personal communication
[**] Robert Kuwalek, personal communication; see also Kuwalek 2006

religious authority but also the influential position of Hasidim in the city and region of Lublin, despite the government's official hostility to Hasidism. Actually, after his father's death, Abraham did not wish to become rebbe. However, his mother, Bubbe Basia, claimed that it would be disrespectful for him to forsake his father's followers, and insisted he take on his mantle. Bubbe Basia was a forceful woman; she was instrumental in having her son installed as rebbe, and he became the leader of the Lublin Jewish community in 1882. He retained this position until his passing in 1914.

As mother recounts, after the death of Abraham Eiger, a split occurred between two of his five sons, revolving around who should succeed him as rebbe. The possibilities were his oldest son, Shlomo (1872-1940), who believed it was his birthright, as was customary, but who had lived much of his life in the town of his wife's birth, Kraśnik, and the second son, Ezriel Myer (1873-1941), who lived near his father's house all his life. At issue, too, was the question of which of the sons had the right to the synagogue located in their father's house, and who would be left with the father's writings. The conflict was never resolved to anyone's satisfaction, but both sons assumed the title of rebbe. The older one inherited also his papers (he also became rector of the Yeshiva Hokhmei Lublin). There were many reasons for the dispute, including the followers' conflicting desires: each of the two brothers had his supporters, who exacerbated the quarrel. The disagreement between the two brothers had reverberations on my mother's life, which can be gleaned from her narrative, especially as it related to her dowry. Whatever the many reasons for the conflict were, it was not resolved even by the beginning of World War II. Unfortunately, the war wiped out most of the Eiger family, including the two quarrelling sons and most of their descendants, as well as any property in the family's possession. Notwithstanding the conflicts between her uncles, my mother observed that until 1939 she knew a beautiful familial world, sprouting in Germany and flourishing in Poland, but when she returned to Poland in 1945 all she found were ashes; later, in her words, "little branches were forming from the ashes, with new generations beginning to bloom."

The two quarreling brothers died in the Warsaw ghetto, Shlomo in 1940 and Ezriel Myer in 1941, and were buried in unknown graves in the Jewish cemetery there. Mother devoted two entire cassette tapes to listing the names of all the people she knew and loved who were annihilated. I was not able to include all of this information in her narrative and could only include some of it in the genealogy (see **Appendix 3**). In the audio tapes she simply names all the members of the family, all of Abraham Eiger's descendants, and then recounts who of the family was left after the war. At the very first moment, weariness befell me as I listened to the recitation of each family member's name, and the names of the very few who had survived. Then I was struck by the realization of the enormity of the disaster, by the simple identification of individual names of all the hundreds of people comprising the kin, the cousins and their children, who were lost. Outrage swept over me as the catastrophe penetrated my consciousness a few hours after I heard the two tapes. I was left heartbroken, not weary.

The Radoszyce Dynasty

Regrettably, I know much less about my father's than I do about my mother's family, or even my mother's birthfather's family. What I find remarkable is that within the context of the history of Hasidism, the originator of my father's dynasty, Issachar Dov Ber of Radoszyce (1765-1843), was known as a great mystic, magician, and healer. Actually, he was often described as the second Besht—Besht referring to the founder of Hasidism **(see Appendix 2)**. Dov Ber was famous as the Holy Grandfather (*Ha-Saba' ha–Kadosh*), for his working of miracles. He was a contemporary of Akiva Eiger , but the two men probably never met, and could not have been more different from one another in their approaches to God. Akiva Eiger, the superb Torah scholar, supreme rationalist, and legalist, rejected beliefs in magic, mysticism, and mystical healing practices, whereas Dov Ber was the ultimate practitioner of the occult. This said, Akiva Eiger would refer people to Dov Ber when he was asked for a cure of sorts.

Dov Ber, a disciple of the Seer of Lublin, was one of the most popular Hasidic leaders in Poland during his lifetime, and was regarded as a great healer and magician, able to exorcise evil spirits: in short, a purveyor of miracles. He ultimately became the representative of the mystical wing of Hasidism, drawing heavily on the Kabbalah, as the founder of Hasidism had done **(see Appendix 2)**. He believed in possession by *dybbukim* (demons, from the singular *dybbuk*), which was regarded as a spiritual sickness, characterized by an evil person's spirit wishing to torment a living being by possessing him or her. The spirit not uncommonly required exorcising from a woman's body.

Dov Ber of Radoszyce began life as an extremely poor man, born to a humble family; he knew hunger from childhood. He was born in Radoszyce, in a village where his mother's family had lived not far from Piotrków, as did his wife, who was raised in similar dire economic circumstances. He attempted to engage in some commerce, but apparently failed. His wife was the breadwinner; thanks to her commercial acumen, his family managed to eke out a livelihood. As my mother remarks in her narrative, it was not uncommon in Hasidic households for the wives to earn the livelihood, leaving the husbands to dedicate themselves to scholarly activities, as was also the case with Bubbe Basia, who originated from a wealthy family.

Dov Ber was not known for his talmudic scholarship, but there are numerous wonderful tales about his miraculous feats and cures. After his mentor, the Seer of Lublin, died in 1815, many of the Seer's other students and followers became Dov Ber's disciples. One scholar of Hasidism (Mahler 1985: 248) observes that Dov Ber's wondrous acts brought men back to Judaism after they visited him. He worked his miracles through devout prayer and the application of healing creams and waters; his hands and his mere physical presence were believed to be endowed with healing powers. He prepared his own ointments, which presumably alleviated people's afflictions, out of paraphernalia used during Jewish holidays: on *Sukkot* citron, date palm, myrtle, willow (*Etrog, lulef shanes*); on Passover the *afikoman;* on Hanukah, oil from the Menorah; and after Yom Kippur, wax from the candles that had been lit on that day. He produced a cream by mixing these ingredients, and prescribed it to his patients. The ointment may have its origins in the Talmud. He also used three grades of amber, each having a slightly different miraculous power. The grades were defined as strong, sacred, or very sacred.

People sought his ministrations even when he would not see them personally; they believed that by just coming to his home they would be healed. He claimed that persons sought his cures when their sickness was far gone, and there was little he could do for them. But he had great confidence in himself, and he too believed that the afflicted would recover from the malady by just reaching his door.

On one occasion, Dov Ber gave a pregnant woman his sacred cord, known as a *gartle*, which is a garment designed to separate the upper from the lower parts of the body **(see Glossary)**. People believed that his gartle had power, and the woman was assured that she would give birth to a healthy baby. According to this story, the promise came to pass—the woman delivered a healthy baby—and then many women wanted his gartle.

Eventually so many people sought his treatment that he could no longer give each person individual attention. He let it be known that those needing ministrations should arrive at his home between 3 and 4 p.m., when he would heal everybody collectively around the well in his courtyard. God gave him a gift to heal the sick during this one hour using these waters, which he claimed were blessed by God. Since he primarily ministered to groups, an individual would not need to wait for weeks to see him, and his healing activities would not take time away from his study of Torah. It is asserted that everyone who sought his care was successfully healed, except those who didn't believe in his cures. Those who were doubtful that the water could heal them received personal treatment in addition to water.

I lack information as to whether he charged for his ministrations; some rebbes may receive a *pidyon*, or a monetary contribution, from a Hasid, particularly when he seeks his advice or a blessing. It is known that Dov Ber grew rich once he became a grand rebbe and famous healer.

Lastly, notwithstanding his mystical beliefs and practices, he was ahead of his time by longing to go to Palestine at a time when rebbes did not encourage their followers to go to the Holy Land.

I find these and numerous other stories about this particular ancestor especially fascinating because when I embarked on my anthropological research on traditional Spiritualist healing years before delving into the history of my family, I was unaware of the similarities between the people I studied in Mexico and Dov Ber, especially the rationales for their successes in healing, healing techniques and treatments. If I were a mystic myself, I would probably say that my professional choice of research topics was not coincidental.

Rebbe Dov Ber had two sons and three daughters; the husband of one of the daughters, Itzhak Finkler, inherited Dov Ber's Hasidic court after his death in 1843. His two sons are also said to have become rebbes. Itzhak Finkler became known as the Radoszyce Rebbe; of his four sons, two became rebbes, Hillel and Lazer Duved **(see Appendix 3)**. Hillel had two daughters and two sons, one of whom, Myer Menahem Finkler

(1862-1912), was my father's father. Hillel moved to Piotrków where he became known as the Radoszyce Rebbe of Piotrków, whereas his older brother Lezer Duved remained in Radoszyce, where he was known as rebbe of that town. Myer Menahem, who is buried in a mausoleum in Piotrków, was also recognized as a sacred man, a tzaddik; he engaged in ardent prayer and charity. My father, Haim Yosef, was the youngest of Myer Menahem's three sons; his siblings were Itzhak Shmuel, Abraham, who died about ten years prior to World War II, and three sisters, whose names I don't know.

As was the custom, my grandfather Meir Menahem's eldest son, Itzhak Shmuel, became his father's official successor. My father, Haim Yosef, refused to become rebbe even though he had numerous followers who urged him to assume that mantle as well. My father dedicated himself chiefly to the study of the Talmud in the rationalist tradition. Tragically, with the exception of one of my father's sisters and his young brother Abraham, who died before the war, his remaining siblings perished during the war and the Finkler line was cut short, leaving very few descendants.

The Modzitze Dynasty

My mother and father were distant cousins. My mother's paternal grandfather Yisrael Taub, known as the Modzitze Rebbe, and my father's mother, Sheva, were half-siblings, having the same father but different mothers **(see Appendix 3)**.

The Modtzitze dynasty is best known for its music; it served God through music and Talmud study. My mother's birth father was quoted as saying, in response to people who complained that some students of the Talmud academy neglected their studies, leaving the academy to hear him sing, "It is said that God chooses the Torah, but it is also said that he chooses songs. Both Torah and song are God's choices. There are those who worship God by studying the Torah, and there are those who worship Him in songs of praise."

Indeed, the nigun, or melody without words, is generally the means by which Hasidim articulate their fervent emotions, their joys, hopes, and agonies, but in the Modzitze court the nigun became the crown of Hasidic life. The nigun suggests recognition that words cannot express powerful spiritual emotions as well as music can. The source of the nigun was the poetry of the heart; it is a Hasidic way to ecstasy in its devotion to God.

The Modzitze dynasty began with Yeheskel Taub of Kuzmir (Kazimierz Dolny, 1772–1856), known as the Kuzmir rebbe, who was succeeded by Shmuel Eliahu Taub (1820-1888), who had two wives. Shmuel Eliahu's son from his first wife, Yisrael Taub (1849-1921), moved from Zvolin to the town of Demblin (Modtzitz), where he became a rebbe and subsequently established what is now known as the Modzitze court. Shmuel Eliahu's daughter, Sheva, from his second wife was my paternal grandmother.

A lot more has been written and is remembered about Yisrael Taub than about Yeheskel Taub of Kuzmir, or Shmuel Eliyahu Taub of Zvolin. One of the few stories I learned about Shmuel Eliyahu Taub is that he was said to have "a wondrous musical talent." Unexpectedly, he stopped singing one day, and did not sing again even once for the rest of his life. He explained that he did this because he "enjoyed singing too much. I believe that a Jew is forbidden from so much joy in this world." The problem may have been that his delight came from the sheer pleasure of singing, rather than from the pleasure of coming closer to God through song.

Yisrael Taub became better known in the Orthodox world than the predecessors of the Modzitze dynasty. When Yisrael was 14 years old, he married the 12-year-old Dobre Brandel Friedman from Ożarów (Ozsharov), becoming the son-in-law of a well-off merchant, Chaim Saul Friedman. The father-in-law wanted him to become a grocer and merchant, but he failed in commerce. Dobre's father therefore supported Yisrael (giving him kest) for 15 years, enabling him to devote himself to the study of Torah. After moving to Modzitz where he became rabbi and rebbe of the Jewish community, he came into full bloom as a composer of "nigunim" (plural of nigun), and his melodies became sacred to his Hasidim.

Yisrael of Modzitz was not the only one to compose music for the liturgy, but he seems to have been one of the few Polish rebbes who based his worship on the nigun, creating and singing the melodies. My Modzitze ancestors did not know how to write or read music, but their music was disseminated by their followers and others who heard them. It became widely known, even though the music was considered sacred. While Yisrael did not master musical notation, he knew enough to apply musical concepts to the study of Torah, which comes into view in his book *Divrei Yisrael* (*Words of Israel*), in which he compares men's ascent on the ladder of life to a musical scale.

According to all accounts, Yisrael Taub was an imposing figure. People recalled that he went out with his sons for a walk every evening, all of them dressed immaculately in fur hats and silk coats. People would come from different synagogues to hear him pray and sing. He left a legacy of melodies for every occasion. One of the best-known is called the "Homeless Nigun," which was composed during World War I, when he witnessed the arrival in Warsaw of thousands of refugees looking for shelter during the German attacks. The song expresses a longing for a permanent home in Palestine (Israel). He also displayed extraordinary self control when he created his other famous composition, *"Azkara"* ("I Shall Remember") in 1913 in Berlin, as his foot was being amputated; it consisted of 36 verses, and he said that creating this music eased his pain during the surgery. It is reported that Jews, and even non-Jews, in his town would gather in his courtyard to hear him sing his beautiful melodies.

Yisrael's wife Dobre Brandel, who died at age 93, had her first child at age 13; in all she gave birth to nine children: five sons, one of whom was my grandfather, and four daughters. Except for one daughter who moved to Belgium, and one son who came to the United States, her children remained in Poland: in Warsaw; in the vicinity of Modzitz; and in Ożarów.

As reported by my mother, during World War I Jews living in small towns were accused by the Russians of spying for the Austrians, and many, including Yisrael Taub, moved to apartments in Warsaw where their families felt safer. It was in Warsaw that my mother met her paternal grandfather for the first time in her life, and there that he received his Hasidim until 3 a.m.

Yisrael Taub passed away in 1921; he was buried in Warsaw, where he now rests in a mausoleum. Before he died, he designated my mother's father, Shaul Yedidya Taub of Modzitz (1886-1947), the third of his five sons, as his successor. He chose him, and not his oldest son as is customary, because he, of all his sons, had the most beautiful voice.

My grandfather, Shaul Yedidya Taub, was rabbi in Raków, near Keltz (Polish Kielce), from 1917 to 1924. His first rabbinical position was in Raków, where my mother visited him around 1918 or 1919. He moved from Raków to Kartchev in 1924 to become rabbi there, and he remained there until 1929, when his followers invited him to establish a Hasidic court in Otwock. There he established a yeshiva for Talmud scholars, and thousands of his followers would congregate to hear him sing and pray, especially on the High Holidays, when extra trains were provided by the Polish rail authorities to accommodate the multitude of people who would arrive in Otwock.

I recall hearing my grandfather pray when we arrived in the United States, and to this day his prayers still ring in my ears; they have moved me very deeply all my life, especially his melody for the prayer *Shma Koleinu* ("Listen to our voice"). Indeed, my grandfather, like his father before him, had a stunning voice. His was a strong tenor, with a wonderful trill. When he allowed the middle notes to vibrate, the walls trembled. He composed over a thousand melodies, which are widely known in the Hasidic world, and even the secular one, until now. For example, some songs of Modzitz, as they are known, were performed by the new-age singer Shlomo Carlbach, who as a young man spent time in my grandfather's home. I have also heard Yisrael's and my grandfather's nigunim played by contemporary klezmer bands, even though, as I have found, such groups may not be aware of their origins.

When my grandfather arrived in Lublin after he married my grandmother, his Modzitze emphasis on song and music was not appreciated. The hostility between the two wings of Hasidism—between the Lublin rationalist and the modified mystics of Modzitz—rose to such a pitch that the young couple could not withstand the strife between the followers of the two different Hasidic courts. This contributed to the divorce, which, according to my mother's occasional musings on the subject, neither one of the pair may have wished for; the conflict between the two Hasidic wings is poignantly captured by my mother in her account of her parents' divorce, which resounds in my life even to the present.

My grandfather was married four times **(see Appendix 3)**. After his divorce from my grandmother, between 1907 and 1908 he married a young woman from Stopnice with whom he had four children, two sons and two daughters. She died during the flu epidemic of 1918; in 1920 he remarried, this time to a previously married woman without children, with whom he had four children as well: two sons and two daughters. After she passed away, he married his niece, his brother's Haim Yeheskel's daughter, in 1936, and had one son with her. Of my grandfather's eleven children, happily, at least nine survived World War II. His last wife and seven of his eleven children came with him to the United States.

APPENDIX ONE

Unlike most Hasidic rabbis, but like Dove Ber, my grandfather was ahead of his time with his very strong bond to the Holy Land. He was one of the first rabbis to travel there when World War I ended. There he was received by the High Commissioner of Palestine, Herbert Samuel. Subsequently, he revisited Palestine several times; on his last trip in 1936, my mother's younger brother, Shmuel Eliyahu Taub, accompanied him and decided to remain there. Shmuel Eliyahu served as a member of the rabbinate in Palestine.

My grandfather was one of a very few rabbis who had the forethought to escape from Poland on foot as soon as the Germans attacked Warsaw. He did so on September 7, 1939, with two of his sons and one son-in-law; they made their way to Vilna (Vilnius, the Lithuanian capital) on foot, by truck, and finally by train—the trip took them eight weeks. Once there, he sent a Pole to collect the rest of his family piecemeal and bring them to him, as my mother relates.

My grandfather remained in Vilna nine months. By the end of this time he gathered all the children who could accompany him; during this period they were supported by the American Jewish Joint Distribution Committee (AJDC). Thanks to the now rightly-acclaimed Japanese Vice Consul, Chiune Sugihara, who, at great risk to his diplomatic career, issued several thousand transit visas through Japan to Jews, my grandfather and his family were able to escape from Vilna. Most of those who reached Japan had nowhere further to go and were subsequently transferred to Shanghai, but my grandfather's brother, Itzhak, who had resided in the United States since the 1920s, was able to arrange American visas for him and his children. The family was thus spared from being sent to China. Once the visas arrived, the family embarked on their trip, a two-month odyssey that took them from Vilna to Moscow, to Vladivostok by train, to Kobe, Japan, by boat, by train to Tokyo, where they remained for a week, and then to Yokohama, from where they departed for San Francisco, reaching the United States in March of 1941. He settled in Brooklyn, where he remained until July 1947, when he left on a visit to Palestine. He passed away there on November 29, the very same day the United Nations declared the partition of Palestine that opened the way for the establishment of the State of Israel. He did not live to witness the celebration of the creation of the State of Israel, but it was still possible for him to be buried at Har HaZeitim (Mt. Olive) in Jerusalem, even though Jerusalem was already under Arab siege once the United Nations declared the partition of Palestine.

My mother's younger brother, from whom she was separated at a very early age, my grandfather's oldest son, was Shmuel Eliyahu Taub (1905-1984). He succeeded their father as Modzitze rebbe in 1947, and was an equally talented composer with an exquisite voice; he built a synagogue in Tel Aviv and continued the dynasty. He composed several hundred songs. I remember him well. He was a handsome man, who walked slowly and upright; he had a lovely smile, and a soft, delicate voice, and his compositions were deeply heartfelt. I often recall his joyful smile when he would enter the room and see me sitting there when I visited him on various occasions during my trips to Israel. He was succeeded by his only son, Don, and currently Don's son continues the Modzitze tradition by being rebbe and composing songs. Of my family, the Modzitze dynasty is the only one that has continued the dynastic tradition.

To complete this chapter on the history of my family, I must make reference to my step-grandfather, known as the Opole rebbe, the man my mother and I called the "Fete" (the "uncle"), Yermiahu Kalish (1873-1942), who was central to her and my life. The Fete was my grandmother's second husband; he was renowned for his holiness. They had three sons and one daughter—Leibl, Avrumce, Binim, and Basia. The Fete, too, originated from a well-known dynastic family of rabbis and rabbes beginning with the Rebbe of Wurke, who was known for his love of humanity and his good deeds in his community. Of all my family, he is one of the handful of people I clearly remember from my childhood and miss most. He met his untimely death in the Warsaw ghetto in 1942, in the manner my mother describes.

APPENDIX 2
Hasidism

Because Hasidism and its variants were central to our lives, and also to the religious lives of Jewish communities in Poland, this appendix will provide a brief sketch of the origins of Hasidism and the ensuing conflicts the movement created both in the community and in our family over the generations.

Hasidism arose in the eighteenth century, ushered in by Israel ben Eliezer; he was born in what is now Ukraine, and was known as the *Ba'al Shem Tov* (Master of the Name of God), or the *Besht* (1698–1760). The Besht placed at the forefront kabbalistic ideas of ecstasy and mysticism as ways of serving God, ideas that some would argue were a reaction to the strictures of talmudic Judaism, which stressed learning and asceticism, as Rabbi Akiva Eiger and his son believed in and practiced. Talmudic Judaism saw the worship of God as being by way of Torah and Talmud study, but the Hasidic approach to the Divine was through joy and intensive, ecstatic prayer, contemplation of God by means of transcendence, and, most important, by a person's involvement in community life. The Besht introduced a unique way of life, which according to Martin Buber (1960) was a great revolution in Judaism.* This is the way of life that my mother describes , in part, in her narration of her childhood.

Hasidism t means "loving kindness," and the rebbe (plural rebbes) was the representative of a Hasidic community; he was considered a tzaddik, or holy man, who engaged in intensive prayer. Unlike a rabbi, who normally receives ordination and adjudicates Jewish laws to the general community, a Hasidic rebbe has numerous followers, or Hasidim, who become bound to him, seeking his advice on important matters in their daily life. The rebbe mediates between heaven and earth and is seen by his followers as being closer to God than the average human being. For this reason, his word, or his blessing, is sacred; his advice possesses the wisdom of the Divine. For example, to get a piece of the bread the rebbe touched, or to eat at his *tish*, or table, is to be elevated into a higher plane.

---

* See also Buber 2001.

One of my uncles, a scholar of Hasidism, likened an "authentic" rebbe to a ruler—he is a leader, or monarch, who is regarded as an emissary, having obligations to his followers. But, unlike a ruler who must earn a mandate from the people, the rebbe receives his mandate from God.

The Besht was such a man. He did not leave any written books, but he passed his thinking and practices on to his followers in numerous letters. During his life he taught the joy of performing God's commandments; that the Divine was present everywhere in the world; and that one must live by three basic precepts: love of God, love of Israel, and love of the Torah. He rejected dualities, such as that between the sacred and the secular, between body and soul, for the flesh ought not to be denied. Unlike some later rebbes, including my mother's stepfather, the Besht rejected asceticism on the grounds that the body is Divine and must not be neglected. Most significant, he opened the way for the average man to unite with the Divine without necessarily devoting himself to learning Jewish law and the Talmud. Some have suggested that the Besht's teachings democratized Judaism.

The Besht was known too as a gifted healer, healing being considered a respectable occupation at the time. He derived his knowledge from folk healing and the Kabbalah and prescribed medicines, as well as amulets, exorcisms, and magical defenses. He traveled between the cosmic realm and the earth, an intermediary between the Divine and the human. In one letter, he describes how his soul actually rose up to heaven during the days of awe (referring to the High Holidays) to protect the Jewish community because Jews were being accused of blood libel and other such fictions.

Since the Besht left no more than letters expressing his thoughts, they could be easily reinterpreted by his followers. Indeed, developments of Hasidism in the nineteenth century led to Hasidic courts of the type seen in our family and, arguably, many of the Besht's magical ideas moved to the periphery of Hasidism, although one of my ancestors **(Dov Ber; see Appendix 1)** was a known practitioner of occult activities. While magical ideas disseminated by the Besht may have lost much of their currency through time, Hasidism introduced into Jewish mainstream thought some kabbalistic notions, especially the notion that human beings yearn to comprehend the Divine and the concept of transmigration of the soul, known as *gilgulim* (rolling over). When a person has failed to fulfill the commandments in his lifetime, his soul may be reborn in the body of another human and thereby repair (*tikun*) itself by performing all the commandments in this new life. God's compassion allows a person to complete his obligations to keep the commandments through rebirth and redemption.

The Besht's successors were charismatic, as he was; the ability to become a rebbe, a tzaddik, a holy man, was dependent on an individual's capacity to attract followers. However, new developments occurred in the second decade of the nineteenth century, when *tzaddikim* (plural of tzadik) each developed a particular way, or style, that attracted followers, and, rather than charisma, dynastic succession became institutionalized in Hasidism. Previously, followers chose a successor to their rebbe based on his allure and on the basis of master-disciple relationships, but by the nineteenth century the power of the father was believed to reside in the son, and yikhes, or pedigree, became central in Hasidic life, creating Hasidic dynasties. Succession became hereditary, normally with the oldest son inheriting his father's place. There was sometimes some contention between two brothers, as was the situation in the Eiger family in my grandmother's generation, as described by my mother, and to a lesser extent in my father's family between my father and his elder brother. The followers played an important role in such succession conflicts; they usually supported one or another contender, fueling the conflict, as was the case with the Eiger family.

With the emergence of Hasidic dynasties, family yikhes began to bestow high status on a person by virtue of the fact that he or she was a member of a dynastic family. At the same time, the individual was required not to blemish the family name by his or her behavior, which is why my mother felt that it would have shamed the family had it been known that she had studied at a university.[*]

Most important, the notion of yikhes was invoked in marriage arrangements. Before the rise of Hasidic dynastic courts, descent was already important among non-Hasidim. For example, Akiva Eiger's offspring, who were most assuredly not Hasidim, were regarded as "bluebloods" because of Akiva's learning. Normally, wealthy merchants sought out mates for their children among Torah scholars, but when Hasidic hereditary dynasties became hierarchically organized, an indi-

---

[*] See an excellent discussion about the importance of yikhes (yihus) in Hasidism, especially in Dynner 2006.

vidual's status was framed by his or her family of origin: his lineage. In effect, marriage established an alliance with a pedigreed family, usually creating a reciprocal relationship between those with scholarship and those with wealth. The wealth of a woman's family supported talmudic scholarship, which in turn promoted the prestige of the family beyond what mere wealth could bestow.

Marriages could, of course, also be arranged between children descended from two dynastic Hasidic lines, or between relatives. Each rabbinical court tended to follow different policies regarding how marital ties were established, beyond linking wealth with scholarship. For example, the Eiger family normally sought wealthy mates for their sons and daughters; other families may have favored only relatives, since cousin marriage is permitted in Judaism, or members of another rabbinic family.

From its inception, Hasidism encountered virulent opposition from many different directions. The Vilna Gaon (1720-1797), the greatest sage of Jewish learning in the eighteenth century, strongly opposed the Hasidic movement from his base in Lithuania. He even attempted to excommunicate Hasidim from the Jewish community. He accused them of idol worship because of their veneration of the rebbe, whose person is, indeed, viewed as sacred. Lithuanian Jewry unleashed numerous other criticisms against Hasidim, chiefly that they engaged in magical practices, which the Lithuanian rationalists opposed; that they failed to attend sufficiently to the study of Torah and Talmud; and that they rejected Torah study outright.

Of course, rationalists and Talmudists still rebuff mysticism and magic, along with kabbalistic practices and beliefs. The rationalists claimed that Hasidim exploited youthful exuberance. As one scholar of Hasidism notes (Hundert 2004, see also 1991), it opened a new avenue to Orthodoxy, to which the elders seem to have objected, as can clearly be seen when Leibl Eiger, my mother's great-grandfather, became a Hasid at a young age, early in his marriage, thus angering his father and father-in-law. It is astounding to read the lengths to which the opponents of the movement—misnagdim—went to persecute the Hasidim. They organized prohibitions against them, including barring marriage and business relations, and may have been instrumental in driving Hasidim out of towns where they lived. The misnagdim would even enlist local government authorities to arrest them.

Hasidim were persecuted by the misnagdim for the first 40 years of the movement's existence, until gradually they became the mainstream of Jewish life in Poland. By then, Hasidim had also established important yeshivas, or talmudic academies, in several different cities, including Lublin. Hasidism began to gain prominence in Poland with the Seer of Lublin (d.1815); his grave, miraculously, was not destroyed by the Germans and remains in the old cemetery of Lublin today, serving still as a pilgrimage site. By the nineteenth century, Hasidism became the establishment rather than its adversary; the conflicts between Hasidim and misnagdim became attenuated, if not completely erased. However, conflicts between the Orthodox leadership and the Maskilim, or followers of the Jewish Enlightenment, between traditionalism—Hasidism—and secularism, became intensified because secularism was considered the royal road to assimilation. This apprehension had been expressed even earlier, before the ascent of Hasidism, by Akiva Eiger and his son Shlomo.

Once Hasidism achieved dominance in the Jewish community, with the proliferation of Hasidic rebbes and dynastic courts, some major splits occurred in the movement in the nineteenth century. To paint in broad strokes, at the risk of some generalization and simplification, in the nineteenth century Hasidism moved in three main directions, which are also mirrored in the history of my family. These can best be described as a rational wing, devoted to Torah study and talmudic scholarship, as exemplified by Leibl Eiger; a mystical and magical wing that the Seer of Lublin propagated, which was exemplified by my father's ancestors Dov Ber and the Radoczyce rebbe **(see Appendix 1)**. The third wing was somewhere in between the rationalists and the ecstatic, so to speak, and included such families as my mother's birth father's Modzitze dynasty, whose offspring were, and are, principal practitioners.

During the lifetime of the Seer of Lublin, the Lublin community split between Hasidism and its opponents and there was a continuous conflict and bitter rivalry between these two branches of Orthodox Judaism until Leibl Eiger established what is known to this day as the Lublin Hasidic dynasty in the town. He was recognized as a holy man, renowned for his learning and ardent prayer. While he and the Lublin Hasidic dynasty were acknowledged rationalists, mysticism is not fully eliminated from Hasidic beliefs by any group, because the followers of any rebbe attribute to him, as they did to Leibl Eiger and to all of my rabbinical ancestors, special powers, which they believe affect them when they receive the rebbe's blessing, or touch his food and thereby reach the Divine.

Unlike books written by talmudic scholars including Akiva Eiger, who like the Tosafists were interpreters and commentators of the law, books written by Hasidic rebbes, such as those my mother cites, consist generally of commentaries on the weekly Torah portion (*parshat hashavua*) and have a specific purpose: to teach ethics and, most important, to show different ways one can come closer to God, thus elevating the reader. Normally, such teachings were prepared remarks that took place during a tish such as during se'udah shelishit, when a rebbe expounded on his philosophy, but my mother's grandfather, Abraham, spoke extemporaneously on the occasions upon which his book is based.

The familial conflicts between the Lublin and Modzitze dynasties vividly depicted by my mother reflected internal conflicts within Hasidism. The Hasidim of each court were also instrumental in leading to my grandparents' divorce, mirroring conflicts revolving around the ways in which an Orthodox Jew must approach God that had initially emerged between Hasidim and misnagdim, and then among different Hasidic dynasties. In general, in the late nineteenth century the rationalists prevailed, establishing an unexpressed hierarchy among rabbinical courts: those who were known as talmudic sages were ranked higher than those who were not. The conflict between the rationalist and the extreme mystic wing of Hasidism, arguably, may have lost its luster; nevertheless, the "in between" dynasties, represented, for example, by the Modzitze dynasty, had enough followers for them to be recognized as an important dynastic court to this day; as my mother notes, this unexpressed dynastic "pecking order" led to resentments and greatly contributed to the dissolution of my grandparents' marriage.

The followers of the Lublin court were decimated to such a degree that the court was unable to reconstitute itself following World War II in Israel or the United States, although the very few descendants who remained have large families; thankfully, the Modzitze court, with its emphasis on song, continues to thrive, especially in contemporary Israel. While I lack the musical talents of my Modzitze ancestors, I have absorbed their love for all music and some mystical tendencies, but have adhered chiefly to the rationalist nature of my Eiger ancestors.

APPENDIX 3
Genealogy

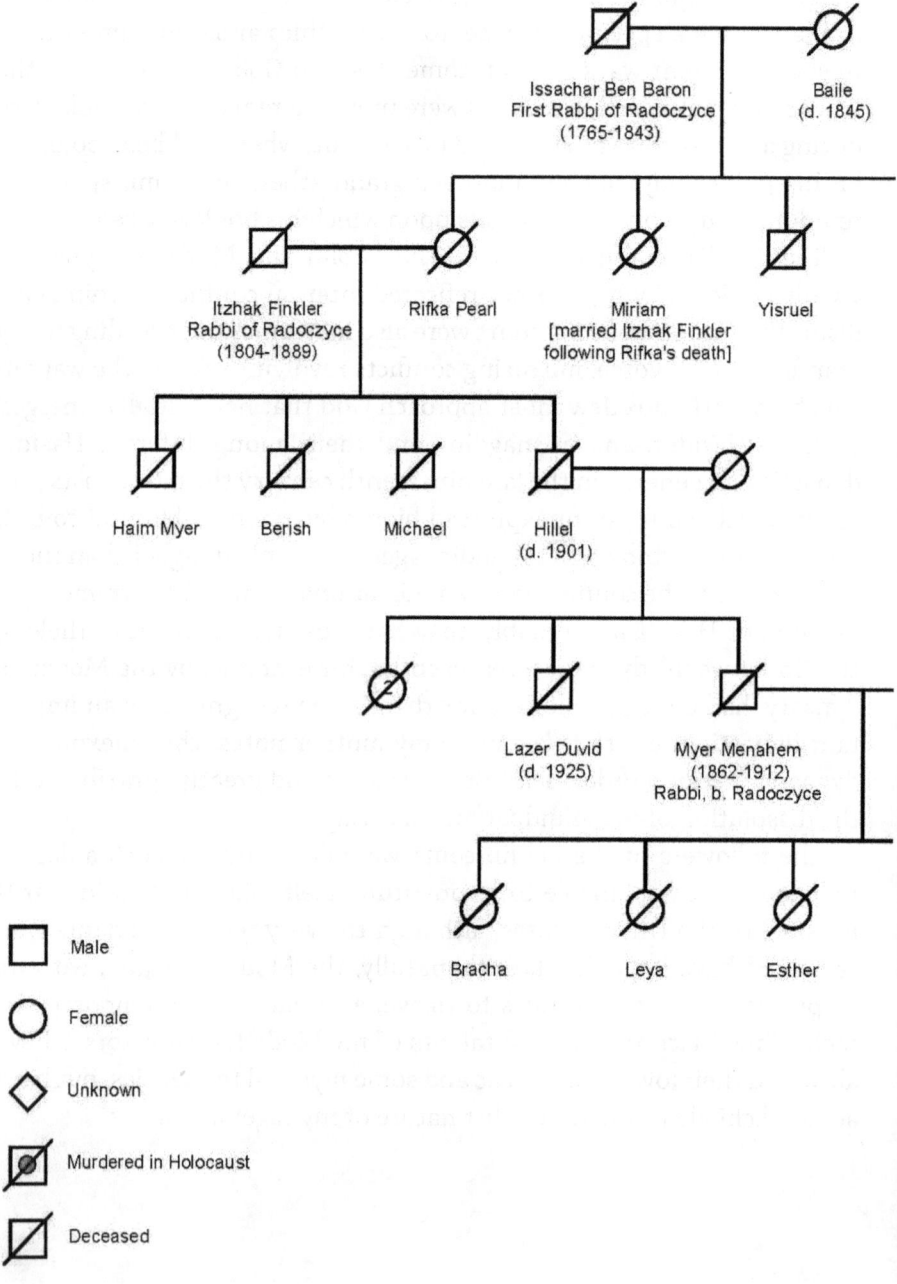

Radoczyce Rabbinic Dynasty
(Finkler family)

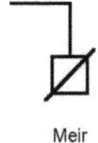
Meir

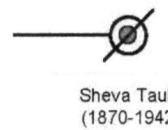
Sheva Taub
(1870-1942)

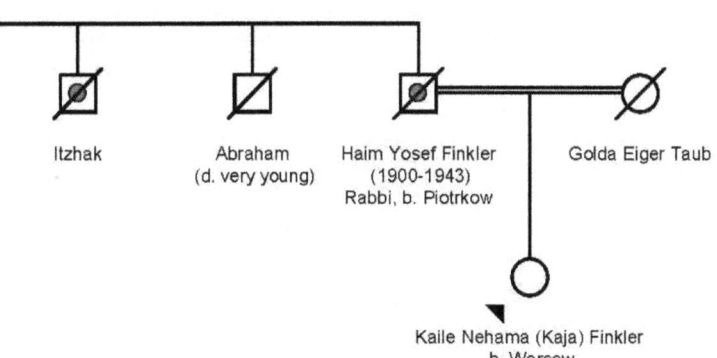

Itzhak   Abraham   Haim Yosef Finkler   Golda Eiger Taub
         (d. very young)   (1900-1943)
                           Rabbi, b. Piotrkow

Kaile Nehama (Kaja) Finkler
b. Warsaw

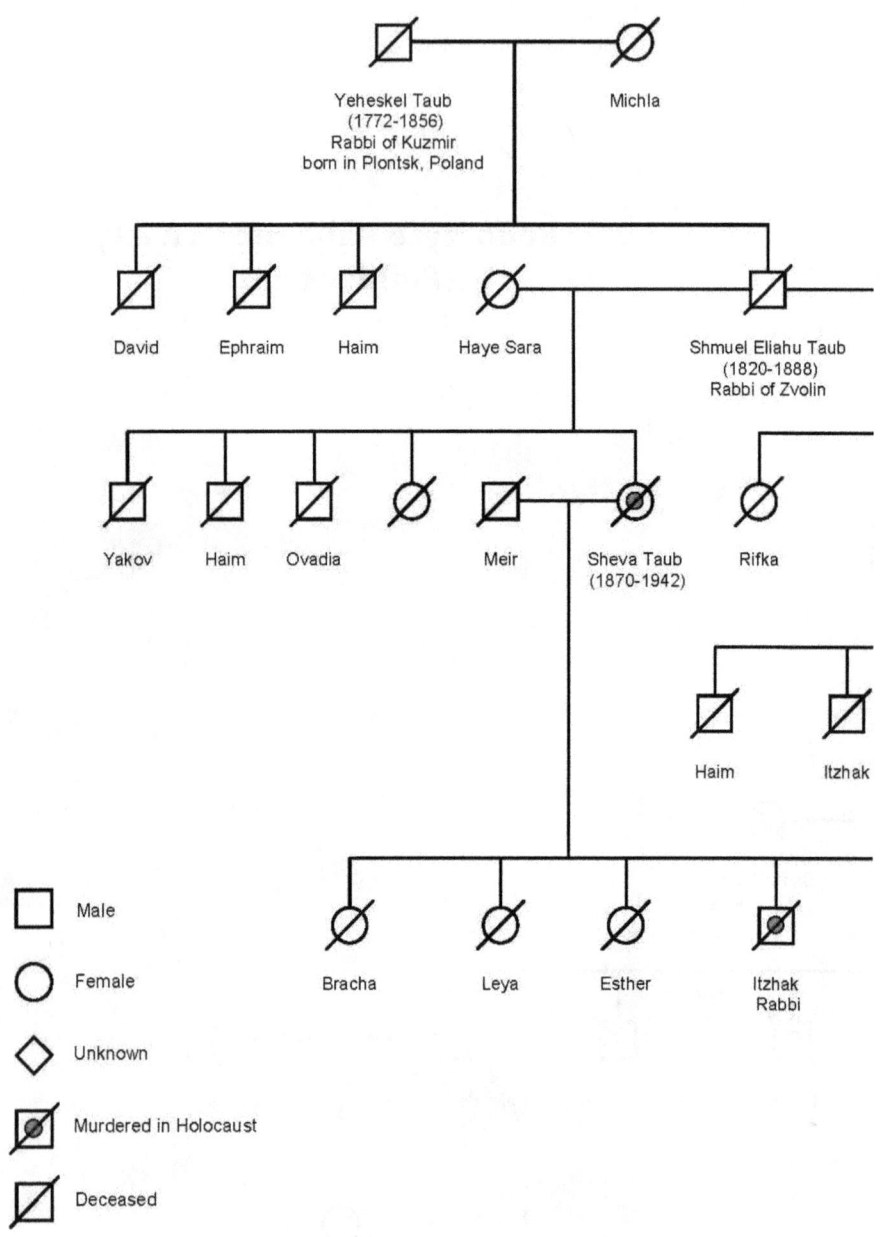

Modzitze Rabbinic Dynasty
(Taub family)

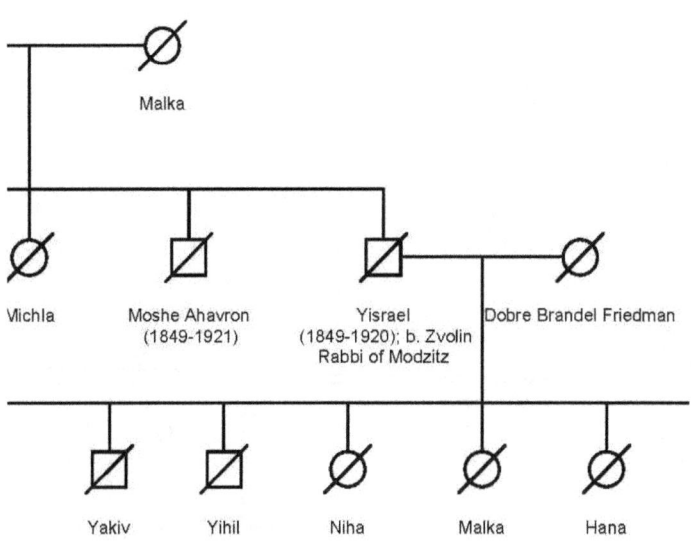

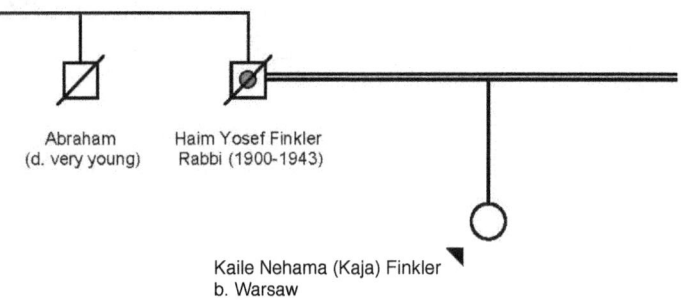

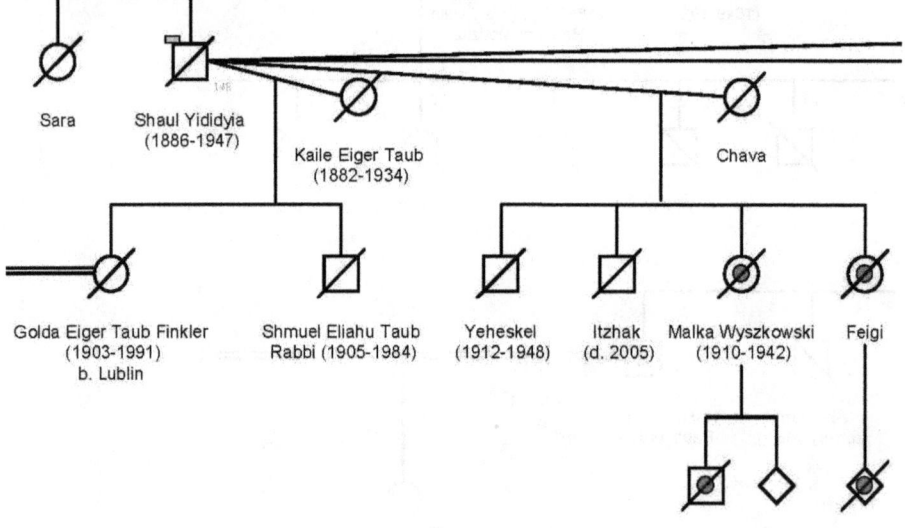

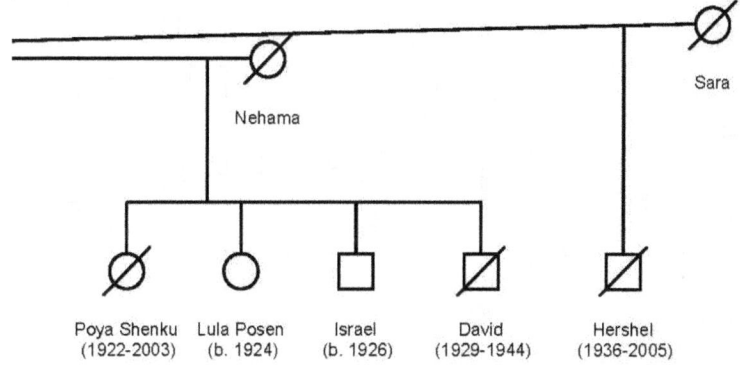

Eiger Rabbinic Dynasty
(Eiger family)

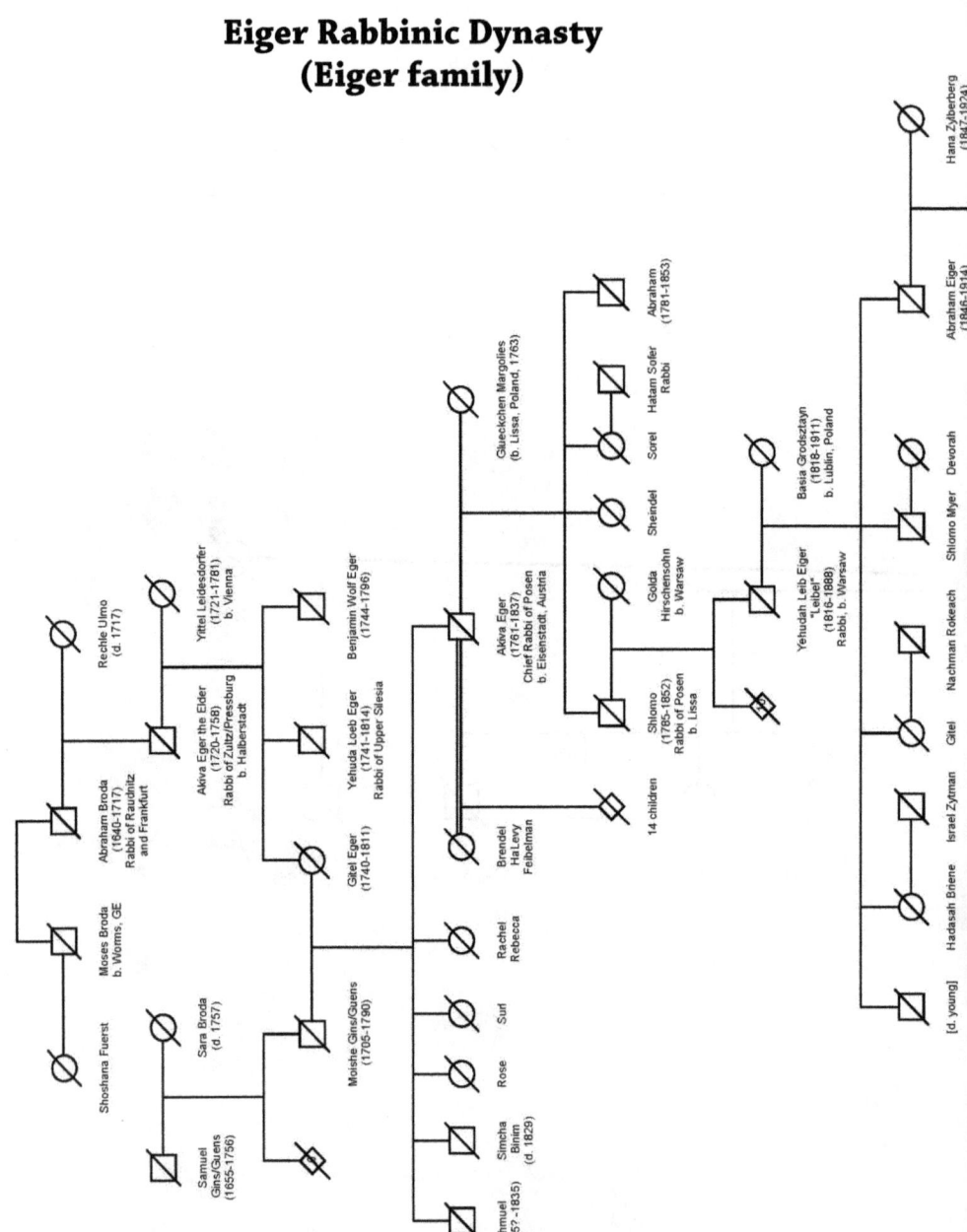

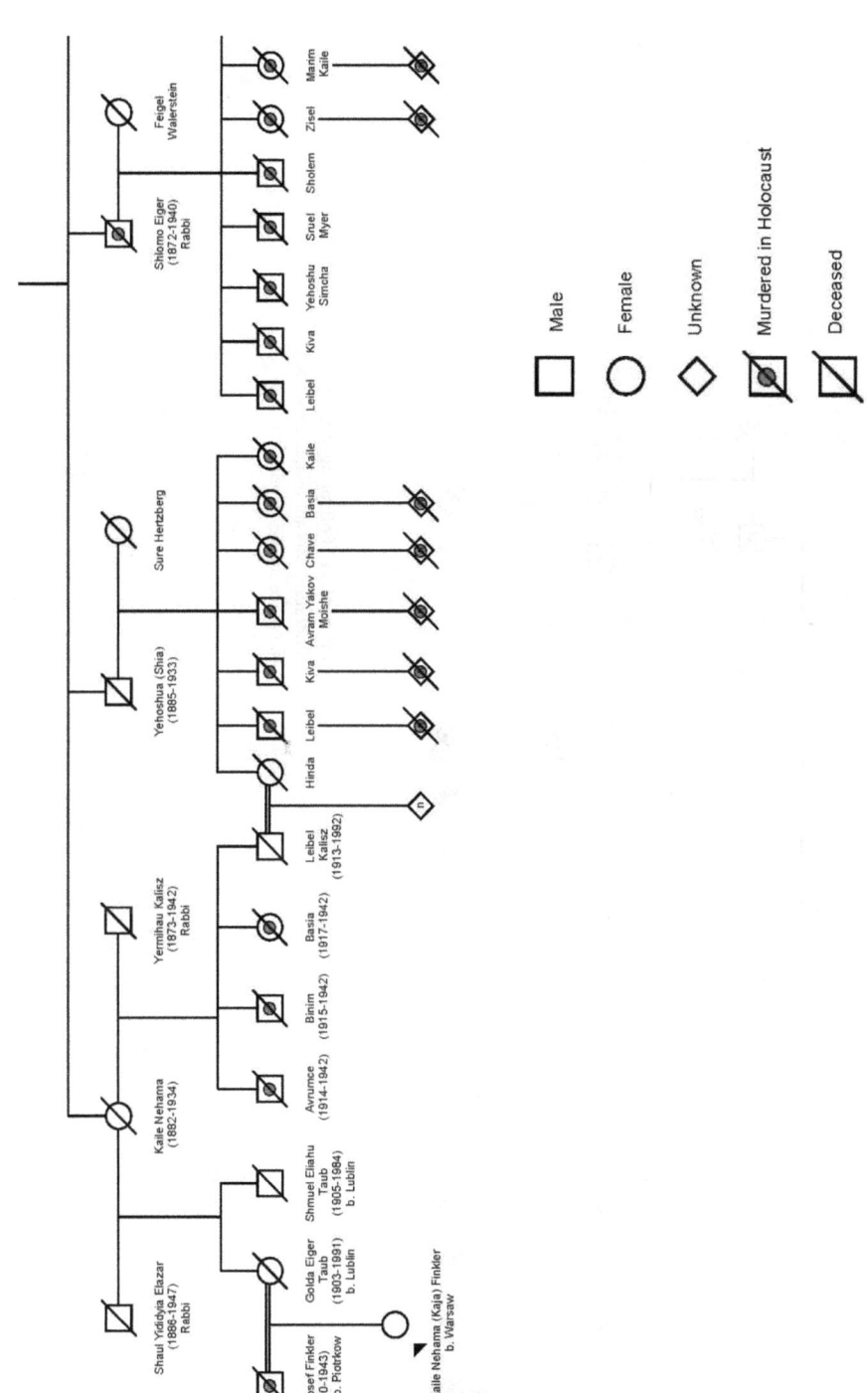

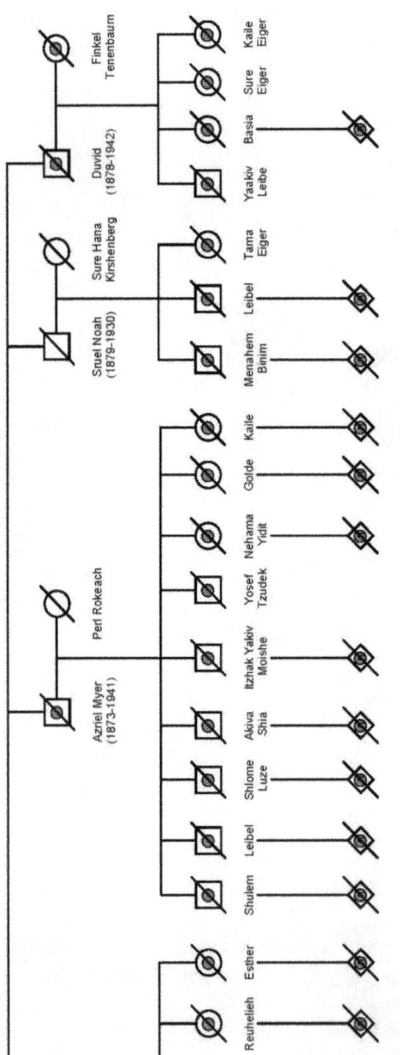

The number of offspring in the last generation was abbreviated due to the space consideration.

APPENDIX 4
Prayers and Calendar of Jewish Holidays Reconstructed by Golda Finkler in Hasag-Leipzig

Selected prayers reconstructed by my mother in Hasag Leipzig camp

1. Birkat Hashahar – Morning Blessings	p. 323
2. Adon Olam – "Lord of the Universe"	p. 324
3. Yigdal – "The living God is great"	p. 325
4. Baruch Ata – "Blessed Are You, Lord"	p. 326
5. V'Natan Lanu – "And gave us Torah"	p. 327
6. Elokai Neshama – "My God, the soul that You have placed in me is pure"	p. 328
7. Velachazot – "Dwell in the House of the Lord all the days of my life"	p. 329
8. Yehi Ratzon – "May it be Your will"	p. 330
9. Al Naharov Babel – "By the rivers of Babylon"	p. 331
10. – 13. Calendar	pp. 332-335

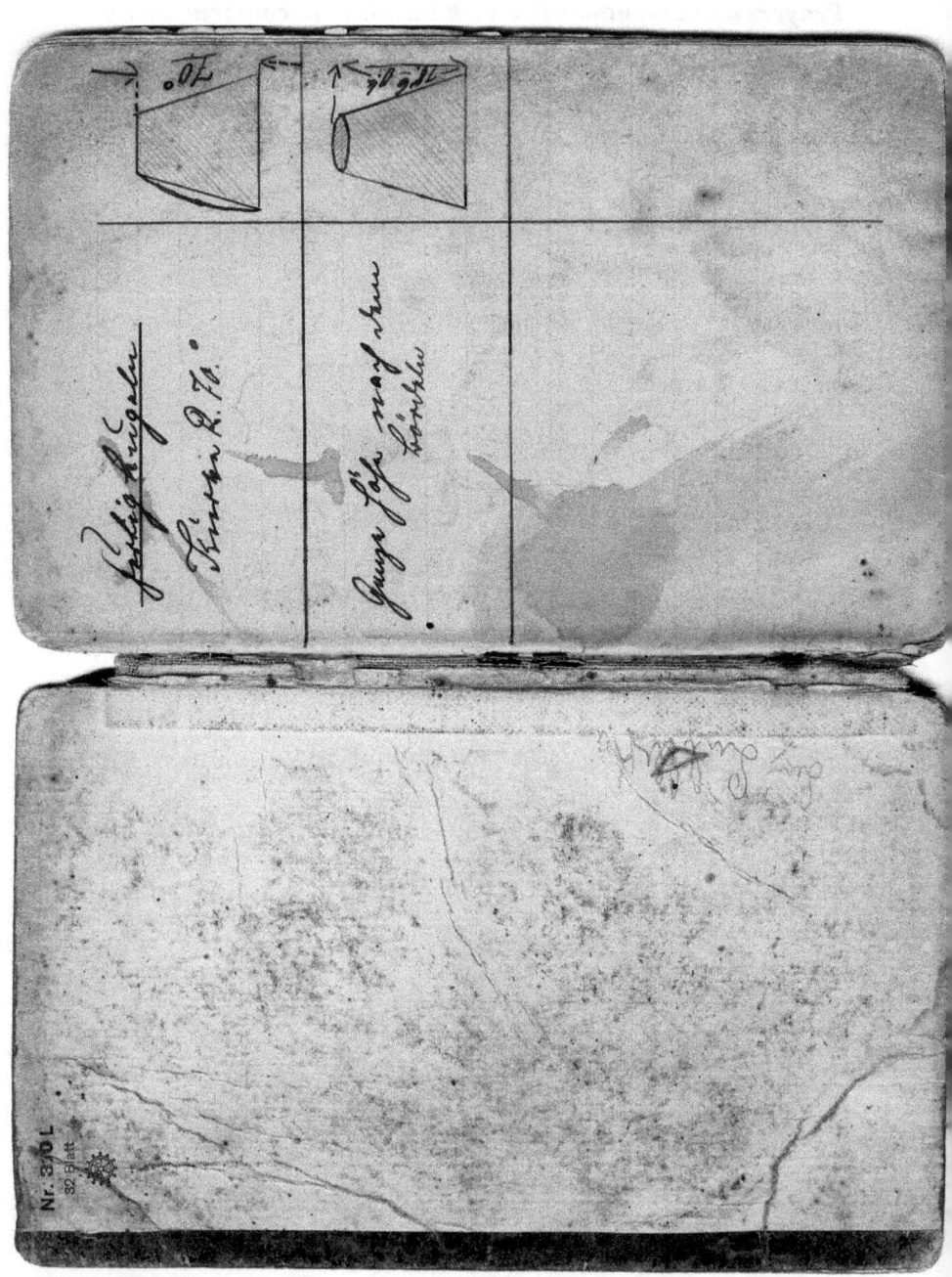

Birkat Hashahar

בִּרְכַּת הַשַּׁחַר

בָּרוּךְ אַתָּה יְיָ אֱלֹהֵינוּ מֶלֶךְ הָעוֹלָם - שֶׁעָשַׂנִי
יִשְׂרָאֵל. שֶׁלֹּא עָשַׂנִי עֶבֶד. שֶׁלֹּא עָשַׂנִי אִשָּׁה.
פּוֹקֵחַ עִוְרִים. מַלְבִּישׁ עֲרֻמִּים. מַתִּיר אֲסוּרִים.
זוֹקֵף כְּפוּפִים. רוֹקַע הָאָרֶץ עַל הַמָּיִם. שֶׁעָשָׂה
לִּי כָּל צָרְכִּי. הַמֵּכִין מִצְעֲדֵי גָבֶר. אוֹזֵר
יִשְׂרָאֵל בִּגְבוּרָה. עוֹטֵר יִשְׂרָאֵל בְּתִפְאָרָה.
הַנּוֹתֵן לַיָּעֵף כֹּחַ. הַמַּעֲבִיר שֵׁנָה מֵעֵינַי
וּתְנוּמָה מֵעַפְעַפָּי.

Adon Olam

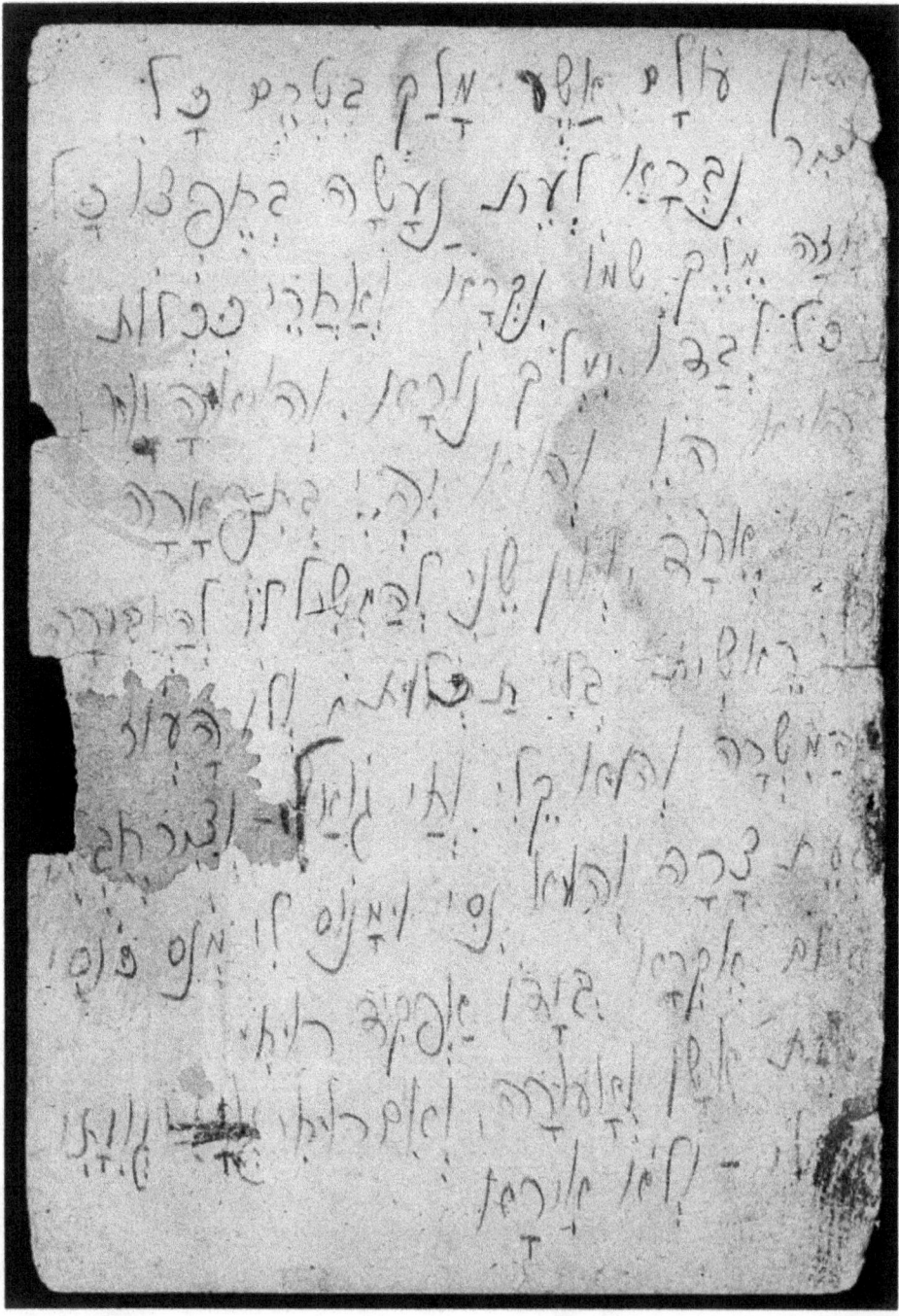

Yigdal

V'Natan Lanu

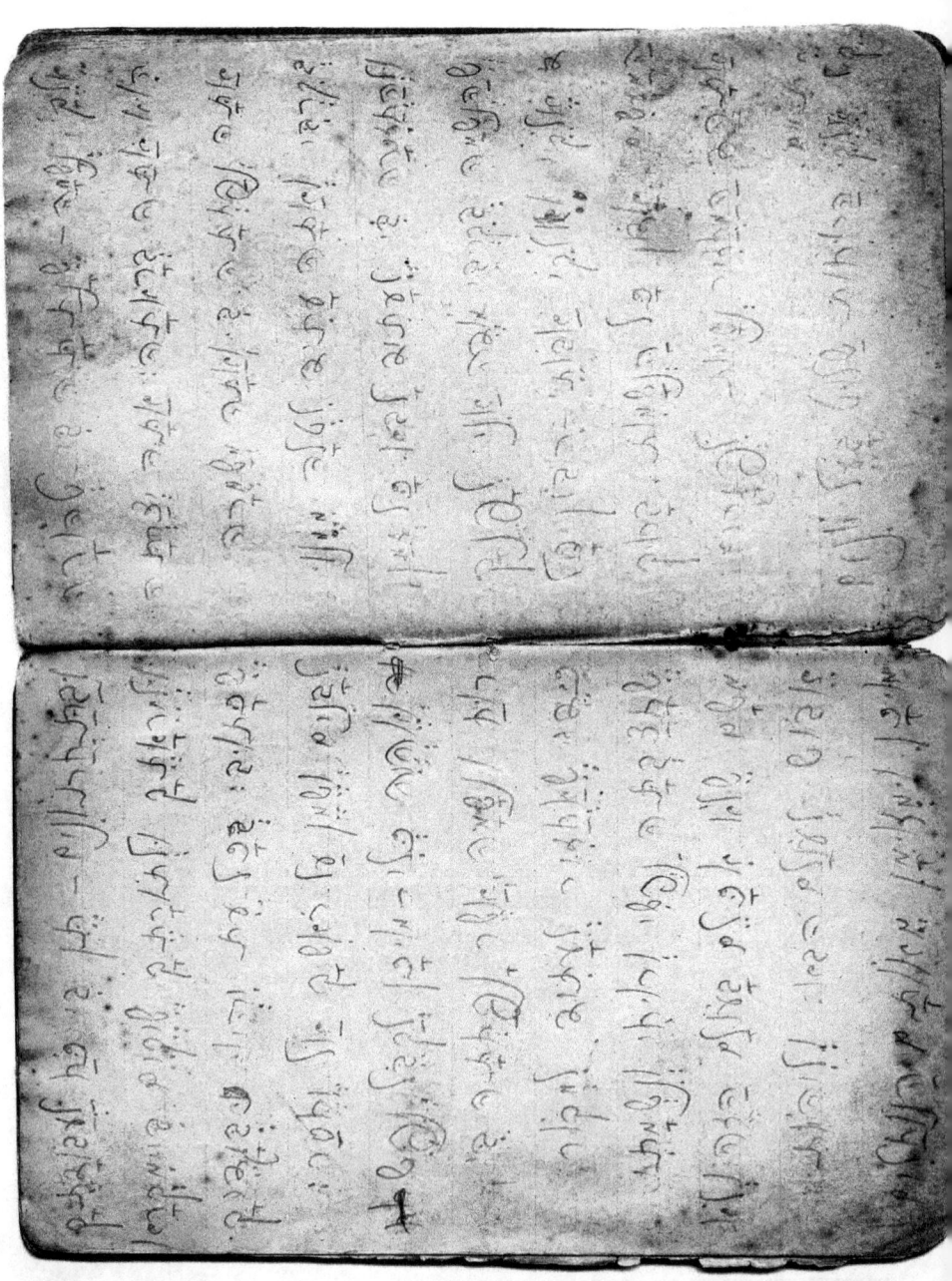

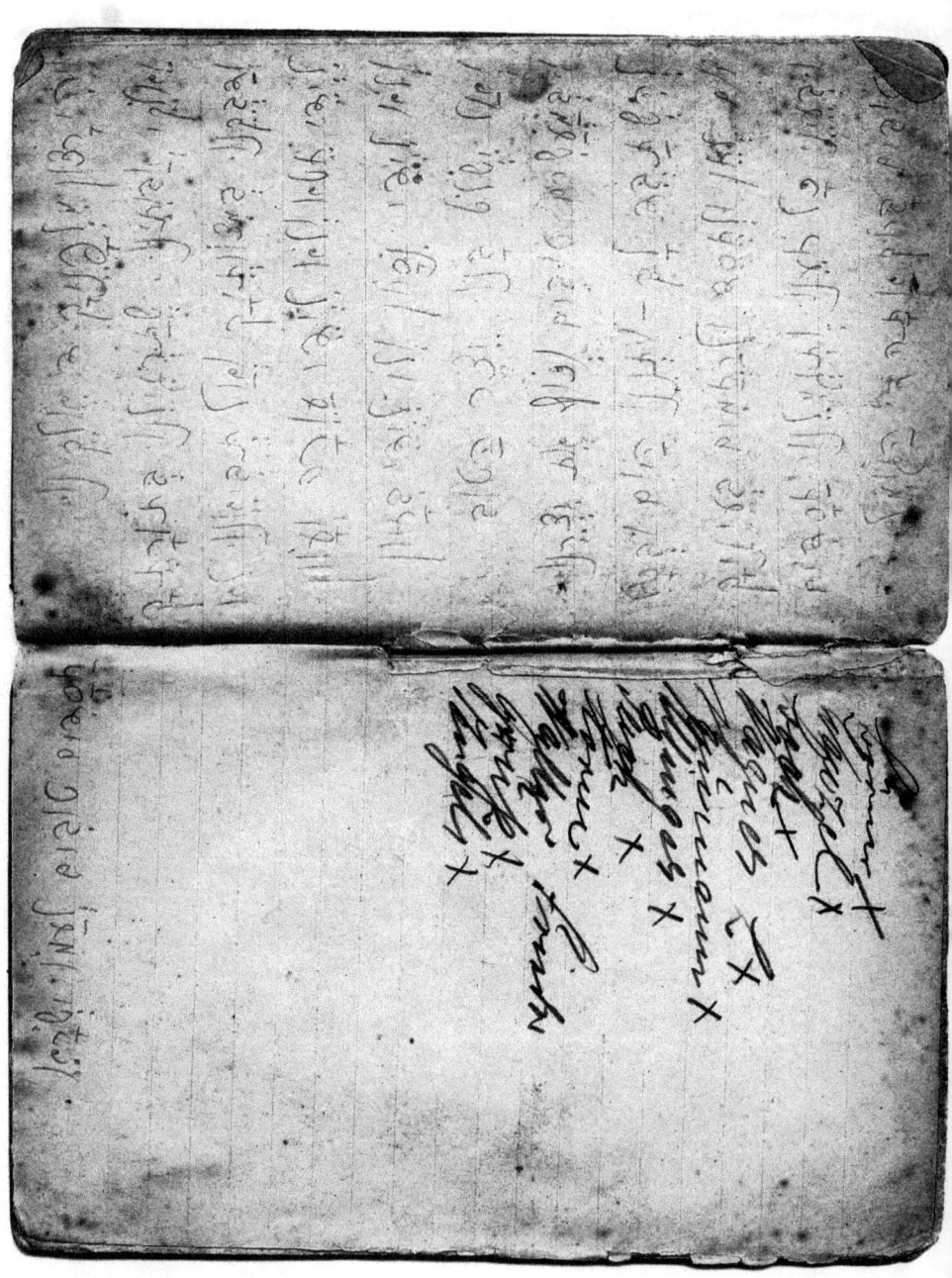

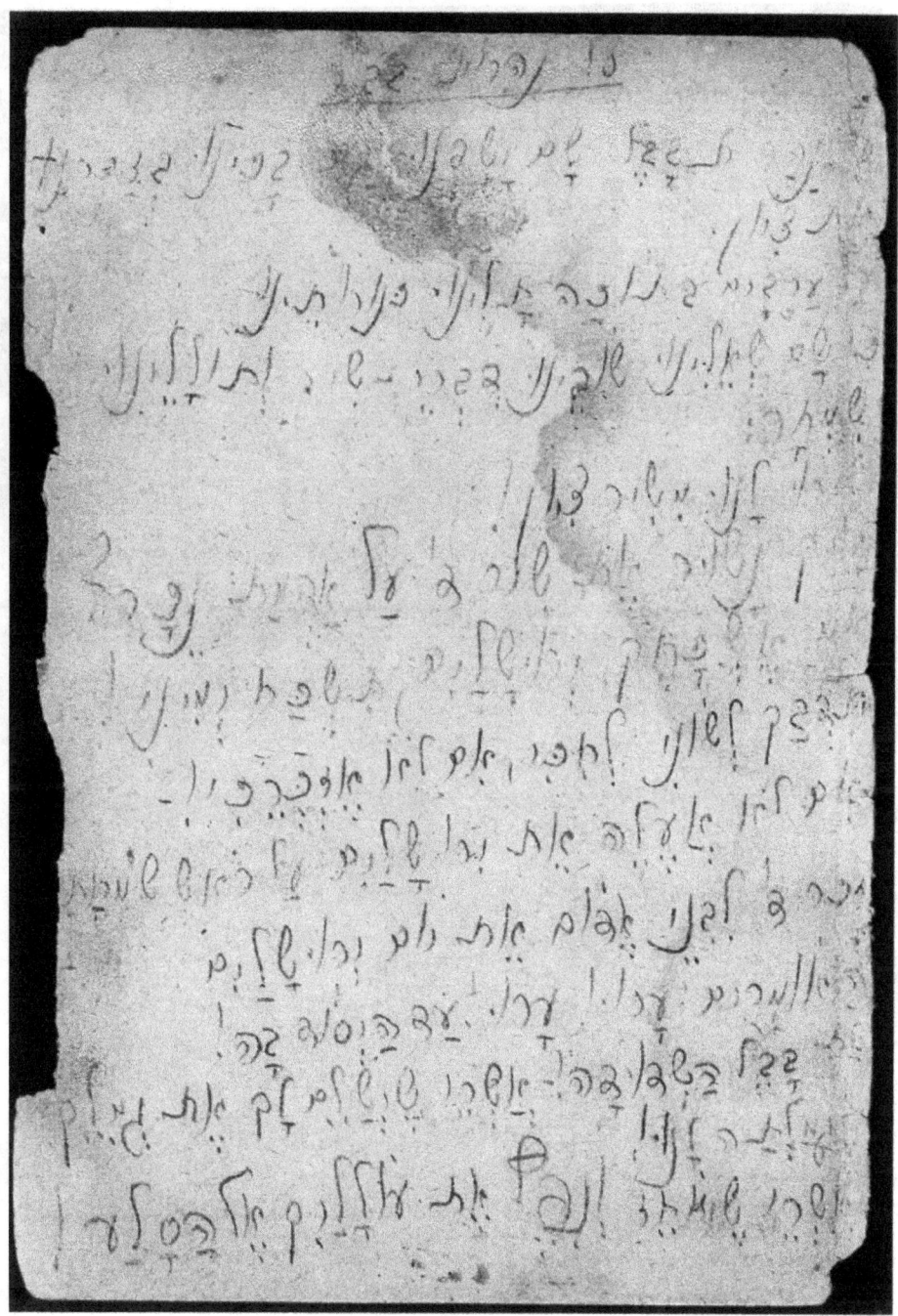

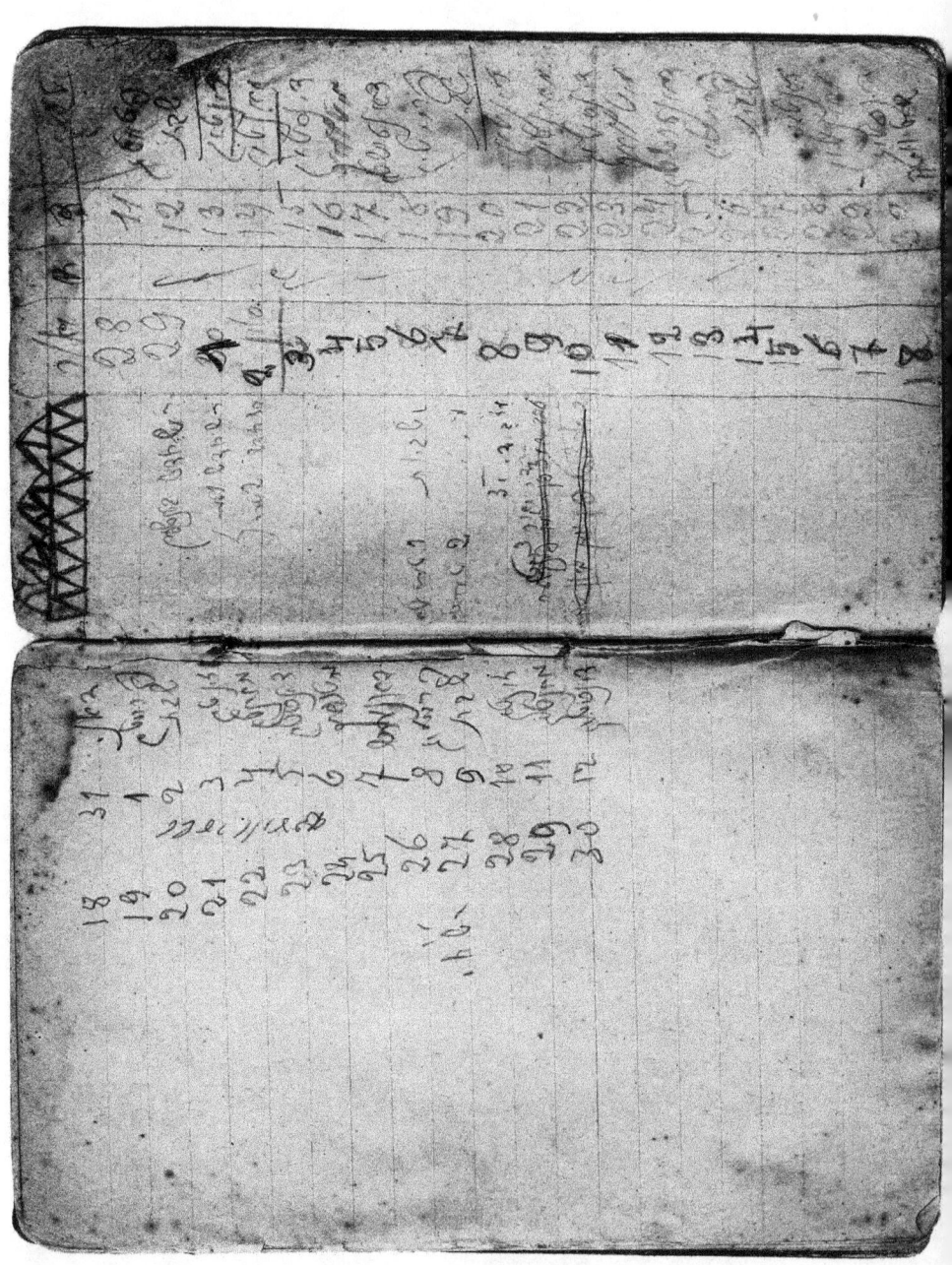

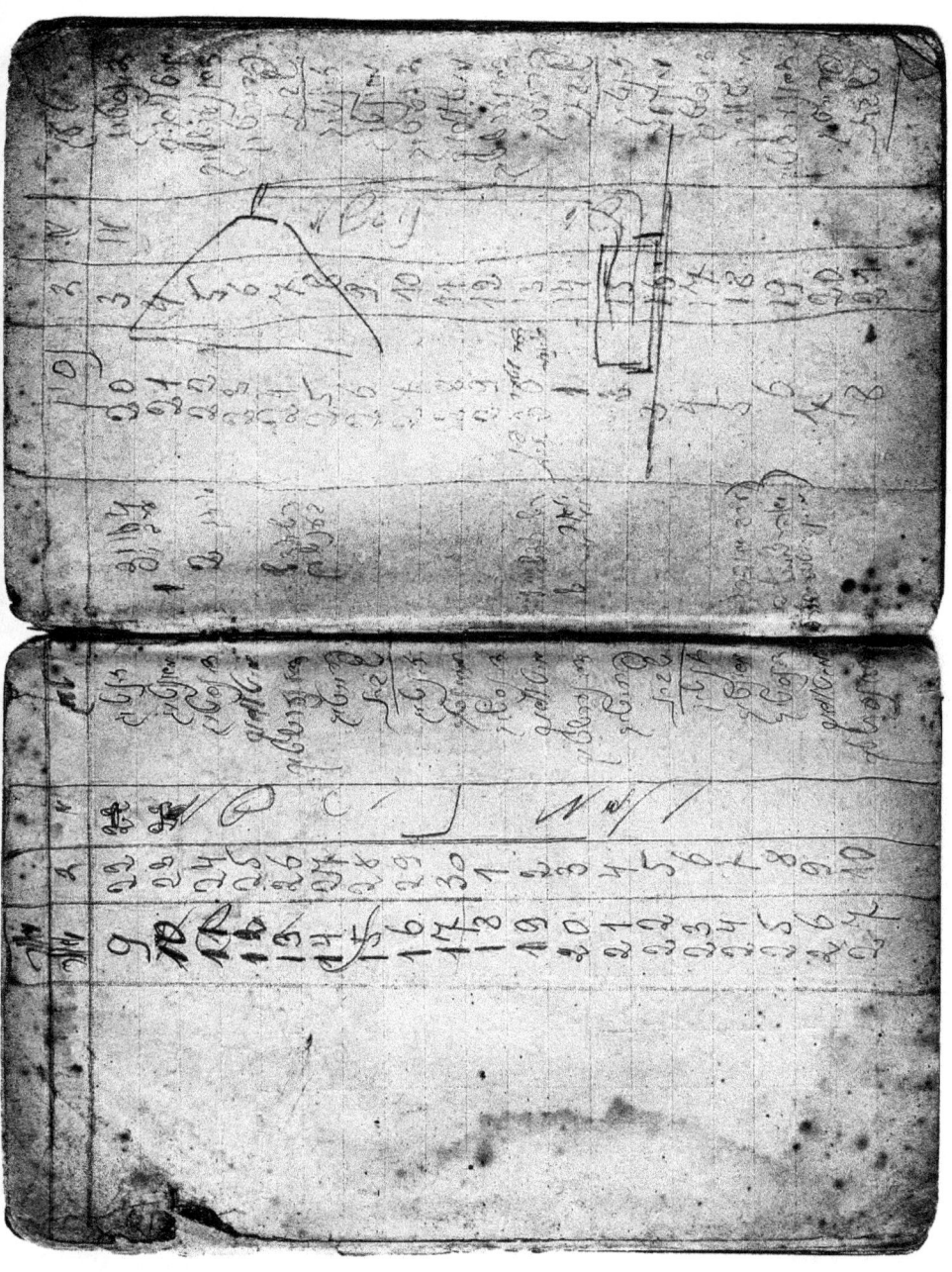

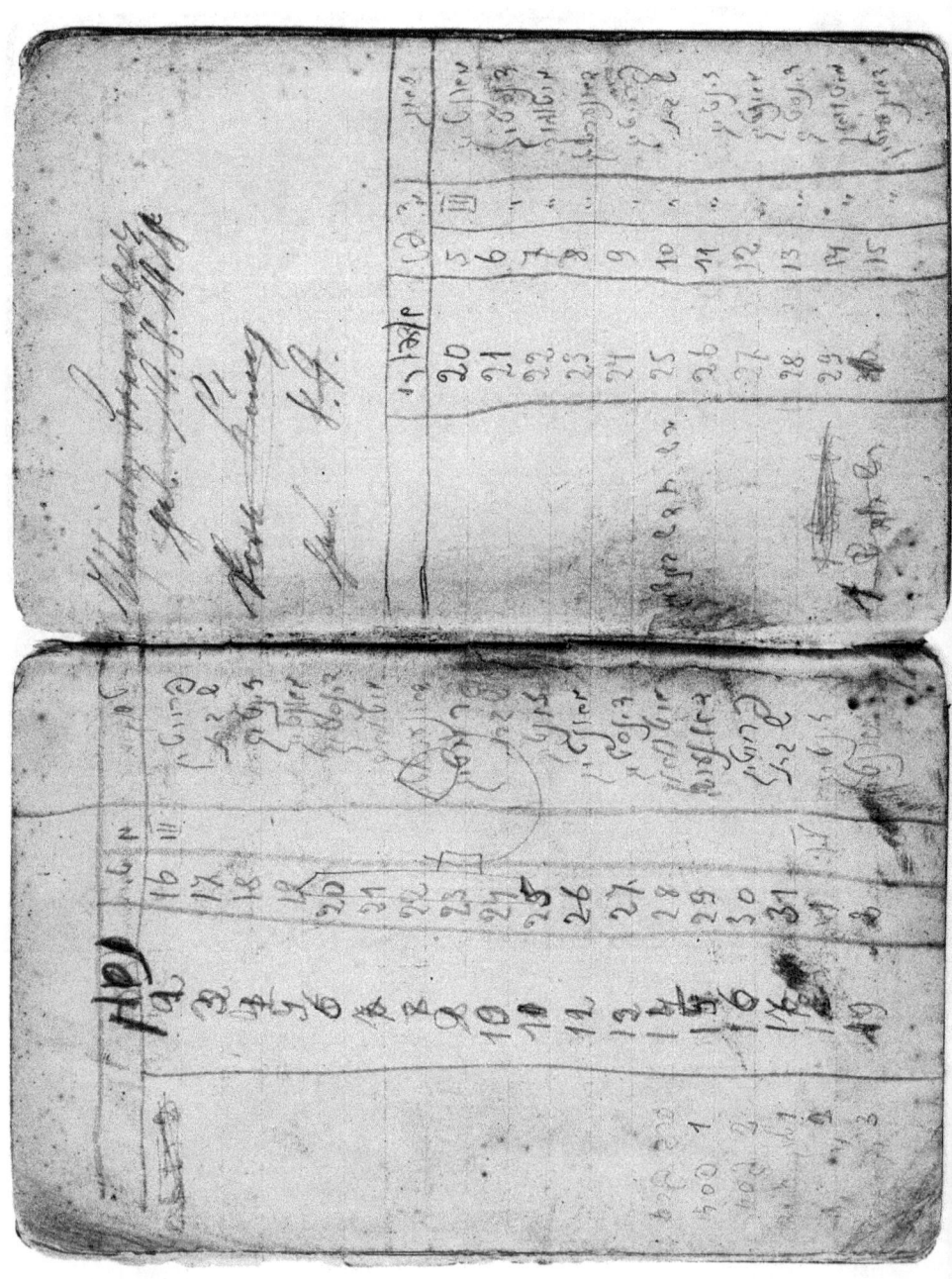

Calendar (cont.)

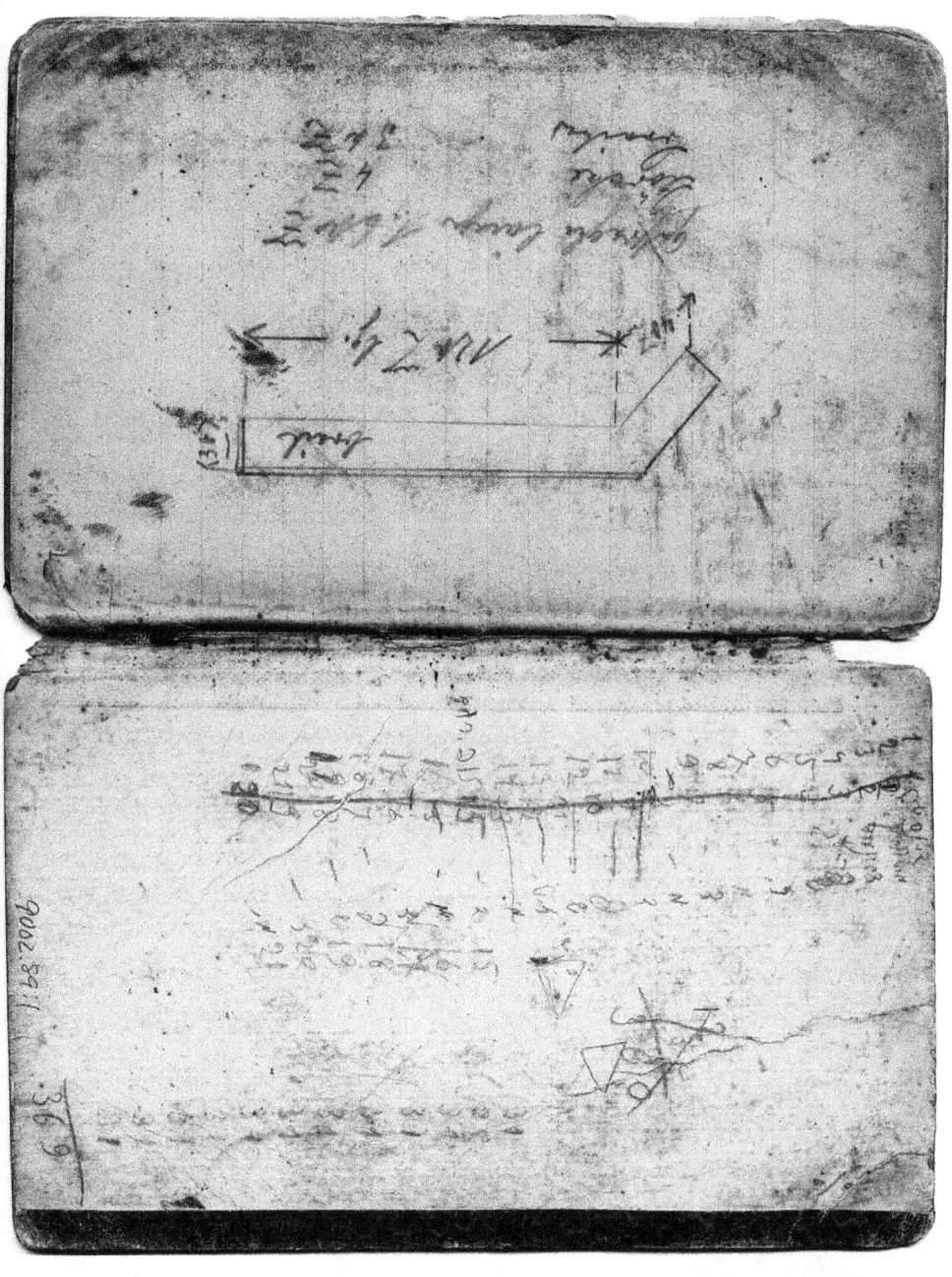

Glossary

Amkhu	Folk.
Aktion	Violent mass roundups conducted by Germans.
Besmedresh [Beit Midrash]	Prayer and study hall.
Beit din	Rabbinical court.
Chuppah	Wedding canopy. The defining moment of the wedding ceremony when the couple stands under the Chuppah.
Dintoyre (Din Torah)	A conflict adjudicated according to the Laws of the Torah.
Dybbuk (Dybbukim pl.)	A malevolent spirit possessing a human body, a demon, often.
Feldscher	A quasi-doctor, a lay family physician, common in Eastern Europe who was sought as the first defense when a person fell ill.
Gartle	A black cord worn daily by Hasidic men around the waist to separate the upper from lower body in keeping with the belief that the upper body is where one's spirituality resides, and the lower part channels body processes.
Gematria	Kabalistic numerology system that gives numerical significance to a word or phrase in the belief that the word, which the number represents, has its own power.
Geystlekh (Geistlich) Geystlekhe (adjective)	Spiritually or emotionally.
Gilgul (Gilgulim pl.)	A roll-over, refererring to reincarnation of the soul.

Halakha	The body of Jewish religious law.
Hasid (Hasidim pl.)	Righteous man, a follower of a rebbe.
Khimesh side (Humash seuda)	A celebration of the day, usually at age five, when a boy begins to study the Pentateuch, the five books of Moses.
Kest (or eating kest)	A common custom among Hasidim, and other traditional Jews. After a couple gets married the pair resides with and is supported by the bride's parents for the first years, enabling the groom to dedicate himself to the study of Torah.
Ktav mehila	A note of forgiveness upon breaking an engagement.
Lomdim	Great scholars.
Meshamish (Shamusim pl.)	A rebbe's trusted assistant, servant and guard.
Mezuzah (Mezizes or Mezuzot pl.)	Pieces of parchment inscribed with prayer that is contained in a box hung at the doorway of every room of a Jewish house.
Misnaged (or Mitnaged; Misnagdim pl.)	Opponent to Hasidism.
Nakhes (Naches)	Taking pride and joy, usually in the accomplishments of one's children.
Nign (or Nigun; nigunim pl.)	A melody, often without words, usually composed by a Hasidic rebbe.
Nisoyen	Temptation, or test (of one's will).
Parshat Hashavua	A Torah portion read each Saturday in the synagogue.
Pidyon	A monetary contribution given to a rebbe.
Rabbi (or rav)	An ordained teacher.

Rebbe (Rebbes pl.)	A leader of a Hasidic group or dynasty.
Se'udah Shelishit	A Hasidic practice wherein the rebbe and his followers have a light meal late Saturday afternoon or on the afternoons of other significant days and he expands on his teaching at the table—"der tish"—to his disciples.
Shidekh (Shidukhim pl.)	Arranged marriage.
Shites (Shitot pl.)	Hasidic ways of being (each Hasidic court may have a different way.
Shimenesre (Shmoneh Esrei)	The core prayer said standing up in silence during daily prayer and holidays. It is comprised of 18 blessings, plus one, and is said three times a day. On the Sabbath and holidays only seven blessings are said. The blessings include praise of God, petitions to God (only said on weekdays), and thanking God.
Shoykhet [Shohet]	Ritual slaughter, or Kosher butcher.
Shulchan Aruch	The oral law codified in the sixteenth century
Sukkah (Sukkahs pl.)	A booth covered with palm branches, usually an impermanent structure, that Jews build for the autumn festival of Tabernacles.
Talmid haham (talmidim-khakhomim or talmidei haham, pl.)	Brilliant student.
Tikun	Rectification.
Tish	When a rabbe of a Hasidic court and his followers gather around a table, or tish, usually at the third meal of the Sabbath, Friday nights, or on another special occasion; a small meal is served and the rebbe expounds on his teachings. The rebbe may distribute a morsel of food to each man present, which is believed to be a blessing.

Glossary

Tnoyim	Conditions referring to the engagement before marriage.
Torah	Pentateuch
Tzaddik (tzaddikim pl.)	A righteous person. Generally designating a holy man, a rebbe.
Tzene Rene	A translation of the five books of Moses in Yiddish.
Yahrzeit	The anniversary of death according the Hebrew calendar (Lunar); a candle is lit and the kaddish prayer is said.
Yikhes (Yihus)	Pedigree, but it may be attained or inherited. Could be grounded in one's own scholarly achievement, or in one's distinguished family and ancestors.

Bibliography

Agassi Buber, Judith. *The Jewish Prisoners of Ravensbrück: Who Were They?* Oxford: Oneworld, 2007.

Bartov, Omer. "Communal Genocide: Personal Accounts of the Destruction of Buczacz, Eastern Galicia, 1944-44." In *Shatterzone of Empires: Coexistence and Violence in the German, Habsburg, Russian, and Ottoman Borderlands*, edited by Omer Bartov and Eric D. Weitz. Indiana: Indiana University Press. In press.

Bartov, Omer. "Setting the Record Straight." *PastForward* (Spring 2011).

Blatman, Daniel. *The Death Marches: The Final Phase of Nazi Genocide.* Cambridge, MA: Belknap Press of Harvard University Press, 2011.

Browning, Christopher R. *Collected Memories: Holocaust History and Postwar Testimony.* Madison: University of Wisconsin Press, 2003.

Browning, Christopher R. *Origins of the Final Solution.* Lincoln: University of Nebraska Press, 2004.

Buber, Martin. *Tales of the Hasidim.* New York: Schocken Books, 2001.

Buber, Martin. *The Origin and Meaning of Hasidism.* New York: Horizon Press, 1960.

Dynner, Glenn. *Men of Silk.* New York: Oxford University Press, 2006.

Hundert, Gershon David. *Essential Papers on Hassidism: Origins to Present.* New York: New York University Press, 1991.

Hundert, Gershon David, *Jews in Poland: Lithuania in the Eighteenth Century.* Berkeley: California University Press, 2004.

Inbar, Yehudit. *Spots of Light: To Be a Woman in the Holocaust.* Jerusalem: Yad Vashem, 2007.

Karay, Felicja. *Death Comes in Yellow: Skarzysko-Kamienna Slave Labor Camp.* Amsterdam: Overseas Publishers Association, 1996.

Kuwalek, Robert. *From Lublin to Belzec: Traces of Jewish Presence and the Holocaust in South-Eastern Part of the Lublin Region.* Tomaszow Lubelski: AD REM, 2006.

Mahler, Raphael. *Hasidism and the Jewish Enlightenment: Their Confrontation in Galicia and Poland in the First Half of the Nineteenth Century.* New York: Jewish Publication Society, 1985.

Morrison, Jack. *Ravensbrück. Everyday Life in a Womaen's Concentration Camp 1939-45.* Princeton: Marcus Wiener Publishers 2000.

Orzeszkowa, Eliza. *The Forsaken or Meir Ezofowich.* Bornemouthe: Delaware Publishing, 1980.

Rothstein, Edward. "Making the Holocaust the Lesson on All Evils." *The New York Times* (April 30 2011): C1-C5.

Weinberg, Gerhard L. *A World at Arms: A Global History of World War II.* New York: Cambridge University Press, 2005.

Index

Anthropology, the discipline of, 275-276; encounter with, 271

Being Bilingual, 221-222; and learning English, 258, 261, 262; and learning Hebrew, 259, 260; and learning French, 268; as natural, 272

Berenbaum, Michael, 9-21

Bergen Belsen: leaving, 249; after liberation, 247; daily life in, 245; described, 245; liberation in, 33, 246-247; living arrangements in, 245; moral dilemma in, 246; sharing in, 245-246, shipped to, 244

Blatman, Daniel, 32, 172, 175

Browning, Christopher, 32, 157, 244

Buber, Agassi, Judith, 32, 241, 243

Bugaj (slave labor woodwork factory): guards in (Jewish and Ukrainian), 239; return visit to, 240; work in, 238-239, 240

Childhood experiences influencing the adult, 277-278, 283

Concentration Camps: *See* Bergen Belsen; Bugaj

Conundrums faced during World War II, 26-27, 35, 103-104, 108-109, 114-115, 233, 236, 282; and "choiceless choice", 13-14

Death March, 172-173; beginning of the, 167-169; disorientation during, 171-172, 175, 173; finding food during, 173, 177, 179, 180, 181, 182; liberated from, 175-176, 178; and caught in battle during, 176-177; and marching without food or water, 170, 177; and walking in circles, 168-171, 173, 176

Divorce: in Hasidic courts 41, 42; and consequences of, 43, 49, 61, 63-64, 283

Dov Ber, Issachar, of Radoszyce, 297, 310; life of, 298; children of, 299-300; genealogy of, 312; and healer, 298-299

Eating kest, 44: *See also* Hasidic customs

Eiger, Abraham (Shevet *mu Yehuda*) (Golda's grandfather), 38, 44-46, 47, 49, 53, 294-295, 296; died, 49; eating habits of, 54; genealogy of, 318-320; se'udah shelishit of, 45 *See also* Hasidic rebbes; Hasidic succession; Jewish Inheritance Laws

Eiger (Eger) Akiva, chief Rabbi of Posen, 38, 297, 311; children of, 38, 53, 287-288, 291-292, 306, 308; genealogy of, 318-320; opponent to Hasidism (misnaged), 53; origins of, 289-291

Eiger, Bat Sheva Grodshtyn (Bube Basia) (Golda's great grandmother), 44, 51, 52, 53-54, 292, 294-295

Eiger family, 40, 295; conflict within, 296; loses in World War II, 296-

297, 308. *See also* Eiger, Abraham; Eiger, Akiva, Eiger, Leibl
Eiger, Leibl (Yehuda Leib), 38, 53; becoming a Hasid and established the Lublin Hasidic court, 292, 293-294, 310; genealogy of, 318-320

Genealogy of: Eiger family, 318-320; Finkler family, 312-313; Taub family, 314-317
German's failure to destroy people spiritually, or their humanity, 12, 14, 15, 16, 26, 35, 93, 143, 146-147, 161, 162, 196, 279
German's invisible tools of oppression, 35, 92; and fear 105, 135; and humiliation 119-120; and disorientation, 153, 171. *See also* death march; World War II
Germany: visit to as an academic, 280-281

Hasag-Leipzig (Slave labor ammunition factory): administered by, 155, 156, 157, arriving in 154, 155, 165; assaults on dignity in, 165-166; bombing near, 166; "bonuses" distributed in, 157, 158, 160; compared with Skarżysko-Kamienna, 155, 156, 157, 161; creating a religious calendar in, 36, 162-163; dealing with hunger in, 160, description of, 155, 156; falling sick in, 159, 162; Liquidation of, 167; origins of inmates in, 154, 157; owned by, 156; prophetic dreams in, 163, and gematria, 165; recording psalms and prayers from memory in, 163; Red Cross in, 157; religious and spiritual life in, 161-162; resisting in, 160; sabotage in, 161; sleeping arrangements in, 155; work in, 162. *See also* German failure to destroy people spiritually and their humanity; Skarżysko-Kamienna

Hasidic courts: class differences among, 40-41; conflicts among, 311; conflicts in about succession, 55; described, 38; difference between, 38, 40; fear of assimilation, 57, 73; holiday celebrations in, 44; and breaking engagements, 70-71, 72; and celebrations for deceased, 56; and divorce, 40-41, 42; and education of girls in Lublin, 56-57; and marriage and marriage arrangements, 10, 39, 40-41, 53, 308-309; and women working outside the home, 77, 223-224, *See also* Holidays, religious; Eiger, Abraham; Eiger, Leibl; Eiger, family; Modzitze Hasidic court; Hasidic rebbe

Hasidic customs: boys fifth birthday celebration, 42-43, and other rites of passage, 78; eating kest, 44; head covers for women, 42, 49, 51, 77; se'udah shelishit, 60, 147, 227 and description of, 45; and breaking engagements, 70-71; and inscriptions on tombstones, 65; and lighting candles for male but not female ancestors, 56; and naming children, and adults, 23, 78; and not being photographed, 233; and not registering children at birth, 62-63. *See also* Holiday celebrations

Hasidic rebbe (tzaddik): eating habits of, 225; role of, 45-46, 66, 68, 306-307; succession of, 308; and birthing, 78; and importance of yikhes (pedigree), 308; and se'udah shelishit, 227

Index

Hasidism: described, 38, 306-307; dominance in pre-World War II Jewish communities, 310; origins of 306; three wings of, 310; and beliefs in protection by righteous ancestors, 106, 164, 232, 273; and conflicts, 40, 296, 303; and establishing learning academies, 310; and healing tradition, 307; and persecution by opponents to, 309-310; and the Besht, 307-308

Holidays, religious: Sukkot, 44; Purim, 46; Hanukah, 52; and preparation for Passover, 50-51; and rhythm of life, 267; and the Passover Seder, 51-52, 257

Holocaust: uniqueness of, 29-30, 214-215, 220-221, 281-282

Israel, leaving for, 202, 259, living in 260-261

Inheritance Laws, Jewish, 54-55; and conflicts over, 55

Jewish Assimilation into larger society, 283, 287, 288; conflicts over, 287-288. *See also* Poland, Positivist movement

Joint Distribution Committee (Joint), 187, 201, 204

Judenrat (Jewish Councils created in ghettos by Germans): functions of 92, 112-113, 157, 234; and Jewish police, 92, 113, 115, 227. *See also* Skarżysko-Kamienna and Jewish policemen

Kuwalek, Robert, 33, 293, 295

Lemkin, Rafael, and the crime of genocide, 75, 212, *See also* Polish Free University

Lublin: Jewish presence in, 286; Hasidic court, 38, 30 and leader of Jewish community in, 296. visit to, 32, 33, 292-293. *See also* Hasidic courts, Eiger, Abraham, Eiger, Leibl, Kuwalek Robert

Marriage: and Hasidic courts, 10, 39, 40-41, 53, 72, 308-309; arranged (shidukhim) customs of customs of, 68-69, 71-72, 295, 302; importance of in Hasidic life, 58-59; and dowries, 55, 72; and dress, 58-59; and women's hair cut before 58, 77. *See also* Hasidic courts

Memory: desire to obliterate it, 117-118; nature of 27, 30-32, 35-36; as tombstone 21, 283; significance of 31, 213, 282; and uniqueness of each individual's, 25

Modzitze Hasidic court, 39, 40; continuity of 305, 310; origins of, 301; role of music in, 42, 300-301, 302. *See also* Hasidic courts; genealogy, 315

Organization of book, 23-24, 33-36

Otwock, suburb of Warsaw, 47, 77, 222; Modzitze Hasidic court established in 303

Parent-child relations, 20, 27, 59-61, 64, 79, 255-256, 263-264, 273-275, 279, 283

Piotrków: described, 231-232; visit to, 32, 239-240;

Piotrków large ghetto, 36; hiding in, 107, 233; life in, 102, 105, 106, 232; liquidation of 103, 234-235; and description of hide out, 107-108, and being discovered in hide out, 109; and people captured to work in slave labor factory in, 113-114, 235-236

Piotrków little ghetto, 111; and life in little ghetto, 237-238; and transfer to, 235, and slave labor camps life in, 111-112,

Poland: being back after end of World War II, 186-188, 189-196; escape from during World War II, 88-89; division of after loss of Independence, 67, 286-287; and anti-Semitism after Independence, 288-289; and persecution of Jews resulting from division, 67, 302; Independence of, 62; Jewish persecutions in (Chmielnick Revolt) in 286; market towns in, 40; Positivist movement in, 70, 288; reasons for increase of Jewish population in previous centuries, 286; returning after World War II by walking back to, 183-184, by train 185-186, and reconstituting one's identity after returning to, 189-190; small towns in, described: Lublin, 292-293, Opole, 66, Piotrków, 102, 231-232; surrender to Germans 85; when Jews first came to, 285-286; visit to 23, 32, 33, 221. *See also* Warsaw ghetto

Polish Free University (Wolna Wszechnica Polska), 72, 210, 211, 289; attendance in, 10, 72-73, and by women 73-74; courses taught in, 75-76; and the faculty of law in, 74; and matriculation in, 74. *See also* Lemkin, Rafael

Ravensbrück (Concentration camp), 156, 224, 239, 253; daily life in, 243, 244, 245; described, 240-241, 242; ration allotments in, 243; roll calls in, 241, 242; selections in, 244; transported to, 104, 241; working in 242-243

Refugees: anthropological insights on, 199, 275-276; feelings of being a, 212-214, 216-217; finding an apartment in New York by, 201, 203; finding work in New York by, 203, 204, 205, 206-208, 209; and workers' relations, 208, 209; finding a career as a, 209-211; living in two cultures, 27, 271-272; losing status as consequences of being, 211-212; problems of 34-35, 258-259; reception on arrival in America of, 200-201, 255-256; and going to high school, 261-262, 263, and working and studying, 265-266, 269-270

Religious rituals: power of, 25-26; and Jewish practices of 26. *See also* Hasidic customs; Holidays, religious

Ritual slaughters (shoykhet), role of in Jewish community, 66-67

Slave labor camps: *See* Bugaj; Hasag-Leipzig; Skarżysko-Kamienna

Selections by Germans, who lives and who dies, 110, 125, 253, 244, 253; during roll calls 125, 135-136; fear of 135. *See also* concentration camps, slave labor camps

Skarżysko-Kamienna (slave labor ammunition factory) 116, 126; arrival in, 118-120; attempts to escape from, 118-120; being transported from, 151, 152, 153; daily life in, 122, 124-125; dealing with hunger in 140-141; description of, 120-122 and factory in, 126-127; falling sick in, 129-130, 132, 137-139; food and living conditions in,

139-140, 141, 142-143; goods exchanged in, 122-123; inmates interacting in, 133, 141, 144, 149-150; Jewish policemen in, 120-121, 125, 127, 129, 130, 138, 141, 142; liquidation of, 150-152; moral dilemmas in 17-18, 134-135; organization of 127-128; religious life and spirituality in, 143-147; resisting the Germans in, 134; roll calls in 125-126, 135; sabotage, 133; sleeping arrangements in, 118-120; type of work done in, 127-128, 130-131

Sources for this book, 23, 24, 27-28, 30, 32, 33

Studying and working in Paris, 268-269

Sweden, arrival in 199, 249; departure from, 253; life in 249-250, 251, 252-253; visit to 33

Taub, Shaul Yedidya (father of Golda), 60, 62, 302-303; escaped from Poland, 89, 304; visit to Israel (Palestine), 304

Taub, Israel, 42, 301; marriage of, 302, 303. *See also* genealogy, 314-317

Theological musings, 273, 280

Traditional healing remedies, 47, 50-51, 298-299. *See also* Dov Ber Issachar, of Radoszyce

Warsaw: bombing of, 85-86, 87, 226; defense committee established in, 90; destroyed, 187; under siege, 91-92, 93; visit to, 32, 221

Warsaw ghetto: a willed death in, 14, 101, 229; capturing people for slave labor in 96-97, 227; curfews in, 97; daily life in, 12, 94-96, 97, 226-227; described 93-94; diseases in, 94-95, 98, 228; escaping from, 98, 99-100, 228, 229; Jewish uprising in, 102; liquidation of, 101

World War II: beginning of 81, 85, 88, 282-283; disbelieve in Jewish destruction, 13, 101, 228; lack of information about 83-84; preparation for 81, 83, 86-87; and uncertainty, 13, 10, 80-81; and Ronald Reagan, 214-215, 245

Weinberg, Gerhard, 32, 158, 179